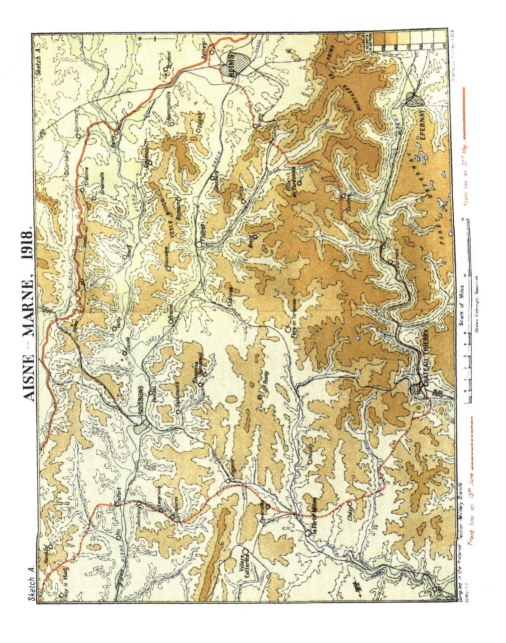

Sketch A. AISNE – MARNE. 1918.

HISTORY OF THE GREAT WAR

MILITARY OPERATIONS

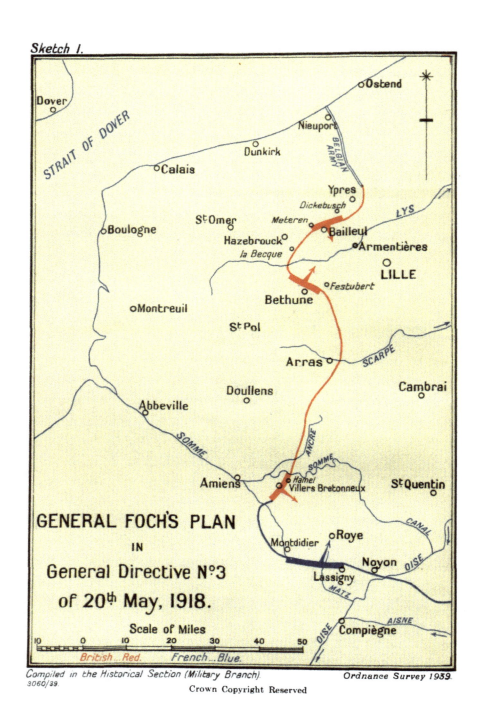

HISTORY OF THE GREAT WAR

BASED ON OFFICIAL DOCUMENTS

BY DIRECTION OF THE HISTORICAL SECTION OF THE
COMMITTEE OF IMPERIAL DEFENCE

MILITARY OPERATIONS

FRANCE AND BELGIUM, 1918

MAY–JULY: THE GERMAN DIVERSION OFFENSIVES AND THE
FIRST ALLIED COUNTER-OFFENSIVE

COMPILED BY

BRIGADIER-GENERAL SIR JAMES E. EDMONDS
C.B., C.M.G., Hon. D.Litt. (Oxon.), R.E. (Retired), p.s.c.

SKETCHES AND MAPS COMPILED BY

MAJOR A. F. BECKE
Hon. M.A. (Oxon.), R.F.A. (Retired)

The Naval & Military Press Ltd

in association with

The Imperial War Museum
Department of Printed Books

Published jointly by
The Naval & Military Press Ltd
Unit 10 Ridgewood Industrial Park,
Uckfield, East Sussex,
TN22 5QE England
Tel: +44 (0) 1825 749494
Fax: +44 (0) 1825 765701

www.naval-military-press.com
www.military-genealogy.com
www.militarymaproom.com

and

The Imperial War Museum, London
Department of Printed Books

www.iwm.org.uk

There took part in the compilation of the
first draft of this Volume :

Major-General H. R. Davies, C.B.
Lieut.-Colonel R. G. B. Maxwell-Hyslop, *p.s.c.*

In reprinting in facsimile from the original, any imperfections are inevitably reproduced and the quality may fall short of modern type and cartographic standards.

PREFACE

THIS volume covers three months, from the beginning of May to the beginning of August 1918, that is the period between the close of the two great German offensives of the 21st March–5th April and 9th–30th April against the British and the opening of the Franco-British offensive of the 8th August, General Ludendorff's " Black Day ". In this period there were a few interesting but minor British operations ; our forces were, in the main, reorganizing and recuperating after the strenuous fighting of the previous six weeks ; our Ally had to bear the brunt of the fighting. The German Supreme Command made three great diversion offensives against the French (who now, for the first time, had American divisions in their ranks on the active fronts) for the purpose of drawing away the Allied reserves from Flanders preparatory to delivering a final knock-out blow to the British. This result was to be achieved by an offensive, of which the code-name was " Hagen ", directed against the Hazebrouck—Ypres front, followed by the isolation of the Belgian Army and the rolling up of the British line. The preliminary German offensives against the French were, first, that of the 27th May, officially known as the Second Battle of the Aisne, but usually called the Chemin des Dames offensive ; secondly, that of the 9th June, the Battle of the Matz, designed to blunt and widen the salient in which the Germans found themselves after the unexpectedly easy success on the Aisne ; and thirdly, the Reims—Soissons offensive of the 15th July, called the Second Battle of the Marne, intended to secure a good defensive line behind that river, so as to enable all possible reserves to be diverted to " Hagen ". Then, in the midst of this last attack of the German Armies on the Western Front, came Foch's counter-stroke of the 18th July, led by General Mangin's surprise attack near Soissons. It was carried out by French and American troops against the western shoulder of the German salient, and continued against the eastern shoulder and apex until the enemy had abandoned his gains between Reims and Soissons and retired behind the Vesle and the Aisne.

In these operations British divisions played a relatively small but important part. Five of them were involved in the disaster on the Chemin des Dames, having been sent to that front for rest—for it was considered a quiet one—under a system of exchanging tired British divisions for fresh French formations, inaugurated by General Foch, now in command of the Allied Forces on the Western Front. These tired divisions, in the IX. Corps, under Lieut.-General Sir Alexander Gordon, took the place in the front line of the French XXXVIII. Corps of three divisions, which thus became available to join General Foch's General Reserve west of Amiens. There it was well placed to support the British, who almost to the end of the period, remained under the threat of " Hagen " ; for Crown Prince Rupprecht of Bavaria's Group of Armies had made all preparations to attack, and until the latter part of July had a reserve of more than thirty divisions on the Hazebrouck—Ypres front.

Another four British divisions, as the XXII. Corps under Lieut.-General Sir Alexander Godley, fought in the French counter-offensive in July ; they were drawn by General Foch from the British reserves in order to help the common cause.

In view of the employment of these nine divisions in the ranks of our Ally it has been thought necessary to say more than usual about the operations of the French ; not only because detached British divisions took part in them, but also because without knowledge of the Allied operations as a whole it is impossible to form a just estimate of the consummate skill with which General Foch handled the Allied reserves—at one time draining Sir Douglas Haig of his last available division. His disadvantage as compared with Ludendorff, who besides " interior lines " had a homogeneous force under his control, requires no stressing. With Armies in the process of recovering from the effects of six weeks' almost continuous fighting, General Foch had, day by day, to balance the respective claims of the British, whose left in Flanders was threatened by the vast accumulation of men and guns under Crown Prince Rupprecht of Bavaria, and of the French, whose Armies under General Pétain from Reims to Montdidier were from the

27th March onwards in actual combat with the enemy. At the same time he had to bear in mind the very natural claims of the Americans for the formation as early as possible of a separate Army.

Further, as British divisions sent to the French area were serving sometimes under French corps commanders and always under French Army commanders, an opportunity is presented of studying our Ally's methods, which may be of service in securing smooth co-operation should occasion arise in the future. It will be noticed that the French higher commanders did not accord a free hand to the men on the spot as is the custom in the British Army, but maintained control by means of both messages and liaison officers empowered to act on emergency in their name.[1] On the other hand, French orders (of which some specimens are given in the Appendices)[2] seem to give the subordinates who receive them a better idea of the general manner in which the commander considers the action should be conducted, and the general objectives to be achieved, than do the British, though in our case the information was often given at personal interviews. Unless aware of the differences, British generals, accustomed to short matter-of-fact instructions and orders without explanation or reference to principles, might resent being reminded whilst a battle was in progress of the simple principles of strategy and tactics. Some differences in the practice of the issue of orders and of the methods of administration are also noticed.

In the series of battles in the period under review will be seen the gradual mastering of the German methods of break-through. This was accomplished by gradual change in the initial deployment of the defensive forces, so that finally, against General Gouraud's Army, no success whatever was achieved. The secret of the defeat of the enemy methods, acquired by costly experiment in a series of combats—which remind one of the processes of " Duffer's " Drift " (written at the close of the S. African War of 1899–1902 by Major-General Sir Ernest Swinton)—might instead have been learnt by a closer study of the changes in the German defensive and offensive battle.

In May 1917 French G.Q.G. formed a special (instruc-

[1] See, in Appendix III, the messages sent by the G.O.C. French Sixth Army at 8.45 A.M. on 27th May.

[2] They will be found in translation; the original French is available in the French Official Account.

tion) section of the 3ᵉ Bureau (Operations), which was charged with the study of the enemy's tactics in offence and defence. In February 1918 it issued a study of the preparation and execution of the German attack against Riga, 1st–5th September 1917, copies of which were presented to G.H.Q. So little, however, was brought to notice about German methods that on the 16th June 1918 Maréchal Foch himself, as Generalissimo, issued a Note pointing out the features of the enemy "attaque brusquée" (see Appendix X.). No attempt was made to forecast and provide against possible variations in the enemy's tactics, although in 1915, 1916, 1917 and 1918 they were constantly changed, in fact, after every battle.

The location of every German division was carefully and correctly followed; but the General Staff G.H.Q. was content to translate such out-of-date enemy pamphlets on the defensive battle as fell into its hands and to issue instructions for future action based on them. No pamphlet on the defensive battle, however, was put forth until May 1918, when S.S. 210, "The Division in Defence", was published. In S.S. 135, "The Training and Employment "of Divisions 1918", published in January 1918, nothing whatever was said about defence except in a short section on the "organization and strengthening of the captured "position".[1] Although S.S. 135 dealt with attack, it contained no word about preparations to meet and foil the action of the German reserves (*Eingreifdivisionen*).

In June and July 1918, for the first time on the Western Front since 1914, the Allies had not the unavoidable task of attacking defences developed by months of labour, as they had been forced to do at the Somme in 1916 and in the various offensives of 1917. Some of the operations, for instance those of the British XXII. Corps in the Ardre valley, had almost the character of open warfare. In these, as in trench warfare, the enormous power of the machine-gun in the hands of resolute men in defence was markedly apparent: it not only inflicted heavy losses but also compelled the attackers to go warily and this gave the Germans time to improvise fresh lines of defence in rear, so that initial advantages obtained by surprise could never be exploited to the full. Neither aeroplanes nor tanks achieved any result of importance; in fact, had little influence on the decision: aeroplanes are dependent on

---

[1] In February 1918 S.S. 139/7, "Artillery Notes No. 7. Artillery in "Defence Operations" was drawn up by R.A. Staff and issued separately.

favourable weather and tanks move but " by leave of the " ground "; it was obvious that they were both auxiliary arms. The use of gas was small, for fear of infecting ground over which one's own troops might later have to move. With such support as the artillery could give in open or semi-open warfare, the result depended on the training and valour of the infantry. Mounted men were brought up, but could not be employed; as an American said, " You cannot have a cavalry charge until you have " captured the enemy's last machine gun ". The Germans, though held and then forced to withdraw, were by no means defeated. Their retirement from the Château Thierry salient was not so much due to General Mangin's surprise attack of the 18th July, and the loss of ground near Soissons which they sustained, as to their inability to supply their forces in the salient once the Soissons railway junction was under effective artillery fire.

Ludendorff's theories were correct in so far as by a succession of attacks he had forced Foch to withdraw the Allied reserves from Flanders. But he himself was then left without sufficient forces to carry out the final, as he hoped, attack against the British. He had overlooked the enormous cost in German blood of driving British, French and Belgian troops from their positions. The full enemy losses from the 21st March to the 7th August have never been divulged, but the entirely successful Chemin des Dames offensive 27th May to 13th June had, according to the official monograph, " Wachsende Schwierigkeiten 1918 " (p. 192), cost 4,581 officers and 125,789 other ranks, " who " after previous heavy losses, were irreplaceable "; and the total does not include " the wounded who were likely " to recover within a reasonable time " (German Official History, Vol. XI. p. 41). These may be reckoned at another 30 per cent.[1] The addition of these lightly wounded would bring the enemy total to 169,481; the French and British losses for the same period were 172,419, including 60,000 prisoners. Unlike the Allies, whose forces were daily increasing by the influx of Americans, Germany was unable to replace the men who had fallen. Numbers, whether in 1861–4, 1864, 1866 or 1914–18, are bound to tell in the end, and Ludendorff was forced by lack of numbers to abandon the " Hagen " offensive and surrender the initiative to the Allies.

[1] See " 1916 " Vol. I., p. 497, where it is shown to vary, for Germans, from 27 to 33 per cent.

As in previous volumes, I am greatly indebted to the combatants to whom the draft was circulated for providing explanations, filling gaps and generally furnishing corrections, additions and suggestions. Their names are too numerous to mention them all here ; but I have specially to thank General Sir Alexander Godley, the commander of the XXII. Corps, and the late Lieut.-General Sir Alexander Hamilton Gordon, commander of the IX. Corps, who were the senior officers with the British contingents which served with the French, as regards the operations, and to Dr. C. E. W. Bean, M.A., LL.D., the Australian Official Historian, as regards the Australian operations.

For the French operations I had the benefit of the French Official Account, Tome VI., Volume II. and Tome VII. Volume I. ; but General Blin, head of the *Service Historique* of the French General Staff, was kind enough to read the second draft and furnish corrections and suggestions, for which I am most grateful ; but he is in no way responsible for the form of the narrative or the opinions expressed in it.

The allusions to the American forces have been checked by the very valuable " Order of Battle of the United States " Land Forces in the World War : American Expeditionary " Forces ", prepared in the Historical Section, Army War College ; its two volumes contain a summary of the operations of each corps and division. I have also made use of General J. J. Pershing's " My Experiences in the " World War ".

The German Official History has not yet reached 1918, Volume XI. bringing it to February 1917 ; but the *Kriegsgeschichtliche Forschungsanstalt des Heeres* (continuing the work of the *Reichsarchiv*) published in 1929–30 four monographs on the operations, designated : " Deutsche Siege 1918 ", with the subtitle : " The Advance of the Seventh " Army over Ailette, Aisne, Vesle and Ourcq to the Marne, " 27th May–13th June " ; " Wachsende Schwierigkeiten ", with the subtitle " Vain Struggle before Compiègne, Villers " Cotterêts and Reims " ; " Der letzte deutsche Angriff ", with the subtitle, " Reims 1918 " ; and " Schicksalswende", with the subtitle " From the Marne to the Vesle 1918 ". Of the bombardment of the 27th May there is a detailed description in Colonel Bruchmüller's " Die deutsche Artillerie in den Durchbruchschlachten des Weltkrieges ".

The names of the officers who took part in the most laborious task of compiling the first draft of this volume are printed opposite the opening page of the Preface; but I have also received very great assistance from other members of the staff of the Historical Section (Military Branch), particularly from Mr. A. W. Tarsey as regards clearing up points raised by correspondents; also from Captain W. Miles in revision and preparation for the press. I have again had the benefit of the invaluable criticism of the final draft by my brother-in-law, Mr. W. B. Wood, M.A. (Oxon.), and by Lieut.-Colonel H. G. de Watteville, C.B.E., M.A. (Oxon.), *p.s.c.* R.A. (retired).

All officers interested may not have seen the draft or proofs. I beg, therefore, as I have done in previous volumes, that any corrections or additions, and criticisms thought necessary, may be sent to the Secretary of the Historical Section, Committee of Imperial Defence, Audit House, Victoria Embankment, E.C. 4. At the same time, I offer my thanks to those who so kindly furnished corrections for the earlier volumes. A sheet of " Addenda and Corrigenda " is enclosed in this volume.

J. E. E.

March 1939

NOTES

THE location of troops and places is written from right to left of the front of the Allied Forces, unless otherwise stated. In translations from the German the order given is as in the original; otherwise enemy troops are enumerated like the British. Where roads which run through both the British and German lines are described by the names of towns or villages, the place in British hands is mentioned first, thus: " Albert—Bapaume road ".

To save space and bring the nomenclature in line with " Division ", " Infantry Brigade " has in the text been abbreviated to " Brigade ", as distinguished from " Cavalry Brigade " and " Artillery Brigade "; " Regiment " similarly means " Infantry Regiment ".

The convention observed in the British Expeditionary Force is followed as regards the distinguishing numbers of Armies, Corps, Divisions, etc., of the British and Allied Armies, *e.g.* they are written in full for Armies, in Roman figures for corps, and in Arabic for smaller formations and units, except Artillery Brigades, which are Roman; thus: Fourth Army, IV. Corps, 4th Cavalry Division, 4th Division, 4th Cavalry Brigade, 4th Brigade, IV. Brigade R.F.A.; but for artillery brigades with numbers higher than one hundred, Arabic figures are used.

German formations and units, to distinguish them clearly from the Allies, are printed in italic characters, thus: *First Army, I. Corps, 1st Division.*

The usual Army abbreviations of regimental names have been used: for example, " 2/R. West Kent " or " West Kent " for 2nd Battalion The Queen's Own Royal West Kent Regiment; K.O.Y.L.I. for the King's Own Yorkshire Light Infantry; K.R.R.C. for the King's Royal Rifle Corps. To avoid constant repetition, the " Royal " in regimental titles is sometimes omitted. To economize space the 63rd (Royal Naval Division), the 14th (Light)

Division, etc., are usually described by their numbers only.[1]

First-line and Second-line Territorial Force units are distinguished by a figure in front of the battalion or other number, thus : 1/8th London, 2/8th London, 1/3rd London or 2/3rd London Field Company R.E., or, when the First-line and Second-line had been amalgamated, simply 3/London; but in the case of First-line units the figure in front of the battalion number is sometimes omitted.

Abbreviations employed occasionally are :
B.E.F. for British Expeditionary Force ;
D.A.N. for Détachment d'Armée du Nord ;
G.A.C. for Groupe d'armées du Centre ;
G.A.E. for Groupe d'armées de l'Est ;
G.A.N. for Groupe d'Armées du Nord ;
G.A.R. for Groupe d'armées de Réserve ;
G.H.Q. for British General Headquarters ;
G.Q.G. for French Grand Quartier-Général (usually spoken as " Grand Q.G.") ;
O.H.L. for German *Oberste Heeresleitung* (German Supreme Command). *N.B.*—" G.H.Q." in German means Grosses Haupt-Quartier, that is the Kaiser's Headquarters, political, military and naval, as distinguished from O.H.L.
R.I.R. (on maps) for Reserve Infantry Regiment.

The spellings of " lacrymatory " and " strongpoint " are arbitrary, and were selected as being shorter than the usual ones.

Officers are described by the rank which they held at the period under consideration. To save space the initials instead of the Christian names of knights are generally used.

The German pre-war practice of writing the plain name without " von ", when it is applicable and no rank or title is prefixed, has been adopted, *e.g.* " Falkenhayn " and not " von Falkenhayn ".

Both belligerents had adopted Summer Time, the Allies on the night of the 9th/10th March and the Germans on that of the 14th/15th April, so throughout the volume German time is one hour ahead of British time.

In order to save the repetition of words, to indicate that a division or brigade had been reduced by fighting to a mere remnant of its establishment, the abbreviations of " Divn " and " Bde " are employed.

---

[1] The Yorkshire Regiment is usually called in the text by its ancient name " The Green Howards ".

MAPS AND SKETCHES

The principal operations described in this volume are the battles fought from the 27th May to the 7th August over the country which lies between the rivers Aisne and Marne: between Soissons and Château Thierry and Reims and Villers Cottérêts. It was decided to illustrate these operations as far as possible by sketches bound in the text, in order to reduce the number of maps to a minimum, and to dispense with a separate map volume. Acting on this plan it was found that only three maps were indispensable for the study of these operations; these maps are placed in a pocket at the end of this volume.

The layered end-paper, Sketch A, has been designed to show the configuration of the ground over which the Aisne—Marne battles of 1918 were fought, and a general layered map has not been included. A map (2) shows the general arrangement of the defensive position occupied by the French and British forces before the German attack was launched between Soissons and Reims on the 27th May; the British dispositions in detail are given in a sketch (3). The German bombardment on the 27th May is illustrated by a copy of Colonel Bruchmüller's Barrage and Target Map. The inclusion of this map (3) will enable all readers to appreciate the hurricane to which the Allied troops and defences were subjected on that May morning. The German formations—Armies, corps, and divisions—are given on all sketches illustrating the fighting covered by this volume. End-paper Sketch B shows the results achieved by the German offensives between March and June; it indicates also that the ground gained by the Germans in the Battle of the Matz linked up the Aisne—Marne battle area with the Somme battle area. In addition Sketch B shows the four positions in which the "Paris " guns " were emplaced between the 23rd March and the 5th August 1918.

MAPS AND SKETCHES

All the Maps and Sketches contained in this volume were drawn for reproduction by the late Mr. J. S. Fenton (late R.E.), the senior draughtsman of this Branch, and they were his last work for the History of the Great War. The loss which this Branch suffered from the death of Mr. Fenton was put on record in the Notes on the Maps and Sketches in the volume of this series published in 1938 (" 1916 " Volume II.).

A. F. B.

CONTENTS

CHAPTER I

	PAGE
A Pause in the Operations, 1st to 26th May 1918	1
Notes : I. Distribution of British Forces	25
II. Distribution of German Divisions	26
III. German Plans for the Continuation of the Offensive	27

CHAPTER II

The German Offensive in Champagne. The Battle of the Aisne. The Allied Situation Before the Battle . 30

CHAPTER III

The Battle of the Aisne, 27th May 1918. The Assault . 47
Note : The German Preparations for the Attack . . 69

CHAPTER IV

The Battle of the Aisne (*continued*), 27th May 1918. The Defence of the Green Line . . . 73

CHAPTER V

The Battle of the Aisne (*continued*). The Germans on the 27th May 86

CHAPTER VI

The Battle of the Aisne (*continued*), 28th May 1918. Retirement from the Vesle and Loss of Soissons . 102
Note : The Germans on the 28th May . . . 117

CHAPTER VII

The Battle of the Aisne (*continued*), 29th May 1918. Retirement across the Ourcq 120
Note : The Germans on the 29th May . . . 133

CONTENTS

CHAPTER VIII

	PAGE
THE BATTLE OF THE AISNE (*continued*), 30TH MAY 1918. RETIREMENT TO THE MARNE	135
Note: The Germans on the 30th May	142

CHAPTER IX

THE BATTLE OF THE AISNE (*concluded*), 31ST MAY–6TH JUNE 1918. CESSATION OF THE PURSUIT . . . 143

CHAPTER X

THE BATTLE OF THE MATZ, 9TH–14TH JUNE 1918, AND THE DISPOSAL OF THE ALLIED TROOPS DURING THE ENSUING QUIET PERIOD	172
Note: Distribution of German Divisions on 12th June	192

CHAPTER XI

BETWEEN THE STORMS. MINOR AFFAIRS IN JUNE AND EARLY JULY 1918. THE ACTIONS OF LA BECQUE, HAMEL AND VAIRE WOODS, AND METEREN	193
Note: German Morale in June 1918	215

CHAPTER XII

AWAITING ATTACK, 1ST–14TH JULY 1918 . . . 217

CHAPTER XIII

THE LAST GERMAN OFFENSIVE AND THE FRENCH COUNTER-STROKE. THE FOURTH BATTLE OF CHAMPAGNE, 15TH–18TH JULY 1918. THE SECOND BATTLE OF THE MARNE, 18TH JULY–6TH AUGUST 1918 (FIRST THREE DAYS)	228
Notes: I. Date of German Attack against the British in Flanders	251
II. German Troops left on the Eastern Front	253

CHAPTER XIV

THE SECOND BATTLE OF THE MARNE (*continued*), 21ST–26TH JULY 1918	254
Note: German Accounts of Fighting on the Eastern Wing, 21ST–26TH July	269

CONTENTS

CHAPTER XV

	PAGE
THE SECOND BATTLE OF THE MARNE (*continued*), 27TH–28TH JULY 1918. BUZANCY	272
Note: German Accounts of Buzancy	280

CHAPTER XVI

THE SECOND BATTLE OF THE MARNE (*continued*), 29TH–31ST JULY 1918	282
Note: The German Retirement, 25th–31st July	289

CHAPTER XVII

THE SECOND BATTLE OF THE MARNE (*concluded*), 1ST–6TH AUGUST 1918	293
Note: The German Retirement 1st–2nd August	309

CHAPTER XVIII

PLANS FOR AN ALLIED OFFENSIVE	311
Note: German Plans after the Retirement behind the Vesle	320

APPENDICES	323
INDEX	371

TABLE OF APPENDICES

ORDERS OF BATTLE

	PAGE
A. British Forces: IX. Corps, 27th May 1918	325
XXII. Corps, 20th July 1918	327
B. French Forces: Groups of Armies and Armies, May–July 1918	329
C. French Forces Engaged in the Battle of the Aisne	332

DOCUMENTS

I. War Commissions and Committees	333
II. General Foch's General Directive No. 3 (translation)	339
III. Messages sent by General Duchêne, commanding the French Sixth Army, 8.45 A.M. 27th May 1918, at the beginning of the Battle of the Aisne (translations)	342
IV. Operation Order No. 105 of the French XI. Corps, issued at 12 noon 27th May 1918 (translation)	343
V. Operation Order No. 3101 of the French Sixth Army for the 28th May, issued on the evening of the 27th (translation)	344
VI. Operation Order No. 3115 of the French Sixth Army, issued on the evening of the 28th May (translation)	345
VII. Operation Order No. 111 of the IX. Corps, issued on the 28th May in the afternoon	346
VIII. General Foch's Memorandum of the 1st June 1918 (translation)	347
IX. Instructions of the Secretary of State for War to the Field-Marshal Commanding-in-Chief, British Armies in France (War Office, 21st June 1918)	351
X. General Foch's Note of the 16th June 1918 (translation)	352
XI. Operation Order of the French Tenth Army, 22nd July 1918 (translation)	356
XII. Letter from General Foch to the General Commanding-in-Chief the Armies of the North and North-East, 23rd July 1918 (translation)	357

TABLE OF APPENDICES

		PAGE
XIII.	Operation Order No. 8 of the 15th Division, 28th July 1918	359
XIV.	Translation of a Captured German Divisional Operation Order of the 31st July 1918	360
XV.	Order of the Day by General Berthelot, commanding French Fifth Army, 30th July 1918	362
XVI.	Letter from General Fayolle, commanding Groupe d'Armées de Réserve (G.A.R.), to Field-Marshal Sir Douglas Haig, 2nd August 1918	363
XVII.	Letter from the G.O.C. French 17th Division to the G.O.C. 15th (Scottish) Division, 27th August 1918 (translation)	364
XVIII.	Letter from Field-Marshal Sir Douglas Haig to General Foch, 17th July 1918	365
XIX.	Letter from General Foch to Field-Marshal Sir Douglas Haig, 20th July 1918 (translation)	366
XX.	Memorandum by General Foch read at the Conference held by the Commanders-in-Chief of the Allied Armies, 24th July 1918 (translation)	367

MAPS AND SKETCHES

MAPS

(In Pocket)

1. 1st May 1918, Distribution of Divisions.
2. Chemin des Dames, 27th May 1918.
3. German Barrage and Target Map, 27th May 1918.

SKETCHES

(Bound in Volume)

A. Aisne-Marne, 1918 (layered)	*End-paper*
1. General Foch's Plans in General Directive No. 3 of 20th May 1918	*At beginning*
2. Chemin des Dames, 27th May 1918	*Facing* p. 31
3. Chemin des Dames, 27th May 1918 (British dispositions)	,, ,, 51
4. Chemin des Dames, 28th May 1918	,, ,, 103
5. Battle of the Aisne 1918, 27th May–13th June	,, ,, 121
6. IX. Corps, 29th May–2nd June 1918	,, ,, 125
7. The Matz, 9th–14th June 1918	,, ,, 173
8. La Becque, 28th June 1918	,, ,, 195
9. Hamel and Vaire Woods, 4th July 1918	,, ,, 197
10. Meteren, 19th July 1918	,, ,, 209
11. The Last German Offensive, July 1918	,, ,, 229
12. Battle of the Marne, 18th July–7th August 1918	,, ,, 241
13. Battle of Tardenois, 20th–31st July	,, ,, 243
14. Battle of the Soissonais and the Ourcq, 23rd July–2nd August 1918	,, ,, 265
15. The Marne 1918, the German Retirement	,, ,, 269
16. The Marne 1918, the Result, 18th July–7th August	,, ,, 305
17. The Sea to Reims, 7th August 1918	,, ,, 311
B. The German Offensives March to June 1918	*Inset* pp. 322-3

LIST OF BOOKS

TO WHICH MOST FREQUENT REFERENCE IS MADE

AMERICAN ORDER OF BATTLE : " Order of Battle of the United States Land Forces in the World War. American Expeditionary Forces." Prepared in the Historical Section, Army War College. (Washington, D.C.: Government Printing Office.)
  First volume : " General Headquarters, Armies, Army Corps, Services of Supply and Separate Forces ".
  Second volume : " Divisions ".
  In addition to the order of battle and names of commanders and staff officers, these volumes contain a succinct diary of the movements of each formation.

BRUCHMÜLLER : " Die deutsche Artillerie in den Durchbruchschlachten des Weltkrieges ". By Colonel G. Bruchmüller. (Berlin : Mittler.)
  Colonel Bruchmüller, an artillery expert, planned the artillery attack of the German *Eighteenth Army* against the Fifth Army on the 21st March 1918 and of the German *Seventh Army* at the Chemin des Dames. His book gives many details with target maps.

FRENCH OFFICIAL ACCOUNT (F.O.A.) : " Les Armées françaises dans la Grande Guerre ". Ministère de la Guerre. État-Major de l'Armée. Service Historique. (Paris : Imprimerie Nationale.)
  Tome VI. Volume II. and Tome VII. Volume I. cover the period dealt with in this volume.

HARBORD : " The American Army in France 1917–1919 ". By James G. Harbord, Major-General U.S. Army, retired list. (Boston : Little-Brown & Company.)
  Major-General Harbord was the first Chief of the Staff of the American Expeditionary Force, and, being allowed to go to the front, commanded the Marine Brigade at Belleau Wood and the 2nd Division in the Soissons offensive, described in this volume.

HINDENBURG : " Out of My Life ". By General Field-Marshal von Hindenburg. (London : Cassell.)
  Translation of " Aus meinem Leben ".

LIST OF BOOKS

KUHL: " Entstehung, Durchführung und Zusammenbruch der Offensive von 1918 ". By General von Kuhl. (Berlin: Deutscher Verlag.)

This is a most valuable source.

The author, the well-known Chief Staff Officer of General von Kluck in 1914, and later of Field-Marshal Crown Prince Rupprecht of Bavaria, was one of the three technical assistants of the *Reichstag* Commission which enquired into the causes of the loss of the War. His book contains the report which he made to the Commission, divided into five parts : The Relative Strengths, the Reinforcement and Supply of the Armies, the Decision to Attack, the Spring Offensives and the Defensive Battle in the Summer of 1918.

LUDENDORFF: " My War Memories 1914–18 ". By General Erich Ludendorff. (Hutchinson & Co.)

Translation of " Meine Kriegserinnerungen ".

MONOGRAPH I: " Deutsche Siege 1918. Das Vordringen der 7. Armee über Ailette, Aisne, Vesle und Ourcq bis zur Marne (27. Mai bis 13. Juni)." By Major von Bose and Oberarchivrat E. Otto " im Auftrage und unter Mitwirkung des Reichsarchivs ". (Oldenburg : Stalling.)

A very detailed official monograph on the Chemin des Dames offensive. In spite of its sub-title, it goes only to the 30th May.

MONOGRAPH II: " Wachsende Schwierigkeiten. Vergebliches Ringen vor Compiègne, Villers Cotterêts und Reims." (Oldenburg : Stalling.)

Same authors, etc., as Monograph I. This is a continuation of Monograph I. and covers the period 30th May–13th June, including the Battle of the Matz.

MONOGRAPH III: " Der letzte deutsche Angriff. Reims 1918." By Archivrat A. Stenger. (Oldenburg : Stalling.)

The last German attack.

MONOGRAPH IV : " Schicksalswende. Von der Marne bis zur Vesle 1918 ". (Oldenburg : Stalling.)

Same author, etc., as Monograph III. The turn of the tide by the French counter-stroke.

MORDACQ: " Le Ministère Clemenceau. Journal d'un témoin." By General Mordacq. (Paris : Plon.)

General Mordacq was Chief of the Military Cabinet of M. Clemenceau, the President of the Council of Ministers and Minister of War in 1918. He seldom left M. Clemenceau's side and kept a full diary.

PAQUET: " La Défaite militaire de l'Allemagne en 1918 ". By Lieut.-Colonel Paquet. (Paris : Berger-Levrault.)

The author, a member of the French Intelligence Staff, was attached to the Intelligence Branch, G.H.Q., in 1918. His book contains an analysis of the German losses and reinforcements.

LIST OF BOOKS xxvii

PERSHING EXPERIENCES : " My Experiences in the World War ". By John J. Pershing, Commander-in-Chief American Expeditionary Forces. (Hodder & Stoughton.)
    General Pershing's personal story founded on his diaries.

RUPPRECHT : " Mein Kriegstagebuch ". By Field-Marshal Crown Prince Rupprecht of Bavaria. (Munich : Deutscher National Verlag.)
    A diary full of interesting details kept by the commander of the Group of German Armies which faced the British.

SCHWARTE iii. : " Der deutsche Landkrieg ". Edited by Lieut.-General M. Schwarte. (Leipzig : Barth.)
    A compendium of the War in 12 volumes. Volume III. covers the operations on the Western Front from the time Hindenburg-Ludendorff took command until the Armistice, and contains extracts of operation orders and other useful matter.

SCHWERTFEGER : " Das Weltkriegsende ". By Colonel B. Schwertfeger. (Potsdam : Athenaion.)
    Colonel Schwertfeger, like General von Kuhl, was one of the three technical assistants of the *Reichstag* Commission which enquired into the causes of the loss of the War. His book contains much valuable information.

Note :

" 1918 " Vols. I. or II. signifies " The Official History of the Great War, Military Operations, France and Belgium ". Volume I. covers the period of the March offensive to the 26th March, and Volume II. from that date to the 30th April.

WAR IN THE AIR : " The War in the Air ". By H. A. Jones. (Clarendon Press.)
    The Official History of the part played by the Royal Air Force.

CALENDAR OF PRINCIPAL EVENTS

Mainly extracted from "Principal Events 1914–18" compiled by the Historical Section of the Committee of Imperial Defence, London. His Majesty's Stationery Office. 10s. 6d. net.

	Western Theatre.		Other Theatres.		Naval Warfare and General Events.
			MAY 1918		
1st.	Versailles Executive War Board dissolved.	1st.	*Russia*: Sevastopol taken by Germans.		During this month 60 British merchant ships (gross tonnage, 192,436) were lost by enemy action.
4th.	(4th–6th) Australians advance front near Morlancourt.	4th.	*Palestine*: 2nd Action of Es Salt ends.		
		7th.	*Balkans*: Treaty of Bukarest between Rumania and Central Powers signed. *Mesopotamia*: British enter Kirkuk. *Finland*: Civil war ends.	7th.	Letter from Major-General Sir F. Maurice to the press putting the blame for the March retreat on Mr. Lloyd George.
				9th.	Blocking of Ostend.
18th.	Australians advance front at Ville sur Ancre. Cologne bombed (1st British retaliatory air raid).			17th.	150 Sinn Fein leaders arrested for communicating with Germany.
				19th.	32nd and last German night air raid on London.
23rd.	Fifth Army reconstituted under General Sir W. Birdwood.	24th.	*N. Russia*: Major-General F. C. Poole arrives at Murmansk to organize forces.		
		25th.	*East Africa*: British advance from N. Rhodesia begins.		

xxix

CALENDAR OF PRINCIPAL EVENTS—(continued)

	Western Theatre.	Other Theatres.	Naval Warfare and General Events.

MAY 1918—(continued)

	Western Theatre.	Other Theatres.	Naval Warfare and General Events.
27th.	Battle of the Aisne (Chemin des Dames) begins.		
26th.			*Caucasus*: Georgia and Armenia declare independence. Republic of Azerbaijan proclaimed.
31st.		*Macedonia*: Battle of the Skra di Legen.	

JUNE 1918

	Western Theatre.	Other Theatres.	Naval Warfare and General Events.
			During this month 51 British merchant ships (gross tonnage, 162,990) were lost by enemy action.
5th.	Independent Air Force constituted.		*Arabia*: Sherif of Mecca begins revolt against Turkey. *Russia*: Don province declares its independence.
6th.	Battle of the Aisne ends. General Guillaumat appointed Governor of the Entrenched Camp of Paris.		
8th.		*Russia*: Germans land at Poti. Bolshevik Government order Entente forces to leave N. Russia.	
9th.	Battle of the Matz begins.		
10th.		*Arabia*: Turkish garrison of Mecca surrenders.	
12th.		*Caucasus*: Tiflis occupied by Germans.	

xxx

14th. Battle of the Matz ends.
15th. *Italy*: Second Battle of the Piave begins.
18th. *Macedonia*: General Franchet d'Espérey appointed Commander-in-Chief Allied forces.
23rd. *N. Russia*: British Expeditionary Force lands.
24th. *Italy*: Second Battle of the Piave ends.
24th. *Germany*: Kühlmann's pessimistic speech to *Reichstag*.

JULY 1918

1st. *East Africa*: Germans reach most southern point in Portuguese East Africa.
    During this month 37 British merchant ships (gross tonnage, 165,449) were lost by enemy action.
4th. Action of Hamel and Vaire Woods.
6th. *Albania*: French and Italian forces begin offensive.
9th. *Germany*: Hintze succeeds Kühlmann as Foreign Minister.
13th. *Siberia*: Irkutsk occupied by Czecho-Slovak forces.
15th. Last German (Reims) offensive begins.
16th. *Austria*: Field-Marshal Conrad von Hötzendorf ceases to be C.G.S. of the Austro-Hungarian forces.
16th. *Russia*: Ex-Tzar murdered.
18th. Second Battle of the Marne begins. Last German offensive ends.
19th. Action of Meteren.

CALENDAR OF PRINCIPAL EVENTS—*(concluded)*

	Western Theatre.	Other Theatres.	Naval Warfare and General Events.
		JULY 1918—*(continued)*	
24th.	Foch's conference at Bombon at which it is decided to press the offensive.		
20th.			*United Kingdom:* Last (unsuccessful) German aeroplane raid.
30th.			*Russia:* German commander in the Ukraine assassinated.
			During this month 41 British merchant ships (gross tonnage, 145,721) were lost by enemy action.
		AUGUST 1918	
1st.		*N. Russia:* capture of defences of Archangel.	
3rd.		*Siberia:* British troops land at Vladivostok.	
4th.		*Caucasus:* British forces arrive at Baku.	
5th.			*United Kingdom:* Last (unsuccessful) German airship raid.
6th.	General Foch created Maréchal de France.		
7th.	Second battle of the Marne ends.		

CHAPTER I

A Pause in the Operations

1st to 26th May 1918

(Map 1 ; Sketch 1)

THE first weeks of May were a period of uncertainty and uneasiness. A German wireless message in secret code, intercepted on the 1st May, stated that the attack in Flanders was to be discontinued for the moment; yet this aroused suspicion rather than allayed doubt. As each day passed, however, without the enemy making any visible attempt to resume offensive operations, the fears of the Allied High Command dwindled and the spirits of the troops rose. That the Germans should remain inactive after accomplishing so much and after creating two great salients in the Allied front, towards Montdidier (Amiens) and Hazebrouck, with long, weak flanks, seemed to indicate that they were more exhausted than their British opponents, worn and weary as the latter might well be. On the other hand, they still had in reserve a large number of divisions, so that as the general enemy front in the West formed roughly a right-angle, having the French on one face and the British and Belgians on the other, General Ludendorff was in a position to throw the weight of these reserves either southward or westward.

Actually, on the 1st May, opposite the front of 300 Map. 1. miles stretching from Switzerland to the Oise at Noyon, held by 58 French, one British, 3 American and 2 Italian divisions, the Germans had 57 divisions (44 of them fresh), including 3 in reserve ; between the Oise and the sea, 160 miles, held by one American and 45 French divisions (45 miles), 54 British (90 miles) and 6 Belgian [1] (25 miles), there were 139 German divisions (only 12 accounted

---

[1] " Divisions d'Armée ", containing 2 normal divisions.

fresh), but including 65 in reserve.¹ Ten more enemy divisions known to be on the Western Front were not yet located by the British Intelligence Branch ; so the total enemy reserve was 78.² During the next three weeks, with the exception that the number of divisions out of the line was increased by 11, the German dispositions did not appear to change greatly. By the arrival of two divisions from the East the total rose from 206 to 208 ; the number between Switzerland and the Oise fell from 57 to 54 (2 in reserve), and north of the Oise rose from 139 to 145 (78 in reserve); out of the total reserve of 89, only 9, according to the British Intelligence Branch, remained unlocated. Of the 78 in reserve north of the Oise, 56 (besides 54 in the line) were opposite the British and Belgians, and the remaining 22 (reserves of the *Eighteenth* and *Second Armies*) were within twenty-five miles of the Oise, and within thirty miles of the front of the French Sixth Army, which held the Chemin des Dames, east of the Oise, although there appeared to be only 8 (according to the British Intelligence) or 9 (to the French Intelligence) actually opposing that Army. Behind these were possibly the 9 divisions whose position was not known.

The French, with 103 divisions and 6 cavalry divisions, had 45 divisions and 3 American divisions in the line between Switzerland and the Oise—of these only 13 and 2 American were east of the tip of the St. Mihiel Salient on 150 of the 300 miles. In reserve south of the Oise, arranged in four groups, were 13 French divisions, 2 Italian (which had been sent to France on the 18th April) and one British (50th), sent for rest on a quiet front; and, near the river were 3 cavalry divisions. Immediately north of the Oise were 16 French divisions and one American, with 9 behind them in reserve. In Flanders, with the British Second Army, was the Détachement d'Armée du Nord (D.A.N.), with 4 divisions in the line and 6, with 3 cavalry divisions, in reserve. In General Foch's General Reserve were the French Fifth Army (7 divisions) behind the French left, where his own headquarters lay at Sarcus, and the French Tenth Army (3 divisions) behind the British centre, west of Doullens—St. Pol.³

¹ See Note II. at end of Chapter on the distribution of German divisions on 1st and 24th May and Map 1.
² The French Intelligence showed not 10 but 47 unlocated.
³ General Foch was enabled to assemble the General Reserve of 10 divisions because, to replace French divisions, the Americans had given him

Of the French divisions, 22 had fought in the Picardy battle in March, and four (the 22nd, 56th, 66th and 133rd) had suffered severely; two had fought in the German "Archangel" attack on the Ailette, and four, besides cavalry, in the Lys battle, the 28th with heavy casualties. According to the French records, altogether 43 divisions and 6 cavalry divisions had been engaged in March and April, with a gross loss of 100,000 officers and other ranks.[1]

There had been a general drift of the French Armies to the left. To replace losses, General Pétain had, on the 4th April, asked that 200,000 of the youngest of the 1,200,000 men mobilized as fit for service in the interior should be drafted into the ranks, in particular the miners thrown out of work by the German advance in the Béthune area. The Minister of War could offer only 40,000 before the 15th June; but he promised to send for instruction in the Zone of the Armies on the 1st July the infantry and engineer contingents of the 1919 Class, which would normally not be mobilizable until October. These, with 59,000 coloured troops and 15,000 Poles and Czechs, would make up the numbers and render it unnecessary to break up any divisions, as General Pétain had threatened to do.

The alarming features of the situation were the wastage of the British Armies, and the danger from the air to which the troops and multifarious establishments, particularly those of the Second Army, were now exposed, crowded together as they were in a narrow coastal area. Enemy bombers, often in relays, came over the line nearly every night, clear or dark; the ports of Dunkirk, Calais and Boulogne were specially attacked; even G.H.Q. did not escape; the hospital establishments at Etaples and Abbeville suffered considerably; the villages in the Somme valley and the railway bridges received special attention: the long brickwork railway viaduct over the Canche at Etaples, on the one line now left between Calais—Boulogne and Abbeville, over which a hundred military trains passed daily, was bombed almost nightly in May, but only touched once in the early morning of the 31st.[2] With the exception that an ordnance depôt at Saigneville (5 miles north-west of Abbeville) was set on fire and 5,600 tons of ammunition

---

4 American divisions, each, with an establishment of 28,105 men, approximately double the strength in infantry of a French division; in addition the Italians had sent 2.

[1] F.O.A. vi. (ii.), p. 3.   [2] See Chapter IX.

destroyed on the 21st/22nd, and that in a dump at Campagne (15 miles east of Calais, Second Army area) a thousand tons were similarly lost on the 18th and 19th, no material military damage was suffered. In fact, from the point of view of the fighting troops, enemy air bombing did very little more than interrupt sleep and cause annoyance. A double line of powerful searchlights gradually organized behind the front under the Inspector of Searchlights, Lieut.-Colonel W. C. H. Prichard, R.E., did much to keep enemy fliers high up in the air and save at least the forward areas.

As regards wastage, nearly the whole strength of Sir Douglas Haig's command had been called upon to withstand the superior weight of two great enemy attacks, first in the " March offensive " between the 21st March and 5th April, and then again, in the Battles of the Lys, between the 9th and 30th April. Of the total of 59 divisions (49 British, 5 Australian, 4 Canadian and one New Zealand), 43 besides the 3 cavalry divisions had been engaged in the former, and 24 in the latter—17 of them in both battles. The casualties in the two offensives had been 177,739 and 82,040, total 259,779.[1] The troops badly needed rest, reinforcements and time for reorganization and for training their drafts.

According to the return of the Adjutant-General in France dated 6th May, the reinforcements received had numbered 133,092, mostly boys of $18\frac{1}{2}$ and wounded who had recovered : 27th to 31st March, 26,384 ; 1st to 30th April, 102,698 ; 1st to 5th May, 4,010. In addition, 26,220 had been sent up from the base. Lieut.-General Sir G. Fowke put the excess of officer casualties over replacements at 3,009, and made the infantry total 48,000 less than on the 20th March, to which, to envisage the whole deficit, must be added 75,000, the shortage of infantry before the battle.[2] The field artillery was over 3,000 short and the heavy artillery nearly 2,000. On the 15th May the Adjutant-General put the decrease in fighting troops since the 1st January 1917 at 93,000, from which, for comparison, should be deducted 14,100 added to the air forces ; but the increase in non-combatants on ration strength had been 328,650, of whom no less than 308,100 were on

---

[1] See " 1918 " Vol. II., pp. 490-3. A final report of the Adjutant-General in France, dated 6th May, reduced, as might be expected, the total by nearly 20,000, that is about 8 per cent, to 9,704 officers and 230,089 other ranks.

[2] See " 1918 " Vol. I., p. 27.

Transportation and Labour services, and 4,100 W.A.A.C. There were now 50 British divisions in France (inclusive of the newly-arrived 52nd from Egypt), which were made up of 9 infantry battalions each instead of 12 [1] since the decision had been taken on the 10th January by Mr. Lloyd George's Government to reduce them to a lower establishment. Out of these, 15 had battalions with a strength of 900 other ranks, so that the rifle strength was under 8,100 instead of being 11,136 as in 1914; in 19, it was between 800 and 900; in 6, below 800; and 10 ranked as exhausted. The Commander-in-Chief had already received authority to reduce to cadre nine divisions which averaged under 3,500 infantrymen apiece, but only eight were actually so treated.[2] One of the weaker divisions, the 50th, had already been sent to the French Sixth Army, and four more were earmarked to follow,[3] under a system of " roule-" ment " suggested by General Foch, whereby tired British divisions were to be used to free French divisions which were holding quiet sectors, in order to make the latter available for the General Reserve.[4] For fighting purposes, Sir Douglas Haig had therefore only 37 British and 10 Dominion divisions, to which must be added the 74th (Yeomanry) Division, which began to reach France from Egypt on the 1st May. The Portuguese divisions could no longer be counted as fit for battle.[5]

Of the eight cadre divisions, the 30th and 34th were to be reconstituted as first line divisions with battalions from Egypt and Palestine; but this could not be done until July, and meantime they were, with the 39th and 66th, to be employed in training American troops; the

[1] The 52nd Division was not reduced until 28th June.
[2] Reduction to cadre usually meant that the infantry battalions were reduced to 10 officers and 45 other ranks, the surplus being sent to the base depôts. The artillery, engineers, machine gunners, etc., were attached to corps or other divisions for employment.
The 14th, 16th, 30th, 31st, 34th, 39th, 40th, 59th and 66th Divisions were selected for reduction. Except the first two and the last, they had fought in both battles, but even these three in one battle suffered losses of 5,793, 7,149 and 7,023. Ultimately the 31st was not reduced.
[3] The 8th, 21st, 25th and, later, the 19th. The strength of their battalions was to be maintained at 700. All except the 8th, which suffered 4,869 casualties in the March offensive, had been in both battles. The 8th and 21st were completed by drafts, as was later the 19th. It was proposed to reconstitute either the 25th or 50th with battalions from Salonika and send the cadre of the other to England, but this had not been done before the battle on the Chemin des Dames.
[4] See " 1918 " Vol. II., pp. 367, 378.
[5] For the distribution of the British forces, see Note I. at end of Chapter and Map 1.

40th and 59th were to be filled up with "B" men from England as garrison divisions; and the 14th and 16th sent to England for reconstitution.

General Foch protested very strongly against the reduction of any divisions until the crisis should be past. He suggested that, in order to increase the General Reserve on which future success depended, all or the greater number of the divisions under sentence should be sent to the French front to replace fresh divisions, at least until August, by which time plenty of British reinforcements should be coming along. He said that he was sure that out of "the 1,400,000 men wearing khaki in England",[1] 100,000 could be obtained to fill out nine divisions sufficiently to hold a quiet part of the front and release fresh divisions for the General Reserve. Sir Douglas Haig could only promise to communicate with the War Office, receiving the assurance that M. Clemenceau would impress on the Prime Minister the urgent need for sending soldiers to France. Eventually General Foch obtained from General Wilson, the Chief of the Imperial General Staff, an assurance that, over and above the 20,000 reinforcements per month, which it had been settled should be sent to France during the three weeks commencing the 20th May, 70,000 more would be sent. In the end, this addition, and the arrival of battalions from Egypt—Palestine, enabled the gaps to be filled, and by the end of June six of the eight divisions had been reconstituted, and during July, one more; only the 39th was left—it had been fighting in the later part of the Lys battle as a brigade-division of 4 battalions—its staffs and cadres continuing to be employed in training American divisions and administering a number of attached cadres and reinforcements which were engaged in constructing back lines.[2]

The ammunition situation on the 1st May was entirely satisfactory, and continued to improve. On that date there were in France, for instance, 7,582,772 rounds for the 3,109 18-pdr. guns; 2,182,523 rounds for 982 field

---

[1] See "1918" Vol. I., p. 52, where a War Office return of 1st January 1918 is quoted giving the total in the United Kingdom, excluding Dominion troops, as 74,403 officers and 1,486,459 other ranks, with 607,403 trained "A" men available, and 359,270 "unavailable" (cadres, administrative duties, recruits, etc.).

[2] The 14th, 16th and 66th were filled up with drafts; the 30th and 34th with battalions from Egypt and Palestine; the 40th and 59th with "B" men.

howitzers; 1,368,292 rounds for 990 6-inch howitzers. The number of tanks was increased at about the rate of twenty a week; on the 16th May the strength was, 129 Mark V., 387 Mark IV. and 82 Whippets.

Sir Douglas Haig spent some part of each day during this period in visiting the various divisions; he learnt they were in good heart; the " B " class men seemed as efficient as the rest, except that they had been insufficiently exercised in marching, and so found a 10-mile tramp a considerable trial.

The French and British measures to supply effectives did not even succeed in bringing all the existing divisions up to establishment, whilst they left few men available to replace losses, and none for an expansion to equal, if not exceed, the number of German divisions. The only solution of the Allied difficulties as regards man-power in the field appeared to be the hastening of the transport to Europe of American forces.

On the 1st May there were in France seven American divisions and parts of two others. The 1st Division (Regular Army) was in the line near Montdidier, the 2nd (Regular Army), 26th (National Guard) and 42nd ("Rainbow", National Guard) were in training in Lorraine on quiet fronts, but now fit to take a more active part; the 32nd (National Guard) was employed on the lines of communication; the 41st (National Guard) was the depôt division; the 3rd (less artillery and engineers, Regular Army) was in a training area, and did not move up to the front until the 30th May; the 5th (Regular Army) had begun disembarkation at Brest on the 7th April, but did not complete it until the 19th June (it remained training in a French area until the 14th July); the 77th (the first of the New Army divisions) arrived between the 13th April and the 13th May. The total strength of the American Expeditionary Force in France on the 30th April was 23,548 officers and 406,111 enlisted men. During May, the 82nd, 35th, 28th, 4th, 33rd, 27th, 30th and 80th Divisions began to arrive, so that the total on the 31st May was 32,642 officers and 618,642 enlisted men. Under the Pershing—Milner agreement of the 24th April,[1] the infantry, machine gunners, engineers and signal troops of six American divisions, and the headquarters of divisions and brigades were to

---

[1] See " 1918 " Vol. II., pp. 444-5.

be brought over in British and American shipping during May for training and service with the British Army in France, the troops necessary to make the divisions complete being transported in surplus shipping if available. The disposal of the American troops formed one of the subjects of debate at the Fifth Session of the Supreme War Council on the 1st and 2nd May at Abbeville, where it reassembled for the first time since the German March offensive and passed several resolutions.[1] It was, amongst other things, agreed : first, in view of the powers conferred upon General Foch, to dissolve the Executive War Board ; secondly, to send a commission to Salonika to confer with General Guillaumat (the Allied commander) for the purpose of arranging with him the immediate withdrawal of some battalions—12 British were eventually withdrawn ; thirdly, to urge the Italian Government to accept an arrangement for the increase of naval forces in the Ægean prepared by the Allied Naval Council ; fourthly, to approve of arrangements for the transportation of Czech troops from Russia ; and, fifthly, to extend General Foch's powers of co-ordination to the Italian front.

It was the debate upon the disposal of the American troops which absorbed the greater part of the two days. General Pershing, very naturally, desired to form an American Army as soon as possible—the Canadian Government also at this very time was anxious that their troops should form a separate Army, and the Australians held similar views. The French and British representatives, in face of the situation, argued that the system of sending over divisions less artillery and services, arranged for May, should be continued during June, and the troops should be brigaded, by battalions or smaller units, under British and French divisions. A somewhat heated discussion took place, as M. Clemenceau and General Foch maintained that Lord Milner had taken an unfair advantage of them in making a separate agreement with General Pershing for May ; but the American Commander-in-Chief declined to be coerced. Finally, with a view to meeting the present emergency, it was agreed that the programme of transporting the infantry, engineers and machine guns of six divisions during May, should be continued during June ; to this end,

[1] There were present the Prime Ministers of France, Italy and Great Britain, and Mr. A. H. Frazier, First Secretary, U.S. Embassy in Paris, with Lord Milner, 24 naval and military officers, including General Foch and the Commanders-in-Chief, Sir Maurice Hankey and an interpreter.

the British Government would furnish transportation for a minimum of 130,000 men in May and 150,000 in June, with the understanding that the first contingent of six divisions should go to the British for training and service, and that troops sent over in June should be allocated to training and service as the American Commander-in-Chief might determine.

The Council also formally resolved : " it is the opinion " of the Supreme War Council that, in order to carry the " War to a successful conclusion, an American Army " should be formed as early as possible under its own " commander and under its own flag ", the American infantry and engineers serving with the British and French Armies being withdrawn and united with their own artillery, etc., into divisions and corps as soon as the present emergency had been met.[1]

By the 14th May there were training with the British under the cadres of the 30th, 34th, 39th and 66th Divisions, 18 American battalions : 12 of the 77th Division and 3 each from the 35th and 82nd Divisions ; by the 23rd, the infantry of the 28th and 4th Divisions had begun to arrive, and the American strength with the British was reported as 2,379 officers and 74,283 other ranks (the strengths in the divisions varying from 19,951 in the 77th to 6,025 in the 4th).[2] The numbers carried across in March and April had been 64,200 and 93,128. In May, "thanks to British tonnage ",[3] the number rose to 206,287, of whom 176,602 were combatants, and 140,024 of these were infantry.[4]

Many weeks must obviously pass before the Allies

[1] General Pershing appositely quotes in his " Experiences ", p. 386, the very explicit instructions given by Louis XVI. to the Count de Rochambeau, the commander of his troops sent to America to aid in the Revolution : " the intentions of the King are that the French troops shall not be dispersed " in any manner and that they shall serve at all times as a corps d'armée " and under the French generals, except in the case of temporary detach- " ments, and then they should rejoin the main body within a few days ".

[2] One brigadier of the 77th asked that, if his battalions were sent into the line, British officers and N.C.O.'s might be left, " because it would be " little short of murder to send his men into the trenches in their present " ignorant state without them ".

[3] F.O.A. vi. (ii.), p. 31.

[4] The distribution at the end of May given in F.O.A. vi. (ii.), pp. 31-2, is : two divisions (1st and 2nd) battle-fit in Picardy at the disposal of the French ; three divisions (26th, 32nd and 42nd) in quiet sectors of the G.A.E. ; two divisions (3rd and 5th) completed disembarkation ; five divisions (4th, 28th, 30th, 35th and 82nd) in course of disembarkation ; four divisions (27th, 33rd, 78th and 80th) in transport ; and one depôt division (41st). This omits the 77th training with the British.

could take advantage of the increasing strength of the American Army to stage an attack, but fortunately a pause in the operations seemed likely. The Germans, though perilously near success, had lost heavily in their two great offensives, and had used up a great number of divisions. According to the Intelligence reckoning, no less than 140 had been engaged, of which 60 were definitely accounted " tired ". They, too, needed time to recuperate and reorganize.[1] Nevertheless, if the enemy intended to try to force a decision before the initiative, which he still retained, might pass from him, and before the weight of the American Army began to make itself felt, further attacks could not long be delayed. For the moment, the enemy was on the defensive ; but this phase was not likely to last. A hopeful factor was that it had taken him twelve days to accomplish the difficult and intricate manœuvre of shifting his " battering train " of heavy guns, trench mortars and aeroplanes together with their accompaniment of ammunition and material from the Amiens—Arras battlefield to the Lys region for the offensive of the 9th April. Whether he decided to continue the battle for Hazebrouck and the north, or to attack a new sector, it now seemed certain that he must allow the Allies some respite. For in the first case he would be compelled to expend at least several weeks in reorganizing and extending his railway communications. In the second, there would be at least a dozen days, probably more, before the preparations could be completed. Whatever the enemy did, the Allies must play for time, using every possible means to discover what the enemy's intentions might be, and taking no risk of their own line being broken.

To improve the position at the front and to keep the enemy from imagining that he could shift troops as he pleased, a number of small operations were undertaken, mainly on the fronts of the Fourth, Third and First Armies. On the night of the 2nd/3rd May, the 4th Australian Division (Fourth Army), in co-operation with the French, carried out a small operation in front of Villers Bretonneux, and secured 21 prisoners ; but it was unable to hold the ground gained as the enemy brought up reinforcements

[1] From prisoners and captured documents of 16 German divisions, summarized on 7th May, it appeared that these divisions had lost more than 40 per cent of their infantry in the recent fighting ; some companies were down to a strength of 9, 18, 20, 23, 29, 30-35 men. The *26th Reserve Division*, still in the line on 1st May near Arras, was said to have lost over 60 per cent. It left the line on the 14th.

MINOR OPERATIONS

which eventually amounted to five divisions. During the night of the 3rd/4th, the 3rd Division (First Army) slightly advanced its line north of the La Bassée canal. On the other hand, the enemy retook the wood near Locre in the French sector of the Second Army. On the night of the 4th/5th, the 3rd Australian Division (Fourth Army) began operations to improve the front near Morlancourt, and continued them on the 5th/6th, advancing five hundred yards on a 2,000-yard front and taking 150 prisoners. On the 8th, in reply, the enemy attacked the junction of the D.A.N. and the XXII. Corps (Second Army) near Kemmel; but after an initial success he was ejected. A local operation by the 37th Division (Third Army) on the 9th, east of Bucquoy, and another by the V. Corps (Third Army) near Aveluy Wood, failed to retain their gains.[1] On the 13th, the I. Corps (First Army) discharged gas from 5,000 cylinders—more than the total used at the battle of Loos in 1915—in one vast cloud between Hulluch and the Hohenzollern Redoubt, and a thousand drums were projected near Cité St. Elie (south of La Bassée) and Le Cornet Malo (north of Béthune). On the 18th/19th, the 2nd Australian Division (Fourth Army) captured Ville sur Ancre, established its line 3,500 yards beyond it and took about 400 prisoners. On the 19th/20th, the D.A.N. carried out an operation to improve the French position south of Kemmel, and captured over 300 prisoners. On the 21st, the 5th Division (First Army) successfully closed a re-entrant north-west of Merville, and the 63rd Division (Third Army) recovered four posts lost to the enemy in the Aveluy Wood sector on the previous day. On the 24th, 4,000 gas cylinders were successfully discharged by the Third Army in the Mericourt—Avion—Lens sector.

Throughout the period 1st-26th May, the Royal Air Force was very active, particularly in the fine weather which prevailed from the 15th to the 23rd, and in air fighting maintained the upper hand. In every 24 hours, bombs were dropped on railway junctions, depôts and billets, the number of tons varying according to the weather, from 57, 37, 35, 34 down to 3, 2, and $1\frac{1}{2}$. Long-range flights by British squadrons, based on an aerodrome near Nancy, reached Metz, Thionville, Saarbrücken and Mannheim; whilst the Royal Naval Air Force dealt with Bruges,

---

[1] In the early hours of the 10th, an attempt was made to block the entrance to the Ostend docks with H.M.S. *Vindictive*; she was duly sunk in the channel, but obstructed only one-third of it.

Zeebruge and Ostend. The general result was disappointing, and had no greater effect on the issue of operations than had the German bombing of the small British area.

Proposals were now taking shape for the establishment in France of an independent air force intended for the bombing of enemy territory in accordance with orders received from the Air authorities in London. In discussing this idea with the Commander-in-Chief on the 17th May, Major-General Trenchard stated that he considered such an organization quite unsound. But, as will be seen, it was subsequently forced upon Sir Douglas Haig.

It had been agreed between General Foch and Sir Douglas Haig that four tired British divisions, and possibly a fifth, should be sent, under the G.O.C. IX. Corps, Lieut.-General Sir A. H. Gordon, to some " secteurs calmes du " front français "—the Chemin des Dames sector was selected by General Foch—in order to allow him to add fresh French divisions to the General Reserve. On the 30th April, General Foch had written suggesting that the number should be increased to 10—15, " to begin with ", as he had already reduced his reserve by the 10 divisions which he had sent north. He now thought that a further exchange of forces between the active and quiet fronts was more indispensable than ever. Sir Douglas Haig replied that arrangements were being made to despatch the 8th and 21st Divisions at once, and that the 25th would follow as soon as relieved by the D.A.N. : the despatch of further divisions would depend on the situation. General Foch, however, pressed for an answer to the proposal to send 10–15 divisions, promising to consider the relief of two divisions of the XXII. Corps by extending the front of the D.A.N. northwards with one division. He insisted that his reserves were altogether insufficient, that their low total constituted a veritable danger, and in particular he deplored his consequent inability to maintain a General Reserve of at least four divisions in the St. Pol area and northward.

During their presence at the meeting of the Supreme War Council at Abbeville on the 1st/2nd May there was an amicable discussion of the matter between the two commanders. Sir Douglas Haig fully admitted the necessity of forming a strong General Reserve, and agreed to send two more divisions. On the 8th, however, the Generalissimo expressed his uneasiness about the smallness of the reserve near Amiens, and said that no more French divisions could be brought to this area until relieved by the British. To this the British Commander-in-Chief replied that he did not think it wise to send away any more British divisions from the north in the present crisis. Finally, General Foch admitted that, given the figures of the reinforcements which were being received from England, it was impossible for Sir Douglas Haig to do more, but again urged him to insist with his Government upon the importance of some large increase of the number of reinforcements to be sent. Such an increase, he declared, was necessary in order to place the Allies in a position to face with success the enemy's total of two hundred or more divisions during the critical months of May, June and July.

The British authorities had by now quite disabused themselves of the idea that General Foch was trying to secure entire control of the British forces by mixing them with the French in small packets of a few divisions, and admitted the correctness of his views in the endeavour to create a General Reserve. Being a strategist, however, with only a small operations staff,[1] he had overlooked the administrative difficulties of placing British troops in French areas and vice versa; these must inevitably arise, since the ammunition, material, even rations, hospital arrangements, and system of making up supply trains, were quite different in the two Armies. To meet the situation of supplying the British divisions in French areas, it was eventually agreed to adopt as far as possible the French system of bulk trains from ports to regulating stations without the use of advanced bases.[2] The proviso was accepted that the bulky stores in use by both Armies, such as hay, straw, oats, petrol, and engineer material would be supplied on the spot by the French and replaced in kind at a convenient centre. Two days' supplies were to be kept at the regulating stations against emergencies.

The question of pooling all Army supplies had been raised by the Italian Permanent Military Representative at the Supreme War Council at the end of February, and brought up again in a letter of General Pershing to the Prime Minister on the 28th April. The Americans were already

[1] He had no administrative staff until August. See "1918" Vol. II., p. 1.
[2] That is, each train contained one sort of supplies only, e.g., food rations, wood, oil, engineer or ordnance stores; at a "regulating station" these were broken up and sorted out into mixed trains to meet the requirements of divisions. See "1916" Vol. I., p. 101.

in difficulties and had begun purchasing in Europe what the Homeland had failed to send.[1] Sir Henry Wilson saw in the suggestion an attempt of the French " to take us " over administratively as well as strategically ", and he proved to be right. An Inter-Allied conference was held in Paris on the 6th May to consider the co-ordination of the military supply and transport systems, and construction in the Allied rear areas in France. At this meeting, Colonel Dawes represented the U.S.A.,[2] Colonel Payot, the head of the services of Supply and Transport, France, and General Sir John Cowans, the Quartermaster-General to the Forces, the British Empire. Definite suggestions were made to pool food, oil, tanks and aeroplanes. In theory, pooling seemed a simple matter which would benefit the cause and all the Allies. But the British authorities saw many and various practical difficulties in the idea. It would, in the first place, involve the collection of statistics and an enquiry into the resources of each nation—when it was already a daily problem for the administrative staffs to keep their Armies supplied from the stores which they had collected in depôts ; in the second place, they obviously could not be responsible for the maintenance and feeding of their troops if some higher authority could pounce on their depôts and send the contents to another Army ; further, the proposals for co-ordination, if adopted, would mean the pooling of locomotives and rolling stock, mechanical transport vehicles, and labour, also the reallotment of storage and dock accommodation, and the reduction of the American and British ration, since the former was double that of the British and the British slightly larger than those of the other Allies ; it might eventually result in the evacuation of British wounded in other than their own hospital trains, and their treatment in hospitals other than their own, where accommodation was less elaborate ; a situation could not be gauged by counting the supplies in France—the Americans, for instance, might have a great accumulation, but, as their communications with the Homeland were liable to be interrupted, their supplies might be required to last a long time ; in some cases the failure of supplies to reach our Allies had not

---

[1] Ten million tons of military material were thus gathered, whilst only seven million tons were sent over from the U.S.A. See " The American " Army in France 1917–19 ", by Major-General J. G. Harbord, who was first Chief of the Staff and later Chief of the Service of Supply.

[2] Later Br.-General ; a Chicago banker, with a temporary commission in the U.S. Engineers, known to us as General Dawes.

been due to lack of them, but to indifferent administration. The British Quartermaster-General pronounced the scheme unworkable, but stated that the Allied Munitions Council in Paris was preparing to deal with the pooling of many military supplies. It was decided to investigate the subject further.[1]

On the 1st June an agreement on the pooling of supplies made on the 22nd May between M. Clemenceau and General Pershing was suddenly announced and laid before the Supreme War Council. It contained the proposal that a Board consisting of representatives of each of the Allied Armies should be constituted, with the safeguard that only the unanimous decision of the Board regarding allotment of material and supplies should have the force of orders. The Board was set up in July, with, eventually, no less than 73 members representing all the nations of the alliance against Germany. A tendency was soon apparent to make the Board an agency for placing the material resources of the Allies at the disposal of the Generalissimo, and the position became one of great delicacy. The British were fully prepared to assist the Allies who were in want, but not to throw everything into a common pool.[2] A crisis was averted by the action of Colonel Dawes. An Inter-Allied reserve of lorries for troop movements was formed; French and American ammunition was pooled; and a number of measures tending to a more effective use of combined resources without interfering with the internal administration of any one Army were adopted or put in hand. But the Board was only in the early stages of its usefulness when the War came to an end.

A question of greater urgency to the British than pooling supplies was the reorganization of the railway system.[3] All four Armies had lost some of their railheads

[1] The manifold complications which arise in a national war are well illustrated by the number of councils, committees, etc., it was judged necessary to set up. A list of those in existence in March 1918 is given in Appendix I.

[2] General Dawes says in his book " A Journal of the Great War " (3rd July), p. 132. " The English are co-operating like the thoroughbreds they " are ". In this book and in the " R.A.S.C. History of Transport and " Supply " Vol. II., p. 148 *et seq.* by Colonel R. H. Beadon, who was the British representative until replaced in September by Major-General R. Ford, interesting details of the working of the Military Board of Allied Supply will be found.

[3] On 19th March the experiment of placing " Transportation "— railways, light railways, canals, roads in rear areas, docks—in charge of a civilian railway magnate had been abandoned, and Major-General S. D'A.

during the German offensives—the Fifth Army every one —and had had to take unprepared stations in rear into use as they found them. Great parts of the light railway system had been abandoned; nevertheless it was decided that, with a few exceptions, no new light lines should be built until the situation became more stable. As regards the standard gauge lines, the most pressing needs were new ammunition railheads and facilities for unloading tanks, besides new lines and connections. Labour was short, so a definite programme was got out;[1] but it was not until September, more than four months after the close of the German offensive in the north, that the Director-General of Transportation was able to report the practical completion in the back areas of all standard gauge works which had been adjudged indispensable.

In view of the anxiety and danger caused by the maintenance of large depôts in the now restricted zone occupied by the British Armies, exposed as it was to intensive bombing, and, in the event of a resumption of the enemy's operations, even to long-range artillery fire, the Quartermaster-General had already taken steps to relieve the northern area of certain stocks of ammunition, workshops, hospitals and depôts by removing them southwards.[2] He suggested that reserves of supplies, ammunition, ordnance stores, guns and spare parts, R.E. and Transportation stores, over and above 14 days' normal expenditure, should be kept in the south of England. This measure it was not found necessary to put into practice.

Schemes for the evacuation of personnel, stores and animals, in view of various contingencies, such as the loss of the southern line of communications should the enemy break in between the French and British near Amiens, or the evacuation under his pressure of the whole area north

---

Crookshank, R.E., appointed Director-General of Transportation. In June the D.G.T. and his department reverted to the control of the Q.M.G., from whom " Transportation " had been detached on the advent of Sir Eric Geddes in 1916, and its establishment of personnel was reduced. See " 1916 " Vol. II., p. 548.

[1] See " Transportation on the Western Front 1914–1918 " by Colonel A. M. Henniker, pp. 411-19.

[2] Thus one ammunition depôt at Bourbourg was closed, and two, at Zeneghem and Audruicq, reduced; two M.T. repair shops moved from Bergues and St. Omer to Honfleur and Rouen; the hospitals at Calais and St. Omer removed, and those in the Etaples area reduced and sent to Trouville.

Beaurainville was completed as a petrol depôt to replace Calais.

DOUBT AS TO GERMAN INTENTIONS

of the Somme, had been under consideration since the 26th March. For the latter contingency a complete scheme was drawn up to fit in with General Plumer's plan for a withdrawal of the front to a series of successive back lines. In such a case the Navy undertook to give assistance and assumed responsibility for the destruction of the docks of Dunkirk. But so many authorities were involved that it was not till early in June that the scheme was ready. At a rough estimate, it involved 250,000 persons and 600,000 tons of stores. At first it was hoped that such an evacuation might be carried out in 14 days, but detailed calculations showed that it would take at least 28.

It was suggested to Sir Douglas Haig by the Chief of the Imperial General Staff, on behalf of the War Cabinet, that, in view of the complicated problems of modern war, he should take an eminent civilian as his engineer adviser; but he replied that he was perfectly satisfied with his Engineer-in-Chief. During May, however, the War Cabinet sent out a party of four eminent civil engineers, including two past Presidents of the Institution of Civil Engineers and one who was destined to become President. After a week's tour of the front during which the party repeatedly came under fire, they informed the Commander-in-Chief that they considered things were running so well that advice from them would be superfluous.

Until the very eve of the 27th May, when the Germans attacked the French Sixth Army, complete doubt and uncertainty reigned at G.H.Q. and G.Q.G. as to where, if it should come, such a blow would fall, although the Intelligence Branch of the American Army at Chaumont handed in to the Supreme War Council on the 25th April a shrewd forecast based on logical grounds, that the sector Reims—Montdidier, which included the Chemin des Dames and the Matz, seemed the most probable enemy objective. The Germans had lost the Chemin des Dames ridge in October 1917, and ever since it had been a quiet sector,[1] in spite of the concealed approaches afforded by the wooded nature of the country lying to the northwards: there were as many as a hundred German divisions con-

---

[1] It had been undisturbed, too, from 10th January 1915, when the French were pushed off it and over the Aisne, until 16th April 1917, when General Nivelle had launched his offensive. The Germans called the sector "the sanatorium of the West" (Goes, "Chemin des Dames", p. 87).

veniently handy to the sector, whilst the Allies had, at most, 62 : the railway facilities from north to south of the Somme were much in favour of the enemy, he had three double lines and one single track against the two French single tracks : surprise in force was thus easy. Such views found " no converts at French " G.Q.G." [1]

The first appreciation of the situation made at G.H.Q. was that the Germans would continue the battle in the north, but not towards Hazebrouck, as in that area they were now stuck in the mud, tired-out and suffering all the consequent miseries : the bulk of the enemy's reserves were still in the Somme area, and he might very rapidly concentrate them against the Somme—Arras front, probably between Albert and Arras. This view was confirmed by a statement made on the 2nd May by a captured airman. This was not, however, the opinion of General Foch, who, on the 3rd May, wrote that the enemy's offensive on the Bailleul—Ypres front might be renewed any day, and that the best method of countering would be by an attack from the front Festubert—Robecq towards Merville and Estaires ; a similar French offensive, he said, was in preparation ; and he suggested that the Canadian Corps, which had hardly been engaged, might be employed. Sir Douglas Haig replied on the same day that preparations for the very offensive proposed were already in hand, that the Canadian Corps (less one division) had been withdrawn for the purpose, and that the attack could be carried out at short notice : but, as the Germans were evidently making preparations for an attack on a considerable scale on the British front, he might require all available reserves to resist it : consequently he did not consider the time suitable for the operation suggested. General Foch then expressed great anxiety that no retirement should be made voluntarily without reference to him, and that close connection should be kept with the Belgian Army. Sir Douglas Haig was able to reassure him upon both these points.

On the 5th May the Generalissimo addressed a tactical note to Sir Douglas Haig, General Pétain, the G.A.R., the D.A.N. and the four French Armies nearest to the British,

---

[1] Pershing " Experiences ", p. 408. Harbord, p. 269. General Tasker Bliss, the American Military Representative on the Supreme War Council, noted on the paper that he presented it in person to the Supreme Command on 25th April, " but the American views were not accepted ".

GERMAN PREPARATIONS

on the subject of preventing a rapid penetration of the Allied positions by the enemy. He ordered that, without delay, they should develop the organization of the positions now held, increase fire-power by bringing up more artillery and whilst combining the fire of artillery and infantry, should prepare counter-attacks. There was no question, he wrote, of outpost lines and lines of resistance : " any " retirement, even a very limited one, plays the game of " the adversary ". Sir Douglas Haig duly forwarded copies of the Note, without comment, to his Army commanders.

The enemy continued real or feigned preparations for attack at a number of places. By the 7th, these seemed to point to the possibility of attacks on the 18-mile front Albert—Neuville Vitasse, astride the Scarpe on a 7-mile front, and astride the La Bassée canal on a slightly smaller front. On the 8th, information obtained from prisoners seemed to indicate an attack between Albert and Arras, whilst the enemy's airmen fought hard to prevent British squadrons reconnoitring on this front. But white signposts were noticed south of La Bassée near Hulluch, similar to those observed in places before the 21st March, and other indications north of the La Bassée canal were noted. On the 10th, the enemy, though organizing defensively from Merville to Kemmel, seemed to have offensive intentions farther north, where preparations were more advanced than in the Albert—Arras—Lens sector. General Debeney (French First Army), on the other hand, was convinced that an attack was imminent near Villers Bretonneux. On the 11th and 12th, definite signs of attack astride the La Bassée canal were found to be increasing. The statements of prisoners left no doubt that an attack had been planned for the 10th, but the operation cancelled for reasons unknown. North of Kemmel the enemy was obviously only strengthening his defences ; the front Montdidier—Moreuil also was reported as being organized as a quiet sector. The shelling of the centre of the Third Army with mustard gas on the 11th, 12th and 13th seemed to preclude the possibility of an offensive against that front for five days at least. On the 15th there was little enemy movement, and on the La Bassée canal front his wireless was suspiciously quiet—this was now a normal indication of attack. Captured, possibly bogus, diaries, spoke of an attack on Italy as imminent, although it was certain that no German troops had gone to Italy and that another division had arrived in France, making the total 208.[1] The 17th brought to notice that a systematic artillery preparation against the centre of the Third Army appeared to be beginning, whilst an obviously truthful captured airman divulged that the attack astride the La Bassée canal could only be a feint, as it was known that the British were expecting such a stroke, a fact which perhaps explains the cancellation of the German order on the 10th, mentioned above. On the 18th and 19th, the Intelligence Branch considered that evidence was accumulating to show that the enemy's main blow would fall between Albert and Arras, whilst an attack astride the Scarpe was probable. In the north, the enemy was obviously trying to simulate an imminent attack, his measures including the display of thirteen large motor barges on the coast. The "Weekly Appreciation of the Situation" issued on the 19th attributed the pause in the enemy's operations as probably due to the necessity for training new drafts and the shortage of horses: the enemy was evidently making preparations for an offensive on a broad front, but the only definite information obtained from prisoners pointed to its falling on the sector immediately north of Arras.

The next two days brought nothing fresh, and according to air reports the enemy was very quiet behind the front opposite the British. On the 22nd, 23rd and 24th, no important change was reported; the signs of an approaching attack on the Albert—Arras sector continued to increase, and on the Kemmel front the enemy was working hard on his communications; it was learnt that in occupied territory and in neutral countries German agents were spreading rumours that the next attack would be against the Reims sector. On the 25th and 26th the enemy's artillery was rather more active than usual all along the British front, gas shell being used south of the Somme, which ruled out attack against that sector for several days. But on the 26th Br.-General E. Cox, the head of the Intelligence Branch, reported the movement of four enemy divisions southwards from Belgium, of heavy artillery from near Dinant—Namur towards Laon (9 miles

---

[1] The accuracy of the British Intelligence information is confirmed by Kuhl, pp. 6-7. He states that by the middle of March there were on the Western Front 192 divisions and 3 brigades, and that between the middle of March and 22nd May there arrived 15 more divisions, making a total of 207 divisions and 3 brigades.

due north of the Chemin des Dames sector), and of field artillery from Ciney camp (15 miles south-east of Namur) in the same direction. He also produced a letter, captured in the Ypres sector, written by a soldier from Ciney, which made it clear that the writer expected a large attack to develop shortly on the Laon front. Sir Douglas Haig remarked that an attack against the Chemin des Dames seemed very likely, as the French were there holding a wide front, in which three tired British divisions were responsible for 25,000 yards. The information was forwarded to French G.Q.G. and the IX. Corps, which both reported during the morning, " no signs of attack on " Aisne ". The " Weekly Appreciation of the Situation " issued on this day stated that the enemy had 89 divisions in reserve, of which 62 were fit to attack, and all but two of the latter were between the Oise and the sea : the enemy appeared desirous to draw attention by his wireless to the sectors between Moreuil and the Luce, and between the Comines canal and Ypres, and was suspiciously quiet astride the La Bassée canal, but was constantly increasing his dumps of ammunition on the Albert—Arras front : elsewhere on the British front sufficient ammunition did not appear to have been accumulated for an offensive on a large scale. It concluded, " there are no signs of offen-
" sive intentions on any part of the front east of Moreuil,
" except in the Laon sector, where there are indications
" which need investigation. In considering the possibility
" of any diversion, it must be remembered that the enemy
" has never yet weakened the force of his main blow by a
" holding or subsidiary attack. In Galicia in 1915, at
" Verdun in 1916, and in March this year, he concentrated
" every available man and gun for one attack. It is
" possible, of course, that the enemy may consider that the
" Allied front on the Somme must be weakened before he
" can hope to attack it with success. If he does think
" so, he is likely, as far as the British front is concerned,
" to attack south-west of Ypres, where a short advance
" would not only threaten the evacuation of Ypres, but
" would also threaten the whole of the Allied left. Such
" an attack, however, as well as an attack on the Chemin
" des Dames would have to be made in considerable
" strength for it to have any chance of succeeding in
" drawing in reserves, and would materially weaken the
" enemy's main attack."

" During the period 1st-16th May ", to quote the

French Official Account,[1] " the (French) Intelligence Service " was unable to locate the greater part of the enemy " reserve divisions (47 being unlocated on the 1st May, " 48 on the 16th and 45 on the 26th)."[2] It should be " noted that the trace of the front and the numerous " transverse lines which the enemy could use gave him " the power of rapidly shifting his mass of reserves, which " seemed disposed in the area north of the Oise, towards " a sector between that river and Switzerland. The " Intelligence Bureau of G.Q.G. calculated on the 14th " May that the German High Command would be in a " position to launch an attack on a large scale in Champagne " from the 20th May onwards and in Lorraine from the " 6th June."

General Pétain ordered suitable aeroplane reconnaissance and stimulated the enterprise of his troops by offering prizes for the capture of prisoners. " But no indication " of any value in assisting the command with precise data " was gained." The greater part of the information obtained seemed to show that the enemy was returning to his " original [sic] idea of separating the British and " French Armies ". " Nevertheless, some pieces of in- " formation, less numerous but not negligible . . . obtained " principally from prisoners, deserters or escaped French " soldiers, indicated the possibility of an attack having as " its object the conquest of the crest of the Chemin des " Dames. But the various statements thus collected were " not corroborated by any definite signs. . . . Reims " was also mentioned as a possible objective, and even, " but not so likely, the Verdun—Nancy sector. Whatever " might happen, until the 25th May, the French High " Command considered that the front between the Oise " and the sea was most immediately threatened by the " next enemy offensive."[3]

[1] F.O.A. vi. (ii.), pp. 8-9.
[2] Neglecting the division in Upper Alsace, there were no German reserves on the French front until the 24th, except over against the French left next to the British right ; viz. 2 opposite the Sixth Army (on the Chemin des Dames), south of the Oise, and 37, rising to 42, opposite the French Third and First Armies, north of the Oise (see Note II. and Map 1).
[3] The French Intelligence reports will be found in F.O.A. vi. (ii.) Annexes 275, 276 and 334. The last, dated the 26th, and marked transmitted to G.Q.G. on the 27th, ends with the summary that if the rumoured attack is a diversion, 12 divisions would suffice to make it ; if it is an attack " à " fond ", 25 to 30 divisions. " The Crown Prince's Group of Armies is " actually in a position to assemble 20 divisions which have had more than " a month's rest. Of these divisions, 13 are very good, 6 are good, 1 is " mediocre."

On the 22nd the Generalissimo had expressed his opinion to General Plumer that the German offensive would be directed against the Albert—Arras sector; but after issuing general instructions for the defence he was mainly concerned with the collection of a General Reserve and the contemplation of counter-offensives. He had on the 20th, after discussions with Sir Douglas Haig and Generals Pétain and Fayolle (G.A.R.), addressed to the British Commander-in-Chief a covering letter, "General "Directive No. 3", which placed on record the proposals first suggested on the 3rd May, and a "Note" on "opera- "tions between Oise and Somme", followed by a second "Note" on "operations in the region of the Lys".[1] The Notes went into considerable detail as to how the operations proposed should be carried out, a curious interference with the prerogative not only of the Commanders-in-Chief, but even of the Army commanders. The objects in view were: in Picardy, to thrust back the enemy so as to free Amiens and the Paris—Amiens railway from the inconvenience of long-range fire, and, in Flanders, to free the mining area from similar interference; in either case with full exploitation of any success gained.

In both cases General Foch proposed to make use of the enveloping positions which the Allies held round the salients gained by the enemy at Montdidier and Haze- Sketch 1. brouck. In the former area, attacks were to be made northwards by the French from the line Lassigny—Montdidier, and eastwards from the Villers Bretonneux front by the left of the French and right of the British (who were asked to provide 5 or 6 divisions in all): the French troops situated between the two attacks would also press forward as opportunity offered: possibly, the major attack might precede the other by one or two days, as it would start from a broader base with larger forces: and surprise was essential. He asked that the British should provide two hundred tanks and that General Rawlinson should put himself into communication with General Debeney in order to combine operations. Similarly, in the Note on the operations in the Lys area, he proposed an attack by 14 divisions northward from the line Festubert—Robecq and south-eastwards from Meteren—Dickebusch, also by 14 divisions, towards Armentières: since the numbers available might not permit of simultaneous

[1] See Appendix II for translation of the Directive; the originals are in F.O.A. vi. (ii.), pp. 16-17 and Annexes 214, 215, 216 and 221.

attacks—the most effective form of operation—it might be possible to carry out at least one or other of them.

In conclusion, he pointed out that, should the enemy attack before the opportunity arrived for the launching of the offensives proposed, they would form a suitable riposte ; but, as the forces necessarily absorbed in meeting the enemy attack might not leave sufficient available for these operations at full scale, reduced forms of them might be carried out. " The Lys operation, less costly in every " way, of which the front could be reduced if necessary, " should therefore be ready."

The reasons why General Foch did not anticipate or fear an attack against the Chemin des Dames happen to have been recorded.[1] When, on the 28th May, M. Clemenceau, as Prime Minister and Minister of War, with General Mordacq in attendance, visited him, the Generalissimo " viewed the situation with great calm. He did not believe " in a very powerful attack by the Germans in that " direction. . . . In any case, he thought that the affair " of the Chemin des Dames might very well be only a " feint. In consequence, he did not see for the moment " any necessity to shift the bulk of his strategic reserves " (which were mainly in Flanders and in the Somme " area)." General Mordacq continues :

" M. Clemenceau was very astonished. Still more so " when I told him, directly I was alone with him, that I " shared the opinion of General Foch entirely. I explained " the reasons to him. From the strategic point of view, " this attack of the Germans on the Chemin des Dames was " not very easy to understand : it could not lead to any " result of very great scope. So far [that is on the morning " of the 28th] it only seemed to be an operation of a purely " tactical order, which might, however, be a feint to attract " to this sector our strategic reserves, and then to execute a " very powerful manœuvre of the strategic order, in conse- " quence very dangerous, against some strategically sensitive " part of our front. It was therefore prudent, as General " Foch thought, to wait before shifting the bulk of the " strategic reserves." The diagnosis of the two generals was, as we now know, quite correct. The tactical success obtained by the Germans only involved them in strategic difficulties. It was in fact for them the beginning of the end.

---

[1] By General Mordacq in his " Le Ministère Clemenceau " ii., pp. 42-3. He was Chief of M. Clemenceau's Military Cabinet, and is the author of the well-known book " Stratégie ", published before the War.

NOTE I

DISTRIBUTION OF THE BRITISH FORCES ON 28TH APRIL 1918

The situation from North to South on the 28th April, the nearest day to the 1st May for which there is a contemporary situation map (Map 1 was compiled for the 1st May and differs slightly from this Note of the distribution three days earlier), was as follows:—

	Front Line. Divisions.	Reserve. Divisions.	G.H.Q. and Army Reserve.
Second Army. (from Boesinghe—Belgians—to 3 miles North of Merville, facing left of German *Fourth Army* and right of *Sixth*.)	II. Corps. XXII. Corps. French II. Cavalry Corps. French XXXVI. Corps. XV. Corps.	36th, 41st. 6th, 21st,† 49th, 25th.† French 39th, 31st. French 34th, 133rd. 1st Australian, 29th.	59th,* 34th.* 9th, 19th,† 30th.* French 32nd. French 27th. 31st.*	VIII. Corps. (33rd, 39th,* 40th,* and 66th* Divisions.) French 129th, 154th, 168th, 2nd Cav., 3rd Cav., and 6th Cav. Divisions in D.A.N. Reserve.
First Army. (from Second Army to a little South of Arras, facing left of German *Sixth Army* and the right of the *Seventeenth*.)	XI. Corps. XIII. Corps. I. Corps. Canadian Corps. XVII. Corps.	5th, 61st. 4th, 3rd. 46th, 55th, 1st, 11th. 3rd Canadian, 4th Canadian, 1st Canadian. 56th.	51st, 52nd. 14th,* 15th,* 16th.	Cavalry Corps. (1st, 2nd and 3rd Cav. Divisions.) XVIII. Corps. (20th and 24th Divisions.)
Third Army. (from First Army to Albert (exclusive), facing left of German *Seventeenth Army* and right of *Second*.)	VI. Corps. IV. Corps. V. Corps.	2nd Canadian, 2nd, Guards. 37th, 42nd, New Zealand. 12th, 17th, 35th, 38th.	32nd. 57th, 62nd. 63rd.	
Fourth Army. (from Third Army to Villers Bretonneux (inclusive), facing left of German *Second Army*.)	Australian Corps.	{2nd Australian, 3rd Australian, 5th Australian, 4th Australian.	8th,† 47th.	III. Corps. (18th and 58th Divisions.)

Note: 50th Division was in the French Sixth Army area.

* Earmarked for reduction. † Earmarked to go to the French.

25

NOTE II
DISTRIBUTION OF GERMAN DIVISIONS

	1st May. Divisions. Total per army.	Total per Group.	24th May. Divisions. Total per army.	Total per Group.
Between Switzerland and the Oise.				
Duke Albrecht of Württemberg's Group of Armies. (Switzerland to St. Mihiel Salient (exclusive))				
B Detachment	6 Divisions (1 in Reserve)		5	
A ,,	4 ,,		5	
Nineteenth Army	4 ,,	14 (1 Reserve)	5 (1 Reserve)	15 (1 Reserve)
Gallwitz's Group of Armies. (St. Mihiel Salient to Varennes)				
C Detachment	9 Divisions		9	
Fifth Army	7 ,,	16	6	15
German Crown Prince's Group of Armies (part). (Varennes to Oise)				
Third Army	8 Divisions		8 (1 Reserve)	
First Army	8 ,,		8	
Seventh Army	11 ,, (2 Reserve)	27 (2 Reserve)	8	24 (1 Reserve)
Between Oise and the Sea.				
German Crown Prince's Group of Armies (part). (Oise to Moreuil)				
Eighteenth Army	35 Divisions (22 Reserve)	35 (22 Reserve)	35 (22 Reserve)	35 (22 Reserve)
Crown Prince Rupprecht's Group of Armies. (Moreuil to the Sea)				
Second Army	31 Divisions (15 Reserve)		33 (20 Reserve)	
Seventeenth Army	17 ,, (7 ,,)		20 (9 ,,)	
Sixth ,,	27 ,, (10 ,,)		24 (8 ,,)	
Fourth ,,	29 ,, (11 ,,)	104 (43 Reserve)	33 (19 ,,)	110 (56 Reserve)
Totals				
Switzerland to the Oise	57 (3 Reserve) (44 Fresh)		54 (2 Reserve)	
Oise to the Sea	139 (65 ,,) (12 ,,)		145 (78 ,,)	
Unlocated	10 (10 ,,)		9 (9 ,,)	
	206 (78 ,,)		208 (89 ,,)	

NOTE III

GERMAN PLANS FOR THE CONTINUATION OF THE OFFENSIVE [1]

" The unfavourable position of the Germans in the salients near
" Montdidier and Armentières was of no consequence as long as they
" retained the initiative and continued the offensive. It portended
" danger if they rested on the defensive."

As early as the middle of April, in view of the possible failure of the attack then in progress, Crown Prince Rupprecht, whose Group containing the *Second, Seventeenth, Sixth* and *Fourth Armies* (the two latter being engaged in the Lys offensive) extended from near Moreuil, south of Amiens, to the sea, put forward proposals for the continuance of offensive operations.[2] He suggested two schemes. The first was a renewed attack in Flanders (to be called " New George ", but the name was later changed to " Hagen "). The first objective of this was to be Strazeele—Flêtre—Mont Noir—Reninghelst—north edge of Ypres, and the final objective Borre (2 miles east of Hazebrouck) —Godewaersvelde—Poperinghe—Boesinghe, which would cut off the British Second Army and the Belgians. The second attack as suggested (" New Michael ", later changed to " Wilhelm ") entailed a resumption of the northern half of the March offensive, " Michael ", from the Somme—Arras westward towards Doullens : if a great result was desired, a third attack, " Hubertus ", from the Béthune sector in the direction of St. Pol, could be prepared so as to increase the breadth of " New George ". " The object of these attacks must " be to break through the British line on a wide frontage, to break " down the Arras defence by envelopment, and drive the British " against the coast " : if the forces available were insufficient, " Hubertus " would have to drop out. When on the 29th April it was decided to stop the Flanders battle, as it had come to a standstill, a decision had to be taken. After some discussion, Ludendorff decided on the 5th May " as a result of yesterday's conference in " Tournai, in the first place New George and in the second New Michael " will be prepared." In the interests of secrecy, Crown Prince Rupprecht ordered the simultaneous preparation of both attacks, with the result, as has been seen, that G.H.Q. was left in doubt as to the probable front of attack.

Earlier, on the 17th April, however, Ludendorff had ordered the preparation of an attack in another sector, against the Chemin des Dames, in the area of the German Crown Prince's Group of Armies. " There it might be hoped to find a weak spot in the French front, " and compel the French to bring their reserves to it from Flanders ". The O.H.L. order of the 1st May stated " This attack has the object " of disturbing (literally ' loosening ') the present united front of the " Entente opposite Crown Prince Rupprecht's Group of Armies and " thereby creating the possibility of a victorious continuance of the " offensive against the British ". As General von Kuhl puts it, " It

---

[1] See " Kuhl ", Monograph I and Schwarte.
[2] Details will be found in Kuhl, pp. 158-164.

" was a matter of an attack to draw off the enemy reserves. The old
" main object, defeat of the British, still remained unaltered. The
" great offensive against the British was to follow the diversion attack
" against the Chemin des Dames as soon as possible." Tentatively
the date of the latter was fixed for the 20th May, and the renewed
offensive in Flanders for the middle of June. The pauses both before
the renewal of the offensive and between the Chemin des Dames and
new Flanders offensive were long, but were unavoidable as the shifting of the " battering train " and the accumulation of ammunition
and supplies took time.

About 90 divisions had fought in the " Michael " offensive and
36 in the " Georgette " (Lys) attacks. Orders were given on the 1st
May to pull out for rest all the troops which could be spared :
divisions, field and heavy artillery, engineers, trench-mortar companies, signal units, etc. Many critics maintain that Ludendorff
would have done better if he had spent the month of May in improving the German communications in the Lys area and had renewed
the offensive there : even a small further advance would have probably cut off the British Second Army and the Belgians. The First
Quartermaster General's view was that a renewed attack would meet
with strong opposition as the greater part of the French reserves had
been brought by General Foch to the Somme and Flanders to support
the British : that the conditions for a great victory over the British
no longer existed and no success was attainable until the British front
was denuded of the mass of the French reserves : and that the weakness of the troops on the Chemin des Dames offered the prospect of
a rapid success. General von Kuhl in his report to the Committee
of the *Reichstag* which enquired into the loss of the War considered
that Ludendorff's decision was justified in the circumstances.

According to the German records, the original objective of the
attack was the line of the river Aisne, which meant the capture of the
Chemin des Dames ridge between the Ailette and the Aisne. During
the preparations in the course of May the objective was extended to
the heights between the Aisne and the Vesle and then to the Vesle
itself. A few days before the attack the objective was definitely put
" some kilometres beyond the Vesle ", because the prospects seemed
favourable, and a threefold superiority in infantry and a still greater
superiority in artillery and trench mortars could be reckoned on
during the early days of the attack. The frontage of attack on the
other hand was narrowed. At first it was fixed as from Brimont
(5 miles north by a little west of Reims) to beyond Soissons. The
German Crown Prince wished it lengthened on both flanks, that is
beyond Reims on the east and as far as Compiègne (23 miles west of
Soissons) on the west. In view of the situation on Crown Prince
Rupprecht's front, where at many points there were " sore places "—
at Kemmel, on the Ancre and the Avre—which were grave dangers,
and occasioning serious losses, Ludendorff felt unable to provide the
necessary heavy artillery and infantry for the extended attack.
" The greater part of the divisions of Crown Prince Rupprecht's
" Group now pulled out for rest in preparation for the proposed
" Hagen attack would have to be brought to the Aisne, which would
" mean weakening the main attack in Flanders and postponing the
" whole plan of operations."

O.H.L. therefore decided to make the diversion attack against
the Aisne sector in two parts. First an attack on the Chemin des

Dames (code name " Goerz ") by the right of the *First Army* and left and centre of the *Seventh Army* from Brimont to Leuilly (7 miles N.N.E. of Soissons), with later a thrust, now known as the Matz offensive, of the right of the *Seventh Army* and the *Eighteenth Army* on the west bank of the Oise from the front Leuilly—Noyon (code name " Yorck "), with an extension as soon as possible as far as Montdidier (code name " Gneisenau ") in the direction of Compiègne.

It was settled that the first attack could not take place before the end of May, although the German Crown Prince's Group of Armies had been warned about it as early as the 17th April. The preparations and the placing in position of the assault divisions when rested would take a considerable time and could not be hurried, and for a successful attack of such a strong position most careful artillery preparation and the collection of a huge amount of ammunition and supplies were required.

Thirty divisions and 1,150 batteries stood ready for attack on the morning of the 27th, and other divisions were en route. A total of 41 divisions was engaged; of these 30 were provided by O.H.L. and 11 were already in position. Of the total 15 divisions were fresh, the others having taken part in the March offensive, but none of those employed in the April (Lys) offensive were included, so that all had enjoyed at least 7 weeks' rest.

How this mass of men and material was assembled unknown to the French Sixth Army is described in a later Note.

CHAPTER II

THE GERMAN OFFENSIVE IN CHAMPAGNE

THE BATTLE OF THE AISNE

THE ALLIED SITUATION BEFORE THE BATTLE [1]

(Map 2 ; Sketches A, 2)

WHEN General Foch, desiring to form a General Reserve, had pressed Sir Douglas Haig for " roulement ", that is the exchange of tired British divisions for fresh French divisions withdrawn from a quiet part of the front, the British Commander-in-Chief, after correspondence with the authorities in London, agreed to the proposal. But he consented to the transfer of no more than a small number, not the 10-15 divisions which General Foch had suggested. Finally, on the 23rd April, it was arranged that four divisions, under the staff of the IX. Corps (Lieut.-General Sir A. H. Gordon), should be sent to the French Sixth Army (General Duchêne), on the Aisne front west of Reims, and one division, under the VIII. Corps (Lieut.-General Sir A. Hunter-Weston), to the French Fourth Army (General Gouraud) near Châlons sur Marne.

Although the British General Staff at the time did not know of the American appreciation mentioned in the previous chapter, they viewed the Aisne front with considerable suspicion ; for the sector was known to be one of those prepared by the enemy for attack and it was thought that Ludendorff, having already extended his original " Michael " front of attack to the right (north) in the Lys offensive, might now try the left (east). Major-General J. H. Davidson (Major-General, General Staff for Operations), when attending a meeting held at General

---

[1] For the French and British forces engaged see " Order of Battle of " the IX. Corps " and " French Forces Engaged " at the end of the volume.

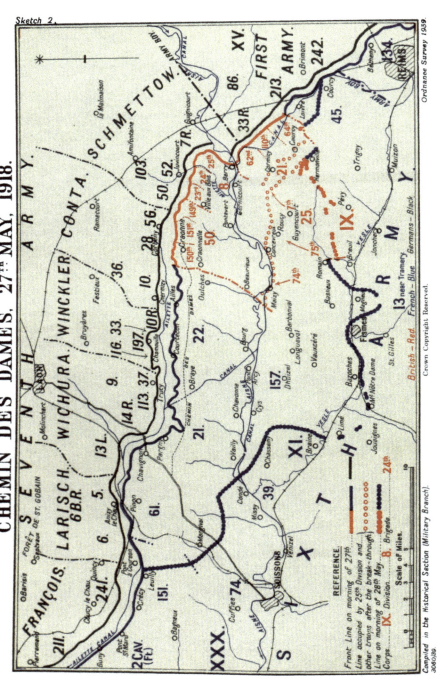

Foch's headquarters at Sarcus on the 3rd May, expressed this view. He further stressed the anxiety felt regarding the destination of the British divisions. He was, however, assured by both General Weygand (Foch's Chief of the Staff) and General Barescut (Aide-Major-Général, that is Assistant Chief of the Staff to General Pétain), that the front selected was suitable and quiet.

The five divisions detailed were, as we have seen, the 8th, 19th, 21st, 25th and 50th. All these divisions had suffered very heavy losses during March and April,[1] and had been only partly filled up to establishment, mainly with drafts of imperfectly trained young recruits. Casualties among the more experienced officers and N.C.O.'s had been exceptionally heavy, so that a period of rest for reorganization and training was most necessary to render the divisions again fit to take part in active operations.

The IX. Corps staff reached the new area on the 26th April, and next day opened offices at Fère en Tardenois, Sir John French's headquarters during the Battle of the Aisne in 1914. The 50th Division (Major-General H. C. Jackson) arrived on the 27th and 28th, followed on the 3rd and 4th May by the 8th Division (Major-General W. C. G. Heneker), on the 5th and 6th by the 21st Division (Major-General D. G. M. Campbell), and on the 10th and 11th by the 25th Division (Major-General Sir G. Bainbridge). The 19th Division (Major-General G. D. Jeffreys), on its arrival on the 18th and 19th, was stationed in the area of St. Germain la Ville, 7 miles south-east of Châlons, the headquarters of the VIII. Corps, in which neighbourhood were also in reserve three French and two Italian divisions.

The French Sixth Army was holding a sector the front of which extended for about fifty-five miles from a point three miles north of Reims to the vicinity of Noyon. Earlier in the year it had occupied a shorter frontage from near Juvincourt (13 miles north-west of Reims) to Barisis (13 miles west of Laon) where it made contact with the British Fifth Army (General Sir H. Gough). But the events of March-April had led to its taking over a further ten miles on its right from the French Fifth Army, whose staff was then transferred to the Reserve, and to the extension of its left westwards for nearly twenty miles.

Map 2. Sketches A, 2.

---

[1] Amounting, as returned, to no less than 42,830, but from this total about 8 per cent can probably be deducted for stragglers and missing who subsequently rejoined.

A corresponding increase in the number of its troops was arranged, so that its strength at the end of April had risen from three corps and a cavalry corps with one division and one cavalry division attached, to four corps and a cavalry corps, with three divisions and two cavalry divisions attached. The average number of divisions, 16, then remained the same until the battle, although they were differently organized, the four corps and three attached divisions being represented on the 26th May by three corps and four divisions directly under the Army. Thus the average front per division was about $3\frac{1}{2}$ miles: suitable for a quiet but not an active front.

On the right, before the British came into the line, stood the 45th Division (General Naulin), directly under the Army, on a frontage of about seven thousand yards opposite the strong German position on the wooded heights of Brimont, which General Nivelle had failed to capture in May 1917. Next came the XXXVIII. Corps (General Piarron de Mondésir), with the 74th, 71st, 51st and 157th Divisions on a 15-mile front. To its left, in the centre of the Army front, on the Chemin des Dames ridge, was the XI. Corps (General de Maud'huy), with the 22nd, 21st and 61st Divisions, all in the line, on a long front of nearly twenty miles. In the left sector was the XXX. Corps (General Chrétien), with the 151st, 2nd Dismounted Cavalry, 19th and 55th Divisions, all in the line, on a 17-mile front. In Army reserve were the 39th Division and eventually the British IX. Corps.

The main feature of the Sixth Army sector, in its centre, was the Chemin des Dames ridge, the summit of which the British, with General de Maud'huy's XVIII. Corps on their right, had managed to reach in September 1914. During the following winter it had been lost by the French, but recovered, after several changes of hands, in the Malmaison offensive of October 1917.[1] It is a narrow, bare range of heights, with a flat top 350 to 400 yards wide, except one portion between Braye and Pargny, which is gently rolling and nearly half a mile in breadth, and another near Soissons, where two slight dips break the level of the ridge. It extends in an unbroken line

---

[1] Prior to April 1917 the French had two small footings on it. As a result of the Nivelle offensive they recovered the whole of it except two very short sections, but in the latter part of May, and in June and July, were pushed off a great part of it by a long series of local German attacks. In October 1917 it was wholly recaptured.

THE GROUND

between the parallel valleys of the Aisne and the Ailette (some four hundred feet below its crest) from the "Californie plateau", its buttress at the eastern end (north-west of Craonne), for some twenty-four miles towards Compiègne. The road from which the ridge takes its name runs along the narrow, flat crest eastward from about Soissons, without ditch or hedge; at the time it was to some extent obliterated, for the previous fighting had turned the summit of the ridge into a tangle of shell craters. The view to the front from the crest is short, not extending beyond the next ridge, although on the map it might appear to be commanding. The northern face is generally very steep. To-day it is thickly wooded, but in 1918 it was covered with the stumps of trees and bushes, which offered a considerable obstacle, even when not wired, to any troops except small bodies of skirmishers. At its foot, the canalized Ailette, below the basin where it is joined by the canal from the Aisne (which passes beneath the ridge in a tunnel), constitutes a serious military obstacle, its breadth being 60 feet and double as much from bank to bank of the cutting. Above the basin the Ailette is only a few feet wide—north of Courtecon six to eight feet—but marshy, in places pure marsh.

The slope occupied by the Germans north of the Ailette was dotted with copses, but not thickly wooded except between Corbény and Chermizy; the shelter afforded was good enough to provide adequate cover for batteries and bridging apparatus, but not to conceal large concentrations of troops and material; for that purpose the great woods farther north, including the forests of Samoussy and Coucy (some 9 and 6 miles, respectively, north of the Ailette), provided ideal hiding places within a day's march.

The southern side of the Chemin des Dames ridge is cut by numerous valleys, with sides often so steep that in places the ascent is a matter of climbing on hands and knees. In these recesses nestle a number of small villages, well known to the British in 1914,[1] but in 1918 represented by a few battered ruins. Between them lie long, generally wooded, spurs, terminating in knolls which reach down to the Aisne, with its wide fertile valley, lying four miles from the crest of the ridge. The winding river, sluggish except when in flood, is as far as Condé accompanied by a navigation canal called the " Canal Latéral ", about sixty feet

[1] See " 1914 " Vol. I.

wide, in places running alongside it and at others as much as half a mile away, the intervening space being flat, covered in May 1918 with high grass, but offering no other cover. Above the junction of the river and canal, where the Vesle also flows into it, the Aisne is fifty to seventy feet wide, but below it broadens out, and at Soissons is about a hundred and eighty feet wide. The river winds so much and is so screened by trees that unless it were held by a continuous line of posts it would be hard to prevent—as it proved—small parties slipping across.

The valley of the Vesle also is flat and was then under cultivation; at Braine it is about one and a half miles wide. The stream itself, 35 feet broad at Fismes, has wooded banks, and is quite a serious military obstacle. The Ardre, which enters it, is little more than a winding ditch, but its valley is deep and imposing for so small a stream.

The ridge between the Aisne and Vesle, which it will be convenient to call the Vesle ridge, has some similarity to the Chemin des Dames, but also presents differences, all in its favour as a defensive position. Its section is a broad, flat curve, on top at least twice the width of its fellow to the north, in places a mile wide, and the spurs on the southern slopes are not wooded and form excellent supporting positions which command the valleys. The rear edge facing north forms an almost ideal "Wellington" position adapted to the range of modern infantry weapons, with excellent howitzer positions behind it—field guns would have to be further away south of the Vesle. Along the top no lateral communication existed.

Eastward of Craonne the Chemin des Dames ridge ends in a long, broad hook-shaped spur which trends south and south-west, limited by the Miette stream, to enclose Ville aux Bois, and the ground then falls to the plain around Reims. The "hook" has fine long views, but even east of the Laon—Reims road there is a fair amount of woodland which acts as a partial screen. To the westward of Soissons, the Chemin des Dames ridge opens out into a series of plateaux, divided by the valleys of the tributaries of the Aisne and the Oise.

Between the evening of the 6th and the morning of the 8th May, the infantry of the British 50th Division, by General Duchêne's orders, contrary to expectation, was withdrawn from rest in order to relieve the French 51st Division, in the left sector of the XXXVIII. Corps front;

of the artillery, half of each battery took over on each of the two following nights thus completing the relief. A French officer said to the staff to whom he handed over: "You are rats in a trap. If you keep quiet all may be well." On the 9th General Franchet d'Ésperey (G.A.N.) called on Lieut.-General Gordon and informed him that he had decided that the IX. Corps should take the place of the French XXXVIII. Continuing the relief, therefore, the 8th Division between the 11th and 13th May, and the 21st Division between the 13th and 15th May, took over the centre and right sectors of the XXXVIII. Corps from the French 71st and 74th Divisions.[1] Major-General Campbell (21st Division), after going round his sector, said to the French commander whom he had relieved that he was not satisfied and could not hold the position for 24 hours; he received the reply that it had been held for two years. The French left on the position two "groupes" of field artillery, four "groupes" of heavy guns, nine machine-gun companies, two Territorial battalions, an air squadron and a balloon company to be attached to the British. By General Duchêne's instructions, the strength of the infantry dispositions in the First Position (Forward Zone) was not changed. Lieut.-General Gordon, with headquarters at Jonchery (on the Vesle, 8 miles west of Reims), assumed command of the former XXXVIII. Corps sector on the 17th. The 25th Division remained in General Duchêne's reserve, together with the French 39th, 74th and 157th Divisions;[2] on the 23rd the division concluded its marches and settled down in the valley of the Vesle around Montigny (divisional headquarters), eight to ten miles behind the front of the corps, with two brigade groups north and one south of the river.

In addition to medical units and workshops, the XLI. and LXXVII. Brigades R.G.A., and two labour companies were subsequently sent to the IX. Corps. No. 52 Squadron R.A.F. from an aerodrome at Fismes (on the Vesle) provided air co-operation, distant air reconnaissance remaining

---

[1] According to F.O.A. Order of Battle volume, the 51st Division had not been in battle since July 1917 ("Third Ypres"), but in the line since 9th March; the 71st, not in battle since June 1916 (Verdun), but in the line since 16th March; the 74th not in battle since October 1916 (Verdun), but in the line since 22nd February. The 157th Division, originally in the XXXVIII. Corps, had on the 30th March become an Army division.

[2] The 2 divisions of the XXXVIII. Corps just relieved began entraining on the 20th for Aumale (27 Miles S.S.W. of Amiens) to join the French Fifth Army, ready to intervene towards Béthune or Arras in support of the British who then seemed threatened.

the duty of the squadrons of the French Sixth Army. Very few air photographs showing enemy battery positions were handed over by the XXXVIII. Corps, but the small number of new ones taken before the 27th did not indicate much fresh work on the enemy's positions except some trenches, apparently of a defensive character, and additional telephone communications.

In the Ailette valley, No Man's Land was wide, two thousand yards or more; both sides, however, had listening posts down by the river. Elsewhere it was from two to three hundred yards wide.

Railheads for ammunition and supply for the IX. Corps were organized, the French affording every possible assistance, on the Reims—Soissons railway, which ran in the valley of the Vesle parallel to the front, with one supply railhead near St. Gilles and one ammunition railhead near Savigny on the single line to the south, which joins the main line at Fismes. Fère en Tardenois was the regulating station; but daily supply trains were run right through from the British advanced base at Romescamps (35 miles E.S.E. of Dieppe). Before the battle, 5,000 tons of ammunition had been accumulated in the area.

Beginning on the right, the British sector ran on low ground near the Aisne-Marne canal—with the front line beyond that canal—from north-west of Brimont to Berry au Bac (on the Aisne). Thence, after crossing a small stream called the Miette, it mounted, at first very gradually, but finally by an almost precipitous slope on to the eastern buttress of the Chemin des Dames ridge, the Californie plateau, north-west of Craonne.[1] It was thus to the east of the sector held by the British Expeditionary Force in 1914. The divisional sectors were wide: 8,100, 9,900 and 8,900 yards, and, topographically, disquietingly weak, the front line on the right being beyond a canal; the centre on the hooked-shaped spur, enfiladed from the north; and the left on the main narrow ridge, where, even by putting the front trench on the forward slope, the whole of the three lines of the position, front, support and reserve, had to be crowded into a depth not exceeding five hundred yards; the northern slope too was so steep that only howitzers and 9.45-inch trench mortars emplaced on the southern slopes could fire a close protective barrage.

---

[1] The plateau was called the Winterberg by the Germans, because the bare white limestone exposed on its sides from a distance looked like snow.

STATE OF THE DEFENCES

Good observation, however, was available in the right half of the corps sector from a long crest west of the Reims—Berry au Bac chaussée, which ran parallel to the front, with the tumbled, wooded heights of the Vesle ridge behind it, and from the Craonne spur; on the rest of the front there was only limited observation from the Chemin des Dames ridge, as view beyond the enemy front line and close support trenches was obstructed by woods. Lieut.-General Gordon pointed out that the sectors were too wide for his weak, not yet rested and only partially trained divisions. General Duchêne promised to shorten them, but no action in the matter had been taken when the German attack started.

As regards the state of the defences: west of the Forest of St. Gobain, from the neighbourhood of the junction of the French and British Armies near Barisis on the 21st March, the defensive organization of the recently stabilized front was still imperfect, but comprised a front position and an intermediate position. East of the forest, the sector, in which the IX. Corps now lay, having been undisturbed for a long period, possessed a well developed defensive system. It comprised three positions, corresponding to the British Forward Zone, Battle Zone and Rear Zone (Green Line), which nomenclature will generally be used in this narrative, though called by the French, the First, the Intermediate and Second Positions. The first was " complete and perfectly kept up ", according to French accounts; the British thought it in a bad state of repair. The French had indeed held the sector with a very small garrison for some months, and finding that the existing trenches provided ample cover and that the communication trenches, roads, light railways and cable routes were excellent, had thought that extensive further preparations against attack were unnecessary. There were plenty of gun emplacements, and more trenches and posts than could be occupied, an obvious advantage to the attack. The Forward Zone comprised continuous front and support lines, with strongpoints and fragments of line behind them, very good wire and dugouts. The Battle Zone, consisting of strongpoints and defended localities, was about a mile behind the front and of less depth, and it relied mainly on the cross-fire of machine guns.[1] North of the Aisne, however, it was supported by

---

[1] For further light on the nature of the defences see p. 55, f.n. 2.

groups of strongpoints, many on the knolls on the spurs, called " centres de résistance ". The Rear Zone (Green Line), a mile behind the Battle Zone on the right, but four miles south of it on the left of the British sector, also consisted of strongpoints, somewhat out of date, but in a good state except in the British sector south of the Aisne. Here were to be found some old trenches dug in the previous fighting in this area, but no organized system. The right and centre were two miles or more south of the Aisne; only the left sector commanded the passages over the river; but in the centre the Gernicourt defences, around the village of that name, between the Aisne and the Green Line, held by a special garrison, stood well above the river, commanding all the ground to the front.

As regards the bridges, General Duchêne authorized the IX. Corps to blow up, if necessary, those over the Aisne—Marne canal, in the 21st Division sector, and over the Aisne and the Canal Lateral, but only east of the entry of the Miette, which is situated between Berry au Bac and Pontavert; below this junction, the destruction of all bridges was retained in his own hands.

In general, the French hospitals, ammunition and engineer dumps and railheads, were too near the front unless the sector remained quiet or was to be used as the jumping-off place of an offensive. Including the British, of the fifteen available divisions of the French Sixth Army, eleven were disposed in the front line, providing one battalion roughly per half-mile of front, and four were in reserve.

Of field artillery, there were 45 French " groupes " and 8 British brigades; of heavy artillery, 38 " groupes " and 2 British brigades; and of super-heavy artillery, 19 batteries: 266 batteries in all. On the front of attack the Germans had brought up 1,036.

On the 19th April General Foch had laid down the principles on which the defensive battle was to be conducted on the front between the Oise and the sea:

" On the Franco-British front no ground can be
" lost. . . . It is a matter of defence foot by foot. It
" should be based on a series of defensive positions, one
" behind the other, and the deployment and action of a
" numerous and powerful artillery."

On the 5th May he had drawn attention to the difference between this front and other sectors long organized for defence: in the former, " which covered important " objectives such as the coal mines and railway junctions, " it was imperative that no unit should retire voluntarily " or on the pretext that neighbouring units had been " driven back ". But in the latter, he said, " it was " possible, without serious inconvenience, to abandon a " certain amount of ground in the face of a violent enemy " onslaught ".

To these old-established sectors applied the principles laid down by General Pétain in his " Instruction on " Defensive Actions " and Directive No. 4, dated the 20th and 22nd December 1917, which may be summarized as follows : [1]

The Front Zone (First Position) should not be occupied by more than the minimum of troops necessary to contain the adversary in ordinary times or to slow up and dislocate the assaulting waves on the day when he should launch an important attack.

The position of resistance, Second Position or Intermediate Position (the British Battle Zone), should become the essential factor of the organized field of battle, on which the enemy must be stopped and beaten; it should be chosen so that it could not be reached by the enemy until after a series of actions and situated so far back as to prevent his infantry having the support of the artillery from the latter's initial positions of deployment.

In fact, it was a matter of applying to trench warfare the usual principles of open warfare, the front zone corresponding to what in open warfare is the outpost system.

In spite of these instructions and in spite of the inadequate numbers of troops available, General Duchêne decided, in case of enemy attack, to fight the battle on the First Position (Forward Zone), and General Pétain reluctantly gave his approval of this decision.[2] In the light of

[1] F.O.A. vi. (ii.), pp. 41-2.
[2] F.O.A. vi. (ii.), p. 70. General Pétain, whose Chief of Staff, General Anthoine, was a brother-in-law of General Duchêne, was convinced that the French Army should remain strictly on the defensive and avoid losses " until the moment when the American Army is capable of putting into the " line a certain number of large formations; until then we must, under " penalty of irreparable losses, maintain an expectant attitude ". So he had in his Instruction on defensive actions and in Directive No. 4 (from which the above quotation is taken) prescribed the acceptance of the defensive battle on a position of resistance " in retreat " and enunciated the principles already mentioned in the text. This meant giving up ground whenever and wherever the enemy attacked, without the discrimination laid down by General Foch that there were parts of the front where not a foot of ground should be surrendered by voluntary retirement, and else-

General Foch's instruction such a disposition was correct only for the new front north of the Oise, and for the left sector recently occupied and not yet thoroughly stabilized; but on the 9th April General Duchêne wrongly included the centre (Chemin des Dames) sector and the rest of his front. He made it the unequivocal duty of the divisions between Craonne and the Oise to prevent the crossing of the Ailette and the Oise by the enemy: no elastic yielding of the outposts, with a rally on a position of resistance in rear there to fight the battle out, could be countenanced.

Both General Pétain and General Franchet d'Espérey (G.A.N.) pointed out to the commander of the Sixth Army that the fighting of a defensive battle on the First Position applied only to sectors not affected by the recent operations, that is to those west of the Forest of St. Gobain (inclusive). General Franchet d'Espérey, in fact, laid down the position of resistance to be held, fixing it as the Second Position south of the Aisne as far as Celles (just north-east of Condé), then the switch to Leuilly (7 miles to the north-west) on the Oise canal, behind the Forest of St. Gobain, and thence the First Position. General Duchêne, however, would not accept this. He argued that no ground in a sector directly covering Paris should be voluntarily evacuated, that the sector in question was very strong and had advantages for defence by the weak forces available; and, finally, that it would create a bad impression on public opinion and the morale of the troops if the Chemin des Dames ridge, won at such heavy cost in the Nivelle

---

where nothing given up except in the face of a *violent* enemy onslaught. According to General Laure (see his " Le Commandement en Chef des " Armées françaises du 15 mai 1917 à l'armistice ", pp. 44-6 and 84), then a member of the Operations Bureau of General Pétain's General Staff: " at the front, as in the bosom of the Government, there was stupefaction. " Here was a General-in-Chief who deliberately contemplated the eventual " abandonment of the famous Buttes in Champagne, conquered in 1915 at " the cost of so much blood ; of the advanced lines of Verdun, like Hill 304, " of the heights of the Talon and the Poivre, on which were inscribed the " victories of 1916 ; of the Chemin des Dames and the knolls of Moran- " villers, the capture of which had been the only positive results of the " attacks of the 16th April 1917."

In consequence, M. Clemenceau, supported by the advice of General Roques, whom he had appointed " Inspecteur-général des travaux " d'organisation défensive ", had protested on 8th February, by letter, against this revolutionary doctrine, reproaching Pétain for failing to use sufficient man-power on the defences and to realize the value of obstacles and wire. The contents of this letter, according to General Laure, were known to the higher commanders, " the greater part of whom were not " prepared to abandon their advanced positions to accept battle in a posi- " tion in retreat behind the advanced posts ", and it encouraged them to disregard the General-in-Chief's views.

DISTRIBUTION OF IX. CORPS

offensive of the previous year, were abandoned. It had thus become a matter of removing General Duchêne from command or of giving way, and, as General Pétain felt that the new method had not been thoroughly tried, and might not be successful, he decided, with regret, " to let his " subordinates prepare in their own way a battle of which " they would have the immediate charge ".

General principles apart, however, it was clear to all who knew the ground, or even looked at a contoured map, that the narrow Chemin des Dames ridge, although the position was one to which visitors were taken to be shown an example of a really well fortified front, would be impossible to hold in the face of a strong attack well prepared by a heavy bombardment. Either belligerent could in 1917 or 1918 by adopting such a method gain at any rate temporary possession of any ground he coveted. For the defender to hold the Chemin des Dames in strength would merely increase the initial casualties. Counter-attack from the spurs and ridges behind the main ridge would be difficult. The French Second Position (Green Line) south of the Aisne, so the topographical features seemed to dictate, was that on which to stop and defeat the enemy. General Pétain actually prescribed that none of the divisions in reserve should be sent across the Aisne.

The general distribution of the three British divisions, the 21st, 8th and 50th, in the defences taken over was simple : each division had all three brigades in the line, and each brigade divided two battalions between the Front and Battle Zones, and kept the third in reserve. In detail, counting by infantry companies, there were 46 companies, one field company R.E. (working on the Californie plateau) and one pioneer company in the Forward Zone ; 32 and one pioneer company in the Battle Zone, with 11 companies, 3 field companies R.E. and 2 pioneer companies close at hand ; 2 field companies R.E. and 2 pioneer companies were in the Gernicourt defences ; and 19 companies, including 4 complete and one 3-company battalions, forming the infantry reserves, 3 field companies R.E. and 3 pioneer companies and two French Territorial battalions near the Rear Zone (Green Line). It was a better arrangement than that of the French XI. Corps, which had 26 battalions (288 machine guns) in the First Position ; 5 in the Intermediate Position (120 machine guns) ; and 7 (84 machine guns) behind them,[1] but worse

---
[1] F.O.A. vi. (ii.), p. 83.

than that of the Fifth Army on the 21st March; and, since a much larger proportion of machine guns was now forthcoming—including the French guns left by the XXXVIII. Corps, there were seven instead of four companies per division — less necessity existed to hold the front line so strongly with rifles.[1] Of the 50th Division, all the infantry companies were north of the Aisne; of the 8th Division, all but six; of the 21st Division, seven were east of the Marne—Aisne canal. Three companies of each of the divisional machine-gun battalions were distributed to brigades, and, with the attached French machine guns, were emplaced in the defensive localities and strongpoints for cross-fire; the rest were retained at divisional headquarters. The trench mortars were held in brigade reserve.

The field artillery of the 21st Division, on the right, reinforced by one brigade of the 25th Division (in reserve), was in rear of or in the Battle Zone, but that of the 8th and 50th Divisions, reinforced by a French " groupe ", was all north of the Aisne behind the Battle Zone, with another French " groupe " and the second brigade of the 25th Division south of the river, south and west of Gernicourt. Special sections of field guns were told off to deal with tanks.

Of the six brigades or " groupes " of heavy artillery, 2,000 to 4,000 yards behind the field artillery, the XLI. Brigade R.G.A. (twelve 60-pdrs. and twelve 6-inch howitzers) and the French Groupe Meurier (34 guns, all 155-mm.) supported the 21st Division; the French Groupes d'Ainville (32 guns, all 155-mm.) and Dubarry (28 guns, all 155-mm.), supported respectively the 8th and 50th Divisions, and the LXXVII. Brigade R.G.A. (five 8-inch and ten 6-inch howitzers and ten 60-pdrs.), covered both divisional fronts. All the heavy guns, except Groupe Dubarry and Groupe Gay (18 guns on railway mountings) were south of the Aisne.

The first instructions given to the British IX. Corps and the French 45th Division, on its right, were to hold on—as a minimum " coûte que coûte "—to the Californie plateau in the front line, but thence eastward to localities in the Battle Zone: the Bois des Buttes (south-west of Ville aux Bois), the Gernicourt plateau, and the line of the villages Cormicy, Cauroy, Villers Franqueux, Thil, St

---

[1] In the Fifth Army, counting by battalions, the proportion had been: Forward Zone, 36⅔, Battle Zone, 43⅔, Green Line, 29⅓.

Thierry. " To cover these essential positions, a principal " line of resistance to be defended à outrance and retaken " without delay if all or part of it were lost " was laid down by the Sixth Army. It began at the crest line north and north-east of the Californie plateau, and thence continued along a " switch " to the Battle Zone at Ville aux Bois. In front of this " principal line of resistance " the Forward Zone was to be occupied only by weak garrisons, which in the case of a general offensive were, on principle, not to be reinforced, but were to seek by holding their ground to break up the enemy attacks. In reality, as the garrisons fixed by him were substantial and not to be reduced, General Duchêne's instructions meant that not only the Battle Zone but also the Forward Zone was to be held to the last, that is he exposed a large number of guns to capture north of the Aisne and did not leave sufficient troops to hold the Battle Zone in strength.

The troops of the IX. Corps had at first been well pleased with their new, comparatively peaceful, surroundings in country beautiful as compared with Flanders, in comfortable trenches where shelling was light. They settled down, established by raiding normal identifications on the front and were themselves raided. The general attitude of the enemy's infantry was defensive but alert; that several determined raids were made could not be regarded as anything unusual. But belief in the prospect of the continued peacefulness of the sector gradually weakened among those who had been engaged in the March and April battles. For some days before the attack the front line troops noticed suspicious movements behind the German lines and all the well-known indications of preparation. They reported great activity at night, the sound of troops marching, the rumbling of wagons and the whispered conversation of working parties. When on the morning and evening of the 22nd the IX. Corps airmen reported distant clouds of dust on the roads leading to the Chemin des Dames, Lieut.-General Gordon communicated this information, as symptomatic of enemy concentration, not only to General Duchêne, but to General Franchet d'Espérey and to Colonel W. G. S. Dobbie, of the General Staff, who was visiting him on behalf of G.H.Q. Of the commander of the G.A.N. he asked the question, whether an attack might be expected within a month, or a week, or immediately, and received the reply, " certainly not at " once ". Dust clouds were again seen on the evenings of the 23rd and 24th. At General Duchêne's corps commanders' meeting on the morning of the latter day, Lieut.-General Gordon protested against the untrained recruits of the IX. Corps being left in the front line at such a time without reserves, and against what, in his view, after his experience in the April fighting, was an unsound method of defence. The Army commander's only comment was "J'ai dit". Lieut.-General Gordon was placed in a very difficult position. With a small British contingent he stood amongst French troops, under a higher French commander, defending French soil : he could do no more than report the situation to G.H.Q. But the blow fell before he could be helped.

From the 24th onwards any attempt of aviators to cross the German line encountered greatly increased anti-aircraft fire. Light shelling, which had the appearance of being registration unobtrusively carried out, was noticed. Patrols on the night of the 25th/26th on the front of the IX. Corps and of the French XI. Corps, on its left, were unable to approach the enemy's line owing to the activity of the German patrols. During the 26th, enemy wireless practically ceased until about 8 P.M. ; from this hour onwards Allied wireless was jammed. Abnormal traffic was observed on the roads at numerous points in the rear areas opposite the front of the British IX. and French XI. Corps, yet air reconnaissance carried out by the French in the afternoon could "discover "no signs of attack".[1] Nevertheless cross-examination about noon on the 26th of two prisoners taken by the French XI. Corps extracted the information that an attack on a large scale would be launched at 2 A.M. (German time) either the next day or the day after, the bombardment lasting two and a half hours. General de Maud'huy at once sent on this information direct to Lieut.-General Gordon, who warned his divisional commanders. It was not until " between 4.20 P.M. and 4.30 P.M.", that General Duchêne telephoned to his corps and independent divisions inviting them to order that all troops should be in their battle positions by 7 P.M. ; these moves were to be followed by the " Alert ". Another message, about an hour later, added that the battle was to be fought out on the Intermediate Line (Battle Zone). But no one had the slightest conception that there were 20 divisions with 1,036 batteries ready to fall on the troops between Berry au Bac and Soissons. Little could be done at such short notice except

[1] F.O.A. vi. (ii.), p. 86.

to thin the actual front line to a chain of posts, and move up some reserves for counter-attack. There was no time to bring up horses and shift batteries near the front to emplacements farther back, as suggested by General Duchêne.

In the 21st Division,[1] the reserve battalion was moved up to Cauroy, and the French I./23rd Territorial Battalion to Cormicy, to be under the 62nd Brigade, both places being in the front line of the Battle Zone.

In the 8th Division,[2] the 25th Brigade was reinforced by moving its two reserve companies up to Berry au Bac; the 24th Brigade, by moving the 1/Sherwood Foresters up to the Green Line at Roucy; and the 23rd Brigade, by moving the reserve battalion into close support. The French II./23rd Territorial Battalion was sent to reinforce the Gernicourt defences.

In the 50th Division,[3] the battalions in corps and divisional reserve were restored to their brigades.

---

[1] 64th Brigade (Br.-General H. R. Headlam) on the right, with the 1/East Yorkshire and 9/K.O.Y.L.I. in the front position, and the 15/Durham L.I. in reserve;

110th Brigade (Br.-General H. R. Cumming), with the 8th and 7/Leicestershire in the front position, and the 6th in reserve;

62nd Brigade (Br.-General G. H. Gater), with the 2/Lincolnshire and 12th/13th Northumberland Fusiliers in the front position, and the 1/Lincolnshire in reserve.

The 97th, 98th and 126th Field Companies R.E. and the 14/Northumberland Fusiliers (Pioneers) were in divisional reserve.

[2] 25th Brigade (Br.-General R. H. Husey), with the 2/Rifle Brigade, 2/R. Berkshire and 2 companies of the 2/East Lancashire in the front position, and the rest of the last named battalion and the French II/23rd Territorial Battalion in reserve. Its sector was supported by the 490th Field Company R.E., one mile north-west of Berry au Bac, and the garrison of the Gernicourt defences, the 2nd and the 15th Field Companies R.E. and the 22/Durham L.I. (Pioneers) (less one company);

24th Brigade (Br.-General R. Haig), with the 2/Northamptonshire in the Forward Zone, the 1/Worcestershire and the remaining company of the 22/Durham L.I. in the Battle Zone, and the 1/Sherwood Foresters behind the Green Line, in divisional reserve;

23rd Brigade (Br.-General G. W. St. G. Grogan), with the 2/West Yorkshire in the Forward Zone, the 2/Middlesex in the Battle Zone and the 2/Devonshire in close reserve.

[3] 149th Brigade (Br.-General E. P. A. Riddell), with the 4/Northumberland Fusiliers in the Forward and the 6th in the Battle Zone, and the 5th in corps reserve near the Aisne;

151st Brigade (Br.-General C. T. Martin), with the 6th and 8/Durham L.I. and one company of the 7/Durham L.I. (Pioneers) in the front position, and the 5th in divisional reserve in the Centre d'Evreux;

150th Brigade (Br.-General H. C. Rees), with the 5/Green Howards and 4/East Yorkshire, with the 447th Field Company R.E. in the Forward Zone and on the Californie plateau, and the 4/Green Howards in divisional reserve in the Battle Zone.

The 7th and 446th Field Companies R.E. and the rest of the pioneers were in the Centre d'Evreux.

The 25th Division was returned by General Duchêne to the IX. Corps at 10 P.M. for the defence of the Green Line, but it was not to cross the Aisne. Earlier, at 6 P.M., Lieut.-General Gordon had given Major-General Bainbridge orders to move the division forward two to four miles as soon as light failed: the 7th Brigade to the Guyencourt area, the 75th to the Ventelay area, and the 74th to the Meurival area, some one and a half to three miles behind the Green Line of the 8th and 50th Divisions, south of the Aisne. The three divisions in reserve behind the French XI. Corps, the 157th, 39th and 74th, were also moved forward towards the Green Line, and also the 151st of the XXX. Corps.

General Franchet d'Espérey (G.A.N.) placed four " groupes " of heavy artillery at the disposal of the Sixth Army, and informed General Duchêne that he could have the 13th Division (reorganizing at Romigny, 11 miles south of Fismes), if he required it. He warned the I. Cavalry Corps to send artillery and motor machine guns towards Fismes; and requested and obtained from G.Q.G. the assistance, if needed, of the " division aérienne " and of a heavy artillery " groupe " then unemployed. Lastly, the 1st Division of the Fifth Army, then at Compiègne, was warned to be prepared to move by motor lorry to the battle.

Harassing fire was opened at 9 P.M. by all calibres on the roads and approaches likely to be used by the enemy, as well as on Asfeld railway station (10 miles north-east of Berry au Bac), known to be a railhead, and many explosions were heard. The enemy did not reply. Counter-preparation and counter-battery fire was not opened, as by General Duchêne's order it was not to begin " until "the first discharge of violent artillery fire ", unless movements were seen or the signs of attack were unequivocal.

CHAPTER III

THE BATTLE OF THE AISNE

27TH MAY 1918

THE ASSAULT

(Maps 2, 3 ; Sketches, A, 2, 3)

AT 1 A.M. on the 27th May in the darkness of a moonless night, Sketch 2. the German bombardment opened as had been predicted by German prisoners. The French and British batteries at once began counter-preparation. But those sited to the north of the Aisne, overwhelmed by the violence of the enemy fire, by which many guns were destroyed and a large proportion of the detachments put out of action by gas, in spite of a gallant struggle, rapidly grew less and less effective in their reply.

The enemy fire covered 24 miles of the Allied front, from Berry au Bac to Chavignon (11 miles north-east of Soissons),[1] held by the British 8th and 50th Divisions, and the French 22nd and 21st Divisions. But, for the purpose of deception, the bombardment was extended on either side by enemy corps which were not taking part in the assault, so that it appeared to the Allies to include a frontage of about thirty-six miles from Brimont, near Reims, to Leuilly, due north of Soissons. The last-named town was itself bombarded, and the fire reached back to the line of the Vesle, nearly twelve miles behind the front. Every battery position, village, farm, and railway station, every bridge and road-junction was systematically shelled. On

[1] Bruchmüller, p. 94, says " the whole front of attack was roughly " 38 km. [23·725 miles] ". See Map 3.

On this day the German long-range guns near Laon (see Sketch B) reopened the bombardment of Paris begun on 23rd March (see " 1918 " Vol. I., p. 327). From 2nd to 27th May it had ceased owing to one explosion of one gun, replacement of worn guns (two out of six available were in action at a time), and changing of position.

48   CHEMIN DES DAMES

the right, in the British area north of the Aisne, as far as Craonne, the bombardment of the defences extended to a depth of over three thousand yards, covering both the Forward and Battle Zones ; on the Chemin des Dames ridge it was shallower, from 1,600 to 2,200 yards ; but at one time or another the swept zone, which was divided into four belts to be shelled at different times, covered the entire top of the ridge in addition to the forward slopes and part of the reverse slopes.

Map 3.   This concentration of fire was the masterpiece of the same artillery expert, Colonel Bruchmüller, who had prepared the artillery attack against the Fifth Army on the 21st March, and against the Arras front on the 28th March. He had had five weeks in which to elaborate his plan. By some who had experienced the previous enemy bombardments of the year 1918, that of the 27th May was considered to be far the heaviest, as indeed it was. On the 21st March there had been 1,706 German batteries on a 64-mile frontage, which gives 26·6 per mile ; on the 27th May, 855 batteries were directed on a 24-mile frontage, that is 35·6 per mile, but no less than 466 batteries were concentrated on the $11\frac{1}{2}$-mile frontage of the British 50th and French 22nd Divisions in the centre, that is between 40 and 41 batteries per mile.[1]

The following is a German description of the bombardment : [2]

"Contrary to previous procedure, in which the fire-
"preparation of an attack had begun with the compre-
"hensive engagement of the enemy's artillery, this time,
"from 1 A.M. for the first ten minutes, all guns and trench-
"mortars, using gas ammunition, simultaneously devoted
"themselves at the highest rate of fire to all targets
"within reach. This was designed to create at the very
"start irremediable confusion and moral effect among the

---

[1] There is a complete technical account of the organization of the artillery attack, with maps, in Bruchmüller, pp. 93-111, and a general account in Monograph I, p. 27. The actual total was 1,036 batteries, the distribution being : Sector Schmettow (on the east), 127 ; Conta, 198 ; Winckler, 268 ; Wichura, 151 ; and Larisch (on the west), 181, the balance being super-heavy batteries under Army control. The batteries in Sector Larisch, however, were directed on Soissons and on localities and passages of the Aisne westward of the front of attack. These batteries, with the batteries of the *XV. Corps* of the *First Army*, on the Reims flank, formed the sides of a " box barrage " enclosing the Allied divisions which were attacked. Five super-heavy batteries on the Reims flank fired westwards, enfilading the valley of the Aisne.

[2] Monograph I, p. 27.

" enemy." At any rate, it forced everyone, right back to divisional headquarters, to put on gas masks, a serious handicap in the dark. " After this, the mass of the
" batteries turned their fire for 65 minutes [1.10 to 2.15 A.M.],
" with gas and high explosive mixed, on the Allied ar-
" tillery, whilst the trench mortars set about the system-
" atic destruction of the front defences and their wire.
" During this period all artillery opposition was to be
" smothered and the infantry in the forward positions so
" held down that the outposts of the position divisions
" could occupy a line beyond the Ailette, whilst the
" engineers would be enabled to prepare the passages and
" the assault infantry could thus advance up to and over
" the Ailette bottom without hindrance. Simultaneously,
" all important traffic and communication centres, such as
" bridges, railway establishments, approach roads, head-
" quarters, telephone exchanges and camps were to be
" kept under fire so as to prevent the arrival of reserves
" and reinforcements. The next 85 minutes [2.15 to
" 3.40 A.M.] were to be devoted, by groups specially detailed,
" to steady, systematic counter-battery work, using princi-
" pally gas shell and shooting by the map, so as to crush
" the Allied artillery. All the long-range gun batteries
" were to fire continuously on distant targets up to the line
" Jonchery, Fismes, Braine, Soissons [that is the line of the
" Vesle and thence the Aisne to Soissons]. The rest of the
" artillery took advantage of this fire period, in co-operation
" with the trench mortars, to carry out the thorough
" destruction of all infantry positions, creeping backwards
" and forwards several times over the various sectors. At
" 3.35 A.M. all batteries detailed to form the creeping
" barrage put their fire down on the Allied front trenches."

The continued effect of the guns, trench mortars and gas was indeed overwhelming. All headquarters had been under fire, and most communications had been cut. The Front Zone had nearly everywhere been rendered untenable, the strongpoints obliterated. Casualties in the infantry had been very heavy, and most of the machine guns and artillery were out of action. For the second time in the War, the first having been at Messines in June 1917, what had been so often attempted in vain had been accomplished : so thorough had been the preliminary destruction that all resistance was crushed and the infantry had only to advance to take possession of the front position.

At 3.40 A.M., nearly twenty minutes before it began to

get light, the barrage moved on, and the German infantry, who had pushed up as near as they could, rose for the assault. By this time the greater part of the front was shrouded in a thick mist which had gradually formed; and this had been rendered yet more dense by smoke shells and gas, which prevented the enemy being seen until close to the Allied trenches.

For the first time the front part of the German barrage was gas, followed by high explosive, which not only compelled the Allied troops to keep on their gas masks, but contributed an additional element of surprise.[1]

The heaviest weight of the infantry, as it had been with the artillery, fell on the centre.[2] Opposite the British 21st Division were two German divisions with a third in second line; against the 8th Division, two and one regiment of another; against the 50th Division, three, with another in second line; against the French 22nd Division, five, with two more in second line; against the French 21st Division, three, with one in second line; and against the French 61st Division, two, with one in second line. This made a total of 17 in the first line and 6 in second line, without counting the *Seventh Army* reserves, instead of the five shown on the French situation map of the 26th May, against 6 Allied divisions in front line and 4 in reserve—nearly two and a half to one; but on the 24 miles selected for the break-through, there were 13 in the front line against 4, that is $3\frac{1}{4}$ to 1; and in the centre, against the 50th Division and the French 22nd Division, 8 against 2, that is 4 to 1.

It was on the Chemin des Dames, on the British left, against the front of the French 22nd Division, a division which had been engaged alongside the British in the March battle, that the main force of the enemy's onslaught fell. Besides the original " battering ram " of five German divisions,[3] parts of two others attacked it in the course of the morning. Here the deepest penetration into the Allied defences was made, and as this naturally affected the British, a few words may be devoted to it before the

---

[1] The instructions were that lacrymatory gas might be used 300 metres in front of the barrage with a favourable wind, and 600 metres in front with an unfavourable wind. The Germans were prepared to risk a few gas casualties among their own men in consideration of the advantage to be derived from forcing their opponents to keep on their gas masks.

[2] See Map 2, on which the German divisions were marked by the courtesy of the *Kriegsgeschichtliche Forschungsanstalt des Heeres*.

[3] See Chapter V., " The Germans on the 27th May ".

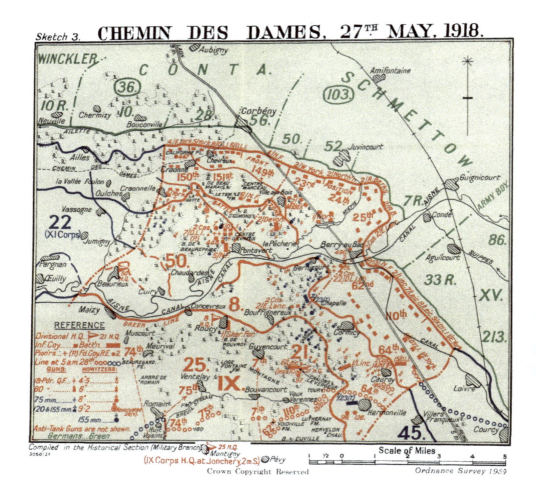

FIRST DAY. 27TH MAY

operations of the IX. Corps are described from left to right.[1]

Against odds of five to one, the French 22nd Division, after its severe bombardment, could offer no prolonged resistance. By 5.30 A.M. the enemy was in possession of the Chemin des Dames in its sector,[2] and by 9 A.M. was nearing the Aisne, his front covered by low-flying aeroplanes and preceded by small parties equipped with light machine guns. By 10 A.M. the bridge over the river at Œuilly (1½ miles east of Bourg), within a mile of the British sector, although covered by a special bridgehead, was in German hands[3] and by midday the bridges at Bourg and Pont Arcy, to the west, had also been lost. Farther to the east, the enemy was across both river and canal from Maizy (by the bridge for which the French were responsible) down to Œuilly. Thus the Aisne line in the 22nd Division sector had been lost, but Villers en Prayères, across the canal south of Œuilly, was well defended and not taken until about 12.30 P.M. On the west, the French 21st Division had also been driven back, and by 11 A.M. the Germans had captured the passages of the Aisne at Chavonne and Vailly, the next two below Pont Arcy, but beyond this a defensive flank had been formed to limit the enemy torrent.[4]

The British 50th Division (Major-General H. C. Jackson) Sketch 3

[1] The 22nd Division was one of the formations sent to the assistance of the British Fifth Army in March. It went into action on the 25th next to the British XIX. Corps, and suffered heavily, especially in the fighting near Montdidier. It was withdrawn for rest and reorganization during 2nd to 20th April, before being sent to the Chemin des Dames sector. The 21st Division, on its left, had not been in action since the Battle of Malmaison in October 1917; the 61st, next on the left, had not been in action since the retreat of the Germans to the Hindenburg Line in February-March 1917.

[2] F.O.A. vi. (ii.), p. 93.

[3] At 4.30 A.M. General Duchêne had authorized the use, to the north of the Aisne, of three battalions (later increased to four) of the 157th Division in reserve to occupy a switch line Bourg—Braye, behind the Oise—Aisne canal, and to hold the bridgehead covering Œuilly. The German advance was so rapid that only two companies of these four battalions actually crossed the Aisne, and these came at once under such heavy fire that they were dispersed.

[4] F.O.A. vi. (ii.), p. 105, gives the following explanation of the failure to destroy the bridges of the Aisne and its canal : " the order arrived too " late at General de Maud'huy's headquarters (11.30 A.M.) [After 12.30 P.M. " at Lieut.-General Gordon's]. The Germans were already masters of " seven passages and held the others under machine-gun fire. On that " account, the order to charge the chambers, given verbally between 8 and " 8.45 A.M. by General Duchêne to the Chief Engineer of the Army, could " not be completely carried out. The engineer parties detailed were caught " at work by the enemy. Nowhere did they receive the order to fire the

had not to face quite such heavy odds as the French 22nd, but was attacked by at least three German divisions.[1]

The Californie plateau, regarded by the Germans as " the key of the Chemin des Dames position ",[2] held by the 150th Brigade (Br.-General H. C. Rees), the left brigade, is flat-topped and steep-sided, standing about three hundred and fifty feet above the Ailette; its slopes were still covered with scattered bushes, but its top had been churned by digging and shell-fire into a welter of shallow ditches and shell craters. Three regiments were sent against it. Avoiding the very steep northern face, the enemy first attacked the north-eastern corner and Chevreux, a village in the line in the low-lying ground east of it, whilst the barrage was kept on the plateau for some time after it had advanced on the rest of the front. By about 4.30 A.M. the Germans were beginning to climb the eastern face of the plateau. At the same time, having broken through the French 22nd Division on the left, they were soon attacking from the west also, so that of the 5/Green Howards and 4/East Yorkshire and their attached troops only small parties managed to escape. From his headquarters at Craonne,[3] Lieut.-Colonel J. A. R. Thomson (5/Green Howards) saw enemy troops on the southern edge of the Californie plateau about 6 A.M., and, with his headquarters and the reserve company of the 4/East Yorkshire, made a gallant attempt to dislodge them by counter-attack; but the ascent was steep and the effort failed with heavy casualties. A company of the 4/Green Howards, the reserve battalion near La Hutte, about a mile south of Craonne, tried, by Br.-General Rees's orders, to join in this counter-attack, but was swept away by the terrific fire falling near La Hutte. A buried cable communicating with the 5/Green

---

" charges in sufficient time, and all initiative on their part was forbidden
" by the defence plan. Moreover, the first enemy parties arrived mixed
" up with the last of the retreating French troops. It was in these circum-
" stances that the bridges between Vailly and Maizy fell intact into the
" hands of the Germans. East of Maizy [where the bridge was specially
" retained under French control], the charging had been carried out earlier,
" on the initiative of the British IX. Corps ; but the order to fire did not
" arrive in time. Nevertheless, the British 8th and 50th Divisions were
" able to destroy part of the passages of the Aisne and the canal ; the
" bridge at Pontavert was blown up, thanks to the initiative of a French
" N.C.O."

[1] F.O.A. vi. (ii.), p. 89, says four. The fourth was in second line.

[2] It was well known to them, as they had lost it in April 1917, regained the summit in May, and lost it again in October.

[3] Craonne has been rebuilt since the War on lower ground, south of the old site.

Howards being intact, Br.-General Rees ordered the survivors of the counter-attack to fight their way out, but few succeeded in doing so, Lieut.-Colonel Thomson being among the killed. Soon after, the 4/Green Howards were attacked on both flanks and eventually from the rear. The remnants retired south-westwards to Craonnelle, where they made a stand amid the ruined houses. But by 8 A.M. nearly the whole battalion had been killed or captured, amongst the dead being Lieut.-Colonel R. E. D. Kent. The headquarters of the 150th Brigade had already left La Hutte, and were making for a chateau (La Terrasse), about three-quarters of a mile south of Craonnelle; but on reaching it they found the enemy already approaching from the west. Several of the brigade staff were wounded, and Br.-General Rees was eventually captured whilst trying to cross the Aisne. By about 8 A.M., therefore, the 150th Brigade, except the usual detachments left in billets for administrative duties, had ceased to exist.

The front companies of the 151st Brigade (Br.-General C. T. Martin), attacked on the left and in front, were soon overwhelmed. The reserves offered further resistance on the Switch Line, and in the Intermediate Line on the northern edge of the Bois de Beau Marais, where the enemy was held up for about three-quarters of an hour. But each position was in turn outflanked and surrounded, until the 6th and 8/Durham L.I., together with a pioneer company (7/Durham L.I.), had been destroyed. Two companies of the 5/Durham L.I., the brigade reserve, in the Centre d'Evreux, covering Pontavert on the Aisne, were ordered forward by Br.-General Martin; but they encountered a German regiment which, having captured part of the Battle Zone, was pushing on, and, after a fight at close quarters, were driven back. Another company of the battalion joined them, whereas the fourth failed to do so, being captured in its dug-outs. A stand was made by the D.L.I. in the Centre d'Evreux, garrisoned by two field companies R.E. and the remaining two pioneer companies, until towards 8 A.M., by which hour the Germans had nearly surrounded them. A shell now killed Br.-General Martin and severely wounded Br.-General Riddell (149th Brigade), who had joined him, besides scattering the Germans who had closed in. The 151st Brigade was no longer an organized formation, but scattered parties continued to put up a fight in various trenches at hand. At Cuiry, on the north bank of the

Aisne, a small force of all battalions checked the enemy advance, and was not dislodged until about 11 A.M., when the village was taken in rear from the west, from the direction of Beaurieux, the headquarters of the 50th Division, where the Germans had arrived from the French area soon after 9.30 A.M. Most of the staff were able to escape, divisional headquarters being re-opened at Breuil, on the Vesle; but three officers and some clerks were captured. Higher up stream, at Chaudardes, some of the 5/Durham L.I., mixed with men of the 149th Brigade, made a good stand.

The 149th Brigade (Br.-General E. P. A. Riddell) had only the 4/Northumberland Fusiliers in the front zone, with two companies disposed as outposts on the hook-shaped spur in which the Chemin des Dames ridge terminates, since it had been decided to hold as the real front a line of posts near the Reims—Corbény road on the reverse slope. To this line, manned by a third company, the survivors of the bombardment withdrew, and there they checked the enemy's advance. But, with the assistance of four tanks, he soon broke through and advanced against the Switch Line, held by three companies, the remaining company of the 4th and two of the 6/Northumberland Fusiliers. Brave resistance was offered; but here again enemy tanks turned and overwhelmed the right flank near Ville aux Bois, and the trenches were lost. Behind these, in the Battle Zone, lay four small French redoubts, including Centre Marceau, occupied by the headquarters of the 4th and 6/Northumberland Fusiliers and the two remaining companies of the latter. But by 6 A.M. the enemy had taken one of the redoubts and the Butte d'Edmond, a post on a knoll behind the left of the line, whose four machine guns had been knocked out by the bombardment. The other redoubts held out much longer; but finally all were surrounded and captured. Lieut.-Colonel B. D. Gibson of the 4/Northumberland Fusiliers was killed, and except for small parties, both this battalion and the 6th had ceased to exist.

At 5.15 A.M. Br.-General Riddell had ordered two companies of his third battalion, the 5/Northumberland Fusiliers in reserve at Pontavert in the valley of the Aisne, to reinforce the Battle Zone. But the message did not arrive until 6.10 A.M., and on approaching the Butte d'Edmond, now in the enemy's hands, the companies received such heavy fire that they were unable to make

FIRST DAY. 27TH MAY

headway. At 6.30 A.M. the two remaining companies, under Major I. M. Tweedy, the second in command, which were suffering from an intense barrage, were ordered to come up to the Centre d'Evreux. But, as already related, the enemy had gained possession of that stronghold before they could arrive. Meanwhile, Br.-General Riddell having been wounded, the command of the 149th Brigade devolved upon Major Tweedy, the remnants of whose companies were now all that remained of its three battalions. It was impossible to hold on facing the Centre d'Evreux, so he withdrew them down the valley of the Aisne to Chaudardes, where, with some of the 5/Durham L.I. (151st Brigade), as already mentioned, a stand was made until about 11 A.M. Then, as the enemy was coming in on both flanks, the survivors of the 5/Northumberland Fusiliers fell back across the Aisne, being the only remaining formed body of the infantry of the 50th Division.

Its artillery (250th and 251st Brigades and French I./203rd Regiment, under Br.-General W. Stirling) had fared no better than its infantry. In spite of heavy losses from the barrage which continued on the battery positions until after 7 A.M., it had remained in action. No sooner had enemy gun fire ceased than the German infantry burst in, so that, by about 8 A.M., the whole of the 50th Division artillery, both French and British, had been destroyed or captured. A few men got away, and were able in some cases to carry off breech blocks and dial sights.[1]

The 8th Division (Major-General W. C. G. Heneker), on the right of the 50th, was attacked by two German divisions and one infantry regiment of a third—21 fresh against 9 battered battalions.

On the left, the 23rd Brigade (Br.-General G. W. St. G. Grogan) had three companies of the 2/West Yorkshire in front line, with the fourth in support.[2] The German

---

[1] Lieut. J. L. Gibson, D/251st, when on the point of capture, struck a German in the face with the dial sight which he was carrying, and was shot down.

[2] Lieut.-Colonel (now the Rev.) C. A. S. Page, 2/Middlesex, 23rd Brigade 8th Division, has kindly furnished the following account of the disposal of the brigade by French orders and the state of the defences : 1 battalion (2/West Yorkshire) was in Outpost Line, 1 battalion (2/Middlesex) in " Première ligne des réduits ", main line of resistance, 1 in Battle Zone (2/Devonshire). (See Sketch 3.) The Middlesex had 2 companies (fight-

assault was held for a short time by the front line; but the bombardment had caused heavy casualties; numbers told and the Germans broke through. Their advance towards the Battle Zone was then very rapid, and between 5 and 5.30 A.M. the three companies of the 2/Middlesex occupying a line of redoubts in front of it, after checking the attackers in the 200 to 600-yard zone, were also overwhelmed. Lieut.-Colonel C. A. S. Page, on his way up to the front line, was desperately wounded and taken prisoner. There remained D Company of the Middlesex and the brigade reserve, the 2/Devonshire, in the Bois des Buttes, a wood which covers a conical hill south-west of Ville aux Bois. This battalion had been sheltered in the tunnels pierced through the hill, and, although gas masks had to be worn, it escaped the heavy losses from the first part of the bombardment which the other two battalions had suffered. No news came from the front, and, as the atmosphere in the tunnels had become almost unbearable, about 4 A.M., directly it got light, Lieut.-Colonel R. H. Anderson-Morshead ordered the trenches on the northern edge of the Bois des Buttes, at the back of the Battle Zone, to be manned by three companies, keeping one company in support in the wood. Shelling was still heavy and many casualties were incurred before the trenches could be reached. Within an hour, by 5.15 A.M., the Devonshire were engaged with the enemy infantry which was advancing in large numbers. The artillery which might have given support was already out of action, and although the Devonshire could rely on their infantry weapons alone, a splendid resistance was made. For nearly three hours they held out, even making charges as the enemy closed in. Meantime D Company of the Middlesex, after acting in a similar way, had been overcome. The Germans, being in far superior numbers, then pressed into the gap on the left of the Devonshire between

---

ing strength of 70) in the line of redoubts; a third held a trench as a refused left flank; the fourth, in reserve, had to garrison a redoubt. The instructions were " se défendre sans se retirer coûte que coûte ". The trenches were old German front-line trenches captured in the previous year, 8 feet deep and as wide as a sunk lane, with a fire step " cut like a mantelpiece " in the side and without a parados. The so-called redoubts (except the one held by the reserve company, which was an oval) had no rear face, some had no right face, and the wiring was poor. Four strong German concrete shelters which held 30 men each were found in the sector. To fight, the 2/Middlesex dug half-moon trenches for half platoons. They were found 4 years after the battle overgrown but almost intact, whilst the redoubts and deep trenches had vanished.

FIRST DAY. 27TH MAY

the Bois des Buttes and Butte d'Edmond now completely open to them owing to the destruction of the 149th Brigade, and enveloped and turned the left flank. Between 7 and 8 A.M. the three Devonshire companies were destroyed, very few men getting away. The headquarters and the support company still held on to the Bois des Buttes hill. It was not till the enemy had broken through the front companies and, on the left flank, was far in his rear, that Lieut.-Colonel Anderson-Morshead decided to retire to trenches south of the hill and fight a rear-guard action back to the Aisne. During this fighting he was killed. By this time the enemy was already in Pontavert, and only about fifty men of the Devonshire, many of them wounded, got back across the Aisne.[1] Of the 2/W. Yorkshire and the 2/Middlesex also very few escaped to tell the tale.

The 24th Brigade (Br.-General R. Haig), holding the centre of the 8th Division, had, like the 23rd, three companies in the front line. These belonged to the 2/Northamptonshire and were on the forward slopes of the ridge, with the valley of the Miette forming their right boundary. Heavily attacked at 3.40 A.M., they fell back gradually on to the Battle Zone. Here the 1/Worcestershire was in position, and, with the survivors of the Northamptonshire, made a fine defence until, towards 5 A.M., the enemy began attacking this line in force. At first he was beaten back; but weight of numbers once more told and the flank was turned by an advance down the Miette valley. Finally the defence was overwhelmed, Lieut.-Colonel C. G. Buckle, commanding the Northamptonshire, and Major J. B. F. Cartland, commanding the Worcestershire, both being killed. By 6 A.M. the two front battalions of the brigade had been destroyed. The headquarters, situated nearly half a mile behind the Battle Zone, were attacked with hand grenades about this time and the staff had to fight their way out. They could obtain no support, for the third battalion, the 1/Sherwood Foresters, was in divisional reserve.

---

[1] The battalion was awarded the " Croix de guerre " by the French, and had truly justified the regimental motto, " Semper fidelis ". Many German battalions were required to dislodge it. Monograph I. (see Chapter V.) says the whole of the *50th Division* was held up. The *158th Regiment* attacked the Bois des Buttes directly. The *39th Regiment* attacked the Butte d'Edmond, and was checked for some time by the fire from the Bois des Buttes, and was not able to get on till a battalion of the *53rd Regiment* was brought in between it and the *158th*. The left flank of the Devon position in the Bois des Buttes was then turned.

The 25th Brigade (Br.-General R. H. Husey) on the right of the 24th, occupied a curved line which formed the right flank of the Chemin des Dames position, and faced north-east round to south-east, on two low hills separated by a depression, the right wing being roughly parallel to, and distant one-quarter to three-quarters of a mile from the Aisne. On the left was the 2/Royal Berkshire, next on the right the 2/Rifle Brigade, each with two companies in the front trenches. The support and reserve companies of the Rifle Brigade were responsible for the line farther south where the Aisne separated the British from the Germans, whilst farther south again, near Berry au Bac, were two companies of the 2/East Lancashire. The enemy attacked the northern half of the sector with tanks, and also crossed the Aisne and made a converging attack on the weakly held southern part of the line. Heavy casualties had already been suffered in the bombardment, so that by 5 A.M., though some parts of the front line could still hold on until surrounded, the enemy managed to break through both the Forward Zone and the Battle Zone. The few survivors of the two and a half battalions involved then fell back across the Aisne.[1] The brigade headquarters, north of Berry au Bac, had been surrounded before it was known that the front line had gone, and the staff had to fight their way out to the Gernicourt defences. The brigade major was killed, whilst later in the day Br.-General Husey was badly wounded, and died three days afterwards in German hands.

The 15th Field Company R.E. in the 8th Division area, and the 446th in the 50th Division area, as the troops retired, blew up or burnt, on the responsibility of the engineer officers on the spot, practically all the bridges over the Aisne and its canal in the British sector, from Berry au Bac (inclusive) to Maizy (exclusive, since for this latter place the French were responsible). The 15th Field Company, which had blown up the bridge over the Miette at 7 A.M., accounted for all crossings in the divisional sector except one, a total of 22; the 446th, for 15 out of 19, suffering a good deal from bombardment, losing 4 officers and 46 men, and thus having the strength of its parties considerably reduced.[2] Without waiting for authority from the Sixth Army, Lieut.-General Gordon had issued orders through

---

[1] The remaining half of the 2/E. Lancashire was in the Gernicourt defences.

[2] The casualties of the 15th Field Company R.E. are not recorded.

FIRST DAY. 27TH MAY

his Chief Engineer, Br.-General G. S. Cartwright, at 12.30 A.M. for the final measures to be taken. Work was started about 4.30 A.M. as soon as boats and other apparatus, including the keys of the demolition chambers made by the French, had been collected; in some cases these keys could not be found and the doors had to be burst open.[1]

The 8th Division artillery (Br.-General J. Lamont) met with the same fate as that of the 50th Division. All the field guns in action, both British and French, were lost.[2]

South of the Aisne, behind the 25th Brigade sector, lay the Gernicourt defences, with a special garrison under Lieut.-Colonel B. C. James (22/Durham L.I.), who was under the direct orders of the division. The village of Gernicourt, as already mentioned, stands well above the river and commands all the ground to the front, but it was liable to be turned through the woods on the west. The garrison consisted of two companies of the 22/Durham L.I. (Pioneers), the French II./23rd Territorial Regiment (less one company), eight British and sixteen French machine guns. In the early morning of the 27th it was reinforced by two companies of the 2/East Lancashire and by parts of the 2nd and 490th Field Companies R.E.;[3] and after

---

[1] Monograph I. shows that in several instances the bridges were blown up under the very noses of the Germans. See Chapter V.

[2] Some details about the British batteries are available, and are given as typical of what happened to the artillery. The two brigades of the 8th Division were in the Aisne valley, north of the river, below the confluence of the Miette.

XXXIII. Brigade R.F.A.

32nd Battery: One gun destroyed by bombardment. When enemy infantry approached guns were abandoned and breech blocks and sights removed.

33rd Battery: All guns put out of action within a few minutes of the opening of the bombardment.

36th Battery: Communication with brigade cut at 2 A.M. At 7.45 A.M., battery position abandoned, dial sights being removed.

55th Battery: Only three men escaped. Undamaged guns continued to fire till overrun from the east. An attempt was made to withdraw the battery, but limbers were driven back by rifle and machine-gun fire.

XLV. Brigade R.F.A.

1st Battery: Three or four guns put out of action. Battery fired till 7 A.M. when it was overrun. Breech blocks were removed, and men fought with rifles.

3rd Battery: Four guns out of the five in action were knocked out. At 7.15 A.M. orders were given to abandon the position.

5th Battery: Fired till about 7 A.M., and then engaged the enemy at close quarters with rifles and Lewis guns till overwhelmed. Only one man escaped. This battery was awarded the " Croix de guerre ".

57th Battery: All guns knocked out by 2.25 A.M. Position evacuated by survivors at 6.15 A.M.

[3] The 15th Field Company R.E., in charge of the demolition of the bridges over the Aisne and its canal, had its headquarters near Gernicourt.

the attack on the front zones, some survivors of the forward battalions also joined it. About 5 A.M. orders were sent by the 8th Division for the 1/Sherwood Foresters and 8 machine guns to move up from divisional reserve at Roucy to the Bois de Gernicourt, on the left of the Gernicourt defences. These troops reached the north edge of the Bois de Gernicourt about 7 A.M., in time to see all the bridges over the Aisne canal in this sector, except one, blown up. They were thus able to take up a position which prevented the enemy from crossing the Aisne canal, and whence they could gain touch on the right with the troops holding Gernicourt. The only bridge left intact being under heavy fire, the Germans[1] were held up on this front for some hours. Meanwhile, other Germans,[2] after taking Berry au Bac, having discovered a practicable crossing west of that place, advanced on the wood south-east of Gernicourt. A right defensive flank facing east was formed to stop them, and here also the attack was checked for a considerable time. On the other flank, the enemy, who had crossed the Aisne and the canal between the Bois de Gernicourt[3] and Pontavert, apparently by a temporary bridge, was able to enfilade the Sherwood Foresters with machine guns.[4] A left defensive flank was therefore formed at the north-west corner of the Bois de Gernicourt, facing west. Pressure on both flanks continued, and about 1 P.M., when nearly surrounded, the survivors of the Sherwood Foresters and the garrison of the Gernicourt defences retired to the Green Line, though the guns of the 110th Brigade R.F.A. (25th Division), and a French "groupe", besides a number of heavy guns, had to be abandoned.[5] Isolated parties continued to resist

[1] These belonged to the right regiment of the *7th Reserve Division*, which had originally attacked the 25th Brigade; the two other bridges were blown up under their very eyes.
[2] These were the other two regiments of the *7th Reserve Division*.
[3] Shown but not named on Map 2. It lies south-west of Gernicourt.
[4] The enemy was the left regiment of the *52nd Division*, which had originally attacked the 24th Brigade.
[5] The 110th Brigade was ordered to retire at 12.20 P.M., when the enemy was within 150 yards. Guns were not destroyed, as it was hoped that the position would be re-established by a counter-attack:
A. Battery: Got 4 guns away at 12.40 P.M., but had to abandon them later.
B. Battery: Abandoned position at 1.15 P.M.
C. Battery: Abandoned position at 1.8 P.M., the battery commander, 1 other officer and a sergeant remaining to the last.
D. (How.) Battery: Position abandoned late and personnel caught whilst retiring.

FIRST DAY. 27TH MAY

even up to 3 P.M. Less than ten companies had held up twelve enemy battalions for over six hours.[1]

On the right of the 8th Division, south of the Aisne, on flat ground, the 21st Division held a front of nearly five miles, with all three brigades in the line. Each brigade had two battalions in the Forward and Battle Zones and one battalion in reserve. Between the two zones ran the Aisne and Marne canal, about twenty yards wide, unfordable though not quite full of water, with swampy ground on each side. The front line of the Battle Zone, which consisted of a chain of redoubts running in front of the Berry au Bac—Reims road on the right, and behind that road on the left,[2] was considered the main line of resistance. But, in spite of Lieut.-General Gordon's protest against having to hold the Forward Zone in strength, in view of the obstacle of the canal in its rear, General Duchêne had expressly forbidden any withdrawal therefrom, even if a great enemy offensive seemed imminent. The division was attacked at first by only one German division and part of another, but later, part of a third from the 8th Division front turned it from the north.

All the eleven companies which were east of the Aisne —Marne canal suffered the same fate.[3] In the dark the Forward Zone was quickly broken through, and very few men succeeded in making their way back across the canal, although the three permanent bridges and some of the temporary wooden bridges were intact, for in the darkness and the confusion it had been impossible to judge the correct moment when to destroy or remove them. By 7 A.M. the enemy was attacking the Battle Zone, his pressure being greatest on the left. But here, with the support of the divisional artillery, a good resistance was offered.

In the 62nd Brigade (Br.-General G. H. Gater), the 1/Lincolnshire, in brigade reserve at Châlons le Vergeur, 4 miles in rear of the front, with 4 machine guns, had been ordered, at 5.12 A.M., to the Battle Zone in front and north of Cormicy. On their left the Lincolnshire found the

---

[1] Monograph I. states that Gernicourt village was not finally taken till 1.30 P.M.

[2] The redoubts are not shown on Map 2; they originally formed the rear line of the Front Position.

[3] Two companies of the 12th/13th Northumberland Fusiliers, three of the 2/Lincolnshire, in the 62nd Brigade; two each of the 7th and 8/Leicestershire in the 110th Brigade; and one each of the 9/K.O.Y.L.I. and 1/East Yorkshire, in the 64th Brigade.

French I./23rd Territorial Regiment, which had been placed under the 62nd Brigade, and in Cormicy itself was a company of the pioneers (14/Northumberland Fusiliers).

By 10 A.M. the remnants of the two forward battalions had been driven from the redoubts along the Reims—Berry au Bac road, which formed the front line of the Battle Zone, and were retiring to the Cauroy—Cormicy—Gernicourt line, which the enemy soon began to attack. Three assaults on Cormicy were repulsed by the right companies of the 1/Lincolnshire, and at 2 P.M. they were still in position. North of the village the two left companies and the French Territorials were holding on, but the advance of Germans from the 8th Division front through the Bois de Gernicourt was threatening their left.

In the Battle Zone of the 110th Brigade (Br.-General H. R. Cumming) a good resistance was made. Two attacks were repulsed with rifle and Lewis-gun fire, whereupon the enemy, covered by light trench mortars, resorted to bombing up the communication trenches, and gradually succeeded, between 10 A.M. and 1 P.M., in surrounding and capturing the different strongpoints of which the line consisted. During the course of the morning, the 6/Leicestershire, in brigade reserve, and a company formed from nucleus parties of the 7th and 8/Leicestershire which had been kept back, had been sent up to the Battle Zone between Cauroy and Cormicy. After the gradual loss of the Front Zone, the road between these villages, as in the 62nd Brigade, became the front line.

The front line of Battle Zone of the 64th Brigade (Br.-General H. R. Headlam) held out for some hours, and was not finally in the enemy's possession till about 11 A.M., when the remnants of the 9/K.O.Y.L.I. and the 1/East Yorkshire fell back on the Cauroy—Cormicy line near Cauroy, then held by the 15/Durham L.I., the reserve battalion, which had been moved up during the bombardment, and by the remaining two companies of the pioneers. The 1/East Yorkshire was then withdrawn into reserve.

About noon Lieut.-General Gordon telephoned to Major-General Campbell to inform him that the enemy had crossed the Aisne and that this movement might cut off the 21st Division : he must therefore prepare a plan for pivoting on his right, in touch with the French 45th Division, back to the St. Aubœuf—Guyencourt position, one mile in rear of the Green Line.

Thus between 1 and 2 P.M. the Cauroy—Cormicy line

FIRST DAY. 27TH MAY

in the Battle Zone had become the front of the 21st Division. It had a good field of fire down a gentle slope to the front, but was liable to be turned on the left flank through the thick woods to the north near Gernicourt, and from this flank, except for scattered parties still fighting, the 8th and 50th Divisions had disappeared. Only the 25th Division (less its artillery, previously attached to the forward divisions), which had moved up into the IX. Corps area, remained intact.

The artillery of the 21st Division (Br.-General H. W. Newcome) did not suffer so heavily as that of the other two front-line divisions. The XCIV. Brigade R.F.A., in the Cauroy area, kept up fire on the S.O.S. line till 8 A.M., when, at the request of the 64th Brigade, the barrage was brought back to protect the Battle Zone. The continued advance of the enemy subsequently made a withdrawal of the batteries necessary, and at 11.30 A.M. the retirement to previously reconnoitred positions on the St. Auboeuf—Guyencourt position was begun, the last battery not withdrawing before 3 P.M. The movement was carried out without the loss of a gun.

The XCV. Brigade R.F.A. also brought back its barrage to protect the Battle Zone at 8 A.M. B/XCV., on the extreme left, was threatened by the enemy's advance on the 8th Division front, and was ordered to retire at 10 A.M.; but the order took time to reach it, and before it arrived the battery was surrounded by the enemy, and only one gun out of the six was saved. The remainder of the brigade withdrew between 11 A.M. and 12.30 P.M. to positions behind the Green Line west of Châlons le Vergeur, D/XCV. having to abandon two guns.

The 112th Brigade R.F.A. (25th Division artillery, but under the 21st Division), near St. Auboeuf, was heavily shelled, but was able to maintain its position and cover the retirement of the 21st Division artillery.

The heavy artillery of the IX. Corps had fared little better than the field artillery. The guns covering the 50th Division were all north of the Aisne, and those covering the 8th Division were chiefly in the Bois de Gernicourt. All these, comprising the LXXVII. Brigade R.G.A. and the French Groupes d'Ainval and Dubarry, were destroyed or had to be abandoned. The only heavy guns still available on the left flank of the IX. Corps after midday were nine guns of the LXXVII. Brigade which had not been with it in action, and of these, only two 60-pdrs. could be used, the others being temporarily unserviceable.

On the right of the corps, covering the 21st Division, the XLI. Brigade R.G.A. and the French Groupe Meurier, in emplacements behind the Green Line, were able to maintain their positions, and it was not until the evening that they had to withdraw.

The aeroplanes of No. 52 Squadron R.A.F., the sole British squadron in the area, had not been able to furnish any assistance. Flying over the battlefield to report the German advance and find targets for the artillery they encountered opposition at once from low-flying enemy machines ahead of the troops, and could not hold their own. Their aerodrome at Fismes was systematically shelled with increasing severity as the day went on; so in the afternoon the squadron was forced to move back to Cramaille (10 miles S.S.E. of Soissons).

On the right of the IX. Corps, the French 45th Division, composed partly of Zouaves and partly of African troops, was not so heavily attacked as the troops farther to the west. Although the division could not prevent the enemy from crossing the Aisne—Marne canal, it held its ground behind this waterway, forming a defensive flank on its left when the right of the British 21st Division was driven back.

Away in the west, on the left flank of the French 22nd Division, the French 21st, though fresh, had fared no better than the tired British 50th and 8th Divisions. It occupied a front of about six miles, from a point in front of Braye (exclusive) to the Forêt de Pinon (exclusive), beyond Malmaison. By frontal attack, and by flank attack from the sector of the 22nd Division, it was swept away southeastwards by three German divisions, and its artillery captured. A stand was made in the centre and left portions of the Battle Zone, which here faced northeastwards, by the reserve battalion and the remnants of the garrison of the First Position. But at 10.40 A.M. the divisional commander reported to General de Maud'huy (XI. Corps) that he " judged it a delusion to think of defend-" ing the Intermediate Position (Battle Zone); that his " regiments were at the end of their powers; and that the " Second Position (Green Line) must be occupied. He, " for his part, abandoned the idea of employing north of

"the Aisne the regiment of the 39th Division which he had
"been authorized to send there, and had placed it in the
"Second Position south of the river. At 11 A.M. the
"Germans, turning the defenders of Rouge Maison [the
"right flank of the Intermediate Line], reached Vailly [on
"the Aisne] where they seized the bridges, and Chavonne
"[above Vailly]." [1]

The left division of the French XI. Corps, the 61st, held a bastion of the front about seven miles in length, covered at close range by the Oise—Aisne canal, from the Forêt de Pinon (inclusive) to Vauxaillon (inclusive), thus slanting three miles forward of the Chemin des Dames. It was attacked at first by two German divisions, and later by a third. The two former, avoiding a frontal attack through the Forêt de Pinon, which was marshy, advanced on each side of it. Three French battalions (one of the 21st Division), although surrounded, held out in the forest for most of the day, and considerably hampered enemy progress. The Germans, however, continued their advance up the valleys on each side of the forest, by Chavignon (in the 21st Division sector) on the east and by Pinon on the west. By 8 A.M. they had reached Malmaison Fort and Allemant, and by nine o'clock were on the top of the Chemin des Dames ridge. Here they were held for a time by the French reserve battalions in the Intermediate Position, on the line Ange Gardien—Laffaux. Farther to the left, the French still held Vauxaillon and the hill to the west of it in the First Position.

Next on the left, the 151st Division (XXX. Corps) was little molested. Early in the morning the enemy crossed the Oise—Aisne canal at Pont à Courson and gained a footing on the Mont des Tombes, a hill north-east of Leuilly. But a counter-attack successfully prevented any further German advance in this direction.

Thus, by 11 A.M., the front of the attack was clearly defined as between the French 151st Division on the left and the French 45th Division on the right. The French front then ran, beginning on the west, from the right of the 151st in the First Position to, including Vauxaillon, the 61st Division sector in the Intermediate Position; between this sector and the Aisne, and along that river as far as the British left, a front was still maintained in the Second

---

[1] F.O.A. vi. (ii.), p. 102.

Position (Green Line), but the enemy was, in places, across the river.

The French air service, like the British, had not been able to give either the troops or General Duchêne much assistance. As the bombardment soon destroyed all communication with the front, it was not until after 5 A.M. that French Sixth Army headquarters at Belleu (2 miles south-east of the centre of Soissons) learnt that an infantry attack had been launched and had made a little progress at three or four places. The divisional headquarters knew no more. But messages which arrived between 6 and 7 A.M. left no doubt as to the success achieved against the French 21st and 22nd Divisions and the British 50th and 8th, and made it certain that the enemy infantry after capturing a very considerable portion of the Chemin des Dames ridge and the Californie plateau, were at Ville aux Bois. What was happening on the left flank, on the front of the 61st Division, remained obscure, but the 45th Division, on the right, appeared to be holding its own. The danger point seemed to be between the 21st and 22nd Divisions.

Consequently, disregarding General Pétain's instructions that no reserve divisions should be sent north of the Aisne, at 6.55 A.M., General Duchêne decided to put the 157th Division at the disposal of General de Maud'huy, to be interpolated between the 21st and 22nd Divisions. At the same time, in addition to its original mission of holding on to the Chemin des Dames, he made the XI. Corps responsible for the defence of the Second Position (Green Line) from the boundary with the British, near Villers en Prayères to Cys, that is, behind the 22nd Division and the right of the 21st Division. All the artillery (9 field batteries, 3 of 120-mm., 5 of 155-mm. and 1 of 145-mm.) present on this position was to remain.

Towards 7.30 A.M. he authorized Lieut.-General Gordon, " who had already asked several times to be allowed to " dispose of the 25th Division, to send one brigade of this " division north of the Aisne, with a view to supporting " the 8th and 50th Divisions."

As early as 5.10 A.M., the French 21st Division too had asked for a battalion to support its right next the 22nd. But not until 7.45 did General Duchêne respond. Then he allotted a regiment of the 39th Division, but he reminded General de Maud'huy that the division was responsible for the Second Position (Green Line) from Cys to Celles, behind the left of the 21st and the right of the 61st, and that the artillery (6 field batteries and 2 of 145-mm.) must remain south of the river. He also decided to order the 39th and 74th Divisions to occupy the Green Line from Cys to Celles, where it left the Aisne, and thence to Margival, near Pont Rouge, in the sector of the 61st Division. Attempts were thus made to hold the whole of the Green Line behind the front where the Germans had broken in. At the same time, General Duchêne requested the G.A.N. to send him not only the 13th and 1st Divisions, but to provide others and the staff of a corps without delay, informing General Franchet d'Espérey that a German prisoner had stated that many divisions were being employed and the intention was, as first object, to reach the Aisne.[1]

None of the information received by General Duchêne between 7.45 and 9 A.M. seemed to indicate that the situation in the centre had grown any worse, although on the left Germans were reported to have reached the plateau south of the Forêt de Pinon. He could do no more than despatch encouraging messages.[2] On the right, however, the British 21st Division had been driven back to the Intermediate Position (Battle Zone), whilst the 45th Division, on its right, was finding some difficulty in keeping connection.

Thus, at 9 A.M., when the Germans were nearing the Aisne, owing to the delay in the arrival of information, the situation appeared to the Sixth Army to be that the enemy had captured the line of resistance selected by General Duchêne, except on the wings. Nevertheless there seemed every hope of stopping or delaying his further advance.

Between 10 and 11 A.M. fresh reports revealed the gravity of the situation and left no doubt that it would be impossible to stop the enemy short of the Second Position (Green Line). At 11.15 A.M. General Duchêne issued the following order to General de Maud'huy :

" Withdraw your troops to the Second Position, which " must remain inviolable. The 39th and 157th Divisions " are placed at your disposal. Wherever the enemy has " crossed the Aisne or the Second Position, he must be " attacked and thrown back." [3]

A quarter of an hour earlier he had delegated to all

[1] Orders for the movement of the 13th and 1st Divisions and the staff of the XXI. Corps were given at once : the 4th Division, then moving by railway to the Third Army, was diverted ; and the 170th and 40th Divisions, in the Oise group, were warned to be ready to move.
[2] Appendix III.
[3] The consequent XI. Corps order is translated in Appendix IV.

his corps commanders authority to destroy the bridges in their areas when thought necessary. The message to the British IX. Corps was not sent off until 12.30 P.M.[1] Fortunately, Lieut.-General Gordon had not waited for such authority.

Map 2.
Sketch 3.
The next phase of the action was the attempt to hold the Green Line.

Sectors of this position had been allotted by Major-General Sir G. Bainbridge to the brigades of the 25th Division, from left to right as follows:

74th Brigade (Br.-General H. M. Craigie Halkett) from Maizy (inclusive) along the Aisne to Concevreux (inclusive);

75th Brigade (Br.-General A. A. Kennedy) from Concevreux (exclusive), where the line left the river, to Bouffignereux (inclusive);

7th Brigade (Br.-General C. J. Griffin), with the 6/South Wales Borderers (Pioneers) attached, from Bouffignereux (exclusive), along a line of redoubts about a mile behind the Green Line to Hermonville (inclusive).

A machine-gun company having been allotted to each brigade, only one company and the 105th, 106th and 130th Field Companies R.E. remained in reserve. The artillery had, as we have seen, been attached to the forward divisions, except one section of each battery of the 110th Brigade R.F.A., which had been retained.

Under instructions from the IX. Corps, Major-General Bainbridge issued orders, at 5.20 A.M., for a nucleus garrison to occupy the Green Line. This was to consist of one platoon from each company and eight machine guns for each brigade front. The sector of the 7th Brigade being a long one, five miles in fact, the whole of the 6/South Wales Borderers (Pioneers) was to occupy as a nucleus garrison the right half of the line. It was not until 7.30 A.M., as we have seen, after repeated requests, that General Duchêne placed the 25th Division at Lieut.-General Gordon's disposal, with permission to send a brigade across the Aisne to support the 50th and 8th Divisions. Instructions were then issued for the full occupation of the Green Line by all three brigades; one field company R.E. was placed by the division at the disposal of each brigade, and four extra machine guns each

---

[1] See p. 51, f.n. 4.

were allotted to the 74th and 75th Brigades. These brigades were in position by about 11 A.M.

The divisional orders took some time to reach the 7th Brigade, and its last troops were not in position till between 1 and 2 P.M.

Under personal instructions from Lieut.-General Gordon, one battalion from each of the 74th and 75th Brigades had been directed, about 8 A.M., to move to Chaudardes and Pontavert, on the Aisne, respectively a mile and two miles beyond the Green Line, to assist the troops in front. But before they could arrive the enemy was reported to be in possession of the two places, and neither of the battalions actually went farther than the Green Line. Remnants of the 50th Division and 8th Division which had retired across the Aisne, some reinforcements from Lewis gun schools and regimental nucleus parties joined the troops of the 25th Division in the Green Line and came under the orders of the brigadiers. But at 1.20 P.M. IX. Corps issued orders (received by the 25th Division at 2.15 P.M.) that the 74th Brigade was to come under the 50th Division, the 75th under the 8th Division, and the 7th under the 21st Division. Thus for a time Major-General Bainbridge ceased to exercise any command over his troops.

NOTE

THE GERMAN PREPARATIONS FOR THE ATTACK [1]

The assembly of thirty additional divisions [2] and some thousand additional batteries, besides trench mortars, on a front of thirty-five miles was in itself a considerable task. Success depended on the concealment of the operation from the enemy and his complete surprise. Allied observation balloons were up on every favourable day, yet, in order not to awaken suspicion, their attack by aircraft might not exceed the normal. The inhabitants of the area were of course hostile; in one corps area alone four baskets of carrier pigeons were discovered, obviously dropped by aeroplane, with directions as to what information should be sent back. The region was certainly thickly wooded, with trees in leaf, practically untouched by the War, right down to the Ailette. Yet the noise of the preparations might be heard, as thousands of guns, hundreds of trench mortars, must be

Map 2.

---

[1] Mainly from Monograph I.
[2] All the fresh divisions which took part in the assault were from the *Eighteenth Army* except the *7th Reserve*, which was taken from the *First Army*. Thus all came from the French front.

dug in well to the front; for weeks innumerable vehicles, night after night, must transport an enormous amount of ammunition and material as far forward as the front infantry line.

In order to deceive the Allies, thirty assault divisions were left opposite the British in Flanders and in the Somme area. Extra bivouac fires were lighted there; large numbers of troops were marched about; telephones, wireless and visual signalling were kept busy; and many air attacks against the rear areas were made in order to distract attention from the Aisne front.

Most thorough precautions for secrecy were, however, taken in the latter area. The following is a summary of the measures ordered:

I. In every corps, division and brigade, every artillery and engineer command, and every anti-aircraft and air formation, members of the staff were to be appointed as responsible executive officers for the measures required.

II. In corps and divisions, officers were to be appointed to test the measures of precaution.

III. Every corps and division area was to be divided into sub-areas, so as to form a network every space of which would be constantly watched.

IV. Only the corps commanders, their chiefs of the staff, and their operations officers were to know of the activities of the above officers. Success lay in the secrecy of the system.

Matters to be watched:

(*a*) In the front positions:

No new work to be done unless at once covered up or camouflaged; in the latter case efficacy must be tested by airmen. No secret papers or secret instructions to be taken beyond the regimental battle headquarters. Observation of telephone and wireless discipline. Guard against enemy overhearing; note behaviour of officers and men when unknown persons—of whatever rank—might appear in the trenches on any occasion. Arrest even on suspicion. Concealment of distinguishing marks of arm and rank when visiting forward positions. Conspicuous articles of equipment and dress (officers' caps, officers' greatcoats, map cases, spread-out maps, etc.) to be avoided. Ploughing over of beaten paths leading to positions, shelters, headquarters.

(*b*) In localities, hutments or on roads, no signboards with number of unit (only the name of the commander). Lights to be covered at night. No wagon park, parade place, refilling point, supply column, to be in the open: either under trees, sheds or gateways, or close to buildings. By day no march column larger than a company or battery except at considerable intervals. Larger movements only by night or in misty weather. During night marches, no noise, singing or bands. Absolute silence as positions were approached, no rattling of equipment; wheels to be muffled; if necessary, noise to be drowned by artillery fire. If enemy aeroplanes appear, take cover at once; keep roads clear, on occasion turn about.

(*c*) Office work: Secret material to be kept locked up by officers. Unobtrusive watching night and day. Test locks of secret cupboards and boxes. Particularly secret matters to be written by officers.

(*d*) Conversations in officers' clubs, canteens, soldiers' homes, etc., to be watched by special confidential agents. Unobtrusive intercourse. Caution as regards orderlies.

(*e*) Refilling points: No assembly on roads; rapidity; no mark-

GERMAN PREPARATIONS

ings on wagons. Observation of transport, and of transfer and issue of postal matter.

(*f*) Area Commandants: Testing of passes. Regulation of movements of inhabitants and workmen. Search of houses. Look out for suspected persons. Inspection of small parties on special duties.

(*g*) Railways: No markings on trucks; rapid unloading and loading. Rapid entraining and detraining and leaving of stations. March from these only at night. Formal parading only if there is cover near at hand. Look out for suspected persons. Examine passes very carefully.

A number of new aerodromes had to be prepared, but no aeroplane might make use of them until the 27th, and even on that day the airmen had to start from the old aerodromes, well in rear. No balloon went to its station until the night of the 26th/27th.

Look-outs were placed to give warning of the approach of enemy aircraft, when all hands must take cover from view.

The air inspection brought a number of new points to notice: *e.g.*, too many horses grazing at the same time, too much smoke, some stations too brightly lit up, motor lorries made too much dust.

In order to mislead the divisions in position as long as possible as regards the arrival of reinforcements, they were informed that a great attack was expected and that a few tired divisions were being rested behind their front. Any registration by the artillery was forbidden. Each gun was allowed to fire only one test round.

Two thousand five hundred miles of telephone cable were provided, principally for the artillery, but for the first advance wireless carried by hand was mainly relied upon; every other kind of signal apparatus, carried on pack animals, was provided, including submarine cable to be laid across the Ailette.

The first batteries began to arrive on the 14th May, the last on the 23rd. The " mass of all batteries " had to be in position before daylight on the 26th, in order to leave the roads clear for the infantry on the last night; but there was not concealment available for all the batteries, so some of them were hidden in woods, villages, gardens, etc., in the neighbourhood, and man-handled into position on the night of the 25th/26th; a few which could not thus be moved were brought up by horse teams during the night of the 26th/27th. All the batteries, except twenty, were dug in by daylight on the 26th. If batteries had to march across the fields, their tracks were ploughed over. The dumping of ammunition ($2\frac{1}{2}$ days' full supply near the guns; 1 day's in the wagons; $1\frac{1}{2}$ days' in divisional dump; and 1 day's in corps dump), should have been completed on the night of the 22nd, but this was not done until four days later. All the work was carried out at night. To give some idea of its magnitude, it is stated that for the 210 batteries of one corps, 320,000 shell of all calibres had been carried. The bringing up of trench-mortar ammunition (30 rounds per heavy, 50 per medium, 100-150 per light trench mortar) close to the front line, gave even greater trouble.

The deployment of divisions, without their artillery, gave less trouble. The reconnoitring officers began to arrive on the 16th to make preparations: the first troops, partly by rail but mainly by march, appeared in the battle area on the 21st, and leaving their baggage behind, moved to assembly places not more than three or four miles behind the line, or to their actual position of readiness when this afforded concealment from view, on the evening of the 24th. All were in position at midnight of the 26th/27th.

On account of the obstacles formed by the Oise—Aisne canal and the Ailette, the engineer preparations had to be very elaborate. An example from the corps opposite the French 22nd Division is given.

"(a) Preparations : construction of 24 foot-bridges in each divi-
" sional sector for the passage of the Ailette, and the dumping of the
" material as far forward as possible and opposite the places where
" it is to be used. Reconnaissance of these places and the routes
" to them.

" Preparation of and placing ready numerous bridges for the
" passage of the marshy ground in the Ailette bottom, after recon-
" naissance. Repair of main roads as far as the southern edges of
" the villages between Grandelain and Neuville. [These villages are
" only about a quarter of a mile from the Ailette.]

" Collection of the necessary material for the passage of the
" cratered zone, for the repair of roads (particularly broken stone)
" between the above-named village line and the crest of the Chemin
" des Dames.

" Collection of materials for the construction of five heavy bridges
" over the Ailette and for bridges over the Aisne.

" (b) As soon as the artillery bombardment begins :

" Picking up and carriage of the bridging material (for foot-
" bridges and five heavy bridges) to the Ailette, erection of the foot-
" bridges and bridges over the marshes, at the same time the removal
" of all obstacles on both banks. Construction of the five heavy
" bridges.

" Completion of up and down tracks from the village line up to
" and beyond the Ailette. All this work must be completed before
" the assault.

" Strengthening of the heavy bridges and further improvement
" of up and down tracks ; advance behind the infantry for repair of
" tracks in the cratered zone, in and beyond the French positions ;
" assistance in the advance of the batteries, the vehicles of the
" infantry, machine guns, trench mortars, etc. For these purposes,
" all three resting battalions of the position divisions should be
" employed ; they were to arrive at the bridges about an hour after
" the beginning of the assault ; their first business would be to assist
" the heavy artillery of the assault divisions up the hill to the top
" of the Chemin des Dames. Reconnaissance and making of cross-
" country tracks alongside the main roads ; bringing up of bridging
" material for the passage of the Aisne ; assistance to divisions in
" bridging the Aisne, if ordered. All this work should begin when
" the infantry assaults."

CHAPTER IV

THE BATTLE OF THE AISNE (*continued*)

27TH MAY 1918

THE DEFENCE OF THE GREEN LINE

(Map 2 ; Sketches 2, 3)

THE Green Line position had not been prepared for defence. Map 2. It consisted, as already mentioned, of some old trenches dug during the operations of the previous year; but no system governed their construction, neither had any exact line of defence been studied or adopted even as a " projet " on paper. The recently arrived 25th Division, in Army reserve until the night of the 26th/27th May, had not been afforded any opportunity for reconnoitring the ground, so that each brigade, as it came on the field, had to settle for itself what position it would occupy in the general line.

The divisional artillery had already been engaged, so that no artillery support was available for the left and centre sectors of the new front, except three remaining sections of the 110th Brigade R.F.A., which, after being formed into a composite battery, came into position about noon behind the centre near Guyencourt. In the right sector, as the 21st Division's losses in guns had been slight, this division and the 7th Brigade with it were still covered by most of the divisional and heavy artillery, though some batteries were on the move and therefore temporarily out of action.

After the overwhelming of the 50th and 8th Divisions, a lull occurred in the fighting whilst the German infantry gradually worked forward and the artillery advanced to new positions from which it could cover the passage of the Aisne and the advance from the Bois de Gernicourt. The almost complete destruction of the British artillery on this part of the front enabled these movements to be carried out with very little interference, and as the French 157th Division had not yet appeared, the prospects of holding the ground seemed gloomy.

In accordance with Sixth Army orders, General de Maud'huy had allotted the defence of the Second Position (Green Line) to the three reserve divisions, directing that the units of the three front line divisions, 22nd, 21st and 61st, should join in the defence of the different sectors as soon as they could be reorganized. To the 157th Division was assigned the frontage from the boundary with the British to Cys (just south of Chavonne); to the 39th, from Cys to Condé; and to the 74th, from Condé to Margival.

Map 2.
Sketch 2.

The 157th Division did not arrive in time. Soon after noon the enemy was across the Aisne and its canal everywhere in the original sector of the 22nd Division: Maizy (exclusive)—Œuilly—Villers en Prayères—Bourg—Pont Arcy—St. Mard (south-east of Chavonne), and had "reached " and crossed the Second Position ",[1] so the 157th, coming up about 1 P.M., could only try, unsuccessfully, to throw back the enemy to the river by counter-attack.

The French 39th Division drove away the Germans who had crossed at Vailly, and occupied its allotted sector in the Second Position. The 74th, also, covered by the 61st, was able to reach its place.

Except, therefore, for a sector where the 157th Division had failed, the Second Position (Green Line) had been occupied by the Allies. But, owing to that failure, a gap of nearly two miles existed between the British left and the French right, which was somewhere south of Villers en Prayères. The enemy, thanks to his aeroplanes enjoying complete command of the air, soon took advantage of this opening. His principal effort, as before, was made in the centre. On the left, the French 74th and 39th Divisions held the western side of the re-entrant made by the enemy in the Allied line, as far as Chavonne; but east of this point Germans had crossed both river and canal and penetrated a mile. The French 157th Division, unable to reach the Green Line, clung until 3 P.M. to a position Longueval—Vieil Arcy—plateau of Grande Roche (west of Vieil Arcy), facing north-east. Between 3.30 and 4.30 P.M. it was driven from this position and fell back south-westwards over the Vesle, which it crossed about 8 P.M. The

---

[1] F.O.A. vi. (ii.), pp. 106-7.

remnants of the 22nd and 21st Divisions, now endeavouring to rally behind the Vesle, were in no position to help. The enemy followed, and reached the railway between Bazoches and Braine, close to Limé. The bridge-heads at Bazoches, covering the railway junction, and at Courcelles, three miles below, were lost. As will be seen, the British left was drawn in slightly to near Romain (1½ miles north of Breuil). The gap between this flank and the stabilized French right at Braine was thus increasing, and by night had grown to some twelve miles. French reinforcements were, however, moving to fill it. About noon, General Martin de Bouillon, commanding the 13th Division, arrived at Lieut.-General Gordon's headquarters and informed him that he had been sent to his help; but whilst they were actually discussing the situation, General de Bouillon received orders to move farther to the left, to Fismes. Later, General Breton, commanding the 154th Division, appeared to impart the same glad news of approaching assistance, but his troops did not appear till next day.

At 1.30 P.M. Lieut.-General Gordon sent the IX. Corps Cyclist Battalion to the left to maintain connection with the French; it endeavoured, with the co-operation of a part of the motor machine-guns of the French 4th Cavalry Division [1] and of parties from French divisional schools sent for the same purpose, to cover the ever-increasing gap. This skeleton force was gradually forced back until towards 4 P.M. the leading troops of the 13th Division came up and dug in north of Fismes, the cyclists remaining to screen them. Nearest the gap, the left sector of the IX. Corps, in the Green Line along the Aisne, under Major-General H. C. Jackson (50th Division), was by about 11 A.M. manned by the 74th Brigade (Br.-General H. M. Craigie Halkett), and remnants of the 50th Divn, with the 9/Loyal North Lancashire (74th Brigade) and some survivors of the 150th Bde, defending Maizy at the western end of the sector. Earlier in the day, about 9.30 A.M., Germans (of the *28th Division*) had reached the

---

[1] The 4th Cavalry Division had just arrived at Dormans on the Marne from the Fifth Army; it was short of two brigades, which had been sent to the centre of France on account of strikes. On the morning of the 27th the divisional artillery and two groups of motor machine-guns were sent north and arrived at Villesavoye (south-west of Fismes) about 11 A.M.; one group of motor machine-guns was called upon by the 13th Division and this group co-operated with the cyclists.

The rest of the 4th Cavalry Division present, that is the Cuirassier Brigade, and the cyclists, came into the battle early on the 28th.

Aisne north of Maizy, but were there held up by artillery fire on the river bridge; later some of them managed to cross by an undefended bridge lower down in the French area. The canal bridge was, however, defended by part of the 9/Loyal North Lancashire, which had just arrived on the scene, and it was not until about 11.30 A.M., after the German artillery had been brought into action on the hill above Beaurieux, to the north, that resistance was overcome. The L.N. Lancashire, with the 74th Light Trench Mortar Battery, 105th Field Company R.E. and a section of machine guns, then swung back and formed a left defensive flank through Muscourt and westward, and the 50th Division Lewis Gun School, coming up with 24 guns to reinforce, extended this flank as far as the hill east of Révillon, on the boundary of the British sector.

In the centre and right of Jackson's sector, the enemy (*5th Guard Division*), having been checked between Maizy and Concevreux by the destruction of the canal bridges and the good defence of the 11/Lancashire Fusiliers and 3/Worcestershire, had begun to work round by the west.[1] As a result, the defenders were driven from Révillon hill, and then, about 1 P.M., from the Muscourt position, when the left flank of the 74th Brigade fell back a mile to the line Meurival—Beauregard Farm. There, in spite of the appearance of German reinforcements,[2] a further stand was made until between 4 and 5 P.M., when the 9/L.N. Lancashire and the troops with it fell back to the long ridge which lies 1¼ miles south of Meurival and runs north-eastward towards Roucy.

Meanwhile the right centre and right of the 74th Brigade, though holding the enemy on their front, were seriously threatened on the east by Germans (of the *50th Division*) who had crossed the Aisne at Pontavert. About 3.15 P.M. the enemy broke through the line of the 75th Brigade (Br.-General A. A. Kennedy), in Major-General Heneker's (8th Division) sector, on the east of Concevreux, where the Green Line left the river and canal and ran eastwards across country. By 4 P.M. the 11/Cheshire, the left battalion of the brigade, was driven out of Roucy. The 3/Worcestershire (74th), being outflanked in Concevreux, was compelled to retire, with the result that by

---

[1] Only two regiments of the *5th Guard Division*, the *20th* and *3rd Foot Guards* were left in front of the 74th Brigade, the rest and the *28th Division* turning off and crossing in the French sector.

[2] The *20th Regiment* from the 74th Brigade front.

5 P.M. the whole of the 74th Brigade and the 11/Cheshire were assembled on the Meurival—Roucy ridge overlooking the Aisne valley.

About 5.30 P.M. the 2/South Lancashire, the right battalion of the 75th Brigade,[1] was also driven back, and then prolonged the right of the 11/Cheshire, in the Bois de Rouvroy, facing north, where the two reserve companies of the 8/Border Regiment were already in position. Supported by some remnants of the 50th and 8th Divns still fighting alongside them, the 74th and 75th Brigades held their ground until nightfall against repeated attacks by the *5th Guard* and *50th Divisions*.

When the 2/South Lancashire retired south-westwards to the Bois de Rouvroy the 1/Wiltshire of the 7th Brigade on its right, now with the 21st Division, also withdrew, though southwards towards Châlons le Vergeur. The 7th Brigade (Br.-General C. J. Griffin), with the 6/S. Wales Borderers (Pioneers) attached, had before noon been ordered to shift to the left and occupy the Green Line west of Chapelle ($\frac{3}{4}$ of a mile west of Cormicy), on the forward slopes looking towards the Bois de Gernicourt, where a good field of fire was obtainable. The whole of the brigade was not in its place until between 1 and 2 P.M.[2] It was then disposed partly in the front trench and partly in the second, the latter dug in the 21st Division area only and some two thousand yards behind the first. The 6/S. Wales Borderers occupied nearly four miles of the second trench [3] from near the Châlons le Vergeur—Cormicy road to the right of the corps boundary, but with a gap on the left between the battalion and the 10/Cheshire. By this time, however, the 21st Division had established itself (left to right, 62nd, 110th and 64th Brigades) on the line Cauroy—Cormicy—Chapelle.

By 3 P.M. the enemy's renewed attacks on Cormicy met with success, as also did his turning movement through the woods against the salient at the left of the 62nd Brigade's line, so that its battalions were ordered to retire to a line of old trenches between Cormicy and La Cendrière, some two thousand yards to the west, facing north, whence the line was continued by the 7th Brigade. This position was successfully held against attacks from the north (*7th*

---

[1] Two companies of the third battalion, the 8/Border Regiment, had been used to reinforce the front line, and the other two were in reserve.

[2] Left to right : 1/Wiltshire, 4/South Staffordshire, 10/Cheshire.

[3] It was only two feet deep, but well traversed and strongly wired.

Reserve Divison) until about 5.30 P.M., when it was endangered by the enemy advance on the left of the 7th Brigade. The left of the latter, 1/Wiltshire, then retired south and the 2/South Lancashire (75th Brigade) southwest, so that a gap was created. An attempt was made to fill it with the 130th Field Company R.E. and brigade trench mortar personnel. They proved too weak for the purpose, and the enemy (*52nd Division*) gradually pushed them back.

At 6.30 P.M. two companies of the 10/Cheshire (7th Brigade) were taken out of the line south of Cormicy and sent to prolong the line of the 4/South Staffordshire (7th Brigade) westwards; but they came under heavy fire and could not extend far enough to prevent the enemy's outflanking movement. Pushing up the Bouffignereux valley between the 7th and 75th Brigades, Germans entered Guyencourt (a mile behind the Green Line), and by 8 P.M. had occupied Bouvancourt (over two miles from the Green Line) and Châlons le Vergeur, to the northeast, whilst others (of the *50th Division*) continued to press the attack from the north against the right of the 75th Brigade in the Bois de Rouvroy. Thus not only were the right flank of the combined 75th and 74th Brigades, themselves forming a left defensive flank facing north-west, and the left flank of the 21st Division and 7th Brigade completely turned, but the greater part of two enemy divisions had broken through the front.

The retirement of the 75th Brigade became imperative. Yet orders were not given by Br.-General Kennedy until 9 P.M. for a withdrawal from the Roucy ridge by the good road through Ventelay, across the valley of the Ventelay stream, two miles southwards, to the next ridge, north of Montigny. The orders to the 8/Border Regiment miscarried, and the companies held on until 10.30 P.M., when, being nearly surrounded, they withdrew to a position north of Ventelay. Here they remained until 1.30 A.M. on the 28th when, learning that the enemy was in Ventelay, they fought their way through to Breuil, and reported to the French 13th Division, which had arrived there during the evening. Reduced to the strength of a single company, with another formed of stragglers of the 8th and 50th Divns, the 8/Border Regiment remained next day with the French.

The withdrawal of the 75th Brigade entailed that of the 74th on its left; so between 10 and 11 P.M. it fell back

FIRST DAY. 27TH MAY

in turn to follow the 75th to the ridge north of Montigny, where both brigades were in place before daylight. The difficulty of organizing the position properly in the dark was great. The brigades, too, were weak in numbers, for casualties had been very heavy: the fighting strength of the 74th on the morning of the 28th was no more than 26 officers and 324 other ranks, and the 75th about the same. Small parties of the 50th and 8th Divns were still with them in the line, and a reinforcement of about six hundred corps details of many different units was sent up to them. Touch, but not immediate connection, was obtained with the French on the left near Romain, but not with the 7th Brigade.

The greater part of this brigade and the 62nd withdrew after 8 P.M. from the Cormicy—La Cendrière position to the wooded ridge, facing north-west, which lies between Bouvancourt on the north and Pévy on the south. Here they were joined by a couple of hundred men of the 62nd Brigade, who had not been in the line. The rest of the 7th Brigade, that is the 1/Wiltshire and part of the 10/Cheshire, with the 130th Field Company R.E. and trench mortar detachment, retired southwards and formed a line due south of Bouvancourt, rather in advance of the left of the main body of the brigade.

Meanwhile, the 110th and 64th Brigades of the 21st Division had clung to the Battle Zone, the French 45th Division supporting them on the right. At 5.45 P.M. Lieut.-General Gordon had issued orders (received at 7 P.M.) for the 21st Division, as already arranged, to fall back at 10 P.M. to the St. Auboeuf ridge, which runs east and west to the north of the ridge on which the 7th and 62nd Brigades established themselves. There the division was to get touch with the 75th Brigade and remnants of the 8th Divn.

Fighting continued throughout the evening on the 110th Brigade front, and though the enemy was gradually working round both flanks, the line was still maintained when the moment for withdrawal arrived. The Germans by this time had come very close, so during the retirement some stiff rear-guard fighting took place; but what was left of the brigade was concentrated by about 2.45 A.M. on the 28th at the eastern end of the St. Auboeuf ridge. No British troops could be found here, as the 75th Brigade (and 8th Divn) were near Montigny, and it was evident that the enemy was to the west in Châlons le Vergeur and

Bouvancourt. The brigade, therefore, continued southwards, to the cross ridge, marked by Luthernay Farm, which connects the various spurs running east and west,[1] halted at the farm and, after getting into touch with the 64th Brigade, which had come up on the right, occupied a line on the ridge west of the farm. Owing to its losses, the brigade was now organized as a weak battalion, but when stragglers had come in next day a second composite battalion was formed.

The 64th Brigade, with part of the 14/Northumberland Fusiliers (Pioneers), held its position all the afternoon, but lost Cauroy about 7.30 P.M., and then, reinforced by the 97th Field Company R.E., occupied a hollow road west of the village. A good defence was maintained there until the brigade order for retirement reached the 15/Durham L.I. on the left about midnight, when with the engineers it withdrew unmolested to Luthernay Farm. The remnants of the centre battalion, the 9/K.O.Y.L.I., did not receive the order and remained in position south of Cauroy all night, getting in touch on the right with the French 45th Division. The right battalion, the 1/East Yorkshire, fell back on Hermonville, in the second line of trenches, about 9.30 P.M. Reduced to about a hundred men, holding a line a thousand yards long by a chain of posts, at midnight it was ordered to the cross ridge south of St. Auboeuf, where it got into touch with the 110th Brigade. A battalion of the French 45th Division having arrived at Hermonville, the 98th and 126th Field Companies R.E. and the headquarters and remaining men of the 14/Northumberland Fusiliers (Pioneers) became available, and were used to prolong the line of the East Yorkshire to the right. By the morning of the 28th, the 64th Brigade and attached troops, with the 6/South Wales Borderers (Pioneers of the 25th Division) were extended from the right of the 110th Brigade to the left of the French 45th Division. One company of the Borderers was left in the second trench of the Battle Zone east of Hermonville, forming a left defensive flank on the northern side. Thus the general situation of the 21st Division may be summed up that it was holding a line, overlapping the French at Hermonville, along the cross ridge, to Pévy

---

[1] The ridges form a rough reversed E, the upright being formed by the Luthernay Farm ridge, the horizontals by the St. Auboeuf, the Pévy (this forks, one branch running north and the other continuing west towards Montigny), and the Trigny ridges.

FIRST DAY. 27TH MAY

ridge as far as the south of Bouvancourt. In front of this line, owing to orders not reaching them, were the remnants of the 9/K.O.Y.L.I., and the left (defensive flank) company of the 6/South Wales Borderers. On the left, after a gap, the 25th Division, with survivors of the 8th and 50th Divns, carried the defence along the ridge north of Montigny to the French sector. The four new divisional headquarters, by Lieut.-General Gordon's orders, were established around his own headquarters in Jonchery : at Prouilly (north-east of Jonchery) for the 21st Division ; Montigny, later Branscourt, south of Jonchery for the 8th ; Romain, later Breuil, for the 50th ; and Savigny (south-east of Fismes) for the 25th.

The new line, thin and disjointed, with several gaps in it, was manned by tired troops with little or no artillery support. The composite battery of the 110th Brigade R.F.A. had done good service in the afternoon, from a position south of Guyencourt, in preventing two batteries accompanying the German infantry from coming into action. In the evening, however, its position became untenable, owing to the enemy's advance, and it lost two guns ; so it was withdrawn across the Vesle at Jonchery. Another battery, consisting of four guns drawn from the Army ordnance reserve with the 8th Division, was sent up at 9 P.M. to the Montigny position, but later was likewise withdrawn. The 21st Division artillery and the 112th Brigade of the 25th Division had remained in action in the St. Auboeuf—Châlons le Vergeur area until about 8.30 P.M., when the enemy infantry advance rendered a retirement necessary; C Battery of the 112th Brigade, in an advanced position, was unable to get its horses up, and had to destroy all its guns. Two of the batteries of this brigade joined the two composite batteries of the 8th Divn south of Jonchery, and these were organized into a brigade under Lieut.-Colonel H. R. Phipps, 110th Brigade R.F.A. The fourth battery also made its way to the south of Jonchery. The XCV. Brigade R.F.A. (21st Division) withdrew to a position half a mile north of Pévy and at 4 A.M. made a further retirement to Prouilly. The XCIV. Brigade remained on the right flank of the 21st Division at Trigny (2 miles south of Hermonville). The heavy batteries on the right wing—those on the left had been lost in the morning—remained in action until times varying between 5 and 7 P.M., when many came under rifle and machine-gun fire, and it was impossible to get them all away, the XLI.

Brigade losing 13 guns out of 24, and Groupe Meunier, 29 out of 34. Those which remained were collected by the morning of the 28th near Jonchery. By the end of the first day's operation the whole of the rounds at the guns had either been fired or lost, and the ammunition dumps near Courlandon, east of Fismes, and Villesavoye, west of Fismes, were in the hands of the enemy. The artillery which remained, therefore, had no ammunition immediately available except what was in the brigade and divisional ammunition columns. Before the attack, however, arrangements had been made by Br.-General J. C. Harding-Newman, the D.A. & Q.M.G. of the IX. Corps to establish a reserve dump at Fère en Tardenois, and the first train reached that station next day.

It will be recalled that the supply railheads were in the process of being shifted to the north of the Vesle, but one, St. Gilles (south of Fismes) remained south of the river. This railhead was shelled in the preliminary bombardment, so supplies were drawn from the other original railheads on the Reims—Fismes—Soissons line. In the evening, part of this line being lost, the supply railheads were moved back to the Epernay—Château Thierry railway, 15 miles to the south, and the supply never failed. As reserves were kept at a minimum, very little fell into the hands of the enemy. He obtained possession of the two casualty clearing stations, at Montigny and Mont Nôtre Dame (south-west of Bazoches). At the former, only forty severely wounded had been left behind, but in the latter, in the French area, 14 miles from the front line, railway trucks or road transport not being available for the purpose, no great proportion of the equipment was saved. The British wounded were evacuated to Dormans, on the Epernay—Château Thierry railway, 17 miles due south of Fismes. Not only was routine supply and evacuation carried on successfully, but the roads were kept clear for use by the troops.

The original divisions in the line, both French and British, on the front selected for break-through by the enemy— the French 21st and 22nd and the British 50th and 8th Divns—had ceased to exist as organized bodies; those on the flanks—the French 61st and British 21st Divisions —were in hardly better plight, and the reserves sent up— the French 39th and 157th Divisions and the British 25th —had been thrown back and the two latter were nearly at the end of their fighting powers. All depended on the arrival of French reinforcements, not only to fill the gap in the front, but to support and hearten the troops holding the sides of the great re-entrant made in the front.

Towards 2 P.M., General Degoutte, commander of the XXI. Corps and the first echelon of his staff, placed at the disposal of General Duchêne by the G.A.N., arrived at Sixth Army headquarters. To relieve General de Maud'huy of his heavy task, General Degoutte was appointed to take command of the right wing of the XI. Corps front from the line Maizy—Breuil, the boundary with the British IX. Corps, to the road (inclusive) Vailly (on the Aisne)—Chassemy—Ciry. This meant the command of the 39th Division, the 22nd and 157th Divns, and the 13th Division, when it should arrive. The instructions given to him, as earlier to General de Maud'huy, were to hold the Green Line at all costs, and counter-attack the enemy who had crossed the Aisne. But at the moment, about 4 P.M., when General Degoutte took over command at Limé (1½ miles south of Braine), the Green Line between Maizy and Cys had already been lost, the 13th Division had scarcely begun to debus and detrain between Breuil and Fismes (both on the Vesle) in the centre of the gap; the 1st and 154th Divisions (directed on the Chassemy, for the XI. Corps, and Jonchery areas, respectively) were not expected until the evening; the 4th Division (directed on the Fère en Tardenois area, 10 miles south-west of Fismes), not until night. General Degoutte, therefore, gave orders that the task of the 157th Divn and the 13th Division should be limited to the defence of the crest of the Vesle ridge, marked by Romain—Blanzy—Vauxcéré. But this had already been lost and the 157th Divn was retiring.

About 4 P.M., alarmed by General Duchêne's reports of a great attack, General Pétain also directed the G.A.N. to send two divisions of the Oise Group, the 43rd Division to Braine, the 170th to the Vic sur Aisne area (14 miles west of Soissons), by lorry and march; and the 20th Division, resting in the Verdun area, was ordered to the Ville en Tardenois area (10 miles S.S.E. of Fismes).

It was not until 8.15 P.M. that the British 19th Division, training near Châlons in the French Fourth Army area, was ordered to be held in readiness to proceed to the battle area; but no movement took place till next day.

The leading units of the 13th Division did not begin to arrive in the area Breuil—Fismes, until after 3 P.M., the lorries having been three hours late in reaching the starting point, and at 3.30 P.M. Lieut.-General Gordon heard that one regiment would move on Romain (north of Breuil) into the gap, another on Merval (north of Fismes), and the third remain at Magneux (1½ miles east of Fismes, south of the Vesle). At 7 P.M. he learnt that part only of the division was entrenched, about one and a half miles north of Fismes. Actually no troops were so far forward.

At the time of arrival of the French 13th Division, the British IX. Corps Cyclist Battalion, the motor machine guns of the French 4th Cavalry Division, and the French 22nd and 157th Division Schools of Instruction, the only Allied troops in the gap, were retiring before the enemy. The crest of the Vesle ridge, between Arbre de Romain (a mile north of Romain) and Vauxcéré, six miles to the west, which General Franchet d'Espérey, who now appeared in person at Fismes, had ordered should be denied to the enemy, was undefended. German infantry was already filtering down the slopes towards the Vesle, and the first battalion of the left regiment of the 13th Division, which passed through Fismes, immediately came under German artillery fire. Nevertheless it managed to establish itself a " few hundred yards " north of Fismes, where another battalion joined it. The right-hand regiment, which later arrived at Breuil, crossed the river about 6 P.M., and its right got touch with the British 75th and 74th Bdes, near Romain. The centre, the reserve, regiment, however, came under artillery fire, and was driven back from the river.[1] At 8 P.M., on account of the retirement of the 22nd and 157th Divns across the Vesle, the 13th Division was directed to extend its left to Bazoches and consider the defence of the Vesle as its task. Thus at night the line of the French 13th Division, much extended, formed a re-entrant between Romain and Bazoches, the right and left just across the Vesle except on the extreme left, the centre nearly two miles south of the river.

In the course of a summer day the enemy had crossed two, and in places three, rivers; he had driven a salient twenty-five miles wide at the base and extending nearly twelve miles into the Allied line; he had destroyed four of the divisions originally in the line, and nearly destroyed two more (British 21st and French 61st), besides two others (British 25th and French 157th) sent up from the reserve.

---

[1] See German account in the following Chapter.

The destruction of the front-line troops had been obtained by surprise and by the employment of an enormous number of batteries. Subsequently, little was to be gained by frontal attack, for rifle fire was sufficient to stop the Germans. Further progress was attained by a method of bold " infiltration " and by the fear of envelopment which this process induced amongst the young Allied soldiers after their few experienced officers and N.C.O.'s had fallen : even machine gunners shot off their ammunition in haste and decamped. Had all the bridges over the river and canal been destroyed the enemy advance would have been stayed until a considerable amount of artillery could have been brought up to cover the construction of passages. This would have afforded the Allies time to bring up reserves. As matters were, only a weak line had been formed round the breach, so weak at its apex near Limé that a length of three miles was covered by no more than scattered parties of the French 157th Divn. The only help close at hand was the French 1st Division, which was beginning to arrive at Serches (4 miles west of Braine).

CHAPTER V

THE BATTLE OF THE AISNE (*continued*)

THE GERMANS ON THE 27TH MAY

(Map 2 ; Sketches 2, 3)

Map 2. Sketch 2. IN spite of their startling success, the Germans by no means gained all that they had hoped. The account given in the German monograph on the battle is so instructive as to the manner in which this great assault was carried out, and shows so authoritatively the fine spirit of resistance exhibited by the troops of the British IX. Corps, that it merits a lengthy summary.

Larisch's corps, on the right (west), with two divisions in the line and one (position) in support, with a fourth, of the Army reserve, behind it in case of need, and having only the left and centre of the French 61st Division on its front, was given the Aisne and the heights south of Soissons as its final objective. It should be noticed that the direction of all the corps was first south to the Chemin des Dames, but then inclined westwards, more on the left wing than on the right. It was recognized that, being on the flank and liable to enfilade fire from the west, owing to the trace of the front, the task of Larisch's corps was difficult. To help it, the *241st Division* of François's corps, next on the west, was to support it by seizing a bridgehead over the Ailette. This, however, it was unable to achieve. The *6th Division*, Larisch's right, suffered much from fire.[1] Of its 14 foot-bridges, only 10 could be made, and of these one was destroyed. The heavy bridge received a direct hit, and could not be used until 10.30 A.M. The infantry

---

[1] In practically every division two infantry regiments assaulted, with the third in reserve. Each regiment engaged 2 battalions in the front line and one in the second. Three or four batteries were detailed as " accom-" panying batteries " to follow the infantry as closely as possible.

lost the barrage, which had to be brought back. At 10.15 A.M. the *6th Bavarian Reserve Division*, from support, was put in on the right to assist the advance of the *6th Division*; but it was not until about 4 P.M., when the French could be seen retiring, that any progress was made, and then the line attained was " not half-way to the final " objective : the success was far below expectation ".

The *5th Division*, next on the east, fared better. It suffered little from fire. Of its 23 foot-bridges, 2 were not ready, but only a few were damaged; the two heavy bridges were ready at 4.50 and 5.20 A.M. respectively. French machine guns, all of which had not been knocked out, caused delay, and resort was made to grenade fighting. But by 7.30 A.M. the crest of the Chemin des Dames ridge was secured. Then there was a pause, as the artillery had difficulty in getting across the marshy ground near the Ailette. It was 1 P.M. before the attack was got under way again. By that time the French 74th Division was coming up, and resistance stiffened. A long fight ensued, and not until 7 P.M. was the first trench of the French Battle Zone reached, and the struggle ceased. Larisch's corps had captured 40 officers and 2,200 other ranks, but it had engaged its third division and had not reached its objective.

The disposition of Wichura's corps, opposite the extreme right of the French 61st Division and the whole front of the 21st, was somewhat strange. Of his 11,500-yard frontage following the course of the Ailette, the *13th Landwehr Division* (a position division in the line) was given 5,000 yards round a bend of the river, its front narrowing as it went forward ; the *9th*, the other position division, became support; the *14th Reserve Division* had half the remainder of the frontage, and the *113th* and *37th* the other half between them. The last three (assault) divisions [1] received lively harassing fire and gas as they came up and deployed, but suffered no losses worth mention, and were not delayed. Only one of the foot-bridges (centre of the *14th Reserve Division*) was destroyed, but the construction of a heavy road-bridge (for the same division) could not be completed until 6.45 A.M.

The *13th Landwehr Division*, which was given two assault detachments to lead it, had to secure the village of Chavignon and the top of the ridge. This was accom-

[1] On Map 2 the *14th Reserve Division* is by mistake marked as a position division.

plished, by 4.30 A.M. and 7 A.M. respectively, with the capture of over a thousand prisoners. It then cleared its western flank of French nests and established touch with Larisch's corps. The *Landwehrleute* had fought so well that the division was relieved at the end of the day.

The *14th Reserve Division*, having a Württemberg mountain regiment attached, put three regiments into the line. The Württembergers, on the left, closely following the barrage, were established on the ridge by 5.30 A.M., and could then afford assistance to the right. The centre and right regiments met with considerable resistance and lost the barrage, so that a united assault became impossible. Then, as the arrival of guns was delayed, each French centre of resistance had to be dealt with separately with trench mortars and grenades. Nevertheless, after Malmaison fort (1 mile south of Chavignon) had been taken, the top of the ridge was reached by the centre about 8 A.M., and by the right between 8.30 and 9 A.M. Then a pause was made to reorganize, but when the division resumed its advance it was, like Larisch's corps on the west, checked before the Green Line by the arrival of the French 74th Division.

The *113th Division* took two mountain batteries with it. The right regiment, though favoured by the slight amount of French artillery fire falling on its area after 3.30 A.M., lost its barrage owing to the ground being very rough. Some men reached the top of the ridge by 6.10 A.M., but the regiment was not collected there until between 7 and 7.30 A.M. The advance to the Aisne was then easy. Leaving Rouge Maison Farm (1,300 yards N.E. by N. of Vailly) in French possession—it was not captured until 3 P.M.—the leaders found Vailly, which they reached at 11.30 A.M., undefended, and its bridge undamaged, and formed a bridgehead (just north of the Green Line). No guns had come up, for there were woods on the front, and as the *14th Reserve Division* on the west had been unable to progress, all further attempts to advance failed. The assault of the left regiment of the *113th Division* was entirely successful: by 5.30 A.M. it was over the ridge, but it then suffered considerable casualties and its advance was slow. The order to cross the Aisne was given at 1 P.M., one undamaged bridge (apparently the light-railway bridge above Vailly) and a weir bridge being available. The guns were late, but there was sufficient fire to prevent the French destroying the bridge. Owing to opposition, however, it was not until 4 P.M. that the river was crossed on a temporary bridge built under the railway bridge; the attackers then waded the canal and formed along its banks. It was 6.30 P.M. before a crossing was possible at the weir, where a small bridgehead was formed. So far, no German had crossed the Green Line.

The *37th Division*, opposite the right of the French 21st Division, accompanied by a mountain battery and two mountain machine-gun batteries, received little fire and kept close to the barrage. The leading men reached the top of the ridge between 4.32 and 4.55 A.M., all but simultaneously with those of three divisions to the east, the *1st Guard*, the *10th* and the *28th*. " Almost without en- " countering any resistance and without receiving any " artillery fire ", they were close to the Aisne by 8.30 A.M., found Chavonne evacuated and two bridges intact. By 9.5 A.M. they were across the western bridge. Then, opposed by the garrison of the Green Line, they were unable to cross the thousand or more yards of open ground between river and canal. Towards 2 P.M. the divisional reserve was brought up and crossed the Aisne on barrel-pier bridges constructed to avoid the artillery fire directed on the Chavonne bridges. It was not until towards 6 P.M., however, that a rush was made which, after considerable losses, reached the canal bank. The bridge south of Chavonne was then seen to be undamaged. After a fire-fight, in which the mountain battery and two field batteries took part, the French were observed to be retiring. At 6.40 P.M. the bridge was secured. More artillery, including 5.9-inch howitzer batteries, arrived, and the pursuit was continued over the Green Line, a mile beyond the canal, until 9.30 P.M., when the top of the Vesle ridge between the Aisne and the Vesle, had been gained. The support division (*9th*) was brought up to the Chemin des Dames.

In Winckler's corps, which was regarded as " the " battering ram ", opposite the left wing of the French 22nd Division, the three assault divisions, the *1st Guard, 33rd* and *10th Reserve*, which were to pass through the *197th*, the position division, were given frontages of only 2,200 yards each. The *1st Guard Division* during deployment suffered a good deal from " lively harassing fire ", which grew progressively feebler after the German artillery opened. The infantry followed the creeping barrage and never lost it; in fact, they were delayed by it. There was little resistance in the first position, except from a farm near the top at the western end of the ridge; but the supports and reserves had to deal with a number of machine-gun nests. The left regiment reached the top of the ridge at 4.35 A.M. and the right at 5.20 A.M., and between 9.15 and 9.30 A.M. both were close to the Aisne at Soupir (1 mile E.N.E. of Chavonne) and Pont Arcy. They found no bridges left standing over this sector of the river, and fire from artillery and the Green Line beyond was increasing. The right regiment edged westward and crossed by the eastern bridge at Chavonne, where the *37th Division* had already arrived; the left got over by swimming and extemporized floats; so by noon the leading battalions were deployed on the southern bank of the river. Now the difficulties began, although some of the artillery had come up; for there was still the canal to cross and the Green Line lay only 200-300 yards beyond it. A culvert under the canal was found, a few men crawled through and formed a covering party; they were joined by others who crossed by punts, or by swimming and wading, so that by 2.45 P.M. the canal was behind the leading battalion. Then began a long fire-fight; but the left was through the Green Line and on the verge of the top of Vesle ridge, west of Vieil Arcy, by 4.30 P.M. The right could not capture St. Mard (in the Green Line) until 7 P.M., but by 8.30 P.M. also reached the edge of the Vesle ridge. By pushing on in the dark a line on top of the Vesle ridge from the west of Dhuizel, north-westward, was secured. The reserve regiment and divisional artillery were brought over the Aisne and its canal. Late in the night patrols found that the French had fallen right back to Braine, but this information did not reach the regiment until the morning hours. The division had captured about two thousand prisoners and many batteries.

The *33rd Division* met with even greater success. It encountered only weak resistance from the left centre of the 22nd Division, and sent back a message : " Quicken " creeping barrage or stop it entirely ". It was on the top of the Chemin des Dames ridge by 5 A.M., and reached the Aisne near Pont Arcy at 9.35 A.M., where it found a heavy temporary bridge. It could not use the two canal bridges owing to fire, but was over both river and canal by 10.15 A.M. Then there was a " many-hours-long halt " opposite the Green Line, and it was found necessary to

THE GERMANS ON THE 27TH MAY

resort to a bombardment by the divisional artillery and trench mortars, which lasted from 2.45 to 3.30 P.M. After that, Vieil Arcy and the Green Line were carried, but the division was held up when it attempted to reach the top of the Vesle ridge, and could make no further progress until Dhuizel (Sir Douglas Haig's headquarters in September-October 1914 and ¾ mile from Vieil Arcy) had been evacuated by the French. By 7 P.M., the leading men were at Vauxtin, one and a quarter miles farther on. At 9 P.M. one battalion crossed the Vesle, two miles still farther ahead, by using trees which it had felled. It then pushed on towards the railway near Limé, and by midnight the whole regiment was slightly beyond it. During the day the division had advanced over twelve miles. Being out of touch with the divisions on the right and left, and the men greatly exhausted after their great effort, a halt was then called.

The *10th Reserve Division*, the left division of Winckler's corps, opposite the centre of the French 22nd Division, took two full hours to reach the crest of the ridge; it had been delayed, " not so much by the defenders as by the " extraordinarily difficult conditions of the Ailette bottom : " marsh and bog and water-filled craters nearly every-" where ". After crossing the ridge, resistance to the right regiment almost ceased, and by 10.15 A.M. its leading battalion had crossed the river and both canals at Bourg, after capturing a general officer and 344 other ranks of the covering force; one hour later its supporting artillery came up. The left regiment met with more resistance, as on the slopes of the southern side of the ridge there stood many batteries. Nevertheless after capturing 57 guns and 40 officers and over 1,400 other ranks, it reached the river bridge east of Bourg, just as advancing French (157th Division from reserve) were crossing the canal bridge; the latter, however, was stormed. After further fighting, by 1.40 P.M. the woods along the road one mile south of the canal were occupied by the right regiment. Then, as more of the French 157th Division appeared, the advance slowed down, and it was not until 4.40 P.M. that the edge of the Vesle ridge west of Longueval was secured, with 500 prisoners, mostly of the 157th Division. The way to the Vesle was open, the river was reached south of Paars (1½ miles north-west of Bazoches) about 8 P.M., and by 9.15 P.M. two battalions were established on the railway on the left of the *33rd Division*. The right regiment, having to clear a number of woods, did not quite reach the Vesle, and stopped on the high road just north of it about 8 P.M., pushing patrols out to the river.

Sketch 3.
The front of Conta's corps was divided unequally : the *10th Division*, opposite the right of the French 22nd Division, had 5,500 yards ; the other two assault divisions, opposite the 150th and 151st Brigades of the British 50th Division, had received, respectively, the *28th*, 3,850, and the *5th Guard*, 2,200 yards of frontage. The *36th*, position division, was in support.

The *10th Division* carried all before it right to the Vesle. The effect of the artillery bombardment was " excellent " ; there was little reply ; the infantry kept close to the barrage and all went according to plan. Shortly after the ridge had been crossed, a flank-guard company took over five hundred French prisoners. The barrage then began to grow thin, but the fire of trench mortars and of the accompanying batteries, which had closely followed up the infantry, took its place. The fire of these batteries drove the French from the bridges lying ahead, and by 10 A.M. the right regiment was over the Aisne, both river and canal, at Œuilly, whilst the left regiment, which crossed at a river bridge 1½ miles east of Œuilly and a canal bridge west of Maizy, was not far behind. Thus both were over the Green Line, which in this sector was between river and canal, but the French were holding out in Villers en Prayères, on the west. The village was taken by 12.30 P.M., and the attacking line re-formed just before the leading troops of the 157th Division (really the IX. Corps cyclists, the French cavalry machine guns and schools of instruction) began to appear. These were swept aside, and the right regiment reached Barbonval, 2 miles from the Aisne, by 2 P.M., and Longueval, to the west, soon after. But at Bazoches progress was stopped by the arrival of the French 13th Division, and the village was not captured until 9 P.M., when it was too dark to attempt the passage of the Vesle. The left regiment, going a little slower, arrived at Merval by 3 P.M., and reached the Bazoches—Fismes road, just north of the Vesle, by 7 P.M., but was unable to cross the river. The reserve regiment now arrived, intending to cross at Fismes, but, the village still being in French hands, it was halted in a ravine north of it. It was most tantalizing to the men of the *10th Division* not to be able to cross the Vesle ; for, on the far side, before the light failed, they had viewed a tempting scene. On all the roads leading south there was heavy traffic; " the aerodrome south-east of Fismes " was in movement, as if it were a swarm of ants "; batteries were galloping about; armoured cars throwing up dust; troop trains were moving on the railway; and in Fismes fires showed that stores were being burnt.

The western boundary of the *28th Division*—which was opposite the three battalions forming the left of the British 50th Division—coincided almost exactly with that of the French and British as far as the latter went.[1] But the northern four miles of the German boundary, between the front line and Beaurieux, was straight, and ran down the western side of Oulches Wood, whereas the Franco-British line bulged towards the British side, through the centre of the wood. Thus the *28th Division* as it advanced encountered both French and British troops. To start with, however, all three regiments of the division in line, with a battalion of each in reserve, were sent against the Californie plateau in the left sector, which, owing to its command, was regarded as the key of the Chemin des Dames position. Opposite the western sector were swampy woods, likely to hold up assaulting troops, so this objective was assigned to three battalions drawn from the reserve (position) division, which were to get on as best they could.

The bombardment is described as " brilliant "—" after " the first two minutes of it there was hardly an enemy " shot "—and in the first assault the losses were " just " nil ". The trouble was to get over the obstacles: " there was one after another; all the trees were con- " nected by barbed wire; wherever there was a path it " was blocked by chevaux de frise. The final fifty yards " to the top of the slope was a matter of climbing on " hands and knees. . . . The top of the ridge, only about " 550 yards wide, had four lines of trenches, with 5-10 " yards of wire entanglements and shell craters in between " them ". Nevertheless, the top was reached between 4.15 and 4.30 A.M., just a little later than the *10th Division* on the west. The two battalions on that flank then turned west and south-west to fill the gap, originally caused by the swampy woods, and then to roll up the French defences; this they duly accomplished, one company capturing a whole French battalion. So accurate had been the artillery fire—" all were united in astonishment

---

[1] On the French official map, the boundary ends at Perles (2,000 yards north-west of Fismes); the western boundary of the *28th Division* on the German map continues on southwards to Jaulgonne on the Marne.

"at what the artillery had done"—that the entrances to the British dug-outs, and to the tunnels dug into the reverse slopes for the reserves, had been smashed, and their inmates caught, when flame-throwers were used to force them into surrender. Oulches Wood "furnished "pictures of the most fearful devastation . . . the roads "being blocked with smashed transport, whilst Frenchmen "who had quite lost their heads were wandering about "aimlessly". Twelve hundred prisoners and two British batteries were captured in the wood by one battalion. Its southern edge was reached about 8 A.M.; in just over four hours an advance of four miles had been made. Farther east, Craonne, at the back of the Forward Zone, had been taken by 5.10 A.M., with the help of trench mortars, which brought about the explosion of a bomb dump. At Beaurieux (50th Division headquarters) stronger resistance was encountered, artillery fire forcing the centre regiment to deploy once more, and preventing any approach to the river bridge north of Maizy. An unguarded temporary bridge, however, was found three-quarters of a mile to the north-west (inside the French area), so here a crossing was made about 9.30 A.M. Half an hour later a bridge over the canal was discovered still farther west by a patrol, so that, by about 11.30 A.M., Maizy was enveloped. The two leading battalions of the centre regiment, finding the defences abandoned, were soon established south of the canal and preparing to assault the defended heights beyond, east of Révillon (held by the 50th Division Lewis Gun School). The left regiment subsequently managed to cross both river and canal just east of Maizy. The attack of the Révillon heights was then begun, well supported by artillery; but as French reinforcements (2 battalions of the 13th Division), supported by armoured cars, now began to appear, progress grew slow. It was not until 4.20 P.M., therefore, that the Germans, as the south-western direction of their advance was leading them into the French area, came to about one mile from Fismes, where the advance was held up. All three regiments and their reserves were engaged, but in vain. At 8.45 P.M. the divisional commander ordered a short artillery bombardment; but again the attack failed, and the *28th Division* halted for the night north of the Vesle.

In contrast to the definitely hilly nature of the ground traversed by the western divisions, the field of attack of the *5th Guard Division*, which was opposed by the 151st Brigade of the 50th Division, lay over the gentle slopes in which the Chemin des Dames ridge dies away eastward, where no natural obstacles existed to hinder progress until the Aisne should be reached. The main task of this division, in the first stage, was the protection of the left flank of the *28th Division*. The British defences were recognized as strong, but the artillery bombardment was perfect—" no one " had ever experienced such a frightful effect "; yet the trees and branches which it had brought down added to the military obstacles. The garrison of the front trenches was found to be dazed with gas and offered little resistance, but the strongpoints in rear held out for some time and the reserves even counter-attacked, so that " in " places, there was desperate close fighting ". On the right two guns, still firing, were captured, with some twelve others; on the left, after several machine-gun nests which put up a brave defence had been settled, two batteries with their detachments fell into German hands. " Envelopment brought success everywhere." It is mentioned that a farm, under two miles from the front was captured at 5.45 A.M., yet the Aisne river was not reached by the leading elements, at Cuiry, until about 10.30 A.M., and, at Maizy, not until shortly before noon. The right regiment (*3rd Guard Grenadiers, Queen Elizabeth Regiment*) then crossed over the river and canal bridges below Maizy, that is, nearly three hours later than the *28th Division*, next to the west, already deployed on the south bank. The left regiment (*3rd Foot Guards*) at Cuiry was not so lucky; it secured the river bridge, but the canal bridge was at once blown up. The *Elizabeth Regiment*, having drifted into the sector of the *28th Division*, did not help. For several hours, therefore, the *3rd Foot Guards* were checked, and it was not until about 4 P.M. that the reserve regiment crossed at Maizy, and by an enveloping attack dislodged the defenders (9/L.N. Lancashire and survivors of the 150th Brigade). Meantime the *Elizabeth Regiment*, in spite of a rapid advance, had been held up before Baslieux (1½ miles north-east of Fismes), apparently by survivors of the French 22nd Division. At 6 P.M., the German commander, after much consideration, decided to assault. The result was entirely successful, and towards 7 P.M. the leading companies of the *Elizabeth Regiment* crossed the Vesle on the heels of the retreating French, whose reserves (centre of the 13th Division) on the heights to the south were " so unprepared and unready " that they could not prevent the remaining companies from following. The leaders pushed on to Villette and Magneux, capturing, so it is claimed, immense quantities of ammunition and supplies. The reserve regiment (*20th*), after assisting the *3rd Foot Guards*, reached the Vesle at Courlandon at 5.30 P.M., but owing to fire was not able to cross. One company, however, followed the *Elizabeth Regiment* over the Magneux bridge and this led to the mistaken belief that most of the regiment had crossed. The *3rd Foot Guards* were therefore urged to advance. Held up at Romain until it was dark, its commander decided to break off the fight, then to follow the *20th* and cross at Courlandon. When the mistake was discovered, the regiment assembled and spent the night at Baslieux. Except by the *Elizabeth Regiment* of the *5th Guard Division*, the Vesle, though reached, had not been crossed by any unit of Conta's corps.

The three assault divisions of Schmettow's corps had been allotted sectors of different width: the *50th*, opposite the British 149th Brigade and half of the 23rd Brigade, only 2,000 yards; the *52nd*, opposite half of the 23rd Brigade and half of the 24th, 2,500 yards; the *7th Reserve*, astride the Aisne, advanced with seven battalions on a two-mile frontage north of the river, opposite half of the 24th Brigade and the 25th, whilst it sent forward the other two battalions on a one-mile frontage south of the river, opposite the 62nd Brigade. As this last division advanced its sector narrowed, for the position divisions of the *XV. Corps (First Army)* were, if possible, to join in the movements. Tanks were allotted to all three divisions.[1] General von Schmettow gave the heights just beyond the Vesle, Unchair—Branscourt, as the objective; but the divisional commanders in their orders contented themselves with a line beyond the Aisne.

The whole of the Forward Zone was carried according to plan. "Then the situation altered materially." British reserves appeared from the tunnels in the Bois des Buttes hill (Viller Berg). The barrage was lost and the whole of the *50th Division* was drawn towards the hill (defended by the 2/Devonshire). The German artillery could not help in this wooded area, and the tanks which came up were hit and set on fire. One machine-gun nest after another had

---

[1] Mostly captured machines. The number is not given. They were to assist in overcoming resistance in open ground. They suffered " serious " losses and only came into action separately, as they could not keep up " with the rapidly moving infantry ".

to be dealt with, and " the whole attack threatened to " come to a standstill ". The reserve regiment with heavy machine guns and trench mortars was brought up, and then " the powers of the brave enemy began to fail ". One battalion worked round by the west through woods in which there was a strong force of artillery. The machine gunners did their best to cover the batteries, but in spite of their efforts 55 guns (8th Division), some still firing, were captured, " mostly with their detachments and many " officers and hundreds of infantry ".

But " precious time had been wasted ". Parts of one battalion of the left regiment had been able to press on and after reaching Pontavert by 8 A.M. crossed the Aisne by the permanent bridge; but they found the bridge over the canal blown up, so that time was again lost before a field-railway bridge to the south-west was discovered. When a passage over the canal had been extemporized by the engineers at Pontavert, after some delay the left regiment crossed, apparently about 10 A.M., and the reserve regiment closed up on Pontavert. The right regiment as it approached Chaudardes about 11 A.M. saw the Aisne bridge go up into the air, and parts of all three regiments had to be used to clear the village (defended by the 5/Durham L.I. and part of the 5/Northumberland Fusiliers)—where there was " a right obstinate defence "—whilst Concevreux (in the Green Line) below it still held out. But another bridge to the east was secured. The right regiment had, however, " fallen into great confusion " in the long and heavy wood fighting ", and as a result the continuation of the attack faltered in front of the Green Line. Concevreux (held by the 3/Worcestershire) was not secured until 4.45 P.M. A regular attack with all three regiments in line was then made on the Roucy ridge (Roucy—Arbre de Romain, north of Romain, held by the 74th Brigade and the 11/Cheshire of the 75th); but the barrage could not assist beyond the Aisne, after crossing which the division could rely on the help of little more than its accompanying batteries. The resistance at Roucy (in the Green Line, held by the 11/Cheshire) was particularly stout, and it was not until after 6 P.M. that the ridge was taken. Connection with the *5th Guard Division* had been entirely lost.

The *52nd Division*, opposite the inner wings of the British 23rd and 24th Brigades, " had an easier task " than the *50th*. " The first serious resistance was en-

"countered on the north-east edge of the Viller Wald "[woods east of Ville aux Bois]", that is the rear line of the Forward Zone. This was broken with the help of tanks about 6 A.M., two hours and twenty minutes after zero. The resistance in the Forward Zone must therefore have been well sustained. After grenade fighting, the wood was cleared in about half an hour, and many batteries (8th Division) were captured. The leading parties reached the Aisne between Gernicourt and Pontavert, some twelve hundred yards beyond the woods, about 8 A.M. "As only "one bridge was destroyed"[1] the greater part of the right regiment was on the south side of the canal by 9 A.M. Part of the *I./169th*, the left regiment, also crossed close on the heels of the retreating British; the rest of this battalion and the *II. Battalion* were stopped by finding all the bridges broken, and set about improvising crossings under lively fire from the Gernicourt woods. All three regiments, no longer helped by the barrage, were now deployed, and Gernicourt Wood was attacked by the centre and right from north and west. The wood was cleared, and after some obstinate fighting 77 guns (110th Brigade R.F.A. of the 25th Division and a French "groupe") were captured, by 1.30 P.M. The right, which had tried to push on towards Bouffignereux, in rear of the wood, met with increasing resistance from reinforcements particularly from Bouffignereux—Roucy (in the Green Line, held by the 75th Brigade), whereupon it called upon the *50th Division*, on the right, for assistance. It was not until 6 P.M., in co-operation with the *50th Division*, that, after very slow progress, an assault "without artillery "bombardment according to plan"—since all the divisional artillery was not up—was made "on the hill position "on either side of Bouffignereux and Roucy"—that is the Green Line. An advance of 1½ miles was then made by the right on to the top of the Vesle ridge near Loge Fontaine Farm, and then one mile farther down the slope to Bouvancourt by the left.

The first task of the *7th Reserve Division*, opposite the right half of the British 8th Division, with 7 battalions north and 2 south of the Aisne, was to reach the Reims—Corbény chaussée, and capture Berry au Bac, which is on it. "By conspicuously good co-operation of all arms, "including aeroplanes, tanks and trench mortars", the

---

[1] There was only one permanent bridge in this sector, and that over the canal.

northern part of the road was reached at 5.15 A.M., the centre at 6 A.M., and Berry au Bac soon after; 600 prisoners and 4 guns were taken. " The comparatively easy capture " of Berry au Bac [undefended except by trenches in front] " was materially assisted by an attack from the southern " bank of the Aisne." When the bridge at this place was captured, the left regiment, which had been divided, re-assembled on the south bank. The right regiment saw two bridges blown up under its very eyes; as the third was under fire, guns had to be summoned to force a passage. It was not therefore until 8.40 A.M. that the first storm troops got over, and 10 A.M. before the regiment was across. The centre regiment also found the only bridge in its sector damaged, but managed to make it passable and also to find a " utilizable passage nearer Berry au Bac ". This regiment, now on the southern bank and under fire from Gernicourt, was ready to move forward by 9.40 A.M. But the *7th Reserve Division* did not advance for some time, although it should have assisted the efforts of the *50th* and *52nd Divisions* by an enveloping attack towards Bouffignereux. The monograph attributes its inaction to memories of heavy losses (79 officers and 2,104 other ranks in two regiments alone) on the 30th March in a hurried attack; also because the divisions of the *First Army*, on its left, did not stir—" a most unlucky delay ". Possibly the stout resistance of Gernicourt was a deterrent, but this is spoken of as " not particularly strong ". At any rate, the left regiment, now south of Berry au Bac, waited, the centre did not reach the north-east edge of Gernicourt Wood until about 12.45 and it was not through the wood until 2 P.M. This delayed the right regiment, which did not take Gernicourt village until 1.30 P.M., by which time the *52nd Division* had already cleared the woods to the west. The *7th Reserve Division* then halted.

The arrival of the troops of the *First Army* on its left flank about 5 P.M. carried it forward again. For two hours it met with determined resistance in the woods south of Gernicourt Wood. The defence was eventually overcome (the 62nd Brigade was ordered to withdraw at 8 P.M. and the rest of the 21st Division at 10 P.M.), when 30 guns were captured (the narrative has shown that 6 field guns and 42 heavies were lost). At night, the division, with units much intermixed, was assembled east of Guyencourt in touch with the *52nd Division*; a few companies were pushed out in advance just north of Châlons le Vergeur.

The monograph sums up the situation of the corps as follows :

"Thus the *50th* and *7th Reserve Divisions* of Schmettow's "corps had reached their first objectives [those given by "the divisions, not the corps], but the *52nd* had not "fulfilled the hopes of capturing the heights east of "Montigny (3 miles north of Jonchery), although, with its "wedge driven towards Bouvancourt, it had gone farther "than the other divisions. The main task, however, "which was to chase the enemy over the Vesle and get a "firm footing on the south bank, had not yet been "achieved."

The *First Army*, whose delay has been deplored, had ordered its infantry to fall in at 10.30 A.M. Nothing is said of its operations except that the right reached Cormicy about 1 P.M., later (5 P.M.) carried forward with it the *7th Reserve Division*, and at 7.45 P.M. was in possession of the hill 2,200 yards south-west of Cormicy. The British 21st Division, in spite of its hazardous Front Zone beyond the Oise—Aisne canal, had prevented an enveloping attack.

The general remarks in the monograph on the 27th May are, that after the "model preparation", if success had not been achieved it would have been regarded as a "momentous set-back": the success, however, lay not so much in the gain of ground, even of the historic Chemin des Dames, or in the overrunning of five position divisions, as in the defeat (*sic*) of the five divisions brought up from the reserve. "In spite of all, however, the situation of "the *Seventh Army* was not completely satisfactory. "Nearly all the great German attacks on the Western "Front had come to a standstill because the outer edges "of the attack—caught by flanking fire and fallen upon "by hostile reserves—could not keep up with the central "thrust. This characteristic was to show itself after the "first day. So the *Seventh Army* commander had to "consider whether anything could be done to help forward "the wings of the Army which were hanging back." On the left (east), Schmettow's corps had its position division, the *103rd*, still in reserve, and there was an Army reserve division, the *232nd*, available behind it. The troops of the *First Army* might be expected to make more progress, and behind their right flank, the *86th Division* was available. On the right (west), however, Larisch's corps had already engaged its reserve, the *6th Bavarian Reserve*

Division, but the *51st Reserve Division* of the Army reserve was behind it. The commander of the *5th Division*, at 5.15 P.M., begged that the *51st Reserve Division* might be put in between the *5th and 6th Divisions*, as the latter and the *6th Bavarian Reserve Division* were now facing west and could not join in an advance of the *5th*. At 7.45 P.M. this request was refused; the reasons for the refusal are not known. Late in the evening the *Seventh Army* ordered : " The attack troops must do their utmost to keep the " pursuit going even during the night, and to reach the " objectives fixed in previous orders ". Nothing was done to help Larisch's corps, which was not in pursuit, but checked by a foe entrenched and in the course of being reinforced.

CHAPTER VI

THE BATTLE OF THE AISNE (*continued*)

28TH MAY 1918

RETIREMENT FROM THE VESLE AND LOSS OF SOISSONS

(Sketches A, 4)

Sketch 4. ON the 28th May, the second day of the battle, the Germans maintained the ascendancy which they had already gained. The intelligence collected by the Allies as regards their numbers was vague, since very few identifications had been obtained; but it seemed certain that some twenty divisions had been engaged. To oppose them, General Duchêne had on the ground five French divisions (45th, 13th, 39th, 74th and 151st) in good condition, and the débris of four British (21st, 8th, 50th and 25th) and four French (22nd, 21st, 61st and 157th), with less heavy artillery than on the first day, since a third of it had been lost. The wings had held fairly well; it was in the centre, between Breuil and Braine, where the enemy had made his heaviest thrust and had in places crossed the Vesle, that the situation was menacing. Here, under conditions of open warfare, the French 13th Division was opposing at least four German divisions on a frontage of nine miles, whilst on its left the 22nd and 157th Divns [1] were fighting at least three divisions on a four-mile frontage. Against these divisions as early at 4.30 A.M. the enemy, who had been fairly quiet during the night, recommenced operations.

Just as General Duchêne had acted contrary to the first part of Pétain's directions as regards not holding the first position strongly, so he now disregarded the later

[1] The French 21st Divn was eventually re-assembled behind the 39th; the 61st was still in the line between the 74th and 151st.

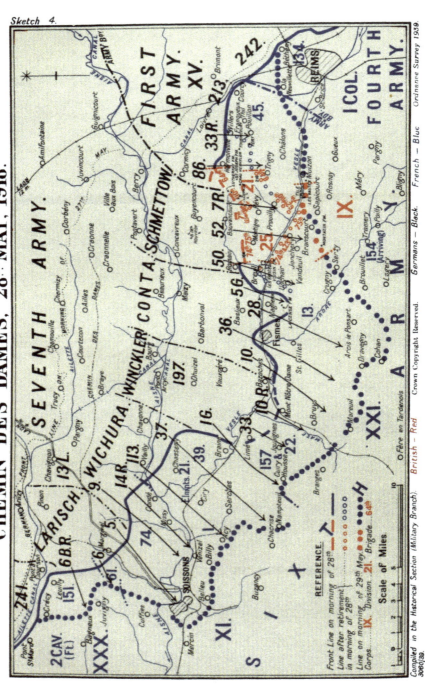

SECOND DAY. 28TH MAY 103

part, which laid down that the reserves of an Army or Group of Armies should be employed: " not only in the " system of counter-attacks in the zone of penetration of " the enemy, but also in counter-offensives either on the " flanks or on a part of the front adjacent to this zone ".[1] As it happened, the German flanks were weak, and both had gaps in them.[2] In any case, General Duchêne ordered such reinforcements as were in sight to meet the enemy frontally: the 154th Division to an area east of Arcis le Ponsart (5 miles south of Fismes) towards the junction of the British IX. and French XXI. Corps ; the 43rd to an area behind the centre of the XXI. Corps ; and the 1st (which had arrived in lorries, less artillery) to the area Ciry —Serches, 6 miles E.S.E. of Soissons, towards the junction of the XXI. and XI. Corps, but, as will be seen, he proceeded to break up this last division to support those already in the line.[3] The I. Cavalry Corps he ordered to Chéry—Chartreuve (6 miles north-east of Fère en Tardenois) in order to cover (1) Fère en Tardenois, which was the supply centre, and (2) the area of assembly of the 43rd Division, which lay four or five miles to the north and north-west of the town. The further reinforcements expected were directed : 20th Division, by order of the Group of Armies, to Ville en Tardenois (11 miles south-west of Reims), ready, like the 154th, to support the British IX. or the XXI. Corps ; the 4th, to Villers Hélon (8 miles S.S.W. of Soissons), to occupy the so-called " Paris Line " ;[4] and the 170th to the west of Soissons.[5]

During the day the Allies fell back, on the average, five miles, less on the right where the British stood, and more on the left, southward of Soissons. But this withdrawal by no means represented the progress of the Germans as a whole ; only a few of their leading units, mainly in the centre, followed up closely, proceeding by infiltration as was done in the previous March. Those which did press

---

[1] See General Pétain's Directive No. 4, Annexe 202, F.O.A. vi. (i.).
[2] Near Breuil and near Braine.
[3] The head of the 154th Division was at Arcis early in the morning ; the 43rd began debusing at 6 A.M. at villages 5 miles north-west of Fère en Tardenois ; the head of the I. Cavalry Corps had reached Mont Notre Dame, 5 miles W.S.W. of Fismes. The Sixth Army operation orders for the 28th are given in Appendix V.
[4] A well-wired line belonging to the outer defences of the Capital, over fifty miles from its centre. See Map 2. It ran from near Fère en Tardenois west-north-westwards. About three miles behind it was a second, similar line.
[5] The first units of the 20th and the 4th Divisions reached their destinations during the morning.

on found the French as sensitive to a threat to their flanks as the British had been; ground was gained not by frontal attack, but by minor envelopment.

On the left, the French still occupied the defences of the various lines between the old front and the Aisne. The 151st Division of the French XXX. Corps at first held its own, as German accounts admit, although it had to cover a front of nearly six miles; but in the afternoon it was forced to give ground, when the greater part of three enemy divisions were turned against it. Its commander, General des Vallières, at one time Chief of the French Mission at G.H.Q., was killed and its situation became precarious, since its right flank was gravely compromised owing to the retirement of the troops on that side. To secure this flank the corps commander (General Chrétien) placed General Hennocque, G.O.C. 2nd Dismounted Cavalry Division, in command of the 151st Division as well as his own formation which was on its left, with orders to cover the corps flank.

The French XI. Corps (General de Maud'huy), now consisting of only the 74th Division and the 61st Divn, suffered a violent attack at 5 A.M., when, after an hour's bombardment, a fresh division, the *9th*, besides the two others in the line, was brought up against it. Four battalions of the 1st Division were sent to its assistance, and crossed the Aisne about 9 A.M. In view of the danger on the right, the bridges over the Aisne from Condé to Missy, as a precaution, were blown up about 10 A.M. By noon, the 61st Divn was reduced to about a thousand rifles and retired into the valley of the Braye (the stream which runs southwards towards Soissons). Here, as elsewhere, the Germans depended upon infiltration, with envelopment when possible, reinforced by machine-guns and trench mortars whereby centres of resistance were to be overcome. The 74th Division, and the four battalions of the 1st with it, lost Fort de Condé about 1 P.M., and, although fighting hard, were gradually forced back. The right crossed the Aisne at Venizel at 6 P.M., blowing up the bridge. The left tried to maintain a bridgehead to cover Soissons, but was chased by low-flying aeroplanes and suffered from machine-gun fire; after running short of ammunition in street fighting, it retired, about 8.30 P.M., over the Aisne, without having time to destroy the bridges sufficiently. Five battalions of the 170th Division [1] had

---

[1] The others were in quarantine on account of an " epidemic ".

SECOND DAY. 28TH MAY

reached Fontenoy (7 miles west of Soissons) about 2 P.M., but had no support from their divisional artillery, which came up two hours later, and so failed to restore the situation. "The enemy penetrated into the town and, managing to "cross the Aisne by the railway bridge, arrived at Point "94 [an isolated knoll] south of the river." The 74th Division rallied during the night south of Venizel.

The XXI. Corps (13th Division, 22nd and 157th Divns and 39th Division), followed up by nine German divisions, after having lost overnight the passages of the Vesle between Breuil and Braine, except that at Fismes, was gradually driven back. In the sector of the 39th Division, all north of the Vesle, General Duchêne in order to counter the threat to Braine from the south, sent three battalions of the 1st Division to its assistance; but at 10 A.M. General Massenet, its commander, found it necessary to order the line of the Vesle to be occupied. The enemy followed so closely that when the bridges were blown up many French units were still north of the river. Ammunition now began to run short, the Germans pushed on by infiltration, and by evening the 39th Division was seven miles behind its morning position : " its line of battle consisted of three " or four groups of a few hundreds of men with an occasional " machine gun ".

The weak 22nd and 157th Divns retired slowly before the enemy, being unable to cover the frontage of 4 miles allotted to them. A gap opened, east of the Maze stream, between them and the 13th Division, so the 4th and 5th Divisions of the I. Cavalry Corps, with three battalions and an artillery "groupe", all of the 154th Division, were early moved up to fill it. Towards 10.30 A.M. the infantry of the 43rd Division also arrived, without artillery, on this flank. There was then a pause in the German advance; but when it was resumed about 1 P.M. the 22nd and 157th Divns and the reinforcing divisions were again forced back.

The 13th Division, on the right of the XXI. Corps, attacked by four divisions, lost Fismes by 7.30 A.M. Nevertheless, assisted by the 11/Lancashire Fusiliers, the rearguard of the 74th Bde, which fell fack on Breuil, it clung to that place until nearly midday. Then, supported by the Cavalry Corps and the 43rd Division, it held a position south of the Vesle until driven back by an enemy attack in the afternoon. During the day it had lost a total distance of eight miles in the centre, but somewhat less on the wings. The line of the XXI. Corps at night, which was

Cuiry Housse—Dravegny—south of Crugny on the Ardre, "presented many points of solution of continuity, particu-"larly propitious to enemy infiltrations on account of the "wooded and ravine-cut nature of the ground. On the "west there was no liaison with the XI. Corps", but on the east contact was established with troops of the 154th Division, as will be seen.

Coming now to the British sector, the front of the IX. Corps lay on the Vesle ridge between Hermonville and Romain, with the valley of the Ventelay stream on its front and left flank, and in rear little valleys, with Trigny, Prouilly and Montigny in them, leading down to the Vesle. On the right and left the French 45th and 13th Divisions gave promise of support; but there were four German divisions on the front. The line had been taken up hurriedly during the night, so that many gaps existed in it. Of artillery support there was hardly any, and at daybreak it was found that German balloons were overlooking the position. Lieut.-General Gordon's orders, issued at 6.30 A.M.—at which hour his headquarters at Jonchery were closed and reopened at Romigny, eight miles to the south—were that the line was to be maintained, but that if this proved impossible, the line of the Vesle was to be held by the 50th Divn (with 74th Bde attached) [1] and the 8th Divn (with 75th Bde attached), whilst the 21st Divn (with 7th Bde attached) should occupy the Trigny—Prouilly ridge, which is separated from the main Vesle ridge by the Prouilly valley.

About 5 A.M. the enemy began to shell the left, the 74th and 75th Bdes, with guns and trench mortars, and almost simultaneously infantry, using machine guns and trench mortars for covering fire, attacked.[2] Without artillery and out-numbered by three to one at least, the weak line was unable to hold on. After offering resistance in the woods and other localities—the brigadiers, with their staffs, riding their horses as in open warfare—the two brigades and the troops accompanying them, between 10 and 11 A.M. retired behind the Vesle, except at Breuil, where the 11/Lancashire Fusiliers, under Lieut.-Colonel G. P. Pollitt made a stand with the French until nearly midday.[3] By this hour the bridgehead was surrounded

---

[1] It would be more accurate to say: the 74th Bde with remnants of the infantry and engineers of the 50th Divn attached, and so on.

[2] *50th* and *52nd Divisions*, with all six infantry regiments in line, the left of the *52nd* covering the gap between the 75th and 7th Bdes.

[3] German accounts say 11.15 A.M.

SECOND DAY. 28TH MAY

and the bridge captured, so that very few of the Lancashire men got away. Lieut.-Colonel Pollitt himself was wounded and taken prisoner.[1]

Meanwhile, about 6 A.M., Br.-General G. W. St. G. Grogan (23rd Bde) had been ordered by Major-General Heneker (8th Divn) to take command of all troops in the Vesle area for about a mile on either side of Jonchery— the 23rd Bde sector on the afternoon of the previous day— and to organize the defence of the south bank. On arrival at Jonchery soon after 7 A.M., he found that men of the 8th, 25th and 50th Divns were already drifting over the bridge and the enemy beginning to descend the slopes of the ridge.[2] These stragglers were easily stopped and, covered by steady rear-guard fighting, the remainder, by 10 A.M., had established a good line along the railway embankment, which here runs parallel to the river.

On the right wing of the IX. Corps, the 7th, 62nd, 110th and 64th Bdes were attacked in front [3] and enveloped on the left through the wide gap on that flank, so that when the enemy appeared on the top of the Vesle ridge soon after 8 A.M. they were ordered to retire to the Trigny— Prouilly position. Crossing the swampy valley of the Prouilly stream under machine-gun fire, although shouldered off the direct route by the enemy blocking Pévy, the three brigades on the left were in the new position by midday. The 64th Bde did not receive the order to retire.[4] The 1/East Yorkshire and the divisional field companies, strung out in a thin line of posts, had been driven in slightly by an attack about 6 A.M., but the remnants of the 9/K.O.Y.L.I., out in front, and the 6/S. Wales Borderers (Pioneers), more to the right, withdrew gradually, and kept touch with the French 45th Division. Not being so directly affected by the enveloping movement on the left, the 64th Bde maintained its forward position until past midday, Br.-General Headlam's horse being hit under him. The brigade, fighting a rear-guard action all the way back, was then able to rejoin the others, but it was 2 P.M. before the

---

[1] The German claim 600 prisoners, French and British; the war diary of the 11/Lancashire Fusiliers states that 14 officers and 319 other ranks were either killed or missing.

[2] German accounts say the southern edge of the top of the ridge was reached about 8 A.M.

[3] By the *7th Reserve* and *86th Divisions*.

[4] The 97th, 98th and 126th Field Companies R.E., the 14/Northumberland Fusiliers (Pioneers of the 21st Divn) and the 6/S. Wales Borderers (Pioneers of the 25th Divn) were placed under the command of Br.-General Headlam, as well as the remnants of his own three battalions.

1/East Yorkshire, reduced to about forty men, came in. Throughout this fighting the left of the brigade had been protected by the 15/Durham L.I., the brigade reserve at Luthernay Farm, which made successive stands, assisted by the 6/Leicestershire, which had become detached from the 110th Bde. The Trigny—Prouilly ridge, where the 2ᵉ Régiment de Marche Colonial of the I. Colonial Corps (in the line at Reims) had been sent up to reinforce the 45th Division, was found, to some extent, to have been prepared for defence—in places there was a trench $2\frac{1}{2}$ feet deep, and some good wire—but woods in front restricted the field of fire.

Thus the position indicated by Lieut.-General Gordon had been occupied, with a French Colonial battalion interpolated on either flank of the 64th Bde. But the Germans had followed close. Soon after 10 A.M. they were attacking Br.-General Grogan's troops on the Vesle line; about 11.30 A.M. they forced a crossing at Jonchery,[1] and a little later, as we have seen, they reached Breuil and les Venteaux, just east of the latter. Grogan's troops then fell back to the slopes between Branscourt and Vendeuil, forming a left defensive flank; for the right of the French 13th Division was $2\frac{1}{2}$ miles away at Unchair.

Sketch A. The country south of the Vesle, between that river and the Ardre was much like that between the Aisne and the Vesle: there was a backbone in the form of a narrow, irregular plateau with slopes furrowed by small valleys in which lay farms and villages. In the course of the morning it suggested itself to Lieut.-General Gordon that the German plan included a strong advance up both sides of the river Ardre with the probable object of gaining the high ground overlooking the Marne valley. The possession of that ground would cover the flank of a subsequent advance westward on Paris or eastward to encircle Reims; it was necessary therefore to dispute every yard.

Grogan's troops, being continuously outflanked on the west by the advance into the gap which had opened on that side during the afternoon, fell back a mile to the high ground between the Vesle and the Ardre, north of Montazin Farm, astride the Savigny—Jonchery road. Here the 414th Regiment of the French 154th Division reinforced

---

[1] Jonchery was attacked by two regiments of the *52nd Division*, which, by concentric attack, took about three hundred prisoners.
The attempt to destroy the bridge failed, the R.E. officer in charge being wounded and the cart carrying the explosives blown up.

SECOND DAY. 28TH MAY

the 75th Bde, which was on the right, and during the night relieved it so that it could go into second line. About 8 P.M. the enemy, issuing in strength from the woods on the left, drove the line off that part of the position which lay west of the road, to the shelter of some old practice trenches.

The new position was commanded from the enemy's side, since the highest point of the ridge, only about two hundred and fifty yards distant from the road, was in his possession. Br.-General Grogan decided it must be re-taken, and sent forward Major A. H. Cope, 2/Devonshire, with 140 men of his own battalion, and a few from other units, to seize the point and prevent the Germans from debouching out of the wood which lay a hundred yards beyond. This task was successfully accomplished, and the Devonshire remained on the knoll, driving back a determined attempt of the enemy to advance from the wood at 3 A.M. on the 29th.[1]

In the meanwhile, just as darkness was falling, the 416th Regiment of the 154th Division had come up, and extended the British left southwards to Serzy (near Savigny).[2]

Farther to the east, the left wing of the 21st Divn was not attacked until about 3 P.M., when the Germans gained a footing on some parts of Prouilly ridge. But it was not

[1] German accounts speak of reaching the dominating height 233 north of Montazin Farm which is just west of the road, at 4.45 P.M. " By this " the task of the *52nd Division* was accomplished : it was now a matter " of taking up a defensive organization." No further operations are mentioned.

[2] F.O.A. vi. (ii.), p. 145, gives the following account of the arrival of the 154th Division on the right and left of Br.-General Grogan's troops disposed between Branscourt and Vandeuil :—" The 154th Division (two " regiments and two ' groupes ' of artillery) [the third regiment and ' groupe ' " had already been ordered by General Duchêne to reinforce the I. Cavalry " Corps at Dravegny, 5 miles south-west of Fismes], entered the line in the " afternoon [this makes the arrival of the 154th Division earlier than do " British accounts] to support the British IX. Corps ; it sent its right " regiment towards Branscourt and the farm Irval [1,500 yards north " of Montazin Farm], where it got into liaison with elements of the left " of the 45th Division, and its left regiment towards Hourges [4 miles " E.S.E. of Fismes] and Vandeuil. But this latter regiment found the " villages strongly occupied by the enemy and quickly suffered heavy " losses. Seeing that it was threatened also on the west by the enemy " advance in the region of Serzy it had to retire. At one moment the " Germans reached the Montazin Farm, whence they were thrown back by " a counter-attack [this is no doubt Major Cope's movement against Point " 233]. Finally, the 154th Division, mixed with units of the British IX. " Corps, managed to establish itself on the plateau between Branscourt " and Serzy, thus ensuring the junction between the 45th Division and the " XXI. Corps [whose right was south of Crugny]."

until 6 P.M. that the 110th Bde was ordered to withdraw behind the Vesle; the 62nd and 7th followed soon after, covered as rear guard by the 1/Lincolnshire, which remained on the ridge and did not retire until 9.30 P.M., after ascertaining that the French battalion on its right had received similar orders. The 64th Bde and the battalions of the 2ᵉ Régiment de Marche Colonial on either side of it had not been compelled to give ground.¹ Br.-General Headlam did not hear of the withdrawal of the left of the line until 11.30 P.M., and it was not until 2 A.M. on the 29th that his force and the French battalions with it fell back across the Vesle, and took position in the general line on its southern bank.

The French 45th Division, attacked by two divisions of the German *First Army*, lost ground in the centre during the afternoon. Being forced back it gave up Fort St. Thierry,² and during the night Thil and Pouillon, farther to the right; but its left near the 64th Bde maintained its position. General Mazillier (I. Colonial Corps), under whom the division had been placed during the morning, gave orders at 6.45 P.M. for its withdrawal, and also that of the 134th Division, on its right, to a new line south of the Vesle from Bétheny (north of Reims) to Muizon, 600 yards from the British flank. This movement was carried out without interference from the enemy, and after the arrival of another Colonial battalion, the greater part of the 45th Division was withdrawn into reserve, the line being held mainly by men of the I. Colonial Corps.

During the 27th General Pétain had directed only a small part of the reserves available between the Oise and Switzerland towards the Sixth Army: two divisions from the Fourth Army and two from the Oise Groupement. This left eleven in the east, although the Germans had not a single division in reserve between Reims and Belfort. Then, during the night he decided to draw on his reserves north of the Oise. The 164th Division (Fifth Army) was ordered to prepare to entrain on the 28th, and the 26th Division (Fifth Army), on the 29th; the II. Cavalry Corps (resting) was to move up north-east of Beauvais; the 131st (First Army) was to entrain in the afternoon of the

---

¹ It will be seen from the Note at the end of the Chapter that Monograph I. comments unfavourably on the " great lack of attack ardour " and the hesitation of the two divisions opposed to the British 21st Divn.
² Marked " Fort " on Map 2, 1½ miles west of Thil.

SECOND DAY. 28TH MAY

28th to detrain south-west of Soissons on the 29th; and the 162nd (First Army) was to make a march towards the Oise.

At 9 A.M. on the 28th General Pétain issued a formal Directive, prepared of course before news had arrived of what had happened during the early hours of the morning and probably drafted on the previous evening. Of this the important paragraphs are : [1]

" III. The enemy seems to be making his principal
" effort in the direction of the valley of the upper Ourcq
" [eastward and westward of Fère en Tardenois].

" This progress must be stopped at all costs by resist-
" ance on the positions actually held, profiting from any
" opportunity to recover lost ground.

" IV. The G.A.N. [Fourth and Sixth Armies] will
" therefore endeavour :

" 1st, to re-establish the integrity of the line of the
" Vesle, driving the enemy back to the north of Mont
" Notre Dame, with a view to recapturing the heights
" between Vesle and Aisne ;

" 2nd, to maintain possession of Fismes and the heights
" of Ventelay [6 miles north-east of Fismes], Villers Fran-
" queux [1½ miles south-east of Hermonville] on the one
" side, and of Braine, Condé and the Pont Rouge [3 miles
" N.N.W. of Missy] switch, on the other [the three last-
" named places were lost during the morning]; as well
" as the line of the Ailette to its junction with the Oise.

" These positions form the two pillars of our resistance.

" The G.A.N., in addition, will hold securely the
" Montagne de Reims [the heights 9 miles south of Reims]
" to guard against an eventual attack against the left of
" our Fourth Army.

" V. The G.A.R. [Third and First Armies] will assure
" close liaison with the left of the G.A.N., and until further
" orders will keep the equivalent of two divisions in reserve
" in the valley of the Oise ".

In passing this Directive to General Duchêne at 10 A.M., General Franchet d'Espérey added :

" You should actually employ all your available forces
" in the Fère en Tardenois region to drive the enemy back
" on the Vesle and make a secure connection between
" Fismes and Braine [where the enemy had nearly broken
" through on the 27th].

---

[1] F.O.A. vi. (ii.), Annexe 519.

"It will then be possible to form a groupement across
"the principal direction of the enemy attack consisting of:
"the 4th and 43rd Divisions [which began to reach the 'Paris
   "'Line' and the Fère en Tardenois area during the morning];
"the 20th, which begins this morning to detrain between
   "Epernay [13 miles S.S.W. of Reims] and Château Thierry
   "[25 miles west of Epernay];
"the 131st, which will begin detraining on the 29th at Villers
   "Cotterêts, Longpont, Vierzy [stations 14, 9 and 6 miles
   "S.S.W. of Soissons];
"the 10th Colonial Division which entrained to-day at Void
   "Sorcy [35 miles south of Verdun] for the direction of Fère
   "en Tardenois.
"I am directing the 20th Division on Coulonges [5
"miles east of Fère en Tardenois], as fast as it detrains.
"It is for you to attach it either to the I. Cavalry Corps
"or the XXI. Corps.
"The 40th Division, which will begin to detrain to-
"night in the Epernay region, is intended to support the
"British IX. Corps and the 45th Division.
"The British 19th Division, whose transport to-day
"reaches the area Tours sur Marne [13 miles south of
"Reims], the rest being moved to-morrow by lorry, will
"have the same mission as the 40th Division."

As news trickled through, it soon became obvious that these measures would take effect too late to give General Duchêne the assistance of which he stood in need. As we have seen, only the 1st and 154th Divisions, the one from the G.A.N. reserve on the left, and the other from the Fourth Army on the right, the infantry of the 43rd Division from the Fifth Army in General Reserve, and two divisions of the I. Cavalry Corps arrived on the field during the day. Apprised of the continued retirement of the Sixth Army, during the morning General Pétain left his headquarters at Provins (45 miles S.S.W. of Fère en Tardenois), and visited Generals Franchet d'Espérey, Duchêne (who had shifted his headquarters back from Belleu to Oulchy le Château), Degoutte and Gordon, and soon after midday issued further instructions as regards the reinforcements. The 164th and 26th Divisions, which had been warned to be ready to move, were now directed to arrange that the former should arrive on the evening of the 29th, and the latter on that of the 30th, in the Villers Cotterêts area, which the 131st would also reach on the

SECOND DAY. 28TH MAY

29th. Two more divisions were ordered up: the Moroccan (Fifth Army), which was to be sent that evening in lorries to Oulchy le Château (8 miles west of Fère en Tardenois) and the 120th (in reserve of the G.A.E.), which was to be despatched in lorries on the 29th to the Montagne de Reims, to form a groupement with the 40th and the British 19th, already ordered to that area, and the 28th, in the reserve of the Fourth Army, which was to come by march. Two cavalry brigades stationed in Lyons and Paris, to cope with any possible disturbances in those cities, and the 10th Colonial Division, from the reserve behind the Fourth Army, were directed to Montmirail (25 miles south of Fère en Tardenois).

To sum up, by General Pétain's order, 4 divisions were to be assembled on the east of the German " pocket " in the Allied front, in the region of the Montagne de Reims, 4 on the west, in the region of Villers Cotterêts and Oulchy le Château, and one other with the addition of two cavalry brigades to the south at Montmirail. But not all these troops would be available before the 30th.

During the morning M. Clemenceau visited General Foch, and, earlier than General Pétain, went on to see General Duchêne, who told him that the Germans were pushing on without a pause, and that he had nothing to oppose to them but mere dust (" de la poussière "). Without complaining, he mentioned that no " grand chef " had been to visit him. M. Clemenceau then went on to General Pétain's headquarters at Provins, where there were many recriminations.[1]

General Foch, in response to requests for help from G.Q.G., for reasons already given,[2] was not prepared to send more than two regiments of field artillery from the Tenth Army (his reserve of 4 divisions behind the British near Doullens); but he warned General de Mitry (D.A.N.

---

[1] See the account by Mordacq (ii., pp. 44-7), Chief of the Military Cabinet, who accompanied him. General Mordacq's view, as he told M. Clemenceau, was that General Pétain was right from his point of view as French Commander-in-Chief in opposing the despatch of reserves to north of the Somme, but General Foch, as Generalissimo, and strategist, was equally right not to listen to him. Unfortunately, the divisions put at the disposal of General Duchêne had been badly employed: " instead of being used to " form barrier positions behind the line of battle, where they would have " had time to organize and on which the retreating troops could have " rallied and clung as to a lifebuoy, they were thrown in almost haphazard " as they arrived wherever there appeared to be a gap in the line. . . . It " was on such an occasion that the higher command should have taken " a hand ".

[2] See p. 24.

with the British Second Army) to be prepared to give up a division. "He was still far from being easy about the "situation on the British front; for Crown Prince Rup-"precht's Group of Armies was equipped for the offensive, "and still possessed, according to the latest information, "important forces in reserve."[1]

General Foch therefore warned General Maistre (Tenth Army) to have everything ready to rush his divisions up quickly wherever they should be required. On the 28th he wrote to Sir Douglas Haig:

"The new offensive launched by the enemy against "the French Sixth Army obliges us to count on having "to engage part of the French effectives in the battle, if "required.

"In these circumstances, the total of the French forces "earmarked to intervene eventually on the British front "will be, for the moment, greatly reduced.

"The Fifth Army [of four divisions and II. Cavalry "Corps, behind the French Third and First Armies] with "the forces which compose it, has just been directed to "the south of the Oise.

"The Tenth Army, constituted of four divisions, now "remains the only French force capable of acting at short "notice to assist the British Armies, if these Armies are "attacked. It is even possible that this Army may have "to be shifted later.

"On the other hand, it is certain that, the enemy having "engaged an important part of his effectives on the front "south of the Oise, the British front is not likely to be the "object of more than an offensive on a reduced scale, but "this always remains possible."

He therefore warned the British Commander-in-Chief that he might be thrown on his own resources and suggested that he should form a general reserve which could be sent in any direction, rather than rely on local reserves.

On the rest of the front during the 28th the enemy was quieter than on the 27th; there was raiding in Lorraine, gas shelling on the front of the French Fourth Army in Champagne and a good deal of air activity between Mont-

---

[1] In fact, Crown Prince Rupprecht had 56 divisions in reserve (about 32 near the Hazebrouck area) as against 43 on 1st May.

The additional divisions for the Chemin des Dames offensive had been taken from the *Eighteenth* and *First Armies* of the German Crown Prince's Group, opposite the French. Crown Prince Rupprecht had been specially directed to show signs of an early attack, and did so effectively. See Note at end of Chapter.

didier and the Oise. On the Allied side an American local attack at Cantigny was carried out with complete success and counter-attacks repelled,[1] whilst east of Dickebusch Lake a local counter-attack restored the line recently lost.

Sir Douglas Haig himself felt that the British front was safe for the moment. In his opinion the enemy would " devote all his energy and divisions to exploiting his " success " on the Aisne front ; " while securing his flank " towards Reims, he will press vigorously westwards " against the French flank in combination with frontal " attacks (as progress is made) towards Compiègne ". The Field-Marshal despatched by aeroplane to visit Lieut.-General Gordon, a liaison officer who brought back a very accurate account of the situation, which was confirmed by a report from Br.-General G. S. Clive, the Head of the British Mission at G.Q.G. Whereupon Sir Douglas Haig wrote a personal letter to General Pétain conveying his sympathy with him in these anxious times.

The situation was not reassuring. During the second day of the battle the enemy had continued to make progress. Seventeen Allied divisions, including four British, and two cavalry divisions had been engaged. Nine divisions, including the four British, had been so nearly destroyed that they could not be expected to do more than furnish a few composite units to reinforce other divisions. General Duchêne could not hope to have more than fifteen divisions in the line of battle and in support next day ; twenty enemy divisions had been identified, but it was thought from the vigour of the attack that many more must have been employed.[2] The enemy, too, had complete command of the air.

The material effect of the blow was great, but its moral effect on the French nation was even greater : the French troops, it seemed, when seriously attacked in May had done no better than, if as well as, the British in March and April, and it looked as if in defeat they might go the same way as the Italians had done during the previous October.

" Not only had the assault of the 27th May in two days " given to the Armies of Boehn and Below a gain of

---

[1] On 27th April, the American 1st Division had taken over the Cantigny sector (4 miles north-west of Montdidier). On 28th May, the 28th Regiment attacked the German salient surrounding the village of Cantigny on a 1,700-yards front, and captured it, penetrating over a mile.

[2] Twenty-four had been engaged, the *9th* and *36th*, and *6th Bavarian Reserve* from the second line having come into the first line, and four divisions of the *First Army* joining in the attack.

" ground which had always appeared to be quite im-
" probable : the possession of one of the ramparts of
" the Ile-de-France, the plateaux of the Aisne, that river
" itself, the plateaux between the Aisne and the Vesle, the
" latter river itself; but the surprise had also been of
" such a character that it had put into German hands an
" unheard-of number of prisoners and an enormous booty.
" Under the protection of the barrier of the plateaux, the
" whole country between Aisne and Vesle on the eve of
" of the 27th May had been filled with accumulated
" material, parks, camps, depôts and hospitals, and all had
" been swept clean away in 48 hours. But more moving
" than these huge figures was the fact that in appearance
" the French troops had disappeared into thin air, volatil-
" ized. The German press accentuated the few lapses, and
" exaggerated them into the grossest caricatures. Cer-
" tainly on the evening of the 28th in France, as in Germany
" and in the Allied countries, there was a feeling that a
" most serious blow had been struck both to French prestige
" and to French armed forces—and perhaps a mortal blow
" to the Entente." [1]

General Duchêne could do no more in his orders than promise reinforcements and fix a line to be held ; this if possible was to include Soissons, already lost.[2] General Pétain therefore decided to summon more divisions : the 167th (Seventh Army in the G.A.E.), directed on Château Thierry; the 2nd and 51st (Fifth Army), and 162nd (First Army) from north of the Oise; and more artillery and aeroplanes.

At 11 P.M. General Pétain issued a fresh Directive. It was obviously impossible to re-establish the line on the Vesle and to counter-attack as previously suggested. His idea now was to limit the German attack by vigorous resistance on the wings ; if the enemy were threatened on his flanks, his forward movement could no doubt be easily mastered. He therefore directed that the G.A.N. should contain the enemy on the front then held. " It is " the duty of all ", he said, " to maintain their positions " without troubling about the thrust of the enemy's " advanced units ". He ordered the Marne bridges to be specially guarded in order to prevent the passage of German raiding parties. On the east the possession of the Montagne de Reims was to be assured, and on the west

[1] Louis Madelin in " La bataille de France " (published 1920), pp. 96-7.
[2] Appendix VI.

the " Paris Line " was to be held as far as Chaudun (5 miles S.S.W. of Soissons), thence a new line, which was to be dug, north-westwards to Vic sur Aisne (9 miles west of Soissons) and thence an existing line as far as Noyon (20 miles north-west of Soissons). Under the protection of the forces holding these barriers of resistance General Pétain expected to collect between the 31st May and 6th June in the region west of the line Château Thierry—Villers Cotterêts—Compiègne (21 miles west of Soissons) " the " Tenth Army, the 73rd Division [Fifth Army, actually in " the British area behind Amiens] and the British reserves " which would be given him ". That is, he proposed to get hold of all the reserves, French and British, which were behind the British front. General Foch had had no such idea in mind when he suggested that Sir Douglas Haig should form his own general reserve.

NOTE

THE GERMANS ON THE 28TH MAY

Late on the evening of the 27th May the *Seventh Army* had ordered " the attacking troops to do all in their power not to allow " the pursuit to slacken even during the night, and to reach the " objectives fixed by previous orders ". No one paid much attention to these orders, as the operations had not reached the pursuit stage, and all were tired after the strenuous exertions of the day. General von Winckler, in the centre, two of whose divisions (*33rd* and *10th Reserve*) were astride the Vesle, alone repeated the orders, and this led to the *1st Guard Division* which was much behind the others moving off at 4.30 A.M. next day. Elsewhere the various divisions resumed operations between 5 A.M. and 6.30 A.M.

In general, little progress was made on the flanks, where stout resistance was offered ; in the centre the objectives of the 27th May, the heights south of the Vesle, were reached about mid-day, after which there was a pause. Orders issued by O.H.L. about 2.30 P.M. for the continuation of the advance " to the line Soissons — Fère en " Tardenois road, then the heights in the general line Coulonges [5 " miles east of Fère en Tardenois] — Lhéry [6 miles further east] " and Savigny on the Ardre ", did not reach the front line units until after 6 P.M., and very little more ground was gained.

The feature of the day was the capture of Soissons. Little progress **Sketch 4** was made by Larisch's corps on the German right until about noon, when the *9th Division*, the reserve of Wichura's corps, came up on its left, and carried forward the *5th Division*. As the bridges over the Aisne were down, the *9th* itself halted on the heights north of the river near Venizel, with its neighbour, the *14th Reserve*, alongside it ; but the leading parties of the *5th Division*, about 7.30 P.M. crossed just east of Soissons by a weir and the railway bridge, which, though damaged, was passable for infantry. Four battalions cleared the town, getting possession of the two permanent road bridges over the Aisne which had been defended. At this moment a telephone message came from the corps ordering that the town was to be evacuated on the grounds that large French forces were being collected south and south-west of Soissons, and therefore on no account was the Aisne to be crossed. Certainly the *5th Division* was isolated, having lost touch with the divisions on either side of it. The troops were therefore withdrawn, leaving only a battalion in a small bridgehead to guard the railway bridge, whilst other parties were disposed to prevent the destruction of the road bridges. The Official Monograph, however, states that the real reason for withdrawing the troops was the fear of excesses and the breakdown of discipline in the event of the troops getting hold of the provisions and luxuries accumulated in Soissons. It is added that earlier in the day a number of men had got drunk in Fismes, also when a supply dump was found behind Pévy, and that there were excesses in Soissons next day.[1]

In the centre there was little difficulty in crossing the Vesle, Fismes was captured after an artillery preparation about 10 A.M. by the *28th Division*; the *36th Division*, from reserve, was brought up alongside it about noon as resistance had stiffened a little. The left wing of Winckler's corps, and all but the left division (*5th Guard*) of Conta's corps reached their objectives of the 27th about noon (the *28th Division*, held back by its eastern neighbour, not till 3.30 P.M.) and then dug in. General von Conta, in anticipation of O.H.L. instructions, actually ordered a continuation of the advance at 1.40 P.M.; but even in this case the orders did not reach the front units until 6 and 6.30 P.M. and the advanced troops did not go forward more than about 3 miles.

The progress of the *5th Guard Division*, of Schmettow's corps (*5th Guard, 50th, 52nd* and *7th Reserve Divisions*) and the four divisions of the *First Army*, against a regiment of the French 13th Division, the fragments of the four British divisions, and the French 45th Division, supported in the evening of the day by the French 154th Division, was not on the average as much as 3 miles.

Breuil, at the junction of the French 13th Division and British 74th Bde, on which the centre of the *50th Division* was directed, making a stout defence, was not captured until 11.15 A.M. When the *50th Division*, after reorganizing went on south-westwards and reached Unchair, 1½ miles to the south, about 1 P.M. it was counter-attacked, but later reached its objective of the 27th, the heights south of the Vesle, where it remained. As the orders for further advance directed the *5th Guard Division* to proceed as soon as the *50th Division* went forward, this division also halted, leaving nearly a 5-mile gap between its flank and that of the *28th Division* to the south and west of it.

The *52nd Division*, which stood opposite the British 75th Bde and the gap between this brigade and the 21st Divn, started at 5 A.M. In spite of " excellent artillery support ", it was 8 A.M. before it reached the northern edge of the Pévy—Montigny ridge on which the British line had been established. Under increasing fire it

---

[1] Ludendorff (ii. p. 629) regrets that the favourable situation at Soissons was not realized and utilized : " our position would have been considerably " better ".

pushed on to the Vesle, which, again well supported by artillery, the infantry crossed on the right (west) between 10 and 11 A.M., by means of a farm bridge and a foot-bridge. In the centre, in spite of a fine defence of Jonchery Mill, the Vesle was crossed soon after 11 A.M.; but the left, which was delayed by " the strongly " defended Jonchery ", did not complete the passage of the Vesle until towards 4 P.M. The attack of the right and centre was continued at 1 P.M., and between 4 and 4.35 P.M. the division " without " much further resistance " arrived on its objective the heights south of the Vesle and, after reorganizing in depth, dug in.

The *7th Reserve* and *86th Divisions* made slight progress against the British 21st Divn : " The infantry of the *7th Reserve Division* " was greatly lacking in attack ardour on this day " and according to the report of a German artillery commander " stopped in the " face of weak resistance, . . . went forward very slowly with " hour-long pauses, without there being a question of any real " fighting ". When they found a supply dump in Pévy " there were " regrettable excesses . . . one saw melancholy sights and cases of " serious drunkenness ". The division crossed the Vesle in the *52nd Division* sector at Jonchery. The brigade and regimental commanders then made personal efforts to get the orders for advance carried out : " but enemy machine-gun and rifle-grenade fire from " the ridge north-east of Montazin Farm and Branscourt sufficed " to prevent " two regiments from going more than a short distance, the third remaining in Jonchery.

The *86th Division* went forward " even more slowly than the " *7th Reserve* and, going no farther than Thil—Trigny, lost all " touch with the Allies ".

The " sack " (pocket) into which their success had led them was beginning to alarm the German High Command.

CHAPTER VII

THE BATTLE OF THE AISNE (*continued*)

29TH MAY 1918

RETIREMENT ACROSS THE OURCQ

(Sketches A, 4, 5, 6 [1])

Sketch 4. IN spite of the unfavourable nature of the ground, General Pétain proposed to deal with the great re-entrant or " pocket " which the German assault had created in the front of the French Sixth Army by attacking its flanks. He collected troops near Reims and near Soissons for the purpose and reinforced his wings. The outcome of his dispositions was that on the 29th May hard fighting occurred on the flanks but little progress was made. Unfortunately the French troops in the centre, at the bottom of the " pocket ", were not in a position to offer a determined resistance, so the Germans made a further, most alarming, advance. As the result the French line fell back over seven miles, ending the day little more than three miles from the Marne. The collapse in the centre of the front naturally embarrassed the left of the British contingent.

Lieut.-General Sir A. H. Gordon's IX. Corps was now reduced to the 21st Divn (Major-General D. G. M. Campbell) with the 7th Bde (25th Divn) attached, the fragments of the 8th and 50th Divns and the rest of the 25th Divn, under command of Major-General W. C. G. Heneker (8th Divn), but the 19th Division was expected to become available during the day.[2] With two infantry regiments of the French 154th Division, which had arrived the

---

[1] Sketch 5 shows the Allied front ; the Germans were not always up to it.

[2] The IX. Corps order of the evening of the 28th is given in Appendix VII.

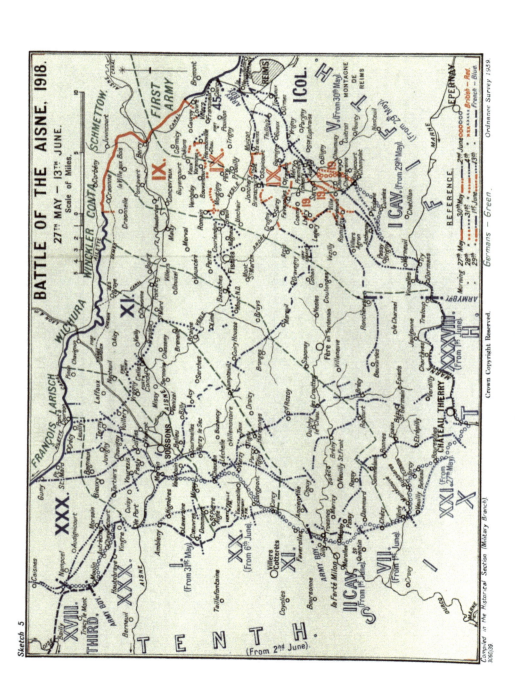

THIRD DAY. 29TH MAY

previous afternoon on the right and left of Heneker's troops, the British force held a position along the Vesle, from les Vautes three quarters of a mile westward to the tile works north-east of Branscourt, whence its line ran south-westwards to Montazin Farm (about 1½ miles south-west of Branscourt). On the British right stood the French 45th Division, not originally attacked, and on the left, the French 13th Division which, after arrival during the 27th, had seen some hard fighting, and was covering a wide front of over five miles.[1]

As the British front was now so narrow, rather less than one-twelfth of the line of battle of the French Sixth Army, it seems best to describe the battle briefly as a whole, and then relate the particular action of the IX. Corps in a little more detail.

Beginning again on the left: the Germans had handicapped themselves by retiring out of Soissons to the right bank of the Aisne on the previous night; and the passages of the river not having been secured at Venizel, to the east of the town (they had been destroyed by the French), delay occurred in crossing in that sector, some of the troops being sent round by Missy. The progress achieved by the Germans on this flank, therefore, was small; yet everywhere they gained ground. On the left, Groupement Hennocque (151st Division, part of the 2nd Dismounted Cavalry Division and some troops of the 55th and 19th Divisions which were in the line farther west) of the XXX.

Sketch 5.

---

[1] According to the British records. In the map for the 29th May in F.O.A. (which records what was thought at French Army headquarters at the time), the front of the IX. Corps and 154th Division is represented as much shorter, extending only from Branscourt to Serzy, thus giving to the 45th Division the 2-mile sector of the British 21st Divn along the Vesle.

The Branscourt—Serzy front was held on the right by the French 414th Infantry Regiment, with the British 75th Bde (less the 8/Border Regiment, remaining with the French 13th Division) in support, and the remains of the 8th and 50th Divns on its left to beyond Montazin Farm; then came the 416th Infantry Regiment, which held Serzy; echeloned to its left, and eventually used to support it, were two very weak battalions: the 9/L.N. Lancashire (74th Bde), sent back for reorganization, with the 74th Light Trench Mortar Battery attached, together numbering only a hundred men, and the 22/Durham L.I. (Pioneers of the 8th Divn), about 220 strong. The dismounted men of the field companies R.E. and the trench-mortar companies were sent up to reinforce the infantry, and the machine-gun companies were distributed amongst them.

Major-General Heneker's advanced headquarters were at Faverolles; those of General Breton (154th Division), 2 miles off, at Lhéry. The troops of the Allies in the Branscourt sector became mixed up in the course of the fighting, and the omission of General Duchêne to unify the command, in spite of the good will of the troops themselves, affected the operations adversely.

Corps, which extended to within two miles of Soissons, was driven back about 2½ miles.

The XI. Corps (General de Maud'huy), now holding from Soissons (inclusive) south-eastwards to Cuiry Housse, had in its sector on the morning of the 29th May the remnants of the 21st, 39th, 61st and 74th Divns and the 1st Division, which had arrived on the previous day. Although reinforced during the day by the Moroccan and 131st Divisions and five battalions of the 170th Division, the belated attack of Wichura's divisions forced the corps westward. Between Chaudun and Taux the Germans were held on the Paris Line, to which the 131st Division had been directed, but east of this sector they carried and crossed it.

Worse befell the XXI. Corps (General Degoutte),[1] which continued the line on to Igny Abbaye in rolling country, masked by many woods with cultivation in the open spaces between them. General Degoutte's orders were " défendre âprement le terrain " and check the enemy's progress so as to permit the arrival of reinforcements. He ordered garrisons to hold certain key points, " but this direction had no effect owing to lack of men ". At 4 A.M. the 43rd Division made a counter-attack, but within half an hour was retiring. Conta's corps (with the assistance of the *10th Reserve Division*, the left of Winckler, and the *50th Division*, the right of Schmettow, Conta's front being overlapped on each side by Degoutte's) then advanced, well supported by field guns and trench mortars, and swept away all resistance. The Paris Line in the sector of Winckler's corps, defended for a time, but outflanked on the east, was eventually lost. Fère en Tardenois, in the sector of the German *10th Division*, the right of Conta's corps, was abandoned. In front of the *36th* and *28th Divisions*, Conta's centre and left, the French " com-" pletely vanished ".[2]

[1] The XXI. Corps was divided into two groupements : on the right, that of General de La Tour (5th Cavalry Division), the 4th and 5th Cavalry Divisions, the 413th Infantry Regiment of the 154th Division, three battalions and two field artillery " groupes " of the newly-arriving 20th Division and the left of the 13th Division ; on the left, that of General Michel (43rd Division), with his own fresh division, and elements of the 1st Division and the newly-arrived 4th Division. In the early afternoon General Degoutte redivided his front from left to right into three sectors : 4th Division, 43rd Division and de La Tour (to be later superseded by the 20th Division).

[2] Monograph I., pp. 150-1. The words are repeated in describing the action of both divisions.

THIRD DAY. 29TH MAY

To use the words of the French account: "towards " midday the Groupement La Tour was driven back to the " line Vezilly—Coulonges—Nesles (south of). The front " was held by groups of a few hundred men without real " connection between them, usually ignorant of the posi- " tion and the plans of their neighbours. The efforts of " General de La Tour to organize command of this scattered " resistance were practically in vain, the enemy giving no " respite." To complete the discomfiture, a gap opened between the Groupements La Tour and Michel. Thus, by noon, " the XXI. Corps, hustled on its whole front " and threatened with the rupture of its centre, was in " a difficult position ".[1]

Soon after noon the commander of the German *28th Division* ordered his troops, leaving their heavier equipment behind, to push on to the Marne. After a rest they started to do so at 4 P.M.; but towards evening French resistance was renewed, so that although the Germans continued operations until nearly midnight and captured Ronchères without a fight, they halted about three miles short of the river, which was their objective.

The rapid disappearance of the XXI. Corps exposed the adjoining flank of the Allied right, now consisting of General Féraud's (I. Cavalry Corps) Groupement,[2] the British IX. Corps and the French I. Colonial Corps. General Féraud had to meet the danger to his flank by sending up the 1st Cavalry Division: one brigade to the Groupement La Tour and one to the 13th Divn in his own groupement. He kept the third to maintain liaison, if possible, with the XXI. Corps; but his troops became involved in the disasters taking place on that flank.

Along the front from the Vesle to Serzy on the Ardre, in the early part of the morning only desultory fighting took place; it was not until between 10 and 11 A.M. that the *52nd Division* and *7th Reserve Division*, the centre and left of Schmettow's corps, advanced. Even then the *86th Division* along the Vesle opposite the British 21st Divn and the French 45th Division made no direct attack. General von Schmettow had prescribed that each division should push on at 1 A.M. independently, in accordance with the Army order, which bade him gain possession of the

---

[1] F.O.A., vi. (ii.), p. 165.
[2] Right of the 13th Divn and the 154th Divn (2 infantry regiments and 2 " groupes " of field artillery, the third regiment being, as already stated, with the Groupement La Tour).

important height 225 (a long L-shaped watershed) south-east of Lhéry, and required that he " should push on " without regard to his neighbours progress, securing " his flanks by echeloning back ". This order, which emanated from the German Crown Prince's Group of Armies for the purpose of ensuring the immediate continuance of the attack beyond the limits first fixed, had a " most unfortunate effect " ; in fact, resulted in confusion and complete lack of co-ordination.[1] The *50th Division* on the right, after only an hour and a quarter's rest, pushed off at 2.15 A.M., and, as we have seen, took part in the success of Conta's corps, when, in spite of the infantry outdistancing the artillery, it advanced five miles and at dusk reached and captured Vezilly. The infantry of the *52nd Division*, having at 2.30 A.M. received a belated order to break off the attack and dig in in depth, did not move at all until the divisional commander, discovering the mistake, about 8.40 A.M. ordered an immediate advance. The right regiment, then went forward at 9.30 A.M. ; the centre, which did not receive the new order until 10.45 A.M., moved about an hour later ; while the left regiment did not fall in until 12.20 P.M. The French 13th Divn, and apparently the greater part of the 416th Regiment of the 154th Divn on the British left, according to German accounts,[2] offered " no resistance worth naming " ; according to the French,[3] " already exhausted by two days of " battle, it did not succeed in holding its ground ".

The delay of the attack of the *7th Reserve Division*—which resulted in its advancing about the same time as the centre of the *52nd Division*—could not be ascribed to bad staff work. As the *86th Division* on its left would not be ready until 7 A.M., that hour was fixed for falling in, " but " as the Allied artillery to the south-west was firing un-" disturbed into the area over which it had to advance, " the hour was postponed until 10 A.M." [4] The front of the division extended from Montazin Farm (inclusive), the British left, to a little over two thousand yards eastwards, and so just included Branscourt. The German attack

---

[1] Monograph I., pp. 152-3.   [2] Monograph I., p. 156.
[3] F.O.A. vi. (ii.), p. 170.
[4] Monograph I., p. 157. The field artillery supporting the composite 8th Divn was Phipps's group (22 guns) and Phillips's group (12 guns), with the French heavy Groupe Hennequin (twelve 155-mm. guns). The remaining nine guns of the LXXVII. Brigade R.G.A. and the three remaining French heavy " groupes," by General Duchêne's orders, had been sent southward across the Marne to defend the bridges over that river.

IX CORPS: 29th May - 2nd June.

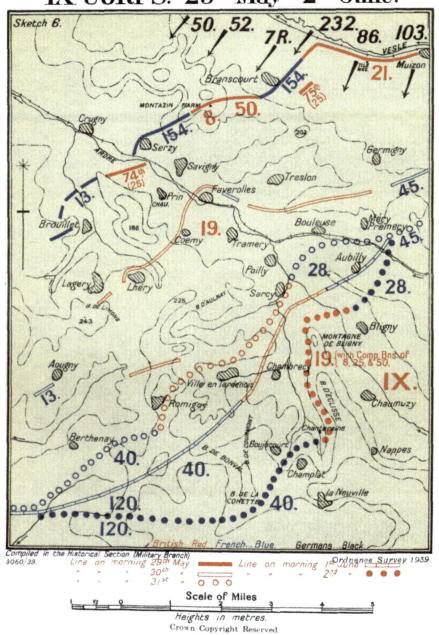

THIRD DAY. 29TH MAY

therefore covered the front of the composite 8th Divn and the 414th Regiment of the 154th Divn.

When, about 11 A.M., Serzy,[1] behind the left flank, was lost by Féraud's groupement, the Allied troops on the Branscourt—Montazin position fell back two thousand yards to the reverse slope of the next ridge, north of Treslon (which lies in a valley),[2] pursued by machine-gun fire and suffering a good many casualties. In spite of their weariness, they were rallied there by the exertions of Br.-General Grogan and other officers, and a new line was established. The enemy then appeared over the crest of the ridge, but was received by such a hot fire that he fell back, and resorted to pounding the line with the 200-lb. shell of heavy trench mortars, the fire being directed by balloon. The first attacks which he made were repulsed; but towards 3 P.M. the fire of the trench mortars, with artillery added, became very intense, machine-gun fire swept the position, and signs of retirement were manifest. Encouraged by Br.-General Grogan, who rode up and down the line, the survivors held on, and fired by his example they maintained the position for some time longer until nearly six o'clock, when the enemy infantry again assaulted and drove both British and French off the ridge.[3]

Sketch 6.

Falling back about two miles across the wooded Treslon valley, they found the 2/Wiltshire of the 19th Division which had now arrived, on the next high ground. This

---

[1] The names of Serzy and Savigny seem to be confused in the French narrative. Both are on the Ardre, the centre of Savigny being about a thousand yards east of Serzy.

[2] German accounts report the Montazin Farm as not taken until 12.30 P.M. by the *7th Reserve Division*.

[3] Br.-General G. W. St. G. Grogan, commanding the 23rd Bde, was awarded the V.C.: " For most conspicuous bravery and leadership
" throughout three days of intense fighting. Br.-General Grogan was,
" except for a few hours, in command of the remnants of the infantry of
" a division and various attached troops. His action during the whole
" of the battle can only be described as magnificent. The utter disregard
" for his personal safety, combined with the sound practical ability which
" he displayed, materially helped to stay the onward thrust of the enemy
" masses. Throughout the third day of operations, a most critical day,
" he spent his time under artillery, trench-mortar, rifle and machine-gun
" fire, reorganizing those who had fallen into disorder, leading back into
" the line those who were beginning to retire, and setting such a wonderful
" example that he inspired with his enthusiasm not only his own men but
" also the Allied troops who were alongside. As a result the line held and
" repeated enemy attacks were repulsed.

" He had one horse shot under him, but nevertheless continued on foot
" to encourage his men until another horse was brought.

" He displayed throughout the highest valour, powers of command
" and leadership."

battalion with four machine guns had been sent at 2 P.M. to hold the ridge in question and it had dug in on a front of nearly a mile. There the exhausted troops rallied, and proceeded to strengthen the line.

In the meantime, no direct attack had been made on the 21st Divn, although it suffered from shelling,[1] and on the right there had only been feeble enemy demonstrations against the French Colonial Corps.[2] Accordingly, in view of the general situation, Major-General Campbell decided to send a battalion from the right to the left.[3] Before it could arrive the officers on the spot had dealt with the situation, and, in order to hold the high ground, which it is convenient to call Hill 202, $1\frac{1}{2}$ miles south-east of Branscourt, had used first all available reserve troops and stragglers of the 110th Bde (about seventy men), and later the 1/Lincolnshire, the reserve of the 62nd Bde.[4] Three companies of the French Colonial Corps also arrived to join the 416th Regiment of the 154th Divn; so that by the time the 8th Divn retired to its second position north of Treslon, its right flank had been secured.

On the other, the left, flank of Heneker's troops, the danger of a gap arising between them and the hard-pressed French 13th Divn had been recognized early in the day, and it soon became a reality. The opportune arrival of the British 19th Division (Major-General G. D. Jeffreys), which for the past ten days had been in reserve to the French Fourth Army near Châlons, recovering from its exertions and losses suffered in the March and April battles, offered a means of filling the gap.[5] The infantry,

---

[1] The *86th Division*, imagining that the British were still north of the Vesle occupying the Prouilly ridge, evacuated the previous evening, sent part of its troops westward to cross the Vesle at Jonchery. It was not until about 10 A.M. that the Prouilly ridge was discovered to be unoccupied. The right wing of the division reached Branscourt " in the evening ". The rest remained as reserve north of the Vesle. Monograph I., pp. 156 and 159.

[2] F.O.A., vi. (ii.), p. 171, speaks of several local attacks during the day, all of which were repelled.

[3] The 6/S. Wales Borderers (Pioneers, 25th Division) was sent, and en route Lieut.-Colonel L. C. W. Deane was mortally wounded. He could not speak, but managed to scrawl on paper : " To my battalion : stick it " boys "—and so died.

[4] Br.-General C. J. Griffin (7th Bde, 25th Divn), having been wounded about 1.30 P.M., the command of his troops was taken over by Br.-General H. R. Headlam (64th Bde, 21st Divn) until the arrival on the 31st of Br.-General C. J. Hickie.

[5] The 19th Division had lost, gross, 4,047 of all ranks in the March offensive, and 4,565 in the Lys battle, including a total of 281 officers ; very few old hands, therefore, were left. Its fighting strength on the 25th May is given as : infantry, officers 237, other ranks 7,214 ; pioneers, 28

travelling in buses, arrived in the area Chaumuzy—Chambrecy (7 miles south of Branscourt), south of the Ardre, in the early morning of the 29th, and divisional headquarters opened at Chaumuzy at 6.30 A.M.[1] Major-General Jeffreys then proceeded to Lieut.-General Gordon's headquarters at Romigny, four miles to the west of Chaumuzy. General Breton (154th Divn), who was already there, stated that the situation was very critical and that already a gap existed in the line, extending from Serzy to Brouillet, $2\frac{1}{4}$ miles to the south-west. Lieut.-General Gordon therefore gave orders that the two brigades of the 19th Division which had already arrived should occupy the line Faverolles—Lhéry (both inclusive), about $2\frac{1}{2}$ miles long, behind the gap, but that, if the villages of Serzy and Brouillet were still in French possession the brigades were to push on and take position between these two localities. The IX. Corps cyclists were ordered to move off at once and hold the Lhéry line until the 58th Brigade (Br.-General A. E. Glasgow) and the 57th Brigade (Br.-General A. J. F. Eden) reached it, which they did about 1 P.M. Later a machine-gun company was sent up to each brigade, and came into position about 4 P.M.

On arrival at Lhéry the brigadiers learnt that not only Serzy and Brouillet, but Savigny also had been lost.[2] The 57th Brigade found that on the left a gap of 800 to 1,000 yards separated it from the nearest French troops; the 58th had no close touch on the right with other troops, as the left of Heneker's troops and such French detachments as were with it, now on the ridge north of Treslon, did not extend as far as Faverolles. Fighting was still proceeding in front, but it was judged better for the two brigades to dig in on the selected position than to go to the support of the front line. In the course of the afternoon the troops of the composite 8th Divn retired and the position of the 57th and 58th Brigades became the front line.[3] To fill the gap on the right the 6/Senegalese Tirail-

---

and 969; machine-gun battalion, 36 and 770; and the wastage to 28th (inclusive) as 16 officers and 456 other ranks. On going into action, the usual " battle reserve " was left behind, which still further reduced the rifle strength.

[1] The artillery and machine guns, moving by road, arrived in the afternoon of the 29th, and the infantry transport and horses on the 30th. The headquarters of the French 28th Division were also in Chaumuzy.

[2] German accounts say Serzy was captured at 11.30 A.M.

[3] The 19th Division General Staff war diary puts the number of men of the 8th, 25th and 50th Divns who fell back and were absorbed into the ranks of the 57th and 58th Brigades as about 500. This number did not

leurs (45th Division) was sent up, but halted in front of Tramery.

The new line was not seriously attacked on the 29th; but the widening gap on the left caused by the retirement of the 13th Divn and the regiment of the 154th Divn remained an ever-present source of anxiety. For the moment the 19th Division could do no more than send a liaison officer to the 13th Divn headquarters. After taking Serzy and Savigny the German *52nd Division* had pushed southwards past the 57th and 58th Brigades, which were in the zone of its neighbour, the *7th Reserve Division*. Galled by fire on the left flank it detached guards to this side, but by night it had established itself south of Lagery, that is beyond the left of the Lhéry position; at that moment the right of the French 13th Divn was at Aougny, 2¼ miles south-west of Lhéry. To guard the British flank, after 5 P.M., the reserve battalion of the 57th Brigade was moved up behind Lhéry. Later, the 74th Bde, part of which had been on the extreme left of the 8th Divn, with the 22/Durham L.I., was used to support the 57th Brigade; it was joined by the 8/Border Regiment, which had been with the French 13th Divn, and reinforced by the 106th Field Company R.E. (25th Divn) and the 1/6th Cheshire, so that it was able to spread out and establish touch with the French 13th Divn near Romigny.[1]

Whilst the Faverolles—Lhéry position was thus secured by the 19th Division, the situation of Heneker's division in its third position on the ridge (Bouleuse) south of Treslon still remained critical. Its position was on a forward slope, with a field of fire restricted by woods which gave almost continuous cover from the Treslon valley to the top of the ridge. The enemy had followed up closely; indeed at one time some Germans had managed to establish themselves on the crest of the ridge, but were driven off by a counter-attack. A composite battalion of details and seven machine guns, organized by Major-General

represent all the infantry that remained of the three divisions. By next day, with the addition of stragglers and reinforcements, the 8th Divn had organized a composite battalion of 800 strong; the 25th, 500 strong; and the 50th, 950 strong.

[1] The 1/6th Cheshire (from the cadre 39th Divn) had arrived by train in the Fismes area at 7 P.M. on 27th May, and was attacked by enemy aeroplanes and fired on by an enemy outpost. A party went out and attacked the outpost, which surrendered and was brought back. The train was then reversed and returned through the French outpost line to Fère en Tardenois. The battalion was eventually taken by train round by La Ferté Milon to Dormans, where it arrived at 2 A.M. on the 29th.

THIRD DAY. 29TH MAY

Heneker,[1] now arrived. As nothing could be seen of the French on the right flank, which appeared in danger of being turned, at Br.-General Grogan's suggestion Major-General Heneker asked for more troops to be sent to this flank. Since the original corps reserve, the 25th Divn, had been put into the front line by General Duchêne's orders, the IX. Corps in response to this call directed the 19th Division to detach two battalions of its reserve brigade (56th). So, late in the evening, the 8/North Staffordshire and the 1/4th Shropshire L.I. prolonged the line to the right, to the angle of the ridge south of Germigny where it turns north-north-west. By nightfall the enemy attacks (*7th Reserve Division*) had ceased, and the position was still held on the morning of the 30th. At 1 A.M. Br.-General R. M. Heath (56th Brigade) relieved Br.-General Grogan in command of the infantry in the fighting line, but the troops on the Bouleuse ridge continued to be under Major-General Heneker, and those on the Faverolles—Lhéry position under Major-General G. D. Jeffreys. The battalion of Senegalese tirailleurs remained interposed between them.

Away to the east in the sector of the 21st Divn, where part of the 414th Regiment of the 154th Divn lay on its left, little had happened until 4 P.M., when a strong German attack was made on Hill 202 from the direction of Branscourt.[2] This was repulsed by rifle and machine-gun fire; but later, when Heneker's troops and the left wing of the 416th Regiment were driven from the Bouleuse ridge, and Faverolles, two miles away, had become the right flank of their position, the situation of the 21st Divn appeared serious. About 7.45 P.M. the line was heavily bombarded by artillery and trench mortars.[3] After this had been suffered in shallow trenches for three-quarters of an hour, Hill 202 was evacuated, whereupon a defensive left flank north-west of Germigny was formed. Under some pressure from the north-east, the right of the 21st Divn line con-

[1] This composite force had about 4 P.M. been ordered to move towards Lhéry at the request of General Breton to meet an attack of German tanks, which turned out to be French armoured cars, so the order was countermanded. Monograph I. claims (twice on p. 150) that tanks were employed by the French in this same area, but it is not so.

[2] This was in the German *86th Division* sector, but the attacks appear to have been made by the *36th Reserve Regiment* of the *7th Reserve Division* (Monograph I., p. 158). It is admitted that the attack did not progress.

[3] Lieut.-Colonel E. S. Chance (Queen's Bays), commanding the 6/Leicestershire, whose skill and courage had done much to maintain the position, was killed.

formed, as previously arranged, so that by about 8.30 P.M. the line ran from the Vesle near Muizon to a point two miles south-westwards. Later the left was withdrawn to bring it nearer Germigny.

Help now came from the French 45th Division, whose infantry regiments were in reserve, since it had been relieved in the front line during the previous night by two battalions of the 134th Division and a Territorial brigade. Lieut.-General Gordon had asked for the relief of his tired and depleted divisions, and General Micheler agreed that the 45th Division should take over the front of the 21st Divn (less its artillery, which remained). The operation was completed during the night, and the remnants of the 21st Divn were assembled around Pourcy (8 miles south-west of Reims).[1] After the relief, the French 45th Division withdrew the left of its line slightly, and so found touch with Major-General Heneker's troops south of Germigny. Thus a more or less continuous front was again formed.

In the early morning General Micheler and his Fifth Army staff, placed at the disposal of G.A.N. by General Pétain, had arrived at Cumières (2 miles north-west of Epernay). At noon, in order to relieve General Duchêne of part of his burden, although the formal change was not intended to take place until 8 A.M. on the 30th, he assumed command of the sector containing the I. Colonial Corps and the Groupement Féraud, including the British IX. Corps. General Duchêne was instructed by General Pétain to move his headquarters to Trilport (near Meaux, 40 miles south-west of Soissons), as Oulchy le Château was too near the front.

When issuing his Directive on the evening of the 28th General Pétain had hoped that pressure on the flanks and an effective resistance in the centre would prevent any further German advance. His measures, adopted too late, had proved ineffective; so, after visiting General Franchet d'Espérey, the Army commanders and several of the corps commanders concerned, he decided that a counter-attack must be launched. On the evening of the 29th, therefore, he issued instructions, beginning:

" The situation requires the immediate launching of a

---

[1] It had in 3 days suffered a loss of about 150 officers and 3,600 other ranks; so the infantry was reorganized, each brigade forming a composite battalion, and these were combined into the 21st Independent Brigade under Br.-General G. H. Gater (62nd Bde).

THIRD DAY. 29TH MAY

" well organized counter-offensive in order to stop the
" enemy progress southwards and throw him first on to
" the Vesle and then on to the Aisne."

As time would be required to assemble the divisions
and place them in position, he fixed the 31st May as the
date for the counter-offensive. This was to comprise two
attacks : the first, the principal effort, from the Soissons
area north-eastwards in the direction of the front Braine—
Laffaux (6 miles north-east of Soissons), to be carried out
by General Lacapelle of the I. Corps with the 2nd, 35th,
51st and 162nd Divisions, none of which had yet arrived,
together with all the troops on the front of attack. The
second was to be made north-westwards from the Ardre
area (where the British 19th Division stood) in the direction
of the front Montigny—Fismes, and was to be carried out
by the Montagne de Reims Groupement (28th, 40th and
120th Divisions, of which one division, the 28th, was
beginning to arrive on the field). The troops in the central
zone were to hold their ground on the understanding that
they would receive a reinforcement of three divisions
(20th, 131st and 164th). One of these appeared on the
30th and went into the line south of Soissons. Every
available detachment, the personnel of schools of instruction, Territorial and L. of C. units, were to be sent to the
Marne Line in order to form a defensive barrier. General
Pershing, for the same purpose, placed the American 3rd
Division (Major-General J. T. Dickman) then in the
Château Villain area (south of Chaumont), its training not
yet having been completed, at General Pétain's disposal.
It arrived on the 30th, less artillery and engineers, at
Château Thierry.[1] In addition to the reinforcements
already on their way, the 73rd Division of the Tenth
Army (General Reserve), behind Amiens, was drawn east-
wards. Accordingly, General Franchet d'Espérey ordered
the Armies of Generals Micheler and Duchêne, " above all,
" to maintain the continuity of their front, engaging a
" minimum of their forces to hold securely [west to east]
" the plateaux of Villers Hélon [$7\frac{1}{2}$ miles east of Villers
" Cotterêts]—Oulchy le Château—Fère forest [S.S.E. of
" Fère en Tardenois and already lost], and assure possession
" of the road Villers Agron—Ville en Tardenois—Pargny.

" They will securely guard the passages of the Marne,
" from Château Thierry to Epernay (inclusive).

" The Sixth Army will use the troops already in the

[1] It moved by lorry to Meaux and thence marched.

"line, and the 131st, 164th and 20th Divisions [which "began to arrive on the 29th] and the 10th Colonial "Division [which began to arrive on the 30th]; the Fifth "Army will only engage such portions of the Montagne de "Reims Groupement as are strictly necessary."

Available information seemed to indicate that the enemy front of attack might be extended westwards: an assembly of five divisions was reported near Noyon, whilst from the French military attaché at Copenhagen came the report that the present attack was only a vast diversion—this much was true—and that the principal German effort would take place between Oise and Somme with a view to breaking the front and marching on Paris—which was not true; for the German gaze, as Field Marshal von Hindenburg has put it, "was still directed steadfastly towards "Flanders".[1]

After ordering special air reconnaissance to discover the location of the German reserves, General Pétain therefore decided to place the French reserves which were then in Picardy so that they could intervene rapidly either on the front of the G.A.N. or G.A.R., that is either east or west of Noyon. The disposition was 4 divisions astride the valley of the Oise, 2 towards St. Just en Chaussée and Breteuil (that is west of Montdidier), and one or two divisions south of Amiens. Further, he requested General Foch to put at his disposal the Tenth Army (4 divisions) of the General Reserve between the Somme and the Lys, behind the British, and to hand over the D.A.N. (9 divisions), in Flanders with the British, replacing it by Belgian or British troops. To do as the French Commander-in-Chief suggested and shift all reserves to the Aisne front was, as we now know, exactly to play the enemy's game. The Generalissimo, viewing the situation as a whole, and no doubt remembering General Pétain's incessant demands for divisions during the Verdun operations in 1916, was not disposed to grant his requests at once. In reply, he pointed out that "the Group of Armies of the Crown "Prince of Bavaria, facing the British Armies, seems to "have kept its reserves intact [39 divisions]; an offensive "on his part remains to be guarded against", and might require the intervention of the Tenth Army. He agreed, however, to ask the Belgian Army, whose front was for the moment quiet, to extend it down to Ypres, so as to economize a British division. To this H.M. King Albert

[1] "Out of My Life", p. 364.

THIRD DAY. 29TH MAY

consented. General Foch also said that the divisions of the General Reserve, without leaving their area, would be moved nearer to their points of entrainment, and that he was keeping the gradual liberation of the D.A.N. in mind.

In response to General Foch's warning of the previous day, Sir Douglas Haig informed his Army commanders that the French reserves in the British area might be reduced or withdrawn, and that the following formations now in Army areas would be held in G.H.Q. reserve : Cavalry Corps, 6 divisions complete with artillery, 8 Army field artillery brigades, 8 garrison artillery brigades, 6 motor machine-gun batteries and one battalion of the Guards Machine-Gun Regiment.

On the 29th M. Clemenceau again went out to see General Duchêne, and made for Fère en Tardenois, where General Degoutte's (XXI. Corps) headquarters had been on the previous evening. When his car reached the Grande Place, he found General Féraud, but the Germans were already on the northern edge of the town. He promptly left and motored to the new headquarters at Fresnes ($4\frac{1}{2}$ miles S.S.E. of Fère en Tardenois). General Degoutte told him plainly that in his opinion the battle was not under control : " we are not fighting a methodical " and organized action in retreat ; we are simply marching " to the rear ". M. Clemenceau then went on to General Duchêne, who could offer " no precise information regard- " ing the battle ", and the same was the case with General de Maud'huy (XI. Corps). At XXX. Corps headquarters (General Chrétien) also, news was scanty, but it was evident that the German pressure on the left wing was less accentuated than on the rest of the front. The general impression derived by the French Prime Minister was that " no one yet knew where he was ". There was nothing to be done except consult General Foch. An interview could not, however, be arranged until the 31st.

NOTE

THE GERMANS ON THE 29TH MAY

The line reached by the Germans on the evening of the 28th formed a great bulging centre whilst the two wings were still hanging back. It was an undesirable situation, nearly " strangulated " hernia ", more especially as the only railway communications into the conquered salient ran through Reims and Soissons, the one still in possession of the French, the other close under their guns.[1] O.H.L. proposed to deal with the situation by broadening the front of attack. Preparations were already in full swing for the " Yorck " offensive, which would extend it some twenty miles westwards towards Noyon, and an Instruction issued at 1.30 P.M. on the 28th called for their punctual completion, so that the operations might begin on the 30th. The *Seventh Army* was warned to be " strong south of Soissons, so as to compel the enemy to evacuate " the ground between the Aisne and the Oise ". Simultaneously the *First Army* was requested to furnish a scheme of attack for the capture of Reims and the ground up to the southern line of its forts. If the pressure near Soissons produced the desired effect, the *Eighteenth Army* (on the west of the *Seventh*) should gain ground east of the Oise in the direction of Compiègne. What O.H.L. had in view was the possession of the line : southern forts of Reims—Fère en Tardenois—Compiègne—Montdidier.

The successes gained on the 29th in the centre and on the right eased the hernia into more or less the form of a triangle, with its apex south of Fère en Tardenois, 25 miles from the Ailette ; the front line had increased from 36 miles to nearly 60 ; the original fifteen attacking divisions had been reinforced by one (*6th Bavarian Reserve*) on the 27th ; three (*9th, 36th* and *86th*) on the 28th, and another on the left, at Bétheny, on the 29th ; the *51st Reserve Division* was moving up to Soissons, and the *232nd* to near Jonchery. The Allies had brought up 13 divisions to reinforce the original seven, so there were now 22 German divisions against nominally 20. This seemed sufficient margin to ensure further success against a beaten enemy.

During the afternoon of the 29th, O.H.L. issued an order : " After reaching the line fixed by the order of the 28th [Savigny— " Lhéry—Coulonges—Fère en Tardenois and Soissons road] the " attack of the left wing of the *Eighteenth Army*, and of the *Seventh* " and *First Armies* will be continued south of the Oise in the direction " of Compiègne—Dormans—Epernay, and the range of heights " between the Vesle and Marne south of Reims secured. The Marne " is not to be crossed."

Owing to the huge depôts of food and drink found in the French area, the problem of supply by road over ridge and river had been greatly facilitated, so the Germans were able to devote their transport resources to the carriage of ammunition.

---

[1] Ludendorff ii., p. 632. The Vauxaillon tunnel on the Soissons-Laon line, nearly midway between these places, having been blown up, this line could not be used for some time.

CHAPTER VIII

THE BATTLE OF THE AISNE (*continued*)

30TH MAY 1918

RETIREMENT TO THE MARNE

(Sketches 5, 6)

As a general result of the fighting on the 30th the enemy Sketch 5. retained the initiative, whilst the Allies again everywhere lost ground, especially in the centre where the Germans reached the Marne. The enemy's progress was achieved in the same way as during the March offensive : a detachment would break in at some weak place or gap and, then turning against the raw edges thus exposed, would induce or force the line on one or both sides of the point of entry to retire. In the effort to keep a continuous line of defence seldom was any effective reply made to this method, although small reserves with a few well-placed machine guns should have been sufficient to cope with it. The doctrine of Colonel de Grandmaison as to the powers of the relentless offensive, propounded before the war, was being curiously justified. The rapid advance of the Germans greatly interfered with the preparations for the counter-attack ordered by General Pétain for the 31st.

On the left, in the French XXX. Corps, the Groupement Hennocque (reinforced during the day by one regiment of the 162nd Division), though twice heavily attacked, according to German accounts, made a good fight and was not finally dislodged until 4 P.M., when it fell back in the centre to Tartiers—Morsain, $2\frac{1}{2}$ to 5 miles. This retirement exposed the right of the 19th and 55th Divisions on its left. By General Chrétien's order, these two made a withdrawal to the 2nd Position (Green Line) Audignicourt—Nampcel. This movement in turn entailed the bending back of the line of the 38th Division, on their left. The

223rd and *105th Divisions* of the German *Eighteenth Army*, and the *221st, 14th* and *241st* of François's corps of the *Seventh Army* followed up, having to bridge the Oise in the *223rd Division* area.

In the French XI. Corps, the Germans, whose artillery in spite of immense difficulties had taken position during the night, broke in on the right and captured Hartennes from the 39th Divn. This loss affected the right of the 131st Division, which had come up on the previous day. The rest of its line held on stoutly, although the 74th Divn, on its left, lost ground, and this retirement in turn occasioned a withdrawal of the Moroccan Division. On the extreme left of the corps, opposite Soissons, the 170th Division, after very heavy fighting, retired about two thousand yards. The progress of Wichura's corps, in consequence of two fresh French divisions (131st and Moroccan) having been thrown in, was small, and " in no way corre- " sponded to the expectations of the German commanders ". At night, since the front of the five divisions of the French XI. Corps was somewhat widely extended, General Lacapelle (I. Corps), being available, was now assigned to the command of its two left divisions.

On the front of the XXI. Corps (Ronchères-Hartennes) " events did not turn out any more favourably " for the French.[1] Winckler's and Conta's corps, reinforced by the *231st Division*, attacking on the right (east) in the early morning, jostled back the 4th and 43rd Divisions and the Groupement La Tour for a distance of five miles and across the Marne. " The instruction given on the previous " evening by General Pétain on the subject of guarding " the passages not having been carried out, General de La " Tour tried to organize bridgeheads at Jaulgonne, Passy " and Dormans, but there was no time to do so as the " Germans pressed on closely without ceasing, in spite of " air attacks by many squadrons." [2] In the evening the Germans (*231st, 36th* and *28th Divisions*) reached the river (part as early as 2.10 P.M.) between Chartèves and Dormans on a front of six miles, measured as the crow flies. The *Seventh Army* orders, issued in the afternoon, stated definitely that the attack was not to be continued beyond the Marne, but that the bridges should be captured. All the bridges were found to have beeen blown up, but one

---

[1] F.O.A. vi. (ii.), p. 184.
[2] Monograph I., p. 180. The action of the air forces is not mentioned in F.O.A.

FOURTH DAY. 30TH MAY

attempt was made to cross, below Jaulgonne, where a small bridgehead was secured.[1]

In the Groupement Féraud,[2] which held a long line with small forces on the left of the British contingent, the Germans of Schmettow's corps attacked the right sector as early as 3 A.M. and during the morning caused the 13th Divn to fall back nearly two miles south-eastwards. The French 120th Division then came up to take over all but the extreme right of the sector. To fill the gap on the left of the Groupement, caused by the retirement of the XXI. Corps behind the Marne, a brigade of the 4th Cavalry Division was sent from the Groupement La Tour during the afternoon. But when a fresh German division, the *5th Guard*, was put in on the western flank of Schmettow, the 120th Division itself was forced back, whilst on the left, from Verneuil to Dormans (inclusive), it was even driven over the Marne. In the evening the 40th Division relieved the remnants of the 13th Divn, which was withdrawn for reorganization.

The British line (now consisting of the 56th Brigade Sketch 6. on the right, a battalion of Senegalese, the 58th and 57th Brigades and the 74th Bde)[3] was attacked on the left centre, about 6 A.M., by three German regiments.[4] Breaking in on the left at the junction of the 57th Bde with the very weak 74th Bde, the enemy enfiladed the left of the 57th. A reserve company of the 10/Worcestershire sent

---

[1] F.O.A. vi. (ii.), p. 185. Monograph I. states, p. 186, that the *28th Division* ordered a bridgehead to be secured south of Jaulgonne and Barzy (¾ mile above Jaulgonne). An attempt was made with the help of a single boat, but on its second trip it was fired on and its occupants were wounded, whilst all of the first party already across were captured. At 2 A.M. on the 31st, however, a whole battalion (less machine guns) was got over in pontoons, then 2 more companies and finally 2 more battalions. French fire prevented a bridge being thrown, but the troops in the bridgehead maintained their position. The place selected for crossing, at a concave bend, was singularly suitable both for covering fire and for forming a bridgehead.

[2] The boundary between the Groupements La Tour and Féraud at the front coincided with that between Conta's and Schmettow's corps.

[3] The line was supported by the following field artillery :
48 guns of the 19th Division (Br.-General W. P. Monkhouse) ;
22 guns of Ballard's (formerly Phipps's) Group of the 8th and 25th Dns ;
12 guns of Phillips's Group of 25th Dn.
A further 29 guns of the 21st Dn supported the French on the British right.
The only heavy artillery was two batteries of the XLI. Brigade R.G.A. They were both ordered to retire during the afternoon.

[4] One of the *7th Reserve Division* and two of the newly arrived *103rd Division* ; the third of the latter attacked the 74th Bde.

to protect this flank was destroyed, losing all its officers and two-thirds of its other ranks, so the 3/Worcestershire (74th Bde) and 10/Worcestershire were ordered to retire and went back about a thousand yards.[1] The attack then spread northwards to the 8/Gloucestershire, which was also driven back. By 9.30 A.M. the 57th Bde was established on its new position, but fresh attacks on its left flank forced it yet farther back, so that, about 11 A.M., whilst the 58th Brigade faced north-west, the 57th was bent round southwards, and was now reinforced by the 10/R. Warwickshire (57th Bde) from the divisional reserve.

Meantime the 74th Bde, reinforced by a composite battalion of the 50th Dn and the 5/South Wales Borderers (Pioneer battalion of the 19th Division), had clung to the high ground south of Romigny, although both its flanks were exposed. About noon, however, the brigade was forced back to the high ground south-west of Ville en Tardenois.[2] To the north, continued pressure of the enemy on the left flank of the 57th Bde, where the two Worcestershire battalions suffered severe losses, made the position of this brigade very insecure, indeed touch was temporarily lost on the right with the 58th Brigade. Consequently it was ordered to make a further retirement to cover Ville en Tardenois; this movement was completed by 1 P.M. and junction with the 74th Bde regained. Later in the afternoon this latter brigade also established touch on the left with the French. After this there was comparative quiet, the only attack made by the Germans, about 5 P.M., being repulsed. At night the 74th Bde was withdrawn into reserve, when the French 40th Division, which had relieved the 13th Divn, took over its front.

Worse trouble befell the 58th Brigade, to the north of the 57th, in front of Tramery. Attacked at 3.30 A.M. by a regiment of the *7th Reserve Division* the Senegalese tirailleurs disappeared, and a platoon of the 9/R. Welch Fusiliers, on the right, was cut off. The left was also exposed by the retirement of the 57th Bde. In the end, the 9/R. Welch Fusiliers and the 9/Welch, in support, were surrounded after making a long struggle, and only

---

[1] The 3/Worcestershire, which had been in close support of the 57th Bde, fought in that brigade during most of the day.

[2] The failure of the regiment of the fresh *103rd Division*, which attacked at Romigny, to do more than make a small gain of ground is a matter of comment in Monograph I., pp. 194-5. It is ascribed to lack of artillery support and the splitting up of the troops, so that only four battalions of the whole division came into effective action.

one company of the latter battalion, out on the right flank, succeeded in making its escape. The third battalion at the disposal of the brigade, the 9/Cheshire (56th Bde), was ordered at 12.25 P.M. to take position on the high ground north-west of Sarcy, about 2,500 yards in rear of the morning front line, and there, about 1 P.M., it was joined by the survivors of the two front-line battalions.[1]

The 56th Bde, reinforced by the composite battalion of the 8th Dn, although attacked by the newly arrived *232nd Division*, and part of the *86th*,[2] and heavily bombarded, repulsed all the early assaults. But, about 11 A.M., the right flank had to be slightly withdrawn as the French 28th Division, on that flank, was falling back. In view of the situation on his left, Br.-General Heath made ready to pivot on his right; but on hearing of the withdrawal on that flank at 12.30 P.M. he ordered a retirement of about a mile to the ridge west of Aubilly, so as to get touch on both flanks. This movement was carried out under machine-gun fire but in good order, the last troops of the brigade leaving the Bouleuse ridge about 2 P.M. An hour later, when Br.-General A. E. Glasgow (58th Bde) had been wounded, Br.-General Heath took over command of both 56th and 58th Bdes. The new position was held until the evening, when the 56th Bde was relieved by the French 28th Division.[3]

Thus the distribution of troops at night was the following: on the right, the French 28th Division held the ridge west of Aubilly with the 56th Bde in support and reserve; then near Sarcy came the 58th Bde (reduced to one battalion 2/Wiltshire, the attached 9/Cheshire, with remnants of the other two battalions), and in front of Ville en Tardenois the 57th Bde, which made junction with the French 40th Division. General Madelin, commanding the 28th Division, placed two battalions at the disposal of the 19th Divn in reserve.

To the British right, the French Colonial Corps lost a little ground, but the situation of the French Fifth Army around Reims did not give rise to any serious anxiety.

---

[1] The Germans claim 600 prisoners. A battalion of the *103rd Division* appears to have supported the attack.

[2] The *232nd Division* had served throughout on the Russian front and, like the *86th*, was of " mediocre combat value ".

[3] The 1/4th Shropshire L.I. remained in close support; the 8/North Staffordshire, 2/Wiltshire (attached from 58th) and 8th Dn Composite Battalion went back two miles to Bligny, where the 8th Dn men were divided among the battalions of the brigade.

During the day, after Lieut.-General Gordon had been to General Micheler's (Fifth Army) and General Franchet d'Espérey's (G.A.N.) headquarters to urge that the British troops ought to be relieved without further delay, as the survivors were quite worn out, some changes in the higher command took place. General Pellé (V. Corps), always a good and courteous friend to the British, took over command of the front held by the British IX. Corps (now represented by the 19th Divn and fragments of four other divisions placed under it at 12.15 P.M.) and by the French 154th Divn which had become mixed up with it.[1] Lieut.-General Gordon handed over command at 2.30 P.M., leaving his own overworked staff to help General Pellé until the V. Corps staff should arrive. Later, the 28th Division was added to General Pellé's command.

The situation on the night of the 30th appeared even more disquieting than on the 29th : the French resistance was growing weak, four British divisions had been reduced to composite battalions and the fifth to brigade strength, while the enemy showed no signs of ceasing his victorious progress in the centre. He had certainly halted for the night on the Marne ; but it did not seem possible that the few troops available could oppose his crossing. The future depended on the counter-offensives ordered to begin next day, even though, seeing that part of the forces intended for them had already become engaged, their efficacy must be reduced. Holding the Marne defensively, the Germans, possessing both local numerical superiority and the initiative, might decide to push southwards from the Château Thierry—Villers Cotterêts front towards Paris, hardly more than forty miles away. Signs growing progressively more definite showed, however, that they were preparing yet another attack with feverish activity ; its front, at first limited to the Noyon sector, was gradually being extended to Montdidier.[2] This would mean an attack on the western flank of the salient which the French front Château Thierry—Noyon—Montdidier now presented, and seemed the more probable as the

[1] " The units of the 154th Divn were very dispersed, and it did " not appear that it could be usefully reconstituted at the moment. Its " troops were left provisionally at the disposal of the British 19th Divn " and the French 28th." F.O.A. vi. (ii.), p. 194.

[2] The signs at this date were marked increase of traffic, railway stations of Ham and Nesle (both to the north of Noyon, see Map 1) well lighted up, bivouac fires, strong anti-aircraft defence ; heavy concentration of artillery at four places between Montdidier and Nesle ; the presence of several divisions known to be in reserve.

FOURTH DAY. 30TH MAY

German reserves on the British main front had not been reduced.

On the original front of attack General Duchêne did not consider that the reinforcements already sent to him were sufficient. General Pétain responded to his further appeal by putting at his disposal the 73rd and the 2nd American Divisions, also the II. Cavalry Corps, besides additional artillery. But General Duchêne asked for still more help in order to replace worn-out divisions and to bar the passage of the Marne. The French situation began to affect the British seriously, as General Foch decided to let his General Reserve, the Tenth Army of four divisions, go to General Pétain, and at midday directed that Army to be ready to entrain its troops next day. At 11.45 P.M. he sent the executive order to move the divisions to such destinations as General Pétain should fix. During the day he had by letter informed Sir Douglas Haig, after thanking him for the constitution of a British general reserve, that for the moment the employment of such a reserve was contemplated only on the British front: but "bearing in mind the possible departure of the Tenth "Army, if, later, it should appear that the enemy is "engaging all the forces at his disposal against the French "front, it is possible that I may be led to appeal for the "co-operation of the British general reserve, either all or "part of it".

General Pershing placed at the disposal of the French the American 5th Division, training since the 4th May in the Bar sur Aube area,[1] and on the 1st June it moved, less artillery, engineers and supply train, to the Vosges front.

M. Clemenceau again visited Generals Duchêne, Degoutte and de Maud'huy. The news at their headquarters was bad: the Germans were coming on because there was no artillery to stop them: the troops "were beginning to get dis- "couraged because, as at the beginning of the War, they "were being bombarded with heavy stuff, and could only "reply with rifles and machine guns: the game was all "one-sided ".[2] In Paris, "the politicians were demanding "not only the head of General Duchêne, but also, above all, "that of General Pétain. Even among the members of the "Chamber there had been aroused an absolutely incredible

---

[1] There were eight American divisions in all training in France at the time: two with the French and six with the British.

[2] Mordacq ii., p. 50.

" fury against the Commander-in-Chief of the French
" Army."

NOTE

THE GERMANS ON THE 30TH MAY

It is claimed in Monograph I. (p. 196) that up to the evening of the 30th " more than 50,000 prisoners, about 800 guns and thousands " of machine guns had been captured ". Further, that " the main " object of the attack had been accomplished : that is the drawing " away of the French reserves stationed behind the British front ", whilst " favourable conditions for the decisive blow planned against " the British were developing ".[1] In spite, however, of the uninterrupted advance for four days and a victory beyond all expectation, " the general situation on the battle front was still unsatisfactory " for German O.H.L." ; the two wings were hanging back and until this disadvantage were remedied a reversion to trench warfare would be inconvenient and costly. " It was essential that from " day to day the front line should assume a form which would " permit a return to trench warfare at any moment." As on the west the French XXX. Corps was falling back, thus rounding off the shoulder of the salient on that side, it would be unnecessary to carry out the " Yorck " offensive (extending the original front to Noyon). On the other flank, however, at and west of Reims, hopes had not been fulfilled and the French resistance had increased. The failure of the *86th* and *232nd Divisions* is ascribed to their having come from the Russian front ; " in the case of the unsatisfactory " course of the battle in the *52nd, 103rd* and *7th Reserve Divisions* " [all of which, so it happens, had had to deal with the British IX. " Corps], the question presents itself whether the prime cause was " not a bad failure (*starkes Versagen*) on the part of the attacking " troops to do their duty ".

[1] Monograph II., p. 5.

CHAPTER IX

THE BATTLE OF THE AISNE (*concluded*)

31ST MAY–6TH JUNE

CESSATION OF THE PURSUIT

(Sketches B, 5, 6)

THE battle which had begun on the 27th May did not finally die down until the 6th June. But as the details of the later fighting present no feature of outstanding interest, the operations lasting from the 31st May to the 6th June may be described in general terms. The period, however, is marked by the continuous shifting towards the centre of both General Foch's General Reserve and the French reserves in the north, and the persistent efforts of General Pétain to secure control of the British reserves. The object of German O.H.L. now was to extend their holding on the Sketch 5. line of the Marne as far as Epernay on the east and Château Thierry on the west, so as to flatten out the awkward salient which unexpected success had created. The flanks of this line were to be secured by special operations designed on the east to reach the southern line of the Reims forts, and on the west, the line La Ferté Milon—Crépy en Valois (10 miles W.S.W. of Villers Cotterêts)—neighbourhood of Montdidier. Entrenched behind this barrier so strongly as to guard against any relieving attacks being made by the French, O.H.L. intended to throw all available forces against the British and drive them into the sea.[1] Although both General Foch and Sir Douglas Haig were of opinion that Crown Prince Rupprecht's Group of Armies was only waiting the opportunity to resume operations against the British, the French High Command was convinced that

[1] Monograph I., pp. 10, 47 ; Monograph II., p. 198 ; Ludendorff ii., pp. 615-6 ; Hindenburg, p. 371.

the German aims were directed against a geographical and political objective, Paris the capital of France. On the 31st May the information issued at G.Q.G. was : " The enemy's " effort has come to a stop on the Marne, but it continues " to be violent between the Marne and the Oise, being " more and more definitely directed towards Paris ".[1]

The counter-attacks to be carried out against the flanks of the German salient by General Pétain's orders on the 31st, failed to materialize except in a reduced form on the west. The operation on the east was not even attempted; the greater part of the three divisions (28th, 40th and 120th) intended to execute it had become involved in the fighting of the 30th, so that General Micheler (Fifth Army), seeing his forces thus reduced, did not consider a counter-attack held out any prospect of success unless the operation against the western flank should make marked progress. On that side, General Duchêne elaborated a plan for a counter-attack on its whole extent which embraced not only the I. Corps (4 divisions), as directed by G.Q.G., but the XXI. and XI. Corps, on its right, and the XXX. Corps, on the left. This was gradually, and of necessity, reduced by the continual fighting, so that ultimately only the 35th Divn (I. Corps) with some units of the Moroccan Division and light tanks advanced south of Soissons, between Chaudun and Vauxbuin, after a short artillery preparation. Just as the number of divisions had been reduced, so the hour previously fixed was changed, owing to various delays, from 9 A.M. to 11 A.M. and then to midday. Towards 6 P.M. the 51st Division joined in. A little ground was gained by the initial surprise and then lost as a result of enemy counter-attacks. General Pétain's plan of reinforcing the

---

[1] F.O.A. vi. (ii.), p. 201. The chapter heading is " Poussée allemande " vers Paris ", and the sub-heading, " Avance allemande en direction de " Paris ".

General Mordacq pointed out to M. Clemenceau that the German strategic objective was not yet clear ; the great battle seemed to be more than a feint. But, admitting, he said, that the objective were Paris, the occupation of the capital would not mean the end of the War : there might be a withdrawal of the front ; but with the French, British and Americans holding the command of the sea the struggle could still be continued under good conditions : the Germans had not the means to continue delivering heavy blows as they had done on 21st March, 9th April and 27th May, and after their last effort " they were not in a position to attempt a strategic " manœuvre which could bring about a decisive result ". M. Clemenceau " listened religiously ", and finally said : " Yes, the Germans may take " Paris, but that would not stop me from fighting. We will fight on the " Loire, then on the Garonne, if we must, even on the Pyrenees. If, at " last, we are chased from the Pyrenees, we will continue the war on the " sea ; but as to making peace, never." Mordacq ii., pp. 53-4.

LAST DAYS. 31ST MAY 145

flanks, however—the one small counter-attack, no doubt, contributing to this result—hindered the Germans from making any further progress worth mentioning on the wings of their attacks near Reims and Soissons. They extended their gains very slightly along the Marne, where the situation otherwise remained unchanged, and they reached Try and the eastern edge of Château Thierry. Between the Marne and the upper course of the Ourcq, that is between Château Thierry and La Ferté Milon, in the sectors of the French XXI. and XI. Corps, however, the enemy made a considerable advance.[1] But, on the whole, O.H.L. regarded the results of the day as " unsatis-" fying " : on the one hand as a result of the French counter-attack, and on the other on account of increased French artillery fire and the fatigue of the troops.

The British 19th Divn, now consisting of the 74th Bde Sketch 6. (with the remnants of the 8th, 25th and 50th Dns), the 57th Bde and the combined 56th/58th Bde (the 58th had only one battalion left), was heavily shelled in the morning and was attacked in the afternoon. But, in common with the French divisions on either side, although it suffered considerable casualties, it lost very little ground.

The 56th Bde was engaged in the severest fighting, part of it being driven off the high ground north of Chambrecy about 3.15 P.M. Lieut.-Colonel W. W. S. Cuninghame (2nd Life Guards), commanding the 9/Cheshire, taking the reserve company with him, rode forward under heavy fire, rallied the retiring troops and led a counter-attack, covered by overhead fire from four machine guns. His horse was shot, but he continued to lead the attack on foot, and the original position was regained. The enemy came on again in large numbers, and, after Colonel Cuninghame had been wounded, succeeded in driving back the 9/Cheshire slightly.

In the meanwhile the report of the loss of the high ground reached Major-General Jeffreys, who was at the headquarters of the 56th/58th Bde. Unaware, as yet, of Lieut.-Colonel Cuninghame's action, he gave orders for a

[1] During 30th May General de Bazelaire with the VII. Corps staff arrived, and was placed in command, taking over next day, of the 4th and 73rd Divisions, the latter just arrived, between the XXI. and XI. Corps. Later, General Robillot with the II. Cavalry Corps staff was given a sector between the VII. and XI., with the 2nd and the 26th Divisions, which came up during the day ; and General Piarron de Mondésir with the XXXVIII. Corps staff took over the front of the Groupement La Tour along the Marne, which contained the 20th Division, the newly arrived 10th Colonial Division and the 4th and 5th Cavalry Divisions.

L

counter-attack by the 2/Wiltshire, which was in reserve west of Bligny. This battalion went forward at 7.20 P.M. under considerable fire and reinforced the 9/Cheshire. The two battalions then made a series of small counter-attacks and succeeded in establishing a line on the plateau sufficiently far forward to prevent the enemy from obtaining observation over the Chambrecy valley. The casualties of the 9/Cheshire on this day were 14 officers and 169 other ranks. The 2/Wiltshire did not lose so many, but was reduced to 5 officers and 120 other ranks.

On the northern flank of the 56th Bde, about 3 P.M., the French 28th Division was driven out of Aubilly and from the high ground west of this village; but the position was regained by a counter-attack of the French and the 1/4th Shropshire L.I.

During the day, first the left half of the 74th Bde and then the right were relieved by the French 40th Division, and the brigade became the reserve of the 19th Divn. Although there was no serious loss of ground on this side, General Franchet d'Espérey was so impressed with the tired state of the troops and the lack of a reserve in the Fifth Army that at 10.30 A.M. he authorized General Micheler to evacuate Reims and thus shorten the front, so as to enable him to form a reserve. This authority was not acted on, and later the prospect of the arrival on the morrow of the 8th and 167th Divisions put a better aspect on affairs.

During the morning of the 31st Sir Douglas Haig visited General Foch at Sarcus, when the possibility of supporting the French with some British divisions was discussed. Sir Douglas Haig said that the French could always rely on the assistance of the British Army to the full extent of its power; but the amount of such help must depend on the situation on its own front. He agreed to investigate the possibility of forming a corps of three divisions as a reserve to support the French in case of grave emergency. As the Intelligence reports showed that not more than two divisions had been withdrawn from Crown Prince Rupprecht's reserve in the Ypres area, which still amounted to over thirty divisions,[1] the British Commander-in-Chief did not expect that he could possibly do more. He suggested shortening the line on some part of the French front which was still quiet before the enemy

[1] Monograph II., p. 151, says that by 3rd June five divisions had been taken from Rupprecht's reserve on the Hazebrouck front.

could take counter-measures to impede a retirement therefrom.

Sir Douglas Haig subsequently proceeded to Paris, where in the evening Mr. Lloyd George with Sir Eric Geddes (First Lord of the Admiralty) and Admiral Sir Rosslyn Wemyss (First Sea Lord) called on him and discussed the possible evacuation of Dunkirk until an air raid put an end to the proceedings.

General Foch in the course of the day visited General Duchêne's headquarters at Trilport (20 miles W.S.W. of Château Thierry), where M. Clemenceau and General Pétain had arrived for a conference. The situation now disclosed was clearer than it had been since the opening of the offensive and was no longer so alarming: each week brought more American reinforcements: time was working for the Allies: the enemy appeared to be tiring or at any rate at the end of this particular effort: he would now probably try elsewhere: there were indications that he was preparing an attack between Noyon—Montdidier. It would therefore be prudent, General Foch thought, to dole out reinforcements little by little. In view of the meeting of the Supreme War Council which was to take place next day at Versailles, he did not come to any decision as regards the demands for reinforcements addressed to him by General Pétain.

General Pétain subsequently drew up and sent to General Foch a written statement of his views, of which the following is an extract:

"Up to the 31st May (inclusive), 32 French and 5
" British divisions have been absorbed in the battle. Of
" these 37 divisions, 17 are completely worn out, 16 have
" been in the line from two to four days, and 4 have come
" in on the 31st. Between the 31st May and the 2nd
" June, 5 more divisions will arrive in the area of the
" battle. Between the 2nd and 10th June there will also
" be available 4 divisions of the Tenth Army, one division
" from Alsace (the only reserve there) and 3 other divisions,
" which will have to be relieved by worn-out troops which
" are hardly fit to hold the line. One Italian division will
" also be available. This makes a total of 14 fresh divisions
" available in the next ten days. It is impossible to take
" more divisions from other parts of the front. In the
" Group of Armies of the Reserve, which is seriously
" threatened with attack, each division holds an average
" front of five kilometres. In the quiet parts of the front

"each division holds thirteen kilometres, and there are no reserves. Besides the 14 divisions mentioned above, which will be used to feed the battle, it is absolutely necessary that I should have a mobile reserve without delay. The only means I can see of providing this is to send American reserves from the British zone to relieve French divisions in the trenches in the Vosges and Lorraine. Also British reserves should be sent to the Oise, and, if necessary, to the Marne. These measures are certainly outside my authority, but it is my duty to propose them to you so that you should have before you all the factors of the problem."

Whilst awaiting General Foch's reply, General Pétain determined to use his reserves with the utmost economy. Against the front of the Fifth Army he judged that the enemy's effort was at an end; so on the 1st June he informed General Franchet d'Espérey that he would send no more reinforcements to this Army. The Sixth Army and the right of the Third, he directed, should continue at all costs to hold the line on which they then stood, with the troops already in the line, reinforced only by the remaining troops of the divisions already partially engaged (26th and 73rd Divisions). Reserves not yet engaged (American 2nd and 3rd Divisions, 15th, 67th, 128th and 133rd Divisions, and the three divisions of the II. Cavalry Corps) were to be organized in positions in rear to form a barrier against an advance on Paris, and not to be sent forward without orders from the Commander-in-Chief.[1] The line of these rear positions was to run south-westward some sixteen miles along the Marne from Château Thierry to la Ferté sous Jouarre, thence a few miles north-westward to the Ourcq, then northward along that river, keeping west of Villers Cotterêts to Pimprez on the Oise, 5 miles south of Noyon.

But at the very moment that General Pétain was

---

[1] The American 2nd Division (Major-General O. Bundy) was near Chaumont and preparing to move north to relieve the American 1st Division. On the night of the 30th/31st it was put into lorries and carried to Meaux. On arrival it was marched towards Château Thierry, finding the roads crowded with refugees and retreating French troops. (Pershing Experiences, pp. 409-10.) It was placed in a second-line position astride the Paris road.

The American 3rd Division (Major-General J. T. Dickman), in training near Chaumont, entrained on the night of 30th/31st May, and on its arrival on 3rd June was used to reinforce the French along the Marne. Its machine-gun battalion, which went by road, was used for the defence of Château Thierry on the 3rd.

sending these instructions, some of the divisions which it was hoped to keep in second line were already engaged, the 128th in the XI. Corps sector and part of the 15th to maintain touch between the Sixth and Third Armies; others did not arrive on the ground for some days.

In reply to General Pétain's letter, General Foch transmitted to him a Note calculated to be soothing in its generalities. It said :—

(1) The line of conduct of the French High Command must be to check the march of the enemy on Paris at all costs, particularly by a route north of the Marne.

(2) The method to be adopted will be a foot-by-foot defence, to the last breath, of the territory in that area.

(3) To ensure that effect shall be given to such a line of action, it is most important to draft orders which will control the conduct of the troops in conformity with it; and to see that these orders are strictly carried out, removing any commander who shows signs of weakening.

(4) The Allied troops have been directed to act in a like manner, and will be engaged in the battle as transportation renders it possible.

The course of the operations on the 1st June was much the same as on the previous day: the Germans could make no progress on the wings; but by throwing in four fresh divisions (*28th Reserve, 47th Reserve, 197th*—a " position division "—and *237th*) in the centre, where there were gaps in the French line, Conta's and Winckler's corps gained two to five miles on a 20-mile front between Château Thierry (where a little more of the town was lost and the bridge was blown up by the French) and Vierzy (7 miles south of Soissons). This German effort, however, was obviously nearing its end; for the enemy was unable to broaden the base of the salient which he had created. On the west, against the front of the French XXX. Corps, where two German corps had been ordered to reach the Aisne and to secure passages over it, François's corps made little progress, and Larisch's corps, already up to the river as far as le Port, was unable to cross. Near Soissons the French I. Corps held its own against Wichura's corps, which " remained hung up ". Along the Marne, from Try to Château Thierry, there was no change, but the Germans began to get alarmed for their small isolated bridgehead at Jaulgonne. The attempt of the German *First Army*, with nine divisions, to break in on either side

Sketch 5.

of Reims, cut off the town and reach the southern fort line, was a complete failure, though there was desperate fighting at Fort de la Pompelle on the south-east side of Reims, where the Germans unsuccessfully used 15 tanks. As a result of counter-attacks by the French I. Colonial Corps, " the whole enterprise came to an end, nearly everything " that had been gained having to be given up again ".[1]

Sketch 6.   Between the Marne and Reims, where (left to right) the French 120th Division, with the 13th Divn and the 40th Division, under the staff of the I. Cavalry Corps (General Féraud), and the British 19th Divn and French 28th Divn, with the much dispersed 154th Divn, faced Schmettow's corps, severe fighting also took place ; but, except a small advance against the 28th Divn, no attack materialized until the afternoon.[2] Then, about 2.30 P.M., a fresh division, the *12th Bavarian*, advancing under an artillery barrage, attacked the French 40th Division, on the left of the British, and after hard fighting drove it back a little. The extreme right of the 40th at first held firm and kept in touch with the left of the 57th Bde, but later in the afternoon the left company of the 10/R. Warwickshire had to swing back to form a defensive flank.

About 4 P.M., whilst this action was in progress, the German *232nd Division* joined in and penetrated the British line at the junction of the 56th and 57th Bdes. Then, turning to the right, the enemy proceeded to roll up the line of the 8/Gloucestershire. The left company stood firm, but the three right companies were driven down a reverse slope. Captain E. B. Pope, 8/Gloucestershire, however, rallied the men in the valley and with great determination led a counter-attack up the hill and retook the position, inflicting heavy casualties on the enemy and capturing twenty prisoners. Commandant A. de Lasbourde, of the French II./22nd Regiment which was in reserve to the 57th Bde, on his own initiative, brought up his battalion and joined in the counter-attack, also for a

[1] Monograph II., p. 75.
[2] Monograph II. says that attacks had to be put off owing to shortage of artillery ammunition, caused partly by the blowing up of an ammunition dump by Allied airmen. The Allied artillery is said to have been definitely superior to that of the Germans in this part of the battlefield. Actually the field and heavy artillery covering the 19th Divn was the same as on the previous day : the 21st Dn artillery, and two batteries of the XLI. Brigade R.G.A. reduced to a total of eight guns, were with the French 28th Divn.

time taking over part of the line whilst the Gloucestershire reorganized.[1]

The situation in the centre of the 19th Divn had thus been restored, whilst the greater part of the 56th Bde had not been attacked at all; but the advance of the enemy on the front of the French 40th Division had completely turned the left of the 57th Bde, and had made it impossible that it could remain where it was. Accordingly, at 5.20 P.M., under instructions of the French V. Corps, Major-General Jeffreys gave orders for a short withdrawal of the division. The movement began about 7 P.M. and was completed by 11 P.M. with little interference from the enemy except in the case of the 2/Wiltshire, which came under artillery and machine-gun fire, and suffered about thirty casualties. On the right, the French 28th Divn had made a similar slight withdrawal, but the 45th had held its own. A gap on the left of the 19th Divn was closed by two platoons of the 25th Divn Composite Battalion, and touch with the French 40th Division thus regained. Against the 120th Division, on the left of the 40th, behind which the 13th Divn had been assembled, the enemy achieved no progress. The German verdict on the day's operations in this quarter is: " Schmettow's corps " had suffered defeat at Navarre Wood [in the 120th " Division sector] and in compensation had achieved a " small gain of ground with the *7th Reserve* [against the " 19th Divn] and a slightly greater one with the *12th* " *Bavarian* [against the 40th] ".

In view of the situation in the centre, General Duchêne decided to allot to the XXI. Corps the American 2nd Division (Major-General O. Bundy), which was beginning to occupy the second-line position on a 12-mile front astride the Paris—Château Thierry road; but he insisted that the infantry of this division should not be engaged without his previous authorization. Having ordered the French 2nd Division, in reserve of the I. Corps west of Soissons, to move south to the II. Cavalry Corps, he authorized General Robillot to employ his three cavalry divisions (2nd, 3rd and 6th), hitherto, by G.Q.G. instructions, held in reserve. General Pétain himself gave orders that the 167th Division (less a regiment), one of the only

[1] The counter-attack of the 8/Gloucestershire and French II./22nd Regiment appears to have caused the enemy some anxiety, as Monograph II., pp. 85-6, mentions that two battalions of the *12th Bavarian Division* were sent to the road leading northwards from Ville en Tardenois to stop any further Allied advance in that direction.

two divisions of the Fifth Army held in reserve, should be transferred to the Sixth : it was allotted to the XXXVIII. Corps and sent to the Luzancy area (11 miles south-west of Château Thierry) to defend the bridge over the Marne. The 133rd Division, coming from the G.A.E., began detraining at la Ferté sous Jouarre (17 miles south-west of Château Thierry), where it remained until the 8th, and the leading units of the 47th, from the General Reserve, reached Lizy sur Ourcq (18 miles west of Château Thierry) where the division remained until the 4th.[1]

General Pétain at this time imagined that " the area " la Ferté sous Jouarre—Lizy sur Ourcq would be athwart " the direction towards Paris which the Germans intended " to follow ". [2] He decided further to reduce the front for which General Duchêne was responsible by directing him to hand over his left wing, the XI., I. and XXX. Corps, to General Maistre and the staff of the Tenth Army, which had become available as a result of the break-up of General Foch's General Reserve. This change was to take effect at 8 A.M. on the 2nd June, when the new headquarters would open at Chantilly. At the same time, he transferred the Tenth Army from General Franchet d'Espérey's G.A.N. to General Fayolle's G.A.R.

As a preliminary to the meeting of the Supreme War Council which was to take place at 3 P.M. on the 1st June at Versailles, the Prime Minister, Mr. Lloyd George, summoned Sir Douglas Haig to a conference at 10.30 A.M. on that day. At this the Secretary of State for War (Lord Milner), Sir Henry Wilson (C.I.G.S.), and Lieut.-General Sir John Du Cane (head of the British Mission at General Foch's headquarters) were also present. On the previous evening the French Government had asked the Prime Minister's agreement to a scheme for sending all American troops training under the British to hold quiet sectors in the French area and thus relieve French divisions for battle. The British Commander-in-Chief was opposed to this idea, first because it would prevent the Americans from completing their training as divisions, and, secondly, because he had inferred from conversations with Generals Foch and Weygand that the French reserves which had

---

[1] The French situation map for this day shows all four divisions (11th, 47th, 48th and 153rd) of the General Reserve in the area between Château Thierry and Paris, and the 133rd moving there from the east.
[2] F.O.A. vi. (ii.), p. 225.

been put into the battle did not last long, but "melted "away like snow", and that this was due to absence of training and preparation after the unfortunate Nivelle operations, to deterioration in the quality of officers and N.C.O.'s, and to general weakening of discipline.[1] In view of the doubtful condition of many French divisions, he thought it a waste of good troops to relieve French by American divisions.

At 2.30 P.M. there was a Franco-British conference in M. Clemenceau's room, when Generals Foch, Weygand and Mordacq represented France, and the members of the previous conference, together with Lieut.-General Sir H. Lawrence (C.G.S.) and Colonel Sir Maurice Hankey, Great Britain. As regards the use of the American divisions, General Foch said that he and Sir Douglas Haig could easily settle the matter, so the question was not discussed. But for over two hours an argument went on, mainly between General Foch and Mr. Lloyd George, as to the state of the British reinforcements. The Generalissimo's point was that the British Government had been fully aware that, unless immediate energetic steps were taken to obtain reinforcements, by the autumn the British Army would be reduced by thirty divisions; yet "nothing had "been done". Mr. Lloyd George denied this strongly and insisted that he had made great efforts to obtain men before the battle of the 21st March began. General Foch then handed in a written statement [2] in which it was pointed out that of the nine British divisions withdrawn from the battle only one had so far been reconstituted, and that now G.H.Q. proposed to reduce two more (of the IX. Corps), whilst the American increase would hardly compensate for the British decrease. His paper went on to show the efforts which France was making to keep up the full number of her divisions. Finally he asked the direct question: "What number of divisions will the British "Government maintain?" Sir Douglas Haig reminded Lord Milner that the War Office had informed him the number would be only twenty-eight. The Secretary of State for War was now of the opinion that this estimate was pessimistic. So it was agreed that General Foch should send an expert to examine the British Man-Power figures. With this M. Clemenceau was for the time satisfied.

[1] A French regimental officer told the compiler about the same time that during the winter the troops had had too much leave and "repos" and no training. [2] Appendix VIII.

The Supreme War Council met at 4.45 P.M., but the only question discussed was the appointment of a Supreme Commander to control all the Allied fleets in the Mediterranean. To this the Italian naval representative objected, as it might mean that powerful Italian ships would be asked to leave the Adriatic. When it was suggested to him that his objections were of a secondary order, he replied, that exposure to the risk of being sunk was not a secondary consideration.[1] A private meeting of the heads of the Governments, for which the meeting adjourned, brought a settlement of the question no nearer.

At the second meeting of the Council on the 2nd June, when, according to General Pershing, " the whole dis- " cussion was very erratic ",[2] a resolution was eventually passed recommending to the United States Government the arrangement made between General Foch, General Pershing and Lord Milner during the previous afternoon, in extension of the programme which had been settled on the 24th April [3] for the despatch of American troops during the month of May. In cabling the resolution to his Government, General Pershing added that " the attitude " of the Supreme War Council, which had been in session " since Saturday [1st June] is one of depression ", and that he considered the situation " very grave ".[4]

The new arrangement assumed that 250,000 men could be transported in each of the months of June and July by the employment of the combined British and American tonnage. The recommendations were :

(*a*) For the month of June :

1st, Absolute priority should be given to the transportation of 170,000 combatant troops (viz. : six divisions less artillery, ammunition trains or supply trains, amounting to 126,000 men and 44,000 replacements for combatant troops) ;

2nd, 25,400 men for the service of the railways, of whom 13,400 had been asked for by the French Minister of Transport ;

3rd, the remainder to be troops of categories to be determined by the Commander-in-Chief, American Expeditionary Forces.

(*b*) For the month of July :

1st, Absolute priority for the shipment of 140,000 com-

---

[1] Procès Verbal of the Supreme War Council, 1st June 1918, p. 7.
[2] Pershing Experiences, p. 421. [3] See " 1918 " Vol. II., p. 445.
[4] Pershing Experiences, p. 426.

batant troops of the nature defined for June (4 divisions, less artillery, etc., amounting to 84,000 men and 56,000 replacements);

2nd, the balance of the monthly contingent to consist of troops to be designated by the Commander-in-Chief, American Expeditionary Forces.

(c) If the available tonnage in either month allowed of the transportation of a number of men larger than 250,000, the excess tonnage was to be employed to carry combatant troops as above defined.

The statement added it was recognized that the troops despatched in July might include some with insufficient training—May recruits in fact; but the present emergency seemed to justify a temporary and exceptional departure by the U.S.A. from sound principles of training, especially as a similar course was being followed by France and Great Britain.[1]

As the signs of impending enemy attack between Noyon and Montdidier (" Gneisenau ") continued to increase, General Foch requested on the 2nd that, in accordance with arrangements made on the 29th May for reciprocal air assistance, five fighter squadrons and three day-bomber squadrons, together with the headquarters IX. Brigade R.A.F. might be moved into the Beauvais area for employment in the direction of St. Quentin and Laon, in order to ensure air superiority.[2]

The operations on the Aisne battlefield during the 2nd June and following days showed distinct signs that the struggle was coming to an end owing to the exhaustion of the troops. They can best be described as local affairs which did not affect the situation.[3] The only fighting of any importance was in the area of the French XI. and I. Corps. There on an eleven-mile front, between Corcy (5 miles east of Villers Cotterêts) and the Aisne, Larisch's

---

[1] The other subjects dealt with by the Supreme War Council did not affect the situation on the Western Front. They were the pooling of military supplies (see Chapter II.); the situation in Russia and the employment of a small Allied force in the Murmansk and Archangel areas; the Czech and Polish questions; and the transport to France via Vladivostock of the Czecho-Slovak troops in Siberia.

[2] " The War in the Air ", Vol. VI., p. 401.

[3] On 6th June the American 2nd Division (stationed since 2nd June in the front line in the Château Thierry area so as to block the Meaux road to Paris) captured Bouresches and occupied the southern portion of Belleau Wood. On the 5th, the American 3rd Division went into the line a little farther west.

and Wichura's corps on the 2nd and 3rd June, reinforced by five fresh divisions (*34th, 45th Reserve, 47th Reserve, 115th* and *11th Bavarian*),[1] first on the left and then on the right, advanced two or three miles without achieving their object. The success gained by Winckler's and Conta's corps on the 1st when pushing forward between the Marne and Ourcq, and that achieved earlier by Larisch's corps near Soissons, whilst François's corps, north of the Aisne, was held up, had only made the German situation more difficult than before. To improve matters and to assist François's corps, Larisch and Wichura had, therefore, been ordered to thrust north-west on the 2nd; but the ground thus gained was "without real importance for the " general situation between Marne and Oise . . . and scarcely " brought the right wing nearer its objective ".[2]

On the 3rd, as an offset to the German success, the French overwhelmed the German bridgehead at Jaulgonne, captured a hundred prisoners and cleared the enemy from the southern bank of the Marne.

French airmen noticed on the 2nd and 3rd that few German troops were to be seen in the rear areas. Only one division, the *10th Bavarian*, was, in fact, left in the reserve of the *Seventh Army*, and seven of its divisions, of Larisch's, Wichura's and Winckler's corps, required relief. Yet the fighting had to be continued, " for to break it off " would not only end the pressure on the enemy which " might compel him to bring new reserves to the Aisne " front, but also would restore to the enemy High Command " the freedom to regroup its reserves as it wished. . . . " All now depended on the forthcoming Gneisenau offensive " and how this would affect the right wing of the *Seventh* " *Army*. . . . Already five divisions had been taken from " the reserve intended for Hagen, the decisive blow in " Flanders." In an instruction of the 3rd June despatched to Crown Prince Rupprecht's Group of Armies, O.H.L. also had to admit : " The employment, which has become " necessary, of several divisions of the German Crown " Prince's Group intended for Hagen, and the withdrawal " of transport columns will probably make necessary a " postponement of Hagen for several weeks."

---

[1] The first three had been in the March offensive, the *11th Bavarian* in the Kemmel attack in April, whilst the *115th* came from Rumania. Monograph II., p. 107, remarks that " the fresh divisions thrown into the " fight had a painful experience, the conditions being very different from " those prevailing at the beginning of the battle ".

[2] Monograph II., pp. 126 and 150.

LAST DAYS. 2ND–6TH JUNE

As a reply to the German tactical successes against the XI. and I. Corps, General Maistre (Tenth Army) ordered the I. Corps to mount a counter-attack. But, as this corps had no fresh reserves and had suffered severe losses in the course of the 2nd, it was unable to comply. As a result, the 87th Division (from the Third Army) was allotted to the Tenth Army for the I. Corps by General Fayolle (G.A.R.),[1] who requested and obtained from General Pétain permission to replace it in his second line by the 153rd Division (Tenth Army) which belonged to the General Reserve. The 67th Division[2] by his orders had also been drawn eastward from the Third Army, so that only three divisions (18th, 152nd and 165th) were left in reserve on the front between Noyon and the Somme. As this small number was wholly insufficient in view of the threatening enemy offensive, General Fayolle suggested that the British should prolong their front by two divisions from the Allied junction near Villers Bretonneux. General Pétain, however, did not forward the suggestion, as he was counting on receiving the three British divisions which General Foch had requested Sir Douglas Haig to hold in readiness for emergency, and the three divisions (69th, 123rd, 126th) of the French XV. Corps on the Lorraine front, which were to be relieved by American divisions from the British area.

During the 4th, 5th and 6th June the battle came to an end. On the 4th the German *Seventh Army* ordered the attack to be continued by Larisch's and Wichura's corps, whilst the others concentrated forces at favourable places; but the results were " quite insignificant. . . . It " was high time to stop the attack on the whole front of " the *Seventh Army*." At the suggestion of O.H.L., General von Boehn made the decision to desist from any further important offensive action, but to resume operations on the 8th or 9th with a thrust, limited in breadth of front and depth of penetration. The preliminaries of this were ordered to be set in hand on the 5th. Sketch 5.

From the 2nd to the 5th June the British 19th Divn, except for occasional shelling and bombing, had been left in comparative peace. The consolidation of the position, Sketch 6.

---

[1] The Tenth Army staff had passed to him from the General Reserve on 1st June, and had taken over XI., XX. (staff and corps troops only) I. and XXX. Corps from the Sixth Army.

[2] Officially it passed to the Tenth Army on 3rd June, but did not reach it until the 6th.

CHEMIN DES DAMES

which consisted of short lengths of trench and shell-holes, was proceeded with, and a reserve line was dug on which to fall back in case of emergency. The composite battalions formed by the 8th and 25th Dns, and the composite brigade, 1,200 strong, of the 50th Dn, under Br.-General F. J. Marshall, were held in support, whilst the composite brigade of the 21st Divn, under Br.-General G. H. Gater, was lent to the French to assist in holding the line of the Marne near Dormans. The few days' rest had exercised a wonderful effect, so that the troops were full of fight on the morning of the 6th June, when the Germans launched a local attack on the front of the 19th Divn and the French 28th Divn, its right neighbour, but particularly against the Montagne de Bligny (a mile west of Bligny), on the British right. This hill, although small, was the highest point in the neighbourhood, and offered good observation and command; its summit was bare, but its lower slopes were covered with high standing corn which gave cover from view to the attackers.

The attack was not unexpected, as there had been premonitory signs of it on the 5th, and counter-preparation was carried out from 2 to 3 A.M. on the 6th, at the close of which the Germans opened a bombardment, with much gas shelling of reserve and battery positions. The troops in the line from right to left were the remnants of the 8/North Staffordshire and 9/Cheshire of the 56th Bde, 58th Bde organized as a composite battalion (460 strong), 8/Gloucestershire, 10/Worcestershire and 10/R. Warwickshire of the 57th Bde, and the 8th Dn Composite Battalion, with the 1/4th Shropshire L.I. (56th Bde), 1/6th Cheshire (temporarily under 74th Bde), 5/South Wales Borderers (Pioneers of the 19th Divn), 50th Dn Composite Brigade and 25th Dn Composite Battalion in support. After about an hour's shelling the German *86th* and *232nd Divisions* advanced, covered by machine-gun fire from the flanks. They captured Bligny from the French and the Montagne de Bligny from the 9/Cheshire, and immediate counter-attacks made with great boldness over the open failed to dislodge them. The retention of the hill was so important, as the British front line could be enfiladed and the artillery positions observed from it, that when, about 11 A.M., news of its loss reached Br.-General Heath, he gave orders for a counter-attack by the 1/4th Shropshire L.I., then in brigade support. Only two hundred strong and under the command of a subaltern, it had a mile of open country to cross under artillery fire in order to reach the front line, from which the counter-attack was launched about 1 P.M. with some of the 8/North Staffordshire on the right, the 9/Cheshire in the centre and the Shropshire on the left. The greater part of the old position was quickly retaken, with about forty prisoners; though a small copse on the left was obstinately defended and cost many casualties until it was evacuated by the enemy after dark. The French 28th Divn front line was also restored by a counter-attack of troops of the 154th Divn, brought up from the reserve, and Bligny was retaken about 7 P.M.[1]

The 19th Divn, reinforced by the composite brigades and battalions of the 8th, 25th and 50th Dns, continued to hold the same sector, under the orders of General Pellé, as French G.Q.G. were unwilling to release them. No further operations were conducted by either side, and at the end of ten days, during the nights of the 17th/18th and 18th/19th June, the British contingent was relieved by the Italian 8th Division, from the reserve of the French Fourth Army. As far as it was concerned, the Battle of the Aisne 1918 had come to an end on the 6th June. The British troops in the area were gradually transferred back to the British area, after some attempts, as will be seen, on the part of the French to retain them longer. Those belonging to the 8th and 21st Dns had left on the 13th and 15th June, respectively; the 50th Dn entrained on the 29th; and the 19th Divn, on the 30th. A number of the survivors of the 25th Dn were used as reinforcements for other divisions whilst the remainder returned to England at the end of June to form a nucleus for the reconstitution of the division.[2]

---

[1] For the successful counter-attack, the 56th Bde was mentioned in French V. Corps orders, and the 1/4th King's Shropshire L.I. in French Fifth Army orders. Both received the "Croix de guerre".

[2] The following were the British casualties between 27th May and 19th June:

IX. Corps:	Officers	Other Ranks
Corps Troops	26	448
8th Division	366	7,496
19th Division	151	3,460
21st ,,	202	4,624
25th ,,	201	4,137
50th ,,	352	7,240
	1,298	27,405

Monograph II. gives the casualties from 27th May to 13th June as follow:

Lieut.-General Gordon's corps headquarters remained until the 28th, and then left for the Fourth Army.

Before the Aisne fighting came to an end, on the morning of the 3rd June, Sir Douglas Haig received from General Foch a letter stating that, with General Pershing's approval, he proposed to move some of the American divisions then training in the British area to relieve French divisions; he further asked that an officer might be sent at 5 P.M. that day to American headquarters at Provins to discuss the arrangements for the details of the transfer. The British Commander-in-Chief of course complied, saying that the divisions were at General Pershing's disposal, so in the course of a few days all five American divisions were transferred, leaving behind the British cadres which had been assisting to train them.[1]

	Officers	Other Ranks
German	4,581	125,789
Allied	5,046	167,373 *

* Including 60,000 prisoners; the Germans claim to have captured 850 guns; 15,000 prisoners were taken between 7th and 15th June.

F.O.A. gives the following casualties 27th May to 6th June:

	Officers	Other Ranks
French	2,424	95,736
American	16	458
	2,440	96,194
and for the 9th to 15th June (Battle of the Matz, Third Army only)	1,051	34,415
British casualties to 19th June were	1,298	27,405
Total Allied Casualties	4,789	158,014

Thus the totals for the Allied losses nearly agree. Assuming that the figures for German losses do not include wounded "likely to recover "within a reasonable time" about 30 per cent. should be added (see Preface to "1916" Vol. II., p. x), bringing the enemy totals to 5,955 and 163,525. So, as often happened, the losses on both sides seem to have been about equal. French calculations, however, put the German casualties for May at 240,000 in the battle and 80,000 elsewhere, and 147,000 on the fighting fronts for June (Paquet, pp. 86-99).

The German Monograph remarks that, though the German losses were less than those of the enemy, Germany, unlike the Allies, was unable to replace the men who had fallen.

[1] The 77th entrained on the 6th for the Baccarat area; the 35th, between the 6th and 8th for the Epinal area; the 4th and 28th, on the 9th to the Meaux area and Gonesse, north-east of Paris, where they continued training under the French; and the 82nd on the 15th, to Lorraine to continue training. (American Order of Battle.)

The 27th Division, which arrived in France between 7th May and 12th July, and the 30th Division, which reached England between 14th May

Early on the following day, the 4th June, General Foch telegraphed to Sir Douglas Haig:

"(1) The development of the battle towards Paris "may take the greater part of the French forces in that "direction, and thus in a dangerous fashion deplete the "rear areas of the French front from Montdidier to the "Somme; it may also call the Allied forces to the great "battle.

"(2) In these circumstances, I request that you will "kindly set three divisions of your general reserve on the "march, by road, without delay, with a view to establishing "them astride the Somme west of Amiens, where they "can act either to the profit of the British or to the profit "of the French Army."

Later, Lieut.-General Du Cane brought a letter confirming the telegram, in which it was stated that it was as yet impossible to determine whether the enemy would pursue his offensive between the Marne and the Oise, towards Paris, or might transfer his attention to some other part of the Allied front: it was therefore with a view to being ready for either eventuality that General Foch had asked that the three divisions of the British general reserve should be moved astride the Somme. But, the letter continued, this measure was only designed to meet the urgent demands of the moment: if the enemy developed an offensive between Château Thierry and Montdidier—as he did—there could be no question but that all the Allied forces in France should take part in the battle, which might very likely decide the fate of the War. General Foch accordingly asked Sir Douglas Haig to prepare in detail:

(1) A plan for the transport, in accordance with the above hypothesis, of all his available resources, general reserve and local reserves; and

(2) a reduction in density of the occupation of the British front. "This reduction, which should be effected "on the part of the front not attacked will permit of the "gradual organization of further reserves, and their "augmentation in case of need."

---

and 24th June, and thence went to France, were sent to the British area, where they remained as the II. Corps (Major-General G. W. Read). The 33rd Division (disembarked between 18th May and 16th June) was in the British area from 25th May to 23rd August; the 37th (from the French area) from 26th October to the end; the 78th (disembarked 18th May–12th June) from 4th June to 20th August; and the 91st from 29th October to 4th November.

162 BOMBING OF BACK AREAS

Sketch B.

Except for night bombing, raids and counter-raids, and a succession of incidents of a minor character, usually terminating in favour of the British, during the Aisne battle the Flanders front had been quiet,[1] although, in addition to the patent enemy preparations for attack against the sectors north of the La Bassée canal, there were now symptoms of an intended offensive near Hulluch and Loos, south of the canal. The enemy night bombing, however, was a source of some anxiety, since the narrow area in which the British were now penned, was crowded with headquarters, hospitals, stores and all the establishments of the Army, so that in spite of anti-aircraft guns and searchlights which caused the raiders to keep high and often to lose their way, the enemy in the end could hardly fail to hit some target of value. But, although he thrice dropped bombs on G.H.Q., Montreuil, damaged the ordnance depôts at Blargies (28 miles south-west of Amiens) and Saigneville (on the Somme below Abbeville), and in a succession of raids, as mentioned earlier, killed 182 and wounded 643 in the hospitals at Etaples, it was at the railway communications that he principally aimed. Early in May traffic on the lateral line St. Just en Chaussée (26 miles south of Amiens)—Amiens—Hazebrouck, had to be abandoned on account of shell fire, and there remained open only the Abbeville—Boulogne line, with a great number of river bridges, amongst them the three-quarter-mile masonry viaduct across the estuary of the Canche at Etaples. Alternative temporary bridges with deviations were made, and other precautions taken: at Etaples a timber bridge was built about a mile upstream of the permanent structure, where the river is only about sixty feet wide. After many enemy attempts against the Etaples viaduct, in the course of which hospitals and other military establishments were damaged, on the night of the 30th/31st May, in the midst of the movement of two French divisions from Flanders to the Chemin des Dames area, a hit was obtained on the western shore end, and one arch collapsed. Within four hours the troop trains were running over the deviation bridge, which was made temporarily usable, and in 23 hours the permanent bridge had been sufficiently repaired for traffic to be resumed.

For its part, during the month of May alone the Royal Air Force dropped 657 tons of bombs on the German back areas,[2]

---
[1] See Chapter XI.
[2] Some details up to 26th May were given on p. 11.

going as far afield as the railway stations at Thionville, Metz and Coblenz, whilst on the 31st May a munition factory at Karlsruhe was blown up. On fine nights as much as 36 tons might be dropped, the highest 24-hour total being 57 tons. On the 6th June, the Independent Air Force, under the command of Major-General Sir H. M. Trenchard, came officially into existence, in the Nancy area, for the purpose of bombing German industrial centres.[1]

Meanwhile Sir Douglas Haig, notwithstanding the difficulties of the situation, had complied with the Generalissimo's request as regards placing three divisions astride the Somme south-west of Amiens; he detailed for the purpose the XXII. Corps (Lieut.-General Sir A. Godley) with the 12th, 37th and 58th Divisions, No. 17 Armoured Car Tank Battalion and some artillery units from G.H.Q. reserve. He further offered to set free the whole of the D.A.N. (the French force under General de Mitry attached to the British Second Army) if General Foch would agree to the five American divisions remaining with him. But he informed the Cabinet of the Generalissimo's request, and on the 4th June made a formal protest in writing to him against the removal—which might prove disastrous—of any portion of the British Army from his command " until it is beyond doubt that most of the reserves available " for Crown Prince Rupprecht's Group of Armies have " been absorbed in the battle ". He pointed out that his reserves were already inadequate, that the enemy's preparations were well advanced, that an attack could be launched at short notice, and that he could not afford to yield any more ground on the front between the Somme and the Lys. He concluded by asking for the return from the Aisne, to an area west of Amiens, of the IX. Corps and the 19th Divn, so that they might be reconstituted. Lieut.-General Gordon's force had lost nearly 30,000 men whilst with the French.

It had come to the Commander-in-Chief's notice that General Foch was withdrawing divisions from the D.A.N. without any warning being vouchsafed to British G.H.Q.[2] At a conference at Second Army headquarters, however, General Plumer declared that he was satisfied that if the D.A.N. were reduced to seven divisions he could still hold

---

[1] See " The War in the Air ", Vol. VI., p. 135 *et seq.*
[2] F.O.A. x. (i.) shows that on 2nd June the D.A.N. numbered 9 divisions; on 7th June, 6 only.

his front and cause the enemy heavy losses if attacked: he was opposed to falling back, in view of the value of Dunkirk as a port for supplies, but he would make all the preliminary arrangements to that end.

General Pétain, on the 4th, sent the Generalissimo a statement,[1] showing that his means did not suffice for a great battle : 5 British divisions (used up), 2 American (just beginning to come into action), 36 French, and 2 French cavalry corps had been engaged since the 27th May : in immediate reserve to the G.A.N. and G.A.R. were 5 and 2 fresh divisions, respectively : behind them were " a certain " number of divisions which had been fighting since the " 27th May, very worn and incapable of further effort " without rest and reconstitution " : these, with the American divisions from the British area, could relieve six good French divisions, but this would take fifteen to twenty days : until then the only reinforcements in sight were 3 French divisions which had long been in a quiet sector, arriving between the 6th and 8th, and 2 from the D.A.N., expected between the 5th and 8th. He therefore made the proposal—more drastic even than General Foch's, as to the disposal of the forces of his Ally—that the British front from the Somme to Dunkirk should be thinned to the utmost, leaving " éléments légers restant " en façade " : under enemy pressure these weak forces should fall back successively on the lines St. Omer—Calais, the river Canche, and the river Authie : with the troops thus economized and those already in reserve, he suggested forming two Allied masses, north and south, one near Beauvais, the other near Epernay : and " with " these two masses to feed the front to cover Paris as " economically as possible, and counter-attack the flanks " of the enemy advance ".

At 9.40 A.M. on the 4th, G.Q.G. by telephone informed General Foch that unmistakable signs of immediate attack were perceptible on the front of the G.A.R., whose left, in the Amiens area, seemed to be insufficiently supported ; it was therefore desired to know when the British divisions whose assistance in such an event had been requested would be set on the move. In reply, General Pétain was told that Sir Douglas Haig had already been asked to send three divisions at once to the Somme and had been further warned to be prepared for a more extended use on the French front of the British reserves.

[1] F.O.A. vi. (ii.), pp. 235-7.

In the evening General Foch wrote to Sir Douglas Haig asking him to hasten the movements of his three divisions, and without delay to complete the preparations for which he had already been pressed, as "the sum of the informa-" tion obtained from prisoners, identifications, agents and air " reconnaissances confirm the probability of an immediate " attack extending from Noyon to Montdidier ".

In reply to Sir Douglas Haig's protest General Foch declined to rescind the instructions given for the withdrawal of the five American divisions from the British zone; but he stated that the British IX. Corps was being assembled in the Vertus area (9 miles south-east of Epernay), and that it would subsequently be sent to the region of Troyes—Méry sur Seine (50 miles south of Epernay), where it should be reconstituted as soon as possible. He asked to be informed of the date when this process would be completed.

The instructions given by G.H.Q. to the XXII. Corps were to the effect that its task was to reinforce the junction of the French and British Armies, and that it must be prepared to move either south to the assistance of the G.A.R., or northwards towards the front of the British Fourth and Third Armies. One of its divisions, the 37th, with corps headquarters, lay to the south of the Somme near Picquigny (8 miles north-west of Amiens), so that to reach the French it would have a march of about eighteen miles to make; the other two divisions were to be echeloned forward north of the river and would have a rather less distance to go.

Sir Douglas Haig informed General Foch by letter on the 5th that he was studying the organization and movement of further forces to the south. Next day he sent him maps showing the movements for the concentration of the XXII. Corps south of the Somme, and for the assembly behind it of the XIX. Corps (Lieut.-General Sir H. Watts), formed of the 38th, 41st and 74th Divisions. He also told him that, in addition to this, the Canadian Corps (Lieut.-General Sir A. Currie) of three divisions (1st, 3rd and 4th), then resting between Béthune and St. Pol, would eventually be available as a reinforcement.[1]

The strength of the British Armies in France at this time, neglecting the 5 divisions which were with the French in the Chemin des Dames area, was 33 divisions in the line, holding on the average over three miles apiece,

[1] The 2nd Canadian Division was in the line.

8 in Army reserve and 7 in G.H.Q. reserve; total, 48, plus 8 cadre divisions. These with the assistance of the French divisions of the D.A.N. and 12 Belgian divisions,[1] faced Crown Prince Rupprecht's Army Group of 100 divisions,[2] and 7 divisions on the right of the line of the German Crown Prince's Group of Armies. Except the 52nd (Lowland) and the 74th (Yeomanry) Divisions, which reached France from Egypt during April and May, two Canadian divisions, one Australian, and two British (11th and 57th), all these divisions had been engaged in one, if not both, of the previous offensives, and were still below establishment, although refreshed by the rest during May.[3] To take away nine divisions to act as reserves to the French would leave Sir Douglas Haig with only six in Army and G.H.Q. reserve. On the 7th, signs of an attack on the Vimy sector were reported, so that, with a view to the future, Sir Douglas Haig thought it necessary personally to inspect a number of rear lines, on which work was proceeding with every man who could be spared from the Armies.

During the day General Foch urged Sir Douglas Haig, in the general interest, to make preparations to carry out a number of minor actions north of the Somme, with tanks, in order to retain enemy forces. " These actions ", he said, " might aim at definite results, such as the reduction " of the loop east of the Forest of Nieppe, . . . or might " be coups de main of marked importance with useful " consequences ". In obedience to this wish, G.H.Q., on the 8th, directed the Armies, in order to assist the French by retaining enemy forces on the British front, to submit at an early date proposals for offensive action of a nature limited to two or three raids or minor operations, involving no more than a few battalions and a limited number of tanks. On the other hand, the XIX. Corps was warned to be ready to move at nine hours' notice.

In view of his responsibility for the British Armies in France, the Commander-in-Chief had communicated Foch's various demands to the War Office. As a result the Prime Minister requested M. Clemenceau, who was Minister of War as well as President of the Council, to discuss the

---

[1] Counting a " division d'armée " as two.
[2] Of these, 63 were fit and ready for action (including 27 in reserve); 15 unfit; and 22 would be fit for action shortly.
[3] There were in Italy, 3 divisions; in Macedonia, 4; in Palestine, 5; in Mesopotamia, 1; in India, 3 (skeleton); in the United Kingdom, 4 and a cyclist division.

DEBATE ABOUT RESERVES. 7TH JUNE

situation with the British Secretary of State for War. Lord Milner reached Paris on the afternoon of the 7th June, accompanied by Sir Henry Wilson, and was there joined by Sir Douglas Haig, Lieut.-Generals Sir H. Lawrence and Sir J. Du Cane. At a meeting at the Ministry of War, Lord Milner explained to M. Clemenceau, who was accompanied by Generals Foch and Weygand, that his Government, in view of the large number of enemy reserves still available for action against the British, had become genuinely concerned about the removal of reserves (French and American divisions) from behind the British front. Sir Douglas Haig then read a paper wherein he stated that, owing to the withdrawal of reserves from behind the British front and the demands now being made that the British Army should be ready to support French troops engaged in the battle south of the Somme, it seemed possible that a situation might arise in which, if he complied with orders to send his reserves south of the Somme, he would endanger the safety of his Armies: in such a case, he would have to appeal to his Government in accordance with the Beauvais agreement: and this he wished to avoid. He then reviewed the situation, recalled the Memorandum of the First Sea Lord, Admiral Sir Rosslyn Wemyss (of the 20th April, which had been communicated to General Foch), in which it was shown " how disastrous " from a naval point of view would be the abandonment " of the Northern French ports ". He concluded his review with the words : " Up to date, I have done every-" thing to meet General Foch's wishes, and I have never " once challenged a single one of his decisions. . . . It is " my firm resolve to do all I can to assist General Foch " *short* of imperilling the British Army ".

In accordance with the normal dictates of strategy, General Foch had reason on his side in reducing the number of troops north of the Somme, and contemplating their withdrawal under pressure, not hastily, but after a step-by-step defence, in a series of rear-guard actions, which would not require reserves ; their position was obviously weak, with the sea at their backs and their front parallel to their main communications by rail through Abbeville ; to shorten the line by retiring behind the Somme would free divisions to add to the reserves. On the other hand the cogency of these arguments was gravely impaired by the special reasons for maintaining a hold on some Belgian territory, the importance of the Channel ports, and the immense amount of material accumulated north of the river.

General Foch, in reply to Sir Douglas Haig's statement, said that, whilst assenting to the last words which had just been read, he could not possibly agree to discuss any order which he might issue as to withdrawing troops from the British front : he was Generalissimo, and his orders and judgment must be accepted as final. In this view, M. Clemenceau and Lord Milner concurred. He agreed, however, that all orders for withdrawal of troops from the British area should go through Sir Douglas Haig, and he expressed his regret that this had not been done in the case of the D.A.N. : he promised that the five United States divisions now with the British Army should remain there until at least their training was completed.[1] General Foch then asked about the state of British man-power and how soon the cadre divisions would be reconstituted,[2] to which the Chief of the Imperial General Staff replied that about 70,000 men would arrive in France shortly ; but he admitted that 60,000 of them were of the " B " category. The Commander-in-Chief explained that he proposed to organize the reinforcements into brigades of six battalions, in which they would be sorted and trained : all men who during training were found sufficiently fit would be drafted to cadre divisions and used in the field.

In order that there might be no misunderstanding, Sir Douglas Haig in a letter of 10th June reported his scheme for the reconstitution, with " B " class men, of six of his eight cadre divisions and two of the IX. Corps. The remaining three divisions of the IX. Corps he could provide with " A " class men. In detail :—

(1) The 8th and 21st Dns from IX. Corps were to be withdrawn at once to an area west of Amiens and reconstituted with " A " men ; but it would be six weeks before they would be fit to go into the line.

---

[1] Two had already left (see p. 160, f.n. 1), and two more followed two days after General Foch had thus spoken. They were soon replaced and it was arranged that five American divisions should be trained in the British area, but that other new American formations which disembarked in June should be re-assembled and trained in French areas. (F.O.A. vi. (ii.), p. 259). On the 18th June the 27th, 30th, 33rd, 78th and 80th were with the British. At the end of August when the Germans were retreating, they were reduced to two, the 27th and 30th, and so remained.

[2] He had previously, in May, suggested in conversation that the infantry of existing divisions might be reduced to 8,000 so as to provide trained men to refill the cadre divisions, and that the number of men retained for defence in England might be reduced, " as the British Isles " are defended on the battlefields of France ".

(2) The 30th and 34th Dns were being reconstituted with battalions from Palestine; as soon as they were ready, they would be sent to the IX. Corps in the French area in order to release the 19th, 25th and 50th Divns.

(3) The 19th would be brought back to the British area and reconstituted with " A " men. Either the 25th or the 50th would be reconstituted with men from Salonika, the other being sent to England, under War Office instructions, to be filled up and reconstituted with " B " men.

(The 50th returned to the British zone between 3rd and 5th July, and was re-formed in the Dieppe area by the 14th July).

(4) The 40th and 59th had already been reconstituted with "B " men; they would require a fortnight for training, and could then go to a quiet part of the front; but they had no artillery and no machine-gun battalions.

(5) The 39th and 66th would remain as cadres for training the five American divisions which would be in the British zone.

(6) The 14th was at present filled with Portuguese and it was proposed to improvise a divisional headquarters for it: the cadres of the 14th and 16th would then be sent to England, under War Office instructions, to be reconstituted there with " B " men.

General Foch expressed himself as greatly pleased by this letter, as it showed a firm will to reconstitute ten divisions as soon as possible, and said that he was hastening the return of the 8th and 21st Dns. He hoped, however, that the inclusion of " B " men was only provisional, and that they would gradually be replaced by men of the " A " class, and he suggested that an allotment of artillery and machine guns larger than the normal should be made to the divisions filled up with " B " men, as " without this " armament, these divisions will not be able to hold even " a quiet front except with the assistance of other forma- " tions, and the object, which is to free these formations " for the battle, will not be achieved ". The " B " class men, however, were found, after a time, to be able to march and fight sufficiently well.

In view of the altered conditions and the now accepted fact that General Foch could dispose of the British contingent in France, Sir Douglas Haig formally asked Lord Milner to modify in writing his responsibility for the safety of the British Armies as contained in his letter of instructions when he took up command. But the Secretary of State for War did not do so until the 21st June, after several reminders; even then the new letter of instructions left matters much as they stood : the Commander-in-Chief could appeal to H.M. Government if the Generalissimo's orders appeared to him to imperil the British Army.[1] Lord Milner seemed to be more concerned about the evacuation of stores if the British Armies had to retire across the Somme ; and on the 13th he sent over high officials to examine the depôts and the plans for removing material.

The feeling at G.H.Q. aroused by General Foch's attitude was somewhat modified when he transmitted to them a copy of a letter, dated the 8th June, which he had sent to G.Q.G., wherein he warned General Pétain that " an important attack in the north by the enemy always " remains possible. The British reserves will be employed " in their entirety in such an eventuality. They may not " be enough. You must therefore face the possibility of " having to send back French forces to the British zone, " and for this purpose you must have plans drawn up for " the transport of a certain number of corps."

The political situation in France during the early part of June had greatly added to the anxieties of M. Clemenceau and General Foch. The attacks in the Chamber and Senate on General Pétain were renewed. Feeling that he might have to yield and to sacrifice the French Commander-in-Chief, M. Clemenceau decided to summon home from Salonika General Guillaumat, as " the only general " having sufficient authority to replace General Pétain if " he were relieved ".[2] He also decided to send as his successor to Salonika, General Franchet d'Espérey, " who " could not be left any longer at the head of the Group of " the Armies of the Centre ".[3]

The military situation continued to improve: the German attacks in the Aisne area against the Sixth Army appeared to have come to an end, and all precautions to meet the imminent attack between Noyon and Montdidier against the Third Army had been taken.

At a meeting between General Foch and Sir Douglas Haig, it was agreed that the D.A.N. should be reduced to four divisions ; that, whilst the VIII. Corps headquarters

[1] Appendix IX.
[2] Mordacq ii., p. 63. General Guillaumat left Salonika on 9th June, and was later appointed Military Governor of Paris.
[3] Mordacq ii., p. 64. On 6th June the G.A.N. became the G.A.C. See French Order of Battle.

SUPERCESSION OF FRENCH GENERALS 171

(Lieut.-General Sir A. G. Hunter-Weston) should be returned without delay, the IX. Corps headquarters should be left at French disposal to command a sector of the battle-front ; and that three out of the five British divisions should also remain in the Aisne area. It was satisfactory, as the Commander-in-Chief said to his staff, to find that General Foch had at last recognized the value of British staffs and their methods as well as the tenacity of British troops. The request that Lieut.-General Sir A. H. Gordon should remain was made more flattering by the fact that not only was the Sixth Army commander, General Duchêne, removed from command (9th June) and replaced by General Degoutte, but the two French corps commanders who had been in the line with the British IX. Corps, General de Maud'huy (XI. Corps) and General Chrétien (XXX. Corps), were superseded.

The disaster on the Chemin des Dames, indeed, marked an important change in Franco-British relations : henceforth, General Foch treated the views and proposals of Sir Douglas Haig with special deference, and, as will be seen, generally gave way to and adopted them; moreover, when the time came to plan the great offensive of the 8th August for the first time he placed a French Army under the British Commander-in-Chief.

CHAPTER X

THE BATTLE OF THE MATZ, 9TH–14TH JUNE 1918, AND THE DISPOSAL OF THE ALLIED TROOPS DURING THE ENSUING QUIET PERIOD

(Sketches B, 5, 7)

DURING the last days of the Chemin des Dames offensive, the attention of the French High Command had been drawn to the activity of the Germans and their concentration of fresh forces, opposite the French Third Army (General Humbert), on the Noyon—Montdidier front between the two great salients created by their successful offensives of the 21st March and the 27th May. From the 30th May onward all the usual indications of coming attack manifested themselves. The activity grew so open and so undisguised that the French Intelligence Branch was for a time somewhat perplexed, since preparations for attack on other parts of the front, notably north of the Somme, were of older standing and well advanced. Doubt was expressed whether the signs observed and reported should be interpreted as an attempt to mislead, and designed to occasion false moves of Allied reserves, or, alternatively, as proof of the haste with which the Germans were hurrying to strike a new and unexpected blow, as is now known to have been the case. During the 7th and 8th June prisoners declared that an attack would take place on the 10th, at latest, whilst the number of German deserters suddenly increased, a sure symptom in 1918 that an offensive was on hand. Other information received on the 8th made it certain that an attack was imminent, while a deserter who came in during the night of the 8th/9th finally revealed the exact date and hour. The only remaining doubt was in what strength the blow would be delivered.

The attack " Gneisenau " carried out on the 9th June by the German *Eighteenth Army* (General von Hutier), the opponent of the British Fifth Army (General Sir H. Gough)

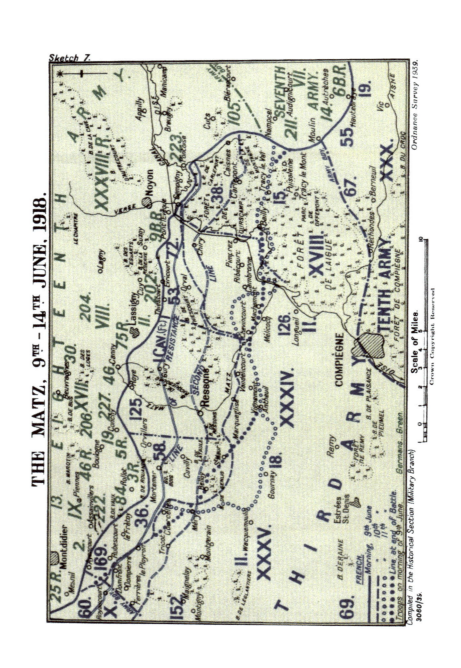

on the 21st March, had originally been planned merely to widen the front of the *Seventh Army* and complete the victory of the Chemin des Dames. The date had not at first been fixed, nor was a definite objective laid down. This subsidiary rôle was altered on the 5th June, when it was clear that the right wing of the *Seventh Army* was held up; whereupon General von Hutier was informed by O.H.L. that the continuance of the operations of the *Seventh Army* depended upon the success of his " Gneisenau" offensive. He was directed to push forward, pivoting on Montdidier, in a single dash of five miles, to the lower, west-east, course of the Matz. No final objective was named, but it was hoped that the *Eighteenth Army*, with eleven divisions in the first line and seven in second and third, would be able to reach, at least, the general line Montdidier—Compiègne, that is, the left would swing forward six miles beyond the Matz. The 7th June was fixed as the date, when the *Seventh Army* also was to attack. But the delays in getting the 600 batteries into position, many of them brought from the Chemin des Dames, caused zero hour to be postponed until the 9th.[1] When, on the 5th June, the corps of Larisch and François (of the *Seventh Army*) on the western flank of the Aisne offensive, could make no further progress, the left wing of the offensive of the *Eighteenth Army* was extended eastwards beyond the Oise by the inclusion of François's corps, so as to give this flank direct assistance and carry it forward.

The country over which the battle was to be fought Sketch 7. contained three distinct sectors : the eastern, up to the Oise, was heavily wooded; the centre, where the French front line ran on the lower northern slopes of the wooded hilly region known as the "Massif" of Lassigny or Boulogne as far as the upper course of the Matz, was undulating with numerous farms, copses, small orchards and hedges; but the western was very open, being, in fact, a continuation of the Santerre. In rear of this sector the ground was flat with large fields—mostly under corn—woods and copses. In its lower course the Matz is about eight to ten feet wide, and not much more than three feet deep, overgrown with rushes and weeds, with water meadows on either side.

Owing to the measures taken by General Pétain and General Fayolle (G.A.R.) at the beginning of June, there were already a number of divisions, besides the II. Cavalry Corps, in reserve behind what seemed to be the most

[1] Ludendorff ii., p. 633.

threatened fronts : in the zone of the Tenth Army (on the western side of the German salient), 3 divisions ; in that of the Third Army (Moulin to Montdidier), 4 divisions, with 3 more shortly expected ; in that of the First Army (Montdidier to the British right south of the Somme), 6 divisions (including 3 of the British XXII. Corps). General Fayolle also had at the disposal of his Group of Armies a considerable air force : the " division aérienne " (4 groupements or brigades), the Groupement Laurens and the British IX. Brigade.[1] He had also 4 groupements of tanks, with a fifth close at hand and available in the First Army area.[2]

The French Third Army had occupied its front in the last days of March, when French reinforcements had been sent to the assistance of the British Fifth Army, and it had filled the space between the original French left and the right of Gough's Fifth Army as it swung back. During the battle of the Aisne only the portion east of the Oise had been affected by any change. Roughly, the defences consisted of a front position, constructed since March and by no means complete as regards dug-outs and communication trenches ; an intermediate position of two lines of partly dug trenches, with good wire ; a second position, about $1\frac{1}{2}$ miles from the front, similar to the intermediate position ; and a third position, merely traced, $1\frac{1}{2}$ to $2\frac{1}{2}$ miles behind the second, along the southern bank of the river Aronde [3] ; and, lastly, two to four miles behind this, the advanced line of the Paris defences.

On the 18th April, after the close of the German offensive in Picardy, General Fayolle, acting on General Foch's instructions, had directed the Third Army " to be " prepared in every detail for a return very shortly to " active operations. He reminded General Humbert that " the present defensive was temporary ; and warned him " to be ready for a general offensive in the direction of

---

[1] The number of machines in a groupement was about 200. According to "The War in the Air", Vol. VI., p. 404, the co-operation in the Battle of the Matz was not happy : there were instances of British pilots attacking French troops and of French pilots and infantry firing upon R.A.F. aeroplanes.

[2] Groupement III. : 2 groupes allotted to the XXXV. Corps and 2 in reserve.
Groupement XII. : 3 groupes in reserve.
Groupement XI. : 2 groupes allotted to the XXXV. Corps and one in reserve.
Groupement IV. : 4 groupes allotted to the XXXIV. Corps.
The number of machines in a groupe was 12 and 3 spare.

[3] Not marked on Sketch 7 ; it flows into the Oise just above Compiègne.

THE DEFENSIVE SYSTEM

"Roye."[1] The First Position was therefore organized as the jumping-off base of an attack. It was not until the 3rd June that, in view of the increasing threat to the Noyon—Montdidier sector, General Pétain telegraphed to the Third Army, it was time to suspend the study of offensive schemes and turn with vigour to the preparation of a defensive battle. It will be recalled that on the 19th April and the 5th May,[2] General Foch had laid down that on the Allied front between the Oise and the sea, which included the sector of the French Third Army, " no ground " can be lost. ... It is a matter of defence foot by foot." The attack was to be received on the First Position, and not on a position of resistance, selected in rear. Acting on these instructions, General Humbert had devoted his main attention to the First Position, and employed only his reserves on the Second Position. These reserves had been successively withdrawn from him, so that as the 9th June approached, although " the First Position was nearly " completed, the Second was only sketched out ". Actually on the 30th May, three days before the receipt of General Pétain's telegram, General Humbert had issued instructions to his Army that all idea of the offensive had been for the moment abandoned and that the echeloning in depth of the infantry and artillery was essential : but " the mission of the corps is to maintain the integrity of " the First Position with the forces at their disposal ". The two generals senior to him in the hierarchy, doubtful of the soundness of the official doctrine of defence, sought to modify General Humbert's instructions. On the 3rd June General Fayolle ordered that the defence works of the Second Line should be pushed on with the greatest activity, and held permanently by the reserves of the front-line divisions. On the 4th, General Pétain directed that the infantry strength in the zone exposed to trench-mortar fire should be diminished. On the same day, in another instruction, General Fayolle recalled the manner in which the Germans had crushed the British front position on the 21st March, once more on the 9th April and again recently in the Chemin des Dames by violent bombardment,[3] notably by trench-mortar fire on the front trenches : therefore, to escape the effects of the preliminary bombardment, the Second Position, or any

---

[1] F.O.A. vi. (i.), p. 466.   [2] See p. 38.
[3] The first French accounts attributed this last disaster to the failure of the British IX. Corps.

favourable position between the First and Second, must be selected as the Position of Resistance, and the artillery disposed as far from the front line as its range allowed.

General Humbert, in consequence, laid down that the line of resistance should be " withdrawn as far as possible " to the rear, to the support line, or to the line of redoubts ", that is the Intermediate Position : if there were time to prepare the Second Position, the line of resistance would be shifted back to it, and there the battle would be fought ; the First Position would then become " a covering " position, an outpost position constituted principally with " machine guns placed, undiscoverable by artillery, singly, " but between them covering all the front with fire ". General Fayolle was not satisfied with these instructions : he wrote next day : " it is not a matter of securing the " integrity of the First Position, it is a matter of break- " ing, where it is possible, the enemy's onslaught ". He ordered that a position of resistance, not necessarily the Second Position, should be fixed without delay, outside the zone of violent bombardments, and the main part of the first-line divisions disposed on it. General Humbert, after a conference with his corps commanders, then selected a position of resistance, which roughly corresponded with the line of redoubts of the First Position. On the average it lay 3,300 yards, sometimes as much as 4,400 yards, from the German trench mortars. It was, he reported, impossible in the state of the work to shift the line of resistance farther back : it would take eight days to complete the Second Position, move back the guns and the munition dumps, and re-lay the signal communications : besides, " a second position is indispensable to form a second zone " of resistance ". General Fayolle was then satisfied ; so that it was on the line thus selected that the Battle of the Matz was fought. But he did stipulate that east of the Oise, where the combat was still raging, "no question of " a covering zone arises : the course of the Oise, in par- " ticular, forms an important barrier, on which resistance " must be offered to the last ". To this General Pétain added that anything was better than offering battle on the First Position : that, in all circumstances, the necessary measures must be taken to stop the enemy at the Second Position : and that the four divisions in reserve behind the Third Army and the three behind the Tenth were to be ready to ensure its defence, and their artillery was without delay to be deployed for the purpose.

In the matter of counter-attack, General Humbert laid down that partial counter-attacks should be used to keep possession of certain important points in front of the position of resistance ; that they should invariably be used to recover any part of that position which was lost, also in the event of the enemy suffering a costly repulse whilst attacking that position : " it is not only a matter of " resisting the attacks of the enemy. He must be beaten."

On the same day, the 6th June, on which General Humbert issued his final instructions, General Foch sent the letter here translated to the French Commander-in-Chief and a copy for information to his British confrère : [1]

" In the different instructions which I have addressed " to the Allied Armies since the commencement of the " German offensive, I have on several occasions insisted on " the *strategic objects* to be pursued, on the *general direction* " to be given to the battle, on the *duties* of commanders, " and on the *spirit* which should inspire all taking part.

" The strategic objects to be pursued are : the denial " of the road to *Paris* to the enemy, the covering of the " northern *ports* whilst keeping possession of the railways " by which troops are transferred ; the last can be ensured " by maintaining indissoluble *liaison* between the Allied " Armies. These objects must be attained at all costs.

" They can only be attained *by a foot by foot defence* " of the ground, this means : defensive organizations, one " behind the other, with plenty of switches ; troops whose " task has been laid down by clear and unmistakable " orders ; the execution of this task assured by echelon- " ing in depth, by power and combination of fire, by the " instant launching of counter-attacks carefully prepared " beforehand and by the occupation of rear positions by " nucleus garrisons intended to prevent any surprise " penetration by the enemy.

" Such a system of defence requires as much activity " of mind from the *commander* as vigilance and will to fight.

" The commander can show his intelligence by his " plans, but he can only show his will to fight *by his orders*, " and his grasp of realities by the care which he takes to " ensure the execution of his orders.

" That is to say he must give clear and distinct orders, " and ensure their execution at all costs ; the *supervision* " of the orders prepared and of their subsequent execution " is a duty of all ranks in their various degrees.

[1] The italics are in the original.

"To conclude, this defence must be conducted by all "with their *utmost energy*. 'Every unit, whatever the "' situation, must defend the position confided to it at all "' costs. There can be no question of falling back either "' of free will or with permission.' [1]

"Not only must the spirit of sacrifice animate all "combatants, but they must also exhibit the spirit of "decision and resolute confidence.

"In order to avoid all divergence on these important "points between the different Allied Armies, and also to "make quite clear how confident is the morale of the High "Command, I should be obliged if you would, without "delay, arrange to publish to the French troops an instruc- "tion insisting that energy and resolution must be applied "to the present battle, and that the vigilance and super- "vision of all staffs are required to ensure the practical "realization of the results desired."

Copies of this letter were transmitted the same day by General Pétain to the commanders of Groups of Armies and Armies, with instructions to promulgate its contents.

At 11.50 P.M. on the 8th the French began counter-preparation fire, anticipating the enemy by a few minutes. The German bombardment, which opened at midnight, was similar to that devised for the 27th May, except that it lasted forty minutes longer—3 hours 20 minutes as against 2 hours 40 minutes. The infantry assault had been fixed for 3.20 A.M., but according to French accounts seemed to be launched at various times between 3 A.M. and 4.30 A.M. in the different divisional sectors, a sign perhaps that, owing to haste, the German staff work had been imperfect.

The four French corps which were affected, the XVIII. (General de Pouydraguin), the II. (General de Cadoudal), the XXXIV. (General Nudant) and the XXXV. (General Jacquot),[2] had placed nearly half the infantry within 2,200 yards of the front line. "The distribution complied "only imperfectly in certain sectors with the principles "laid down," owing, it is said, to the unfinished state of the defences, want of time, the lie of the ground, and "the repugnance of certain commanders to modify the "mistaken practice hitherto followed".[3] In Army reserve

---

[1] A quotation from an earlier memorandum.
[2] The corps were of two divisions, except the last, which had three, with a few attached Territorial battalions.
[3] F.O.A. vi. (ii.), p. 289.

there were five divisions [1] and 3 cavalry divisions, stationed three miles or more behind the Second Position. The artillery to oppose the 600 German batteries numbered 146 field batteries and 161 heavy, with a similar disproportion as regards trench-mortars.

The first assault, by 15 German divisions, was entirely successful, particularly in the centre, as on the 27th May.[2] By their usual method of infiltration, and leaving rearward detachments to deal with centres of resistance, the Germans overran the covering position. By midday they had reached and passed over the Position of Resistance, except at one or two places on the wings. By evening, in the centre, they had advanced six miles, crossed the middle Matz, gained possession of nearly one-third of the Second Position and pushed forward two or three miles beyond it, taken over 8,000 prisoners and put " 3 divisions nearly " hors de combat ".[3] They then halted; but artillery fire continued all night.

The French High Command was not, however, alarmed at the result of the day, for the troops had fallen back steadily, and no rout, as on the 27th May, had taken place; but General Fayolle moved certain reinforcements nearer : the 123rd Division, in reserve to the Tenth Army, was transferred to the Third and sent to the II. Corps, to be replaced in reserve by the 121st from the D.A.N., which was expected next day by rail; the 33rd, from the Verdun area, was ordered to the junction of the Tenth and Third Armies ; and the 133rd, in the valley of the Marne, was warned to be ready to move.

At 7.30 p.m. General Pétain requested the Generalissimo to put the British XXII. Corps at his disposal and send it to Estrées St. Denis.[4] He received the reply that " the " number of enemy forces which appear to have been " engaged to-day and the total of the forces which remain " at the disposal of the Crown Prince of Bavaria do not " yet permit of the British front being deprived of its " own reserves ". General Foch nevertheless requested Sir Douglas Haig to shift one division of that corps, the 37th, southwards to Conty (13 miles south by west of Amiens), to come into his own General Reserve.

Next day the Germans continued their attack in the

---

[1] A fifth, the 69th from Alsace, had been added to the original four.
[2] See Sketch 7, which shows the German advance on each day and the French counter-attack.
[3] F.O.A. vi. (ii.), p. 309. [4] South-west corner of Sketch 7.

centre and on the western wing, and in spite of artillery fire and local counter-attacks once more made progress against the French left centre, but only to the extent of a couple of miles. It was in the French right centre that " a series " of grave events occurred " : the 53rd Division (II. Corps) was driven in, and the 72nd, on its right, conformed to its rearward movement. As a result, General Humbert ordered the retirement of his whole right wing : the XVIII. Corps, which had not been attacked on this day, and the defeated II. Corps, to the northern edge of the Forêt de Laigue ; he thus abandoned an awkward salient in which they ran a danger of being cut off.

General Fayolle had at first hoped to counter-attack on both sides of the pocket formed by the German entry, but the withdrawal of the II. and XVIII. Corps had put an offensive movement on the eastern side, from the Compiègne direction, out of the question. On the western side, however, he had available the three reserve divisions of the First Army and some ten groups of tanks ready to operate in the area of the XXXV. Corps. To these, General Pétain, after a conference, added two more divisions. General Mangin, then awaiting employment at First Army headquarters, was at 4 P.M. placed formally in command of these five divisions and the tanks, together with the XXXV. Corps and all the troops in its area.

The Germans, who had already gained more than their first objective, except on their extreme left, were quiescent on the morning of the 11th, and the artillery preparation for the counter-attack was begun without interference at 10.30 A.M. ; but, owing to lack of time for the preliminary measures, it was " relatively feeble ". The French infantry, four divisions in front line, advanced at 11.30 A.M., accompanied by aeroplanes flying low. As regards the tanks, the orders were quite simple : " the infantry will " attack as if there were no tanks. The groups of tanks, " echeloned in depth and having the same task as the " infantry formations to which they are attached, will " place themselves opposite their objectives behind the last " available cover, so as not to reveal their presence before " the attack is launched. Starting, in consequence, at " the same time as the infantry, but rather far behind it, " the tanks will endeavour to catch up as soon as possible, " and will join in the battle as they pass through the " infantry."

General Mangin's counter-attack, thanks to its deploy-

MANGIN'S COUNTER-ATTACK. 11TH JUNE

ment being favoured by morning mist, made some progress and threw the Germans on the defensive. But between 3 and 4 P.M., the enemy artillery not having been smothered, it came to a stop, " after some thousand prisoners and a " few guns had been captured, pinned to the ground by " the enemy's fire ". Profiting by the morning advance of General Mangin's troops, in the afternoon the right wing moved to the attack and gained ground in two places, in spite of the efforts of the Germans east of the Oise to press forward.

On the 12th the French counter-attack was continued at 3.30 A.M., after half an hour's artillery bombardment; " but it succeeded only on its extreme right and there only " partially ". At 10.30 A.M. General Mangin ordered the assault to be renewed at 5 P.M.; but, in view of the time required for preparation, General Humbert eventually postponed the movement until the 13th. The corps and divisional commanders were, however, disinclined to expend more lives on an operation which had achieved its main purpose, and on the 13th only some local operations were carried out to improve the French position.[1]

Meantime, on the 12th, after an unavoidable delay of 24 hours, the Germans, in order to assist the Matz operation, had launched another attack, " Hammerschlag " (Hammer-blow), on the western side of the old Aisne battlefield south of the river. It was made by the two right corps of the *Seventh Army* (Staabs's, previously Larisch's, and Wichura's), with five divisions in first line and two in second. They were to advance westwards about six miles, with the right directed on Compiègne, and when within twelve miles of that town were to wheel southwards. The attack, launched at 4 A.M. after 1½ hours' bombardment, proved a failure. To quote a German official account:[2]

Sketch 5.

" The ' Hammerschlag ' attack was shattered [mainly " by artillery fire]. On the all-important right wing, where " the *34th Division* was engaged, nothing was achieved, and " even the first objective was not reached by the *51st* " *Reserve Division* and *47th Reserve Division* [right centre, " and left]. The considerable gain of ground by the *11th* " *Bavarian* and *45th Reserve Division* [in the centre and

---

[1] There is a long account of the employment of 144 tanks (72 Schneider, 72 St. Chamond) in the counter-attack of 11th-13th June in " La Revue " d'Infanterie " of February 1938. Of the total, 69 tanks (51 Schneider and 18 St. Chamond) were immobilized by enemy fire or disappeared, that is 47·9 per cent. Of the personnel, 389 or 16·8 per cent became casualties.

[2] Monograph II., pp. 175-6.

"left centre] was not sufficient to carry forward the whole front of attack and bring it nearer the desired objective by any distance worth mention. The hope of pushing the right flank of the *Seventh Army* forward to a more favourable front, in combination with the Gneisenau operation [the 9th June Matz attack] had to be finally abandoned. On the evening of the 12th June O.H.L. ordered both the Gneisenau and Hammerschlag attacks to be stopped." Partial attacks and bombardments were, however, continued without result on both battle fronts until the 15th.

To quote the French Official Account :

Sketch B. "Thus ended in the middle of June, the mighty offensive effort commenced by the Germans on the 27th May at the Chemin des Dames and continued by them without break for [nearly] three weeks. About sixty enemy divisions [actually, 58] seem to have been engaged in the two battles of the Aisne and the Matz. These attacks could only be contained at the cost of heavy sacrifice and considerable losses of ground. The French Army succeeded in covering Paris and even saving Compiègne, and, in the end, mastered the enemy. But it was nearly at the end of its reserves at the close of the long struggle, whilst the German High Command, in spite of the enormous expenditure of divisions which it had just incurred, still kept in hand considerable forces." [1]

"The near future, therefore, remained full of anxieties ",[2] which were not lessened by the opening of the Austrian offensive along the Piave on the 15th June.

On this date the French Army had 70 divisions in the line, and of the remaining 33 only 6 were fresh or in good condition.[3] The British furnished 34 in the line with 27 (10 reduced to cadre) in reserve, the Belgians, 9 in the line and 3 in reserve. The Americans were scattered, with 7 divisions in various parts of the French front and 10 under instruction (5 with the British); but General Pershing was pressing for the formation of an American front.

On the 13th, General Foch addressed the following

---

[1] A total of 62 divisions, of which, however, only 7 were fresh and 44 were in Crown Prince Rupprecht's Group of Armies on the British front. See Table of Distribution of German Divisions at end of Chapter.
[2] F.O.A. vi. (ii.), pp. 345-6. For the casualties, see p. 160.
[3] There were also 6 cavalry divisions and 2 dismounted cavalry divisions.

Note to the Commanders-in-Chief of the French and British Armies:

"According to the information available, the distribution of the enemy's reserves seems to be actually as follows:

"(1) Between the sea and the Somme, a mass of 35 to 40 divisions, of which about 30 are reconstituted or fresh.

"(2) Between the Somme and the Swiss frontier 10 to 12 divisions, of which at least 6 are tired or unfit for battle.

"The latter category may be considered as forming the reserves necessary to supply the normal reliefs of the front between the Somme and the Swiss frontier.

"The other group of reserves, on the other hand, may permit the Germans:

"either (a) to take the offensive against a sector between the sea and the Somme;

"or (b) to continue the attacks begun between Montdidier and Reims;

"or, lastly, (c) to attempt a violent attack by surprise against another part of the front: Champagne, Verdun or Lorraine."

"In the two first cases the Germans would in all probability carry out their concentration movements by night and by road and rail, as they did before the March and May offensives."

The Generalissimo therefore requested that air reconnaissances might be ordered for the purpose of watching all the roads and lines of railway likely to be used, particularly certain transverse routes (" voies de rocade ").

Later on the same day he sent a second Note, suggesting to the two Commanders-in-Chief the studies and plans which should be made:

"At the point at which we have now arrived the German attack on the Montdidier—Noyon front seems to have been defeated.

"The information so far collected indicates that all the available reserves of the German Crown Prince, but only a small number of the reserve divisions of Crown Prince Rupprecht, have taken part in the attack.

"In consequence, the mass of enemy reserves still of an important nature lies at the present moment behind the Armies opposed to the British Armies—and it seems

" reasonable to expect that the next German effort will be
" directed against those Armies.

" Nevertheless, it must not be overlooked that the
" communication facilities at the disposal of the Germans
" in the north of France, permit them to transport their
" mass of manoeuvre rapidly to any point on the whole
" Franco-British front.

" The Allied reserves must take part in the battle wher-
" ever it is fought. They may therefore be called on to
" intervene anywhere on the whole extent of front, in order
" to bring help, as the case may be, to the British or French
" Army.

" In order to ensure this intervention, the General
" Commanding-in-Chief of the Allied Armies has been led
" to request :

" (1) Field-Marshal Haig, by a letter of 4th June, to
" look ahead, and prepare in detail for the case in which the
" whole of the enemy forces are set in action against the
" French front, with :

" (a) a plan for the transport of all his reserves (general and
local);
" (b) a thinning of the forces on the fronts not attacked, in
order to constitute fresh reserves.

" (2) General Pétain, by a letter of 8th June, to draw
" up a plan for the transport of the French reserves towards
" the British zone, for the case in which the enemy directs
" a powerful offensive against the British front.

" The imminence of a new German effort and the
" uncertainty as to its point of application render urgent
" the completion of the general arrangements by detailed
" studies, so that if the movements mentioned become
" necessary they can be carried out without delay.

" It is of course desirable that such studies should be
" made in combination by the General Staffs of the British
" and French Commanders-in-Chief.

" The British and French Commanders-in-Chief are
" therefore begged to regard the matter as urgent.

" The studies will have for their bases :

" 1. As regards the British Army : the preparations for the
transport to the French front of the British general reserve
in the various hypotheses :

        of intervention north of the Oise ;
      ,,   ,,   between Oise and Marne ;
      ,,   ,,   east of Reims.

FOCH'S NOTE. 15TH JUNE

" 2. As regards the French Army : the preparation of a plan for the initial [1] transport towards the British zone of its reserves as they are at present distributed ; it being understood that this plan is constantly kept up to date in relation to the changes in the number of reserve divisions and in their location.

" The results of these studies will be communicated as " soon as possible to the General Commanding-in-Chief the " Allied Armies." [2]

On the 15th, General Foch sent to Sir Douglas Haig by the hand of Lieut.-General Du Cane the following Note on the distribution of the reserves in threatened sectors : [3]

" In view of the pace, now-a-days, of the German " attacks, the only reserves which are of value on the day " of attack are those which are already in place in the " Second Position ; others will arrive too late.

" In the German attacks of the 21st March, 9th April, " 27th May and 9th June, a break-through took place only " because the Somme line, the Aisne line, or the rear " positions were not garrisoned, either owing to lack of " troops ; or because the reserves did not receive, or did " not carry out, the order to hold their positions ; or " because they were too far off to do so.

" In a threatened sector, it is therefore indispensable " that :

" (a) reserves should be stationed beforehand close to the rear positions and should occupy them directly the bombardment commences ;

" (b) the commanders of various ranks ensure that the troops are in place and the orders carried out.

" For example, if an attack seems likely in Flanders, the " reserves should be moved up, as a certain number of " them are too far to the rear to intervene in sufficient " time ; they should be warned and so distributed that " they can be alarmed as soon as the attack appears

---

[1] Thus in the original. The word is possibly the equivalent of " provisional."

[2] Sir Douglas Haig replied on the 19th that north of the Oise the movement would be by bus and rail ; south of the Oise, by the railway facilities which the French could provide ; he could send off two divisions every two days.

[3] He forwarded daily to Sir Douglas Haig a map showing the distribution of the French divisions and was similarly kept informed as regards the British.

"certain, and can jump into their places in the rear lines in the shortest possible time.[1]

"A small number of units placed in time where they are required, will stop short an enemy irruption, whilst reserves arriving too late cannot do so except farther in rear and at greater cost.

"To act as suggested is to hold one's ground and economise one's forces."

By a verbal message, General Foch asked that the British XXII. Corps might accept direct orders to occupy a Second Position from General Debeney, commanding the French First Army next to the British. To this Sir Douglas Haig demurred, because, as he said, the corps would then cease to be in General Reserve: it must take orders from General Foch, but from no one else. General Debeney, nevertheless, issued instructions for the 37th Division of the XXII. Corps to occupy a position close to the front in local reserve in case of attack. On Sir Douglas Haig protesting on the 16th by letter to General Foch, he received a telegram in reply from General Pétain, that the 37th Division would be released on the 19th. It may be added that on the 24th June, General Fayolle, convinced that " Paris was to be the objective of the German Army ", asked that the three northern divisions in General Debeney's Army might be relieved by the British; but this request was refused by General Foch. At a conference on the 18th, General Foch explained to Sir Douglas Haig that he was anxious about the reserves and had to keep strong forces to cover Paris. The methods of meeting German attacks were discussed, and he handed to the British Commander-in-Chief a copy of a long memorandum on the subject.[2] He also expressed his satisfaction with the fighting powers of the American troops which had been in action, as also with the situation on the Piave and on the Asiago plateau, where the Austrian advance was beginning to slacken.

By this time it had become evident to both British and American G.H.Q. that a certain amount of friction had arisen between General Foch and French G.Q.G., and that such existed is borne out by the French Official Account. On the 11th June General Pétain complained, " I have at my disposal only one division fit to be called a reserve ". He made repeated requests for the handing over to him of

---

[1] During a visit on the 18th, General Foch expressed his satisfaction with the disposition of the British reserves.
[2] A translation is printed as Appendix X.

the British reserves, whilst neglecting to ensure that the French First Army should construct its part of the connecting switch behind the Allied junction which it had been agreed should be undertaken. On the 17th June General Pétain wrote a formal letter to the Generalissimo, transmitting a copy thereof to M. Clemenceau, Prime Minister and Minister of War, in which he contested an order to send some additional artillery to the D.A.N.—whose commander, General de Mitry, had also asked that his forces should be reinforced by two divisions, one of them without delay. This letter [1] terminated with complaints, which took a very one-sided view of the situation, that " the French Armies had been engaged in each of the " four battles delivered by the enemy since the 21st " March " and had a great number of very tired and worn-out divisions; " the British Armies had already had two " months' respite to reconstitute themselves and absorb " their reinforcements.[2] They hold their front of 150 " kilometres [nearly 200] with a density of infantry and " artillery which has never been possible in any of my " Armies which have been engaged; they are therefore in " a position to look after themselves and give the French " Armies time to reorganize in their turn so as to be ready " to resist a new shock in the direction of Paris which " cannot fail to materialize. Now, at the actual moment " the resources at the disposal of the French Armies are " barely sufficient to ensure the indispensable reliefs; I " cannot therefore at once reduce these resources for the " benefit of the British front without gravely imperilling " the future."

His arguments had little effect on General Foch,[3] who agreed with the British Commander-in-Chief that all the information pointed to a German attack north-west and south-west from the Lys salient, with perhaps a subsidiary operation just south of the La Bassée canal to support it.

[1] F.O.A. vi. (ii.), Annexe 1604.
[2] General Pétain overlooked the falling infantry strength of the British Armies, 754,000 bayonets in July 1917; 638,000 in January 1918; and 543,000 in the middle of June 1918, as reported by the Adjutant-General.
[3] On 26th June " M. Clemenceau decided that General Pétain should " be placed purely and simply under the direct orders of General Foch ". (Mordacq ii., p. 93.) On the 5th July General Anthoine was superseded as " Major-Général " (Chief of the Staff of the French Armies) by General Buat. It may be recalled that in the Boxer troubles in China in 1900, when Field-Marshal Graf Waldersee was appointed International Commander-in-Chief, only the German contingent refused obedience to his orders.

He stated, however, that in his opinion it was necessary to maintain a General Reserve in three groups :

(a) in the neighbourhood of the Somme, as any advance of the enemy by the Somme route was most dangerous ;
(b) on the routes to Paris ;
(c) in the north : because, although it was the least dangerous, yet, owing to distance, it would be difficult to reinforce it very rapidly.

General Foch requested Sir Douglas Haig to retain the bulk of his reserves in the Somme direction and in the northern part of the British zone. On the 21st, therefore, the divisions of the British XXII. Corps were shifted back so that the right division was immediately behind Amiens south of the Somme, and the other two spread out north of the river, the left division around Thièvres, half-way to Arras.

On the 19th General Foch again wrote to Sir Douglas Haig suggesting the desirability of reassembling the French and British troops in their own zones : General Pétain was anxious to receive back the D.A.N. (six divisions), and, in exchange, was prepared to return the British 19th and 50th Divns and IX. Corps headquarters, and would renounce any claim to the British 30th and 34th Divns, which had been promised to him, when reconstituted, in place of the British 8th, 21st and 25th Divns. General Plumer[1] expressed himself as quite prepared to part with the D.A.N. : as some of the tired British divisions were now partially reorganized—the 40th, 59th, 14th, 16th and 25th had been filled up with " B " class men—he could still hold his front. It was therefore arranged that the relief of the D.A.N. should begin on the 1st July, division by division, and be terminated by the 20th, whilst the British divisions should be sent back in a similar way and five American divisions remain with the British.[2] But on the 23rd General Foch requested that two divisions of the D.A.N. might be sent off as soon as possible ; this, as General Plumer pointed out, entailed a certain amount of risk, but the divisions were despatched. The wireless stations of the D.A.N.

---

[1] His Chief General Staff officer, Major-General C. H. Harington, had been ordered home, at the request of the C.I.G.S., to become Deputy C.I.G.S., and had been succeeded on 29th April by Major-General J. Percy.
[2] The 27th, 30th, 33rd, 78th and 80th. The French had 14. It had been arranged that the divisions with the British should form the American II. Corps, Major-General G. W. Read taking command on 15th June.

INFLUENZA

were kept in action and other measures taken to conceal the departure of the French troops.

About the middle of the month an influenza epidemic made itself felt, principally in the north; but as all reports, since confirmed, showed that it was much more severe among the German troops, to whom it was known as " Flanders fever ", there seemed to be little cause for alarm. More disturbing indeed were the numerous cases of malaria among the troops returned from Salonika and Egypt, as many as ten battalions being incapacitated for a time.

Bad weather from the 15th to the 30th June prevented important air reconnaissances. The enemy's preparations and activity, although he had set rumours in circulation in Switzerland that the next attack would be against Verdun, seemed to the British Intelligence to point to an attack north-west and south-west from the Lys salient, assisted by another immediately south of the La Bassée canal, whilst information obtained by the French indicated that it might be expected between the Somme and the Scarpe, with a subsidiary attack in Flanders. A prisoner taken on the 25th on the Bailleul front stated that most of the batteries for the Lys offensive were in position; another prisoner said that 400 more batteries would arrive in Flanders on the 1st July, but had been ordered to remain silent, and that all other preparations had been completed ten days earlier, but the attack, which was originally timed to be simultaneous with the Austrian attack in Italy, had been postponed for reasons unknown. It seemed at the time that influenza might be the cause, but, as is now known, it was due to the Aisne offensive, by its very easy success, having been carried too far.[1]

Every day of respite was to the advantage of the Allies. They were further cheered by the final collapse of the Austrian offensive along the Piave on the 24th, to which the French XII. Corps and the British troops under General Lord Cavan (7th, 23rd and 48th Divisions) had contributed;[2] also by the report of a speech made on the

---

[1] See Note at end of Chapter XIII.

[2] General Foch in several letters and messages begged General Diaz, the Italian Chief of the General Staff, to exploit the victory he had gained over the war-weary, ill-fed, ill-equipped and disintegrating forces of the Austrian Empire. But the Italian general offered explanations of his inactivity. " At the end of July the situation on the Italian front was " practically the same as at the close of the battle." F.O.A. vi. (ii.), pp. 362-7.

same date by Herr von Kühlmann, the German Minister for Foreign Affairs, in which he stated that there was no hope of ending the War by military means alone. General Foch became so elated that he asked Sir Douglas Haig to arrange for an offensive " at the end of August ", mentioning that the French would also carry out an offensive, but not the Montdidier—Noyon project, as it was more important to drive the enemy back elsewhere. In the meantime, however, on the 28th, he requested the speedy relief of the whole of the D.A.N. (4 divisions, etc.) now remaining in the northern area, as his Government were alarmed about the safety of Paris and wished to have adequate reserves to defend the capital.[1] To this, Sir Douglas Haig replied that he could only relieve the D.A.N. at the moment by depleting his reserves on part of the front; this entailed running a risk, but if Paris were really in danger the risk must be taken, and so he agreed to relieve the French divisions. It was then decided to move the five American divisions under Major-General Read to the Second Army area, and arrangements were made that the relief of the remaining divisions of the D.A.N. should begin on the 2nd and be completed by the 10th July, the withdrawal of the heavy artillery commencing on the 2nd.[2] General Pershing declined the invitation to move two more of his divisions to the British area, saying that he wished to send all American divisions which might arrive during July to the future American area.

On the 28th June the French Intelligence Branch came to the conclusion that the Germans had the choice of two courses : " the first consists in at once attacking with a " relatively weak mass of reserves the Armies of the " Entente before they should be reinforced : the second is " to wait until their forces reach a maximum in numbers

---

[1] At a conference held by M. Clemenceau at General Foch's headquarters on the 15th, it was decided (1) that the defence of Paris must be ensured by a covering force sufficient to stop the enemy ; (2) that if the enemy reached the line Meaux—Creil, the Military Governor of Paris (General Guillaumat) would take command of the Armies covering the direct roads to Paris. General Pétain was of opinion that " the enemy " O.H.L. would continue its offensive against the French front, without " doubt in the direction of Paris, which in this phase of the campaign, " forms the only objective whose conquest justifies the renewal of the " enemy efforts ". F.O.A. vi. (ii.), pp. 375-6 and 391.

[2] The D.A.N. was reorganized in the valley of the Grand Morin (crossed by the British in the Battle of the Marne 1914) as the Ninth Army, in general reserve. During a visit to the front on 26th June to 3rd July, Field-Marshal H.R.H. the Duke of Connaught invested General de Mitry, its commander, with the K.C.B.

"and battle-fitness, with the disadvantage of having to
"encounter an adversary also much stronger". In the
first case the Germans had the fronts in Champagne and
from the Somme to Ypres fully equipped for an immediate
offensive : " but the most probable hypotheses are a con-
"tinuation of the thrust towards Amiens in a renewed
"attempt to separate the British and French Armies, and
"a continuation of the attacks in the direction of Paris by
"the valleys of the Oise and the Marne (in which case a
"delay would be necessary to equip offensively the front
"between the Aisne and the Marne)".

The survey concluded with the words : " it is probable
"that the enemy is resolved to attack only when he has
"concentrated a maximum of the forces at his disposal :
"if he attacks the British it will require a little time to
"reconstitute his reserves ; if the French, by the valleys
"of the Oise and Marne, a delay must occur whilst he is
"equipping his front". In both cases the 15th July was
fixed as the earliest date for the operation. The German
attack did take place on the 15th July, as the date had to
be postponed owing to the gun ammunition not having
been up to time ; but the objective was the Champagne
front, on either side of Reims.

In the uncertainty prevailing at G.Q.G. and G.H.Q.,
and in obedience to General Foch's orders, both Allies took
in hand measures for mutual assistance. Sir Douglas
Haig informed General Pétain that the XXII. Corps could
reach the railway junction of St. Just en Chaussée in two
days, and would then be replaced around Amiens by the
XIX. Corps. He named the centres selected for the
concentration of French reinforcements in case of need,
viz. : south of Doullens, around St. Pol, and between
St. Omer and Dunkirk. General Pétain replied that six
French divisions and a cavalry corps could be concentrated
in the area Doullens—St. Pol about three days after the
receipt of the order for the movement.

NOTE

DISTRIBUTION OF GERMAN DIVISIONS ON 12TH JUNE

	In line		In reserve		Total per Army	Total per Group	
	Fresh	Engaged	Fresh	Engaged			
Between Switzerland and the Oise.							
Duke Albrecht of Württemberg's Group of Armies.						15	(No reserve)
(Switzerland to St. Mihiel Salient exclusive.)							
B. Detachment	6				6		
A. ,,	4				4		
Nineteenth Army.	3	2			5		
Gallwitz's Group of Armies.						18	(3 reserve)
(St. Mihiel Salient to Varennes.)							
C. Detachment	5	4	1		10		
Fifth Army.	3	3	1	1	8		
German Crown Prince's Group of Armies (part).						53	(13 reserve)
(Varennes to Oise.)							
Third Army.	3	3		1	7		
First ,,	1	11		2	14		
Seventh ,, (Battle of the Aisne.)		22		10	32		
Between Oise and the Sea.							
German Crown Prince's Group of Armies (part).						24	(No reserve)
(Oise to Moreuil.)							
Eighteenth Army. (Battle of the Matz.)		24			24		
Crown Prince Rupprecht's Group of Armies.						95	(44 reserve)
(Moreuil to the Sea.)							
Second Army.	2	9	1	10	22		
Seventeenth Army.		11	2	9	22		
Sixth Army.		13		10	23		
Fourth ,,	5	11	1	11	28		
	32	113	6	54	205		
Unlocated			1	1	2		
	145		60		207		

Total fresh . . 39
Engaged . . 168
TOTAL 207

CHAPTER XI

BETWEEN THE STORMS

MINOR AFFAIRS IN JUNE AND EARLY JULY 1918

THE ACTIONS OF LA BECQUE, HAMEL AND VAIRE WOODS, AND METEREN

(Sketches A, 5, 8, 9, 10)

WHILST the Battles of the Aisne and the Matz were in progress, and during the period of comparative quiet following these enemy offensives, in the sectors of the front not directly concerned in meeting the German attacks there was no cessation of activity: bombardment, counter-battery work, harassing fire on batteries and roads at night, small operations and raids.[1] In particular frequent fighting took place on the Second Army front near Locre, 2 miles west of Kemmel, and about Ridge Wood (3 miles

[1] The British Order of Battle (less IX. Corps in the Aisne area) on 2nd June was:
Fourth Army (Villers Bretonneux, inclusive, to north of Albert):
    Australian Corps   (less 1st Division, with XV. Corps);
    III. Corps   (18th, 47th, 58th Divisions).
Third Army (north of Albert to south-west of Arras):
    V. Corps   (17th, 35th, 38th, 63rd Divisions);
    IV. ,,   (42nd, 57th, 62nd, New Zealand Divisions);
    VI. ,,   (Guards, 2nd, 32nd, 2nd Canadian Divisions, and 4th Guards Brigade).
First Army (south-west of Arras to south-west of Hazebrouck):
    XVII. Corps   (15th, 51st, 56th Divisions);
    XVIII. ,,   (20th, 24th, 52nd Divisions);
    I. ,,   (1st, 11th, 46th, 55th Divisions);
    XIII. ,,   (3rd, 4th Divisions);
    XI. ,,   (5th, 61st Divisions).
Second Army (south-west of Hazebrouck to 2½ miles north of Ypres):
    XV. Corps   (9th, 29th, 31st, 1st Australian Divisions);
    French XVI. Corps } D.A.N., 9 divisions;
    ,, XIV. ,, }
    II. Corps   (6th, 33rd, 36th, 41st, 49th Divisions).
G.H.Q. Reserve: 12th, 37th, 59th (just reconstituted), 74th 1st Canadian, 3rd Canadian and 4th Canadian

S.S.W. of Ypres) and Scottish Wood (north of Ridge Wood).[1] To mention the more important incidents: during the night of the 2nd/3rd June, with a view to improving the line, Mont de Merris, a small hill west of Merris (5 miles east of Hazebrouck) was captured by the 3rd Australian Brigade, troops of the 86th Brigade (29th Division) co-operating on the right. On the 10th June, the 7th Brigade of the 2nd Australian Division (Major-General C. Rosenthal) carried out a completely successful night attack on a front of two miles south of Morlancourt (4 miles south of Albert),[2] resulting in a substantial gain of ground and the capture of over three hundred prisoners. On the night of the 12th/13th June the line near Merris was further improved and 36 prisoners taken. On the night of the 14th/15th, starting at 11.45 P.M., the 3rd Division (Major-General C. J. Deverell), using the 9th and 76th Brigades, carried out a surprise attack on a two-mile front between the Lawe and La Pannerie (2 miles north of Béthune), where the wire was known to be weak, penetrated to a depth of four hundred and fifty yards and captured all its objectives and 175 prisoners. The attack was made under a barrage advancing 100 yards in 5 minutes fired by 32 batteries of field guns and 48 machine guns—which were also to deal with counter-attacks — supported by the artillery of the divisions on either flank, whilst the XIII. Corps artillery neutralized all known hostile batteries. The retaliation was very slight.

The comparative quiet prevailing on the British front during the months of May and June and the steady arrival

---

Divisions, and Cavalry Corps (distributed behind the southern wing).
Cadre Divisions: 14th, 16th, 30th, 34th, 39th, 40th, 66th.
American Divisions: 28th, 35th, 77th, 82nd.
„   „   (arriving) 4th, 27th, 33rd, 78th.
Portuguese Divisions: 1st and 2nd.

The Fifth Army headquarters was reconstituted on 23rd May, at Crécy, with General Sir W. R. Birdwood as G.O.C., Lieut.-General Sir J. Monash succeeding him in command of the Australian Corps; at 10 A.M. on 1st July the Fifth Army took over the sectors of the XI. and XIII. Corps, which were transferred to it from the northern wing of the First Army. A proportion of heavy artillery, anti-aircraft, R.E., signals, Air Force, transport, medical, labour and transportation units were allocated to it.

[1] As a general map see Sketch 1, and for details Sketch 31 in "1918" Vol. II. and Sketch 10.

Ridge Wood, in the Second Army sector, changed hands many times and was finally taken on 14th July, with 348 prisoners, by the 18th Brigade (6th Division) and two companies from the 98th Brigade (33rd Division), attached.   [2] See Sketch 5 in " 1918 " Vol. II.

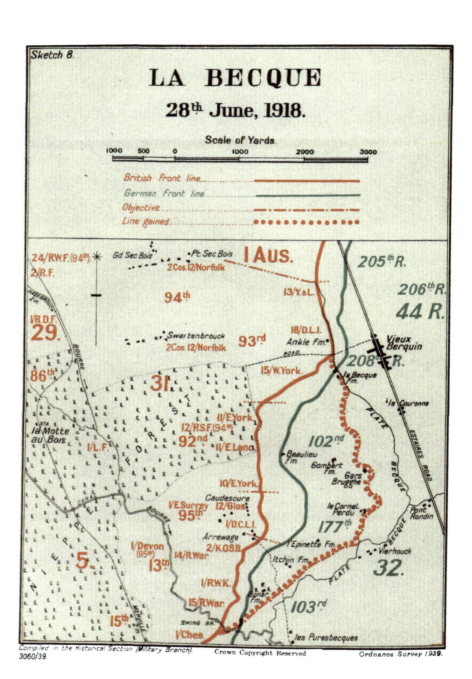

LA BECQUE. 28TH JUNE

of reinforcements had greatly improved the condition of the fighting units; in artillery the Armies were stronger than they had ever been, although many guns were getting worn. Ammunition was plentiful, almost unlimited, but shells, cartridges and fuzes were not uniform in character, so that variation in range, due to change of lots, was definitely appreciable. The situation did not yet warrant a return to a definite offensive policy, as General Foch hoped, since the greater part of the German reserves were still located opposite the British front. Yet towards the end of June Sir Douglas Haig felt that his forces were strong enough to attempt operations on a larger scale than had hitherto been possible in 1918, with the object of improving the defensive line and of preparing the way for future schemes.

As the first of these operations—it had been suggested to him by General Foch on the 6th June [1]—he determined to advance the British line east of Nieppe forest to the extent of about one mile on a frontage of $3\frac{1}{2}$ miles, so as to provide room for an " outpost zone " clear of the forest, which was constantly subject to gas shelling. A plan for this operation had been drafted by Major-General R. B. Stephens after successful raids on the 25th April and 20th May, in order to probe the enemy's intentions and keep up the high offensive spirit of the 5th Division; but it required the assistance of a second division, and so the XI. Corps of the First Army was directed to carry it out. Lieut.-General Sir R. Haking entrusted the attack to Major-General R. B. Stephens's division, the 5th, of the XI. Corps, still 13 battalions strong, as it had just returned from Italy, and the 31st Division (Major-General J. Campbell) of the XV. Corps, but placed for the occasion under the XI. Corps. The date 28th June was chosen and seemed a good omen, as on that date in 1917 the 5th and 31st Divisions had carried out a particularly successful operation near Oppy Wood. Forty batteries of field artillery and the trench mortars of the 5th Division, reinforced by one 6-inch battery from the 61st Division, and the heavy artillery of the XI. and XV. Corps were to support the advance.[2] To mislead the enemy, barrages were fired in the early morning on several days preceding the attack. The existence of Nieppe forest, almost untouched by war, although constantly drenched with gas by enemy

Sketch 8

---

[1] See p. 166.
[2] XI. Corps: G.O.C. R.A., Br.-General S. F. Metcalfe.
    Corps H.A. (Br.-General R. H. F. McCulloch):

bombardment,[1] allowed of the concentration of troops and material being completed unseen immediately behind the front of attack; this circumstance also greatly facilitated the capture of La Becque Farm, from which the action takes its name, Ankle Farm, north of it, being secured by the 13/York & Lancaster on the night of the 26th/27th June.

The ground over which the attack had to be made was quite flat, with corn in places waist high, intersected by hedges and ditches; but the surface was hard and the ditches dry owing to the long continued rainless weather. The Plate Becque stream beyond the German position was only eighteen inches deep at the time.[2] A model of the ground and the enemy trenches was made so that the assaulting battalions had a good idea of their tasks.

From dawn the R.A.F. was very active, so that not a single enemy aeroplane was seen until the afternoon. The assault was launched at 6 A.M. without a preliminary bombardment—some counter-batteries using gas shell—under a creeping barrage of artillery and machine guns moving at the rate of a hundred yards in four minutes. Each division employed two brigades, from right to left, the 13th, 95th, 92nd and 93rd (Br.-Generals L. O. W. Jones, C. B. Norton, O. de L. Williams and S. C. Taylor).[3]

On the left the field artillery of the 1st Australian Division fired a barrage and made a smoke screen with

XXVIII., LXXIX., XLIX., Brigades R.G.A.,
  6-inch howitzers   38
  8-inch   ,,   6
  9·2-inch   ,,   4
  6-inch guns   6
  60-pdrs.   24

XV. Corps: G.O.C. R.A., Br.-General B. R. Kirwan.
Corps H.A. (Br.-General C. W. Collingwood):
  XXXIII. Brigade R.G.A. and XXXVI Heavy (Australian) Brigade:
  6-inch howitzers   26
  8-inch   ,,   12
  9·2-inch   ,,   6
  60-pdrs.   12

[1] The whole staff of the 15th Brigade had become gas casualties on the night of the 25th/26th.

[2] The enemy divisions involved were the *32nd (Saxon)* and *44th Reserve*, the former rated as third class, the latter first. Their defences turned out to be poor: shallow trenches and shell-holes, so that free movement by day was impossible; the dug-outs were only rough weather-proof shelters, and the wire was salved British material, badly erected, with none in the hedges or ditches.

[3] The distribution of the battalions will be seen on Sketch 8. Those of 5th Division used two companies per battalion in the front line; those of 31st, one company. The G.O.C.'s R.A. of 5th and 31st Divisions were Br.-Generals A. H. Hussey and E. P. Lambert.

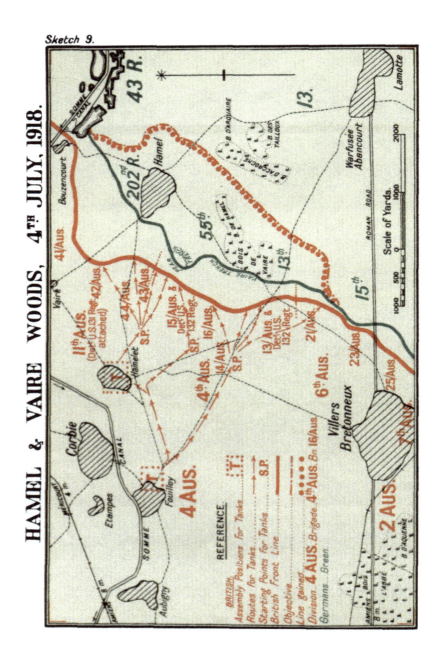

the purpose of deceiving the enemy as to the front of attack; the infantry being extremely enterprising and hating to see a barrage wasted, meanwhile made two raids and carried off 15 unwounded prisoners, 2 trench mortars and 6 machine guns.

The creeping barrage was so good and the troops followed it so closely, it being a principle in the 5th Division to be in the enemy trenches before the barrage lifted, that they were among the Germans, with the bayonet, before the latter had time to bring their machine guns into action, or even to open fire with their rifles. Thus all the objectives were reached and consolidated,[1] and the bridges over the Plate Becque destroyed, without severe casualties except among the 2/K.O.S.B., in front of which battalion the wire of the support line proved an obstacle, and in the 11/East Lancashire, which encountered machine-gun fire. The total losses in the operations of the 27th and 28th in killed, missing and wounded were 72 officers and 1,854 other ranks, with a high percentage of wounded. The motor ambulances were able to get fairly close up and the prisoners did good service in carrying the wounded, so that the advanced dressing stations specialized in hot soup and nourishment rather than surgery. The total captures of the 5th and 31st Divisions amounted to 7 officers, 432 other ranks, 4 field guns, with a quantity of mustard shell (which was returned to the enemy next day), 14 trench-mortars and 77 machine guns. The 92nd Brigade alone buried 135 of the enemy.[2] No organized counter-attack was noticed.[3]

The success of the attack established that the enemy entertained no offensive intentions near the junction of the First and Second Armies.

The action of La Becque was followed six days later by an attack between Villers Bretonneux and the Somme by troops of the Australian Corps (Fourth Army). The date, 4th July, Independence Day, was tactfully chosen by General Rawlinson, as for the first time in France American

Sketch 9.

---

[1] Telephone communication was at once laid down from the front line. One young officer sent a message: " Have captured all objectives but a bottle of whisky would help us to hold on ". He got it.

[2] From three companies of the *102nd Regiment* only a few wounded men returned.

[3] German regimental accounts state that the *32nd Division* ordered a counter-attack at 12.15 P.M. by the *177th Regiment*; this was brought to a standstill by machine-gun fire, and another at 6 P.M. was equally unsuccessful.

soldiers were to fight alongside the British,[1] four companies of the American 33rd Division (Major-General George Bell, Junior) being incorporated by platoons in the attacking battalions. The objective was the ridge which stretches northward from the Villers Bretonneux plateau towards the Somme. On it are situated Vaire Wood and the wood and village of Hamel. The operation entailed an attack on a six-thousand yards front to be carried to a depth of two thousand five hundred yards.

Several advantages could be secured by a gain of ground in this sector. First, the capture of the ridge would materially improve the line of the Fourth Army, giving it increased depth in the neighbourhood of the Villers Bretonneux plateau, the retention of which was vital for the defence of Amiens. Secondly, important observation would be acquired up the valley of the Somme, correspondingly depriving the enemy of his point of vantage on the spur above Hamel. Further, an opportunity would be afforded of testing the strength of the German defence, of ascertaining whether German morale was deteriorating, as was believed, and of making a preliminary trial of the methods in course of elaboration, which it was intended to employ in the operations which must take place at a later date on a larger scale in order to free the Amiens railway centre from danger of capture.

The country about Hamel, being open, was suited to the employment of tanks. General Rawlinson decided, therefore, to engage as small a force of infantry as possible. The Australian Corps (commanded by Lieut.-General Sir J. Monash, with Br.-General T. A. Blamey as his chief General Staff officer) was directed to prepare the scheme. It was entirely successful and a model of its kind.[2]

The strength of the German defences was by no means uniform: Vaire and Hamel woods and Hamel village were well fortified, and a number of strongpoints had been organized; but, as at La Becque, the trenches were as a rule shallow and non-continuous, many of the defenders being in shell-holes; the wire was poor, there were no communication trenches and no shell-proof dug-outs in the foremost trenches. The usual garrison was four infantry regiments.[3]

[1] They had co-operated in China in the Boxer troubles of 1900.

[2] An account of the operation giving technical details was speedily issued to the Armies.

[3] The *13th Division*, rated by the British Intelligence as first-class, which had completed the relief of the *77th Reserve* only on the night of

Only ten battalions of infantry, with five companies (sixty tanks) of the 5th Tank Brigade (Br.-General A. Courage), and the 8th and 9th and 3rd Australian Aeroplane Squadrons, were allotted to the attack, which was entrusted to the 4th Australian Division (Major-General E. G. Sinclair-MacLagan), the centre of the three Australian divisions in the line. Attached to it was the 11th Brigade of the 3rd Australian Division (Major-General J. Gellibrand), then in reserve. On the right, two battalions of the 6th Brigade of the 2nd Australian Division (Major-General C. Rosenthal) were to swing forward to guard that flank.

Surprise was an essential factor for success. As no large woods or other sufficient cover existed to conceal the troops from the air, very thorough measures were taken to ensure secrecy. They proved highly successful, as the enemy gained no inkling of the coming stroke. The additional artillery was moved into position during the five nights preceding the attack. In the early stages of preparation as little as possible was committed to paper, plan and details being arranged verbally at conferences held at Australian Corps headquarters, the final conference not taking place until three days before the attack. All outstanding matters were then settled, and thereafter no change was allowed. No movement of lorries (carrying up ammunition and engineer stores) was permitted during daylight, except in back areas, nor of troops, even in back areas, except at night. The additional troops required were told that they were to be employed to reinforce the line against an expected attack. All units selected to take part were withdrawn from the line before orders were issued to them.

To ensure as far as possible that the frontage and objective of the attack should remain undiscovered, the troops on either flank were to display some activity. On

---

the 3rd/4th provided three, the fourth was the left-hand regiment of the *43rd Reserve Division*. The *13th Division* had lost 40 per cent of its effectives in the March offensive, when engaged in the *Second Army* against the British VII. Corps, and had been reconstituted with returned wounded and recruits who belonged to the 1919 year. It was back in the line on 23rd April in the French Avre sector and carried out some local attacks. It received a draft of 1,300 men on 3rd May and was pulled out for rest on the 18th.

The *43rd Reserve Division*, considered at the end of 1917 a very good organization, was now rated third-class. It had on 9th April signally failed to dislodge the British 55th Division in front of Béthune. It had been reconstituted and rested between 29th April and 24th June.

The infantry regiments in the line had one battalion in the front position, one in reserve, and one resting.

the right, the 2nd Australian Division artillery was to extend the barrage laterally; south of it, the French would carry on neutralization fire, especially directed against two powerful enemy artillery groups near Marcelcave and Wiencourt (3 and 5 miles E.S.E. of Villers Bretonneux), which might enfilade the advance. On the left, north of the river, the 5th Australian Division (Major-General Sir J. J. T. Hobbs) was to carry out a minor operation on a 1,200-yards front. North of the Australians, the III. Corps (Lieut.-General Sir R. H. K. Butler) was to fire a creeping barrage along its whole front, with a proportion of smoke shell intermixed in order to hide the absence of an infantry advance. The field artillery on the front of attack was to fire 10 per cent smoke shell in the first barrage, in order to shroud the infantry advance, at the same time suggesting to the Germans that gas was being used and thereby leading them to handicap themselves by putting on their gas masks.[1] As an additional measure to conceal the attacks, No. 1 Special Company R.E. was to form several smoke screens : one to cover the right flank of the infantry advance; another in three layers, was designed to prevent German observation from the heights north of the Somme.[2] The ground, however, was so hard and the day so calm that, when the artillery fire opened and the tanks moved forward, so much dust was raised as to render smoke almost unnecessary; in fact the tanks were much hampered by it. Harassing fire with a proportion of smoke and gas shell was carried out daily on several mornings before zero day in order to divert suspicion from the real barrage when it should open.

It was a difficult problem to bring up the tanks unobserved to their stations. To drown the noise of their arrival, aeroplanes were detailed to fly up and down the whole front of the Fourth Army during the hours when the tanks would be moving to their starting line, also during the period before zero hour when they would be starting up and advancing to join the infantry. In order to accustom the Germans to the appearance of the aeroplanes, flights were made nightly for some days before the attack.

Since a good many tanks were to be employed, it was

[1] This ruse seems to have been only partly successful; " Regt. No. " 55 " speaks of gassing, but the other regiments concerned only mention " fog " and " thick fog ".

[2] The screen was made in three layers by mortars in three groups, the desired height being attained by a series of high bursts.

deemed essential to make the plan as simple as possible. It was therefore decided to carry out the operation by a direct advance covered by a field and heavy artillery barrage, behind which the infantry and tanks were to follow closely. Some combined training of the two arms was carried out. On this occasion, at the suggestion of Lieut.-Colonel Hon. D. Bingham who was in command of the tanks, "these creatures" were to precede the infantry in the assault, and go "over the top" in front of them, with a tank supporting wave in front of the infantry support line. The great defended localities of Vaire and Hamel woods and Hamel village presented special difficulties. To overcome these it was arranged that the places should be dealt with by special detachments, whilst the troops destined for the final objective should pass by on either side, special precautions being taken with tanks and machine guns to protect their flanks. The attack was then to spread out again, and, after making a halt of ten minutes on an intermediate line about six hundred yards from the starting line, to reorganize and proceed onwards to occupy the final objective.

The artillery of the Fourth Army (Major-General C. E. D. Budworth) was reinforced by five brigades of field artillery and two brigades of heavy artillery; this allowed the total number of pieces allotted to the Australian Corps (C.R.A., Br.-General W. A. Coxen; commander of the Heavy Artillery, Br.-General L. D. Fraser), for the operation to be increased to 326 field guns and howitzers, and 302 heavies. The 18-pdr. barrage provided approximately one gun per 25 yards, and it was supplemented by 111 of the 147 machine guns of the 2nd, 3rd, 4th and 5th Australian Machine Gun Battalions, the remaining 36 accompanying the first line infantry battalions. The machine-gun group positions were chosen with local knowledge of the incidence of hostile shelling, and were for the most part in places usually unoccupied by troops, mainly on the flanks of the attack. As a result, they enjoyed an almost total absence of deliberate enemy shelling. The main volume of the fire of the heavy artillery was to be concentrated on the enemy's guns in the Lamotte—Cérisy valley (running down to the Somme, some two miles east of Hamel), whilst long-range guns dealt with rear establishments and communications. No wire-cutting was to be attempted by the artillery, it being considered that it gave warning of assault and that the infantry, aided by tanks if necessary, could under a protective barrage cut its way through;[1] and it did. Similarly, no preliminary bombardment was allowed—a strictly limited number of rounds were fired for calibration and registration purposes amid a little promiscuous shooting to disguise its purpose; thus the artillerymen were not worn out by days of continuous work before the battle opened. On the night before the attack selected billeting areas were visited by No. 101 Squadron R.A.F., which dropped 350 bombs.

No. 8 Squadron R.A.F. and No. 3 Squadron A.F.C. were to co-operate with the infantry and tanks, flying low over the enemy lines and bombing infantry, guns and transport. At zero plus 30 minutes No. 205 Squadron R.A.F. was to bomb dumps and bivouac areas. No. 9 Squadron R.A.F. was detailed to drop small arms ammunition at pre-arranged points or on ground signal : 93 boxes were thus dropped.

Zero hour was fixed at 3.10 A.M. on the 4th, when the light would be sufficient to distinguish friend from foe at twenty yards.

During the nights of the 2nd/3rd and 3rd/4th, the 4th and 11th Australian Brigades (Br.-Generals C. H. Brand and J. H. Cannan) which were to carry out the main attack, moved up into the line and relieved the 13th Australian Brigade and the right battalion of the 12th, which were then withdrawn into reserve in readiness to take over the new line forty-eight hours after its capture. With the 13th Battalion (4th Australian Brigade) was a company (7 officers and over 200 other ranks) of the American 132nd Regiment; with the 15th Battalion, another company of the same regiment; and with the 11th Australian Brigade two companies of the American 131st Regiment.

On the night of the 2nd/3rd the 60 fighting tanks and 12 supply tanks of the 5th Tank Brigade were brought forward to the vicinity of Fouilloy and Hamelet, a couple of miles and a mile behind the front line, and carefully

---

[1] The first barrage consisted of 60 per cent shrapnel, 30 per cent H.E. with delay-action fuzes, and 10 per cent smoke-shell, fired by 18-pdrs. and was placed 200 yards in front of the infantry starting line. Two hundred yards forward was a barrage of 4·5-inch howitzers, firing 90 per cent H.E. with instantaneous fuzes and 10 per cent smoke-shell. In front of this again was a barrage of 6-inch howitzers. The pace of the barrage was 100 yards in 3 minutes up to the intermediate halt line, and subsequently 100 yards in 4 minutes. This pace was adopted in order to ensure that the tanks could keep in front of the infantry and close behind the barrage.

hidden in orchards, near trees and among the ruined houses of the villages. They were distributed as follows :

To the 6th Australian Brigade (the flank guard), 2 sections (6 tanks), to support the infantry in the attack against the final objective and cover it during consolidation.

To the 4th Australian Brigade: one company (12 tanks), one half being detailed to protect the flanks of the infantry passing south and north of the Vaire and Hamel woods, and the other half to assist in clearing and "mopping up" the woods.

To the 11th Australian Brigade: one company plus 2 sections (18 tanks), 6 tanks being detailed to assist in clearing and "mopping up" the village of Hamel, and the rest to co-operate with the infantry.

Liaison units: one company (12 tanks) to form a link between the 4th and 11th Australian Brigades, 3 tanks being detailed to capture Pear Trench, a salient strongpoint in the centre of the front.

Supports: one company (12 tanks) to move forward, divided between the 4th and 11th Brigades, immediately in rear of the assaulting waves, as far as the intermediate halt line. At that point they were to form a single wave and, like the others, move forward to the final objective and assist in covering the infantry during consolidation. Each fighting tank carried two boxes of small arms ammunition, Lewis gun drums and water for the infantry; in addition, 4 supply tanks carried engineer stores and ammunition, thereby doing, so it was calculated, the work of 1,250 human carriers.

At 10.30 P.M. on the 3rd the tanks moved to their starting line, about a thousand yards behind the tapes from which the infantry was to begin its advance. By 1 A.M. they were in position without any interference from the enemy, the sound of the engines having been drowned, as arranged, by the noise of aeroplanes and of slight artillery activity.[1] The task of getting the tanks up to the infantry unnoticed by the enemy still remained. In order to facilitate this step the barrage opened at zero

---

[1] The experience in this operation seemed to show that, provided the country was suitable, it would be possible to bring up tanks 6,000 yards before an attack from well-covered and secure positions : 4,000 yards at full speed, halt and fill up ; then 1,000 yards on half throttle, and then into action at full speed so as to clear the enemy's barrage. Aeroplane and other camouflage noise which might awake enemy attention would then be unnecessary.

hour, resting on the line two hundred yards ahead of the infantry for four minutes before it crept on, in order to give the tanks plenty of time in which to cover the thousand yards that lay between them and the infantry. Normal harassing fire was put down eight minutes before zero; as soon as it opened the tanks started their advance, so that when the creeping barrage moved forward twelve minutes later they were in position, the last tank arriving dead on time " roaring like a hundred aeroplanes ", without having attracted the attention of the Germans.

The infantry was formed up in four waves, on tapes laid out by the engineers. The waves, in order to avoid the hostile barrage, were well closed up, and, as usual, moved off in this formation, keeping as close as possible to the creeping barrage. Once clear of danger from the enemy's artillery, owing to proximity to the German trenches, the second leading wave took 50 yards' distance, the remainder shaking out into artillery formation of small parties.

All went according to plan, except that some of the shells of the barrage batteries fell short—as much as two hundred yards—hit one tank and occasioned losses among the infantry, notably in the 15th Battalion, which had 42 casualties before the advance began. In general, the barrage was reported as " glorious ". When it came down and the counter-battery guns opened full volume of fire, there was practically no response on the battle front, although half a minute later, German S.O.S. signals were appealing for help. In fact, for some hours after zero, all German guns on this front, except those of one field battery, were practically silent; some artillery fire gradually developed on both flanks, the first sign of any retaliation being a light shelling of the vicinity of Villers Bretonneux seven minutes after zero; but the enemy's fire never attained any density.

On the right, the 23rd and 21st Battalions of the 6th Australian Brigade (Br.-General J. Paton), which had to wheel forward to form a flank, encountered no serious opposition and the two battalions reached their objective with very slight casualties. At 4.49 A.M. a message was sent back to this effect, followed eleven minutes later by another stating that they were in touch on the left with the 13th Battalion. The six tanks proved very useful in destroying small posts of the enemy beyond the final line.

The 4th Australian Brigade had the 13th Battalion on the right, the 16th in the centre and the 15th on the left,

VAIRE AND HAMEL. 4TH JULY

the 14th being in reserve to carry forward stores and establish dumps.

The 13th Battalion had the task of passing south of Vaire Wood on a narrow frontage of four hundred yards and then opening out rapidly to cover twelve hundred yards of the final objective. One company (less a platoon detailed to dig a strongpoint on the right) formed the leading wave. It was followed by two companies each on a two-platoon frontage, the remaining platoons following in lines of sections. The two companies were to pass through the leader at the intermediate halt line, where it was to dig in, and then gradually extend. The fourth company was to advance behind the left in columns of sections prepared to fill any gaps in the ultimate front. Of the three tanks attached to the battalion, two were to guard the attackers as they passed round the southern end of Vaire Wood, and the third to work along the Fouilloy—Warfusée road.

The left company in second line came under fire from a machine gun in Vaire Wood and suffered a few casualties, but the gun was captured by a rush. Whilst moving north to extend beyond the wood opposition was again encountered, but it was swiftly smothered by one of the tanks. So there was very little delay, and the company, preceded from the intermediate halt line, here as elsewhere, by the liaison tanks, reached the final objective at 4.18 A.M., in just four minutes over an hour. There it found the right company, which had overcome the opposition offered half-way and had mopped up a strongpoint, taking 80 prisoners; it added to this number as a result of some unsuccessful bombing attacks by the enemy. The tanks now covered the consolidation of the new line. The fourth company of the 13th Battalion was not engaged until 6 A.M., when it was sent forward to the final objective to fill gaps.

The 16th Battalion, whose business it was to clear and mop up Vaire and Hamel woods quickly and thoroughly in order that the battalions on either side should not be delayed by enfilade fire, placed its six tanks in pairs, on the two flanks and in the centre, well up in line with the leading waves. Strong resistance was encountered on the edge of Vaire Wood; but this was quickly overcome, whilst inside both the woods, and on their outskirts, many strongpoints and machine-gun nests were rapidly brought to surrender. Within an hour and a half the woods had been completely cleared and many prisoners captured. Much useful work was done in the wood fighting by men firing Lewis guns slung over the shoulder to the hip.[1] At 5 A.M. battalion headquarters were informed that the 13th and 15th Battalions were on their final objective, and five minutes later the 16th Battalion was ordered to fall back into reserve.

The 15th Battalion had encountered more trouble. The first lift took the barrage over the salient Pear Trench facing the left of the battalion, and the Germans were able to man their machine guns before the first wave reached the wire, which was uncut; Pear Trench itself was quite undamaged by artillery fire. The wire was finally cut under rifle fire; but men began to fall and it was only after a fierce fight with the bayonet that the garrison was overcome. The falling short of some of the shells of the barrage further delayed the left. Meantime, the right, with three tanks, had pushed on, suffering from enfilade fire from Pear Trench, which at that time was still uncaptured.[2] The defenders of Vaire Trench, which ran along a track from Vaire Wood to Vaire village as a retrenchment to the Pear Trench salient, offered considerable resistance until their trench was taken by assault. No further serious resistance was encountered before the intermediate halt was reached, although fire from strongpoints on either flank caused losses until the garrisons were blotted out of existence by tanks. From the intermediate halt line the advance was preceded by the tanks which had passed through the line during the ten minutes' pause. Flanking fire from the enemy reserve line brought further losses, and on the final objective the Germans made a short stand, but they were driven out with the help of a tank. Consolidation was begun, and by 7 A.M. a good line had been dug. It was then discovered that Germans in some force were on the immediate front; so small parties with Lewis guns were pushed forward to drive them off. The remainder of the day then passed without incident.[3]

[1] For his gallantry in these attacks, Lce.-Corporal T. L. Axford, M.M., 16th Battalion, was awarded the V.C.

[2] The tanks detailed to deal with it did not appear, having apparently gone astray in the mist and smoke which made keeping direction difficult for all the machines engaged.

[3] For his great gallantry in the attack, Driver H. Dalziel, 15th Battalion, was awarded the V.C. "Regt. No. 55" states (pp. 230-1) that, having only just come into the line after a rest following the Chemin des Dames offensive, the night flying of aeroplanes and desultory artillery fire in the evening caused the *III. Battalion* to be on the alert. When the battalion

VAIRE AND HAMEL. 4TH JULY

The 11th Australian Brigade, with its tanks and American contingent, had to capture Hamel and beyond the village re-establish the old French line, which ran down to the Somme east of Bouzencourt. The 43rd and 42nd Battalions were in front line. On reaching their intermediate halt line after little opposition except from the vicinity of Pear Trench, the 44th Battalion " leap-frogged " the 43rd and, on the advance being resumed, divided into two, one half moving south and the other north of Hamel, each supported by six tanks. The 43rd with the six remaining tanks proceeded to clear up the village. Neither of the half-battalions of the 44th, nor the 42nd, encountered much opposition, and the final objective was reached between 4.45 and 4.55 A.M. The " mopping up " of Hamel caused little trouble, as the enemy, surprised in his deep dug-outs, surrendered quickly.[1]

The attack of the 15th Australian Brigade north of the Somme on a 1,200-yards front was also entirely successful. Four companies and one platoon were engaged. They advanced in three lines, supported by a line of small section columns at 10 yards' interval, followed at 25 yards' distance by Lewis guns. Parties were detailed for special objectives and as flank guard. When the barrage came down the Germans replied promptly and, though most of those in the forward position ran, the machine-gunners offered resistance and had to be bayoneted. The new position was consolidated, as previously arranged, by occupying shell-holes at about 50 yards' interval, wired on the flanks. By 5 A.M. it could be reported that the infantry of the brigade was digging in on the whole line of the farthest objective. There was practically no enemy reaction for some hours and even then no serious effort was perceptible.

---

was " overrun "—no mention is made of its fine resistance—two companies of the *I. Battalion* were brought up (no doubt the force seen near the final objective). No counter-attack was made, as by the time the *II. Battalion* arrived the struggle was already ended. It is claimed that a break-through was stopped, but admitted that the small fight cost " a greatly disproportionate loss of men and material ".

[1] " Res. Regt. No. 202 " admits the complete surprise " in thick " fog " of its *III. Battalion*, which was in the front line, and its complete annihilation. It was not until 9 A.M. that the *I.*, the reserve battalion, received orders to counter-attack ; but British artillery fire and bombing delayed the march, so that it was not until the evening that an unsuccessful attack was made against the end of the ridge east of Hamel. It is added that no German aeroplanes appeared until 11 A.M. : they then drove off the British, but retired in an hour, when the enemy aircraft returned.

The casualties of the Australians in the main operation were 51 officers and 724 other ranks; of the Americans, 6 officers and 128 other ranks. Five fighting tanks were disabled and put out of action;[1] all the others rallied by 11 A.M. and by the night of the 6th/7th July the damaged five had been salvaged. Five aeroplanes did not return, but five German fighters and one balloon were destroyed. The captures were 41 officers and 1,431 other ranks, 2 field guns, 26 trench mortars, 171 machine guns and two of the new anti-tank rifles. In the attack north of the Somme the casualties were 8 officers and 94 other ranks, and the prisoners 1 officer and 63 other ranks, with 15 machine guns and other trophies.

This affair completed the Australian operations on the Amiens front. During their progress, in ten attacks between the 28th March and the 4th July, the Australians had gained a belt of ground, between the neighbourhood of Villers Bretonneux and Dernancourt on the Ancre, ten miles wide and averaging a mile in depth; had obliterated the two enemy salients which enclosed Sailly le Sec; and had captured from 16 enemy divisions upwards of 3,000 prisoners, 400 machine guns, 50 trench mortars, and much smaller booty.

On the day following the successful attacks on Hamel, General Rawlinson, before an Army Commanders' conference, asked the Commander-in-Chief for permission to make another attack south of the Somme in order to advance the line of the Fourth Army still farther. Sir Douglas Haig refused on the general grounds that success would mean an extension of the front at a time when reserves were very scarce; but he instructed General Rawlinson to study the problem and to prepare a plan in case troops should become available. He subsequently told Generals Horne and Byng to consider a joint operation to retake Orange Hill, a commanding feature west of Monchy le Preux, near Arras, and of Henin Hill, the ridge between the rivers Sensée and Cojeul, in order to protect from enfilade fire the right flank of the troops advancing against Orange Hill.[2]

On the night of the 12th/13th, six thousand gas cylinders were discharged against the Oppy—Lens—Hulluch front.

---

[1] Two during the actual battle, one by enemy fire, one by our own barrage; a third received a stray shell on the way home, and the remaining two were hit whilst in support during consolidation.

[2] The evolution of the further schemes for offensives is dealt with in Chapter XVIII.

Sketch 10.

METEREN
19th July, 1918.

METEREN. 19TH JULY

Sketch 10.

The capture on the 19th July of Meteren, by the 9th Division (Major-General H. H. Tudor), and of Gerbedoen Farm, a couple of miles to the south-south-west, by the 1st Australian Division (Major-General T. W. Glasgow), formed an operation which presented special difficulties. The 9th (Scottish) Division, reorganized after its heavy losses in the March-April fighting [1] had been filled up with reinforcements from home, so that its infantry when it joined the XV. Corps (Lieut.-General Sir B. de Lisle) and went into the line again on the night of the 25th/26th May near Meteren was mainly composed of boys little more than eighteen years of age.

The principal feature of the sector which it now occupied was the narrow Meteren ridge, a long spur of the Mont des Cats lying at right angles to the general front. This ridge commands an extensive view to the east, south and west, and blocks the road from Cassel to Bailleul. The village of Meteren, at its southern extremity, was in the enemy's hands, so that he was able to observe all approaches to the ridge from the west across the valley of the Meteren Becque and prevent any movement in the valley by day. The French and the Australians had tried and failed to retake Meteren; [2] but the 9th Division was dissatisfied with being overlooked, and Major-General Tudor, having reconnoitred the enemy defences and found that they consisted of disconnected posts and shell-holes, without a continuous belt of wire, was able to convince his corps commander that he could overcome them with slight loss. As the occupation of the whole ridge was requisite for the effective protection of the important railway junction of Hazebrouck, only seven miles away, it was decided to advance the line in order to include the village. All was ready by the middle of June, but, as the French (D.A.N.), on the left, were in the act of leaving and it was essential to keep the front as quiet as possible, the attack was postponed. A preliminary destruction of the buildings of the village was necessary, not only in order to demolish the defensive organizations, but also to enable a creeping barrage to pass over the village without danger to the attacking infantry from falling fragments of masonry.

---

[1] A total of 5,106 casualties in the German offensive in March, and 4,048 in the Lys offensive.

[2] Meteren had been lost on 16th April. Attempts made to retake it by the French 133rd Division on the 16th and by the 3rd Australian Brigade on the nights of the 22nd/23rd and 23rd/24th had failed. See " 1918 " Vol. II., pp. 337 and 373.

For a fortnight before the attack the XV. Corps heavy artillery (Br.-General C. W. Collingwood) fired into it every day, and the 9th Division artillery (Br.-General A. R. Wainewright) and trench mortars co-operated in flattening it out. But such action would convey warning of something on hand; so, in order to mislead the enemy as to the actual time of assault, and train him to expect gas whenever smoke was fired and force him to put on his gas masks, smoke shelling, accompanied by discharge of projector gas, was from time to time carried out by day.

Renewed activity in mid-July on the part of the Germans, both here and on various parts of the front, as will be narrated in the next chapter, made it desirable to make the attempt as soon as possible in order to upset their preparations, in the event of their designing an attack, and to gain an insight into their intentions. Plans were therefore made to carry out the operation on the 19th July regardless of the direction of the wind, although it was desirable that this should be from a quarter favourable to the smoke barrage.

The attack against Meteren was to be made by four battalions, two from the 26th Brigade (Br.-General J. Kennedy) and two from the South African Brigade (Br.-General W. E. C. Tanner),[1] whilst the 3rd Australian Brigade (Br.-General H. G. Bennett) made a subsidiary attack from its sector south of the 9th Division.[2] Zero hour was fixed for 7.55 A.M., when it was hoped that the enemy, after " standing to ", would have turned in and be off his guard. This expectation was realized.

The artillery covering the Meteren operation consisted of seven (including three Army) brigades R.F.A., with portions of three other brigades of the 9th, 29th and 36th Division artillery for the barrage (smoke and H.E.); and the XXXIII. and XXXVI. Brigades R.G.A., assisted by some heavy artillery with the 1st Australian Division on the right, for bombardment and counter-battery work. One 6-inch gun battery of the Australian I. Brigade fired at long range into Bailleul (2 miles east of Meteren) from the south. Light

---

[1] Owing to the heavy South African losses on 24th March (see " 1918 " Vol. I., pp. 416-7), the brigade now consisted of a Composite S.A. Battalion, the 2/R. Scots Fusiliers and the 9/Scottish Rifles.

[2] The 9th Division had opposite it the *81st Reserve Division* (which had suffered heavy losses in the Lys offensive); this had all its three regiments in the line. On its left, opposite the 1st Australian Division, was the *13th Reserve Division* (which had had 3 days' heavy fighting at the end of the Lys offensive).

trench mortars dealt with targets too close for the field artillery. Some trouble was encountered in siting a number of the field guns so as to clear the ridge and yet bear on the enemy lines just below the top on the other side. The barrage was specially planned: smoke at " quarter " strength " was placed one hundred and fifty yards ahead of the field artillery barrage,[1] which opened on the enemy front position at one minute before zero. Three minutes later, in order to establish a straight line, the centre part of the barrage, after falling on the salient which the enemy front line formed, lifted forward until it was level with the flanks, when the infantry moved to the assault. Then the barrage advanced in lifts of only fifty yards per minute until it reached a line just south of the village, where a pause of three minutes was made in order to enable any of the infantry to catch up who had dropped behind in passing through the ruins. It then continued at the same rate to a line roughly 250 yards beyond the objective. A frontal barrage was also put down by the 9th Machine-Gun Battalion, whilst a machine-gun company of the 1st Australian Division fired in enfilade along the front to be attacked by the right (South African) brigade. At three minutes after zero 425 drums of burning oil were projected on the German position south and south-east of Meteren.

Before dawn the S. African Composite Battalion, the 2/R. Scots Fusiliers, the 5/Cameron Highlanders and the 8/Black Watch were in position, so well camouflaged that an enemy aeroplane flying low over them at 7.30 A.M. failed to detect anything unusual.[2] In spite of the very careful preparations the attack began under unfavourable conditions. On the previous day all the battle stores of the South African Brigade had been burnt by fire, and were not replaced until after the infantry had reached its assembly position; the wind was unsteady, varying between south and south-west, the worst direction from the point of view of a smoke barrage;[3] a Stokes mortar detachment moving to the left brigade sector lost its way, wandered into the German lines five hours before zero, and one man failed to return,

---

[1] According to the wind, the smoke was to be in or beyond the field artillery barrage, and of varying degrees of thickness: full, half or quarter.

[2] Two thousand yards of cocoanut matting, the same colour as the turned-up soil, was stretched over the trenches on poles, with gaps only for sentries; to represent the trench a black line about a foot wide was tarred down the centre.

[3] German accounts (" Res. Regts. Nos. 267 and 269 ") say the smoke was very effective and visibility only twenty yards.

an incident which might have given a warning of the attack. To crown the series of mishaps, some howitzers on the right and left flanks opened fire five minutes before the appointed time in order to drop smoke screens round certain suspected O.P.'s in the background.[1]

The effects of the bombardment, however, were excellent and the infantry attack was entirely successful ; for except on the extreme left the enemy was surprised, and at 8.40, 8.27 and 8.25 A.M., respectively, the S. African Battalion, 2/R. Scots Fusiliers and 5/Cameron Highlanders signalled that the final objective had been reached. The delighted divisional commander jumped on to a bicycle and hurried up the Bailleul road to see with his own eyes, and to devise measures against counter-attack.[2] Scores of Germans had simply put their hands up. Serious opposition was encountered only on the left, where wired hedges and uncut wire favoured the defence, with the result that the greater part of the 8/Black Watch eventually fell back to its starting-point. Two platoons of the 7/Seaforth Highlanders were sent up, and, working round the left flank of the Germans holding a hedge, in the course of the next day filled the gap in the line. Contact aeroplanes sent over at one-hour intervals after zero could see no sign of counter-attack ; there was, indeed, no reaction except some artillery fire late in the afternoon.[3]

The casualties of the 9th Division amounted to 25 officers and 497 other ranks, nearly half of them in the 8/Black Watch ; six officers and 348 other ranks, a field gun, 12 trench mortars and 47 machine guns were captured.[4]

The subsidiary attack of the 3rd Australian Brigade was carried out by three companies of the 9th Battalion without any artillery or trench mortar assistance. One company moved out at 8 A.M. as a fighting patrol, whilst the other two supported it with flanking fire of Lewis guns and rifle grenades. The three companies reached a line

[1] German accounts admit complete surprise (" *schlagartig* ") and mention " the unusual hour " : the men had gone back to their shelters and were feeding.

[2] On his return from the trenches—where divisional legend has it that he took prisoner a German officer—the bicycle had disappeared from the place where he had left it.

[3] The confusion on the German side was so great that " not until " 4.30 P.M. was any clarity about the situation obtained ". (" Regt. " No. 269 ", p. 311.)

[4] Five companies of the *269th Reserve Regiment* disappeared ; no history of the *268th* has yet been published ; the *267th* does not give its losses. The *81st Reserve Division* had suffered so heavily that it was relieved next day.

which included the houses at Gerbedoen Farm and le Waton, and there established posts at a cost of only 25 casualties, the Germans losing 98 prisoners, 16 machine guns and 2 trench mortars.[1]

In the course of the night of the 29th/30th, the 3rd Australian Brigade captured Merris, thus extending their new front to the right.

During the period under review, as a result of General Foch's constant pressure, the French Armies were also very active in undertaking raids and small enterprises for the purpose of improving the front positions and encouraging the offensive spirit of the troops.[2]

A more important French enterprise was planned for the middle of July. The value to the enemy of the Soissons railway centre was great. Since he had been unable to gain possession of Reims, he was dependent on it for the supply of the divisions in the Château Thierry salient. On the 14th June, as the Battle of the Matz was coming to a close, General Foch directed that the railway junction should be subjected to methodical bombardment, and preparations made, as soon as circumstances permitted and the necessary means should be assembled, to recover the high ground which dominates Soissons on the south-west. On the 16th he suggested the employment of a strong concentration of artillery and tanks, with a relatively small number of infantry. He preferred this, he said, to an attack near Reims, on the eastern side of the salient, which operation he thought should be cut down or post-

Sketches A, 5.

[1] The account in " Res. Regt. No. 39 " is that the Australians broke through between two companies and then attacked one in rear and rolled up three others, which fought until ammunition was expended.

[2] In the First Army next to the British in June there were " coups de main " in the sectors of Hourges, Sénécat Wood, Autheuil and the Matz. In the Tenth Army, next on the right, near Hautebraye, a knoll and 370 prisoners were captured ; near Montgobert the line was advanced several hundred yards ; and near Le Port a German work and 194 prisoners were taken. The Sixth Army also adopted an aggressive defensive, on one occasion capturing 275 prisoners. It was in this period, on the 25th June, that the American 4th (Marine) Brigade, under Br.-General J. G. Harbord, completed the capture of Belleau Wood, which the American 2nd Division had temporarily occupied on 12th June.

In the first half of July there were still more minor operations. The Fourth Army, in search of identifications, carried out numerous small raids ; the Fifth had fighting on the Montagne de Bligny in the old British sector ; the Sixth, in a German attack captured over two hundred prisoners, advanced its line slightly at several places, whilst the American 2nd Division (Major-General O. Bundy) seized Vaux, taking 250 prisoners ; the Tenth Army was particularly active, making eight attacks and taking over fourteen hundred prisoners ; the Third Army made two good advances,

poned.[1] He did not, however, abandon hope of a general offensive, and, after pressing General Pershing at a conference on the 23rd to speed up the American programme so as to have eighty divisions ready by April 1919, he wrote on the 27th to General Pétain and Sir Douglas Haig inviting them to accustom their subordinates to the idea of resuming the offensive: he hoped that within two months he would have some thirty divisions ready (12 American, 10 French and 7 or 8 British). He also wrote to General Diaz urging him to exploit his recent victory on the Piave and informing him of the possibility of a powerful Allied general offensive in September: if, however, 1918 did not afford the desired opportunity, all the Allies must be ready for a decisive effort in 1919, when, with American help, they should possess the necessary numerical superiority.

When General Mangin (Tenth Army) received orders to press closer to Soissons he had already drafted a plan of attack. This included a preliminary operation for the purpose of securing a bridgehead (3 miles wide and $1\frac{1}{4}$ deep) on the eastern side of the Cœuvres stream, which runs in a deep-cut valley,[2] in order to ensure a rapid start of the advance and facilitate the use of tanks. The main operation aimed at the capture of a wedge of high ground immediately west and south-west of Soissons, on a front of a little over two miles and an average depth of one mile, marked [3] by Corcy (east of Villers Cotterêts)—Villers Helon—Chaudun—Mercin. The preliminary operation was carried out with complete success on the 28th and 30th June by one division and part of a second, assisted by aeroplanes and a few tanks. Prisoners to the number of 1,200 were taken. On the 3rd July, in order to distract the enemy's attention, two surprise attacks were made by two divisions of Mangin's left wing north of the Aisne, and more than a thousand prisoners taken.

The consistently favourable results of the Allied minor operations, particularly those of the Tenth Army during

---

taking about six hundred prisoners; and in the First Army the 66th Division captured Castel, the woods south of the village and Anchise Farm, taking over six hundred prisoners and greatly improving the situation near Moreuil.

[1] The attack by the Fifth Army was designed to gain ground west of Reims, where the British IX. Corps had been.

[2] See Sketches A, 11, 12. On the stream are Cœuvres, Laversine and Ambleny.

[3] See Sketch 12.

the later half of June, induced General Mangin on the 5th July to write to the G.A.N. suggesting that the main operation in hand might be enlarged or exploited so as to obtain the reduction of the whole Château Thierry salient. General Pétain approved of the idea and promised additional troops. Three days later General Degoutte (Sixth Army, on General Mangin's right) also proposed to attack, on a front of eight miles, with the forces at his disposal. These offensive schemes were entirely agreeable to General Foch, and he at once revived the rejected suggestion that the French Fifth Army, on the eastern side of the Château Thierry salient, should attack, but simultaneously with the Sixth and Tenth on the western side, about the 18th July, if circumstances permitted. " These operations ", he said, " will have a good chance of developing successfully against " an enemy who of late has shown signs of feebleness in " resistance."

NOTE

GERMAN MORALE IN JUNE 1918

The distinct falling off in the German resistance to attack seems to have been due to several causes : first, persuaded that they were more skilled than the Allies in open warfare, the Germans, after their successes, had not dug in after the old style—in some cases when ordered to entrench thoroughly they had not done so, although reporting that this had been done ; " continuous trenches and deep " blocks of wire were nowhere to be found. A few dug-outs and " O.P's ; here and there a bit of wire concealed as far as possible ; " a broad ditch or slope of a hollow road deepened a little ; a village " wall organized for defence : that, in general, was all." The defences were truly scattered in depth, but without a strong position anywhere. Secondly, influenza had taken its toll (1,000 to 2,000 cases per division). Thirdly, units were low in strength and the reinforcements of indifferent morale. Crown Prince Rupprecht's diary contains many entries on the subject at this period :—war-weariness of the troops, failure of the supply system, divisions in reserve receiving meat only nine days per month, increasing deterioration of morale, and mutinous resistance of reinforcements being sent to the front. Ludendorff (pp. 643-4) speaks of " a decided deteriora- " tion in the Army's morale resulting from the re-enrolment, after " long leave, of soldiers returned from captivity in Russia ; they " introduced a spirit of general insubordination". He then describes the spirit of the troops in the West as " already weakened by influenza " and depressed by uniform diet "—signs particularly noticed by the British were that the Germans had ceased to trouble about burying or removing the dead, or to make latrines. Ludendorff further told the Crown Prince that the question of reinforcements was causing the greatest anxiety, one division (*9th Bavarian*) had been broken up, and others (ten according to Kuhl ii., p. 394) must follow. (Rupprecht ii., pp. 395-419). According to Kuhl, in the middle of July, the average strength of battalions was 673. Fourthly, with indifferent troops, the " elastic " system of defence failed : the outposts retired at once and gave no time for the counter-attack troops to act

CHAPTER XII

AWAITING ATTACK

1ST–14TH JULY 1918

(Sketches 5, B)

ON the 1st July General Foch had addressed to General Sketch B. Pétain and Sir Douglas Haig another General Directive, No. 4, on the subject of future operations. Translated, it ran :

"To-day, 1st July, the enemy has halted :

18	miles	from	Dunkirk,
36	,,	,,	Calais,
42	,,	,,	Boulogne,
36	,,	,,	Abbeville,
36	,,	,,	Paris,
15	,,	,,	Châlons.

" An advance of 24 miles towards Abbeville would cut
" the communications with the north of France, and separate
" the British and French Armies—a result of considerable
" military importance for the issue of the War.

" An even smaller advance towards Paris—although
" this advance would not have any marked influence on
" the military operations and thereby lead to a decision—
" would make a profound impression on public opinion,
" cause the evacuation of the capital under the menace of
" bombardment, and doubtless hamper the hands of the
" Government, whose free action is so indispensable for the
" conduct of the War.

" Progress of the enemy towards any of the other
" objectives enumerated above cannot offer him any
" comparable result.

" In the defensive attitude which we still maintain
" to-day, 1st July, it is therefore Paris and Abbeville before
" all else which we must cover. Any enemy advance in

218 AWAITING ATTACK

Sketch B.

"those two directions must be checked as soon as possible "and at all costs.

"Putting aside any diversions which the enemy might "make elsewhere in order to distract attention—and his "front is prepared for action from Ypres to Verdun—if he "decides to move against Paris or Abbeville he has no "choice but must launch his attack from the front Château "Thierry—Lens.

"It is therefore opposite this front from Château "Thierry to Lens that we must concentrate our action and "in the greatest possible depth, and make or set about "making the dispositions which defensive war demands, "with a view to a foot by foot defence.

"Opposite this front :

"*defensive organizations* should be pushed on with the "greatest speed—others constructed in rear without delay, "and well connected by switches ;

"*the position of batteries* well chosen, and ranges carefully "registered ;

"*the instructions* issued to the troops detailed to hold the "first and second positions, or to counter-attack, should "be clear, precise and well understood by the participants "(regiments, battalions) ; the execution of these instruc-"tions should, as necessary, be ensured by rehearsals.

"G.O.C.'s should be made to understand that, after "having effected the preliminary dispositions designed to "meet a surprise attack of the enemy without any delay, "to derive the best value from this system they must "personally act with energy and full use of the initiative, "recover as soon as possible the control of the battle, and "be on the ground themselves.

"Finally, neglecting reserves held as a precaution to "guard against possible enemy diversions—in Flanders "and in Champagne particularly—it is to meet attacks in "the direction of Paris and Abbeville that the most rapid "assembly of the strongest possible reserves should be "carried out or arranged :

"French reserves behind the French part ;

"British reserves behind the British part of the front "in question.

"It must be understood, of course, that these reserves "may actually be employed away from the front behind "which they are to be stationed.

"The Allied reserves will go to the battle wherever it

" takes place : the French reserves being engaged for the
" benefit of the British Army if the latter is strongly
" attacked, and, similarly, the British reserves for the
" benefit of the French Armies if the enemy should dis-
" tinctly concentrate his masses in the Paris direction.

" In order to facilitate their proper and co-ordinated
" intervention in the battle, these reserves should be
" organized—at least on paper—into corps or an Army."

In acknowledging the receipt of this Directive, Sir Douglas Haig wrote that he had disposed his reserves and was organizing his defences accordingly : that the XXII. Corps, of three divisions and an armoured motor machine-gun battalion, was located astride the Somme, well placed to check any attempt of the enemy to advance on Abbeville, or to intervene on the French front at short notice : that in place of the XIX. Corps, recalled to the Ypres area in consequence of the removal of the D.A.N., the Canadian Corps, held in general reserve, could follow the XXII. Corps to the French front if wanted : and that three more divisions and the Cavalry Corps were also in general reserve, available at short notice to move wherever required.

General Pétain in his reply to the Generalissimo stated that he proposed to station his reserves as follows : north of the Oise, 8 French divisions (2 tired), a cavalry corps of 3 divisions and 2 American divisions ; between the Oise and the Marne, 10 French divisions (one tired) and one American ; between Château Thierry and Epernay, south of the Marne, 2 divisions and a cavalry corps of 3 divisions ; between the Marne and the Argonne, 3 divisions ; and between the Argonne and the Meuse, 2 tired divisions.

During the 2nd, 3rd and 4th July the Supreme War Council sat in debate at Versailles. The Prime Ministers of Canada, Australia, New Zealand and Newfoundland were present for the first time on the last day of the Council. The subjects discussed were : Allied intervention in Siberia and Russia (including North Russia), a memorandum to be addressed by the British, French and Italian Governments to President Wilson in favour of intervention being approved ; the despatch to Vladivostok of rifles and ammunition for the armament of the Czecho-Slovak forces, which was also approved ; the situation in the Balkans, in respect of which it was agreed that no general offensive should take place until the Military Representatives had made a report. Exception having been taken to the appointment by the French Government of General Franchet d'Espérey to command at Salonika, it was further agreed that the appointment of the Commander-in-Chief of the Allied Army of the East should in future be subject to the approval of the Governments concerned. The recruitment of Yugo-Slav volunteers for the Serbian Army, from prisoners in the hands of the Italian Army, was suggested; and the functions of the Military Representatives as advisers on general military policy were defined. The situation on the Western Front was not discussed, except as regards the relations of the Belgian High Command with the Generalissimo—on this subject no conclusion was reached.[1] As regards the transport of American reinforcements, M. Tardieu, recently appointed " Commissaire Général " by M. Clemenceau, had made certain calculations which he presented to the Council. Mr. Lloyd George took strong exception to the interference of the French authorities in the matter : " the whole of the " shipping in question was supplied ", he said, " either by " the U.S.A. or by the British. It is therefore, I think, " purely a question to be settled by the U.S.A. and Great " Britain." The Council finally decided that :

" (1) General Bliss [the American Military Represent- " ative] be asked to ascertain from the U.S.A. Government " to what extent they can supply the tonnage required to " transport to France and to maintain there in reinforce- " ments and supplies the force agreed upon ;[2]

" (2) should the American Government be unable to " find all the tonnage required, the British Government be " asked to supply any deficiency ; but it is understood that " during the month of August, the British Government " will supply the same quotum of tonnage as in July."

Sir Douglas Haig took the opportunity of meeting General Pershing at the Conference to arrange with him that he would send artillery as soon as possible to the American divisions training in the British area : lack of horses was the difficulty, which meant that for some time the American 27th Division was without guns.

[1] In point of fact, General Foch addressed to General Gillain, the Belgian Chief of the General Staff, any communication which he wished to make to H.M. King Albert.

[2] According to an arrangement made between Generals Foch and Pershing : 46 divisions in October 1918 ; 64 divisions in January 1919 ; 80 divisions in April 1919 ; and 100 divisions in July 1919. Actually 42 divisions (one only partly disembarked) had arrived by 11th November 1918.

At the monthly Army Commanders' conference held on the 5th July, the Commander-in-Chief brought to notice an Intelligence statement to the effect that, although the German preparations for attack were being pressed forward more rapidly in the Lys salient than on any other part of the British front, it should be remembered that preparations for an offensive against the fronts of the Fourth, Third and First Armies had been completed for some time. He therefore pointed out that any part of the front might be attacked, and that this must be guarded against, but that no immediate sign of attack—that is within 48 hours—against the British was apparent.

Meantime the first definite indications of the enemy's intention to move had come to the knowledge of the French. On the 28th June the French Fourth Army (eastward of Reims) reported that detailed information had been obtained from prisoners of reconnaissances and collection of bridging material intended for a projected crossing of the Marne on a 9-mile front between Epernay and Château Thierry: their statements agreed that the attack would take place early in July, and be preceded by diversions, which had already materialized, one south-west of Reims and the other (the Matz) in the direction of Paris. Following on these statements other prisoners spoke of a double attack, one part west of Reims against the Marne line, the other, east of the town between the Argonne and the Suippe (which passes through Suippes). Air reconnaissances confirmed that all the usual signs of an imminent offensive in Champagne could be seen. Other information equally pointed to an offensive in Flanders before the middle of July on a front of 36 miles, in the direction of Hazebrouck and Calais;[1] attacks in the neighbourhood of Arras, Amiens and Compiègne were also mentioned by prisoners. But, by the 4th July, although there was still doubt as to where the blow might first fall, the reports were sufficiently cumulative and concordant to induce General Pétain, with General Foch's approval, to begin shifting reserves to strengthen the Champagne front. The line of the French Fourth Army east of Reims (its left was about five miles east of the town) was strengthened by the interpolation of two divisions, and that of the Fifth Army, next to it on the left, by one division. Behind the right of the Fourth Army three divisions from the east were placed; behind the centre of this Army, two divisions (later three) from

[1] See Note I. at end of Chapter XIII.

Flanders, in addition to the American 42nd Division; and behind the junction of the Fifth Army with the Sixth (Dormans, on the Marne) a new Ninth Army under General de Mitry (formerly commanding the D.A.N.), consisting of three divisions and a corps of three cavalry divisions.[1] Thus, besides extra artillery and air squadrons, the French forces between the Argonne and the Marne, which on the 1st July amounted to 17 divisions in the line and 9 (3 cavalry) in reserve, were increased to 20 in the line and 15 (one American and 3 cavalry) in reserve. In addition, 3 divisions in the G.A.R. area (on the British right) were warned to be ready to entrain at short notice.[2] General Foch asked that a British air brigade, about ten squadrons, might be held in readiness to assist the French; he also convened an Allied conference of heavy artillery experts, including Italian representatives, to arrange for mutual help by the transfer from one national front to another of heavy artillery. On the other hand, he informed G.H.Q. that a reserve of 3 divisions (2 from Alsace and 1 from Flanders) had been ordered to be assembled around Poix (17 miles south-west of Amiens), ready to move to the assistance of the British in 24 hours, to be followed four days later by six others and by the II. Cavalry Corps, which was moved towards Beauvais (35 miles S.S.W. of Amiens).

Sketch B.

Whilst the British Commander-in-Chief continued to think that a German attack in Champagne would be only a diversion,[3] and that the main attack against the British would follow—as, indeed, was Ludendorff's intention—General Foch now altered his views. He was at last convinced, apparently on the 10th or 11th July, by General Pétain of the magnitude of the imminent enemy offensive. The latter had finally written:[4] " it seems certain that the " enemy is about to engage the greater part of his shock

---

[1] General de Mitry received instructions to study the employment of his Army in various hypotheses: to assist the G.A.R., the G.A.C. and G.A.E. F.O.A. vi. (ii.), p. 425.

[2] A few days later the French Fifth Army received a reserve of 3 divisions (one from Flanders and two reconstituted after the Aisne battle) and the Sixth Army, two (one each from the Second and Third Armies).

[3] General Pétain, at any rate on 5th July, considered that " an attack " in Champagne will doubtless be only a manœuvre of diversion, which " may have as its object:
" to attract the bulk of our reserves away from the Paris region and " the zone of the Franco-British junction;
" to capture Reims and get a footing on the Montagne de Reims;
" to bring the Epernay—Châlons—Revigny railway under gun-fire ".
F.O.A. vi. (ii.), p. 424. Revigny is 30 miles E.S.E. of Châlons.

[4] F.O.A. vi. (ii.), p. 440.

"troops". So he yielded to the pressure for making the British bear a greater share of the burden of the War.¹ In the absence of the British Commander-in-Chief, who was on leave in England,² General Foch summoned the Chief of the General Staff, Lieut.-General Sir H. Lawrence, to a conference on the 12th July. At this meeting he said that an attack on the French front from the Argonne to Château Thierry was imminent, that he was convinced that it would be made in great force, and that all French reserves between Montdidier and Moreuil (the British right) were being moved eastwards, and he warned the C.G.S. that the British reserves might be called upon to assist. On the same day, General Foch wrote to Sir Douglas Haig that, in view " of the extensive enemy preparations in Champagne, the " diversion offensive anticipated in Directive No. 4 of the " 1st July may become a large scale operation (' de grande " ' envergure '). . . . In consequence, the probability of a " German attack north of the Somme becomes more remote " and the importance it is likely to assume is diminished." He asked that two British divisions might be moved to the south of the Somme—the 12th and 18th from the reserves of the Third and Fourth Armies were sent—and suggested, drawing attention to his General Directive No. 3 of the 20th May,³ that as the greater part of the German reserves had been absorbed in attacks against the French, the British Armies should be prepared to launch an offensive from the Festubert—Robecq front for the purpose of freeing the Bruay mines and recovering Estaires, with its junction of communications, and asked to be informed of the date on which the offensive would be ready.

¹ General Pétain, on the 12th, wrote: " I have the honour to request a " more complete participation of the British Army in the burdens which " have been weighing on my Armies for three and a half months: either " by the immediate despatch of at least 3 divisions or by an attack launched " before 18th July on a suitable part of the front ". F.O.A. vi. (ii.), p. 436.

² The Commander-in-Chief had an interview on the 12th with the Prime Minister, who was concerned with the state of the reserves and annoyed that, although 15 American divisions had been carried to Europe in British ships since April, only 5 were now in the British zone and in a position to support the British Army in case of attack. Mr. Lloyd George said that the Chief of the Imperial General Staff had been instructed to draft a letter to General Foch pointing this out.

Sir Douglas Haig took the opportunity of his visit to complain to the Military Secretary that the list of proposed honours and awards for the Armies in France drawn up by him and the Army commanders had been ignored by the Army Council.

³ See p. 23 and Appendix II.

The situation of the British reserves at this time was:

	Army Reserve	G.H.Q. Reserve
Fourth Army area	1	5 (XXII. Corps of the 51st, 62nd and, recently re-organized, 8th Divisions, and the two divisions south of the Somme).
Third Army area	2	1
First Army area	..	2
Fifth Army area	..	2
Second Army area	2	1
	5	11 divisions

In addition to these there were three cavalry divisions, five American divisions without artillery, and six British and two Portuguese divisions classified as only fit to man back lines.

Early on the 13th, after a warning given on the 10th, General Foch asked that the IX. Brigade R.A.F., which had been withdrawn after the battle of the Matz, might again be lent to him, and nine squadrons flew south to join the French on the 14th.

At 2.25 P.M. on the 13th he telegraphed in cypher requesting that 4 divisions, two by two, might be sent to the French area, to detrain at stations on the line Revigny—Vitry le François, 20 miles to the south-east of Châlons, behind the French Fourth Army. This was followed by a second telegram, 25 minutes later, requesting that a corps headquarters should be despatched to take command of the British troops, and that a second corps of 4 divisions might be made ready to follow the first. A third telegram, timed 4.40 P.M., stated that the demand for 4 divisions did not cancel the request for 2 made by letter on the 12th. On its coming to General Foch's notice on the 14th that General Pétain, fearing the premature use of the reserves of the Fourth and Sixth Armies, on either side of the sector where he expected the attack, had withdrawn the control of them from the commanders of those Armies, the Generalissimo countermanded the instructions for this limitation of Army powers.

In the absence of the Commander-in-Chief, the Chief of the General Staff, Lieut.-General Sir H. Lawrence, arranged for the despatch of XXII. Corps headquarters

(Lieut.-General Sir A. Godley)[1] and the 51st and 62nd Divisions; but on his return to France at 2 P.M. on the 14th Sir Douglas Haig immediately asked for an interview next day with General Foch, requesting that the despatch of further divisions might be delayed until that interview had taken place. He informed the Chief of the Imperial General Staff of the dangers which would be run by complying with the French request. Later he drew up a second letter, to be handed to General Foch next day, in which he summarized the enemy preparations on the British front, and said: "I beg that you will inform me "definitely of the reasons which have led you to change "your view of the general situation, and to depart from "the strategical plan laid down in your Directive Générale "No. 4 of the 1st July for the guidance of the several "Commanders-in-Chief of the Allied Armies. The informa- "tion now at my disposal goes to show that the British "front is threatened just as much at this moment as when "that Directive was issued,[2] and I submit that in the "circumstances there is no reason for modifying its pro- "visions so far as the English Army is concerned, and that, "consequently, the British reserves should only be engaged "to support the French Armies 'si l'ennemi concentre "'décidément ses masses dans la direction de Paris'. "Such a situation has not yet arisen, nor can it be truly "said that the enemy has begun a concentration with this "object."

During the night a telephone message was received from the Chief of the Imperial General Staff, recorded as follows: "Members of the Imperial War Cabinet have "to-night discussed with the Prime Minister the latest "orders by General Foch for moving British reserves "southward. As information hitherto has pointed to an "attack on your front by Rupprecht's forces as well as "an attack by the Crown Prince on the French they feel

[1] The headquarters included signal units, two casualty clearing stations, two motor ambulance convoys, a mobile X-ray unit, an advanced medical stores depôt, mechanical transport columns, a veterinary hospital, two sanitary sections, a labour company, etc.

[2] The French Intelligence reports of the date 9th July showed that Crown Prince Rupprecht still had 38 divisions in reserve of which 31 were fresh or reconstituted. They stated that the German Crown Prince had 34 divisions in reserve, of which 28 were fresh or reconstituted, and that an attack on the front from the Argonne to the Jaulgonne bend of the Marne required at least 46 fresh divisions; they forecast an attack east of Reims with 16 divisions, and west of the town with 28, with 2 left available to be used on either side.

"considerable anxiety. They wish me to tell you that if
"you consider the British Army is endangered or if you
"think that General Foch is not acting solely on mili-
"tary considerations, they [the War Cabinet] rely on the
"exercise of your judgment, under the Beauvais agree-
"ment, as to the security of the British front after the
"removal of these troops. General Smuts, on behalf of
"the Imperial War Cabinet, will proceed to G.H.Q. to-day
"and confer with you on your return from the conference
"with General Foch."

This, as the Commander-in-Chief remarked, meant that if things went well the War Cabinet and the Generalissimo would take the credit; if ill, he himself would be the scapegoat.

Before the conference met on the 15th at Monchy le Châtel, about half-way between the Generalissimo's château and British G.H.Q., the blow had already fallen. When Sir Douglas Haig arrived about 1 P.M. he found General Foch in the best of spirits. After a three-hour bombardment, he said, the Germans had assaulted at 4 A.M. on two fronts east and west of Reims, respectively 26 and 29 miles wide: the front of 16 miles around Reims had not been attacked: the situation was satisfactory: a great weight had been taken off his mind, for he had feared the attack would extend as far east as Verdun, where he had no reserves.

This news altered the situation, General Foch continued, as regards the destination of the first four British divisions, which, instead of going to Châlons, would be detrained near Provins, 60 miles to the W.S.W., behind the Ninth Army. Sir D. Haig, after reading to General Foch a French translation of the letter prepared on the previous evening, saying that he was still averse to moving reserves from the British front until he knew that Crown Prince Rupprecht's reserves had been transferred to the new battle front, went on to point out that, in addition to many sure indications of attack, 88 additional German heavy batteries had been placed opposite the British in June, and that prisoners and deserters stated that an attack on the Lys salient was to be ready mounted by the 18th July—as actually the case.

General Foch then said that he agreed with the diagnosis, but that his first object was to hold up the present attack at all costs as soon as possible: that he only wanted the British divisions as a reserve in case of necessity; and that they would be in a position to return at once if the British front were threatened. After this explanation the British Commander-in-Chief agreed to allow the second pair of divisions to proceed, and the 15th and 34th Divisions, from the First and Second Army areas respectively, were sent by rail to join the XXII. Corps.[1]

To General Smuts, who arrived at 8 P.M., Sir Douglas Haig reported that he considered the situation satisfactory, but that there was every expectation that he might be attacked soon, probably on the Kemmel front, with the main blow somewhere between Château Thierry and Lens, if the enemy did not previously break the French front about Reims.

[1] As regards the administrative supply of the 4 divisions of the XXII. Corps sent to the French, it was arranged on 15th July that the train regulating station should be Connantre (35 miles south of Reims), with Troyes (65 miles south of Reims) as annexe. Trains from the British bases of Havre and Rouen were to be sorted and made up at Troyes, and then forwarded to Connantre, whence they would be despatched at the proper time to the railheads selected for British use.

CHAPTER XIII

THE LAST GERMAN OFFENSIVE AND THE FRENCH COUNTER-STROKE

THE FOURTH BATTLE OF CHAMPAGNE, 15TH–18TH JULY 1918

THE SECOND BATTLE OF THE MARNE,[1] 18TH JULY–6TH AUGUST 1918. FIRST THREE DAYS

(Sketches B, 11, 12, 13)

THE fighting which began on the 15th July is mainly of interest because it was the last great German offensive; but it also exhibited a further development in the French methods of defence and showed how difficult it is to apply accepted theory to practice in the field.

The general distribution of the French forces for the battle and for the counter-stroke, now designed to follow it, had been made in three great groups : the first, to meet the expected attack between the Argonne and Château Thierry, formed of the Fourth and Fifth Armies and the right wing of the Sixth, 33 divisions in all, of which 3 were American and 2 Italian; the second, for the counter-stroke, formed of the Tenth and Sixth Armies (less the right wing of the latter), 24 divisions (4 American) and 3 cavalry divisions. The third was the general reserve (10 divisions and 3 cavalry divisions) stationed behind the Fourth and Fifth Armies, composed of General de Mitry's Ninth Army, headquarters at Fère Champenoise, now increased in size and containing the XVI. Corps (4 divisions) in Argonne, the XIV. Corps (4 divisions) distributed in the

---

[1] The French authorities decided on two battle names under this heading, which were adopted by the British Battle Nomenclature Committee :

Battle of the Soissonnais and the Ourcq, 18th-28th July, and Battle of the Tardenois, 29th July-6th August.

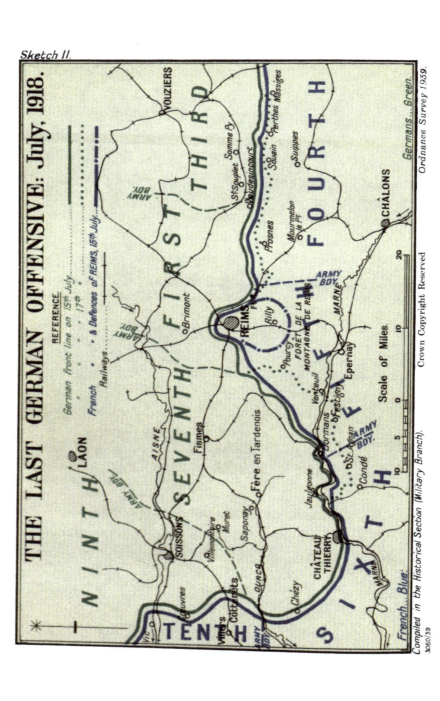

area Châlons—Epernay, the I. Cavalry Corps (3 divisions) in the area Fère Champenoise—Châlons, and the British XXII. Corps (2 divisions), ordered to Vitry le François (S.S.E. of Châlons). To these it was planned to add one more French and two more British divisions. The other French fronts were all but completely denuded of reserves; the British, excluding cavalry, had now 7 divisions, and the Belgians, 1 division in general reserve; and the Americans had 15 in training.

Opposite General Gouraud's Fourth Army stood the greater part of the German *Third* and *First Armies* (excluding the outer flanks), 14 divisions in front line, 6 in second and 5 in reserve; opposite the French Fifth and Sixth Armies, as far as Jaulgonne, the western boundary of the front of attack, were, excluding the unattacked Reims sector, 11 divisions of the German *Seventh Army* with 4 in Second line and 3 in reserve.[1] Thus, excluding General Pétain's reserve and the reserves of Groups of Armies and the troops in the Reims salient, east of this place on the front of attack the French opposed 14 divisions to 25, and west of it, 12 (2 American and 2 Italian) to 18,[2] and, in all, 360 field batteries, 381 heavy batteries and 27 super-heavy guns, to the German 1,047 field batteries and 609 heavy and super-heavy batteries. There were 4 German tank detachments (apparently of 5 tanks each) on General Gouraud's front and one west of Reims. The French were well provided with aeroplanes, the three Armies concerned possessing 42 squadrons, besides having the support of the G.A.C. groupe, the "division aérienne" and the British IX. Brigade, with 9 squadrons[3]; the tanks were being reserved for the counter-attack.

On the western front of the Château Thierry salient, where the French meant to counter-attack, were the rest of the German *Seventh Army* and the *Ninth Army*, 11 divisions in front line and 8 in reserve.

Sketch 11.

---

[1] In order to reduce the responsibilities of General von Boehn during the offensive, on 5th July his three western corps had been formed into a *Ninth Army* under General von Eben.

[2] Of the 22 German divisions which actually attacked east of Reims, 5 were entirely fresh, 2 had fought in the March and Lys offensives, 2 in the March and Aisne offensives, 9 in the March offensive only, and 3 in the Lys offensive only, and 1 in the Aisne offensive only; of the 19 west of Reims (the *86th Division* of the *First Army* joining in the attack of the *Seventh*), 2 were entirely fresh, 10 had fought in the March and Aisne offensives, 3 in the March offensive only, 1 in the Lys offensive only, and 3 in the Aisne offensive only.

[3] See "The War in the Air", Vol. VI., p. 412.

Opposite the British, according to French reckoning, were 48 divisions in the line and 21 in reserve; in all 27 were still unlocated; the British Intelligence put the figures as 38 in the line and 35 in reserve, with no German divisions on the Western Front unlocated.[1]

During the period of waiting the R.A.F. kept a close watch upon the enemy area opposite the British main front, being particularly on the look out for abnormal activity and movements of heavy artillery along roads distant from the front; it carried out almost nightly systematic bombing of railway junctions and trains—it had been found waste of energy to bomb lengths of the permanent way.

After the experience of the battles of the Aisne and of the Matz, in which the front line and the rear line, respectively, of the 1st Position had been chosen as the main line of resistance, it had been accepted by the French commanders that the 2nd Position was the proper place on which to fight out a defensive battle; the 1st Position and Intermediate Position were regarded as forming an outpost zone on which the enemy should expend his artillery bombardment and in which his infantry forces should be delayed and broken up. When it came to apply this very sound doctrine, difficulties arose. In General Gouraud's Fourth Army, consisting of 14 divisions (1 American) east of Reims, where the front had long been stabilized, four positions had been prepared, 1st, Intermediate, 2nd and 3rd, and he intended that the 2nd should be the line of resistance. In distributing his troops, however, he found that he had not enough divisions to occupy both the delaying zone and the 2nd Position. He therefore decided " to assemble the maximum of means " on the Intermediate Position, that is to make it the position of resistance; holding the ground in front of it as " a covering position ", and the 2nd Position as a reserve line, manned by a nucleus garrison (schools of instruction, Territorial units, fortress machine-gun units) until the reserves promised to him should arrive.[2] The artillery was almost entirely disposed

---

[1] Monograph III., p. 16, states that 10 divisions in general reserve were available for the Champagne front: thus the 27 " unlocated " by the French would seem to be 14 (35-21) opposite the British, 10 near the front of attack, and 3 on other parts of the French front.

[2] " La Journée du 15 Juillet 1918 ", by Capitaine P. Waendendries, states, pp. 46-8 and 56, that when the attacks became imminent, " only " a few volunteers, to give warning of the approach of the Boche, were " left in the 1st Position ". The rôle of the advanced troops of the Intermediate Position was " to break up the waves of the assault and force

CHAMPAGNE. 15TH JULY

between the Intermediate and 2nd Positions; but the commanders were warned that it must be " manœuvrière ", and prepared to shift about both for the purpose of deceiving the enemy and bringing surprise fire to bear.

In the Fifth Army (General Berthelot),[1] west of Reims, recently engaged in the Chemin des Dames battle and thrown back, and now containing 11 divisions, of which two were Italian, the defences were, naturally, not so well developed as those of the Fourth Army. The 2nd Position was hardly begun, and the 3rd existed for the most part only on paper. General Berthelot, therefore, decided directly he took over command to make the front of the Intermediate Position the line of resistance, although even this position consisted in many places of no more than a single trench. In the belief, however, that the passage of the Marne ought to be defended and that certain " points d'appui " in front of the Intermediate Line would be of great value in launching an offensive later on, he also decided, with the approval of General Pétain and General Fayolle—an approval subsequently regretted—to hold these " points " d'appui " by means of selected garrisons, which should not retire even if they were outflanked or surrounded. This meant that the 1st Position was held in considerable strength and the outpost line pushed down to the banks of the Marne. Excluding the I. Colonial Corps, charged with the defence of the Reims salient and not seriously attacked, the other two corps of the Fifth Army, the Italian II. and the French V., had in the 1st Position, 16 battalions; in the Intermediate, 27; and in the 2nd, 18. The two corps of the right wing of the Sixth Army, holding the Marne line, the III. and the XXXVIII. (containing the American 3rd Division), had " about one-third of their " effective infantry in the covering zone ", that is the 1st Position.

For several days before the 15th July the Group of Armies of the Centre had been awaiting the attack, even

---

" the enemy to halt under the French barrage-fire ". As a result of General Gouraud's tactics, " a parlementarian informed the Government " of his intention to ask a question on the scandalous abandonment, " without fighting, of ground which it had cost so much to conquer ".

[1] General Berthelot was Assistant Chief of the Staff with General Joffre in 1914; he subsequently commanded the 53rd Division and XXXII. Corps; was head of the French Mission at Rumanian headquarters August 1916 to the beginning of 1918, when he went on a mission to the U.S.A.; on 5th July he succeeded General Buat, appointed Pétain's Chief of the Staff, in command of the Fifth Army.

the code name of which, " Friedensturm " (peace assault), had been revealed by prisoners and deserters. Indications and reports with regard to it were all in accord. Important enemy centres were therefore bombed, and on the night of the 13th/14th all the roads and road junctions in the probable concentration zone were shelled. On the 14th air observers reported the movements of so many small parties of the enemy as to give the impression of an ants' nest. General Gouraud had ordered that at least one prisoner should be taken every day, and on the 14th, by a deep raid, 27 prisoners were captured ; from these it was learnt that the German artillery bombardment would commence at 12.10 A.M. and last three or four hours. The French opened counter-preparation fire " between 11 P.M. and midnight ", thus anticipating by about half an hour the preparation fire of the German artillery, which lasted three hours and forty minutes (instead of five hours as on the 21st March), and catching the German infantry massed for attack.[1]

The morning of the 15th July was overcast and dull, and it was not until 10 A.M. that the aviators could give much assistance. The attack of the German *First* and *Third Armies* against the French Fourth Army, largely thanks to General Gouraud's inspired leading, was a complete failure.[2] Their infantry reached the Intermediate

[1] There is a vivid account by an eye-witness of the German dismay and alarm at French fire falling on them just before zero in Hesse's " Marnedrama 1918 ".

The arrangements for the two bombardments, east and west of Reims, made by the artillery expert, Colonel Bruchmüller, were slightly different:—
East of Reims :
    10 minutes : general fire surprise of every target ;
    75   ,,   increased counter-battery fire ;
    90   ,,   destruction of infantry positions, counter-battery fire and distant targets ;
    15   ,,   as in second period ;
    30   ,,   as in third period, in the last 10 minutes batteries prepare for creeping barrage ;
West of Reims :
    10 minutes : as east of Reims first period ;
    60   ,,   as east of Reims second period ;
    30   ,,   destruction of rearward infantry positions and otherwise as in east third period ;
    120   ,,   as east of Reims third period. At the beginning of the period pontoons moved forward, in the last 10 minutes batteries prepare for creeping barrage.

The periods for the 21st March are given in " 1918 ", Vol. I., p. 159.

[2] There is a very full account of the battle in Monograph IV., which will be found summarized in the " Army Quarterly " of January 1931 under the title of " The Last German Offensive ". The very brief account in the French Official History is summarized in the " Army Quarterly " of October 1936.

Position, the selected line of resistance, and was there held up, units of the American 42nd (Rainbow) Division, from the 2nd Position, taking a distinguished part in stopping them. The German observation balloons were brought down by air attack: the tanks which appeared were knocked out by direct hits.

West of Reims, where a considerable portion of the defenders was in the front zone, the Germans were more successful, and for a time the situation grew disquieting.[1] After the bombardment had annihilated the outpost line, under cover of a smoke-screen they crossed the Marne, and, except in the sector of the American 3rd Division on the left, which counter-attacked, drove the defenders to and beyond the line of resistance. Thus, " in a few hours the " Germans had succeeded in capturing a bridgehead on " either side of Dormans 3 miles deep and 7 to 9 miles " wide ". Between the Marne and Reims they similarly gained this line, the defenders retiring to the 2nd Position, except on the right flank, where the Italian 3rd Division swung back, maintaining touch on the right with the unattacked Reims defences. It would seem that " defence " in depth " had been overdone. The troops were distributed in the outpost position, strongpoints, line of resistance, 2nd Position and even 3rd Position. The resources available were insufficient to go round, so that, although there was depth, there was no strength anywhere, and the French were beaten in detail. At 9.50 A.M. General Pétain telephoned to the G.A.C. " to suspend the pre- " paratory movements for the offensive [of the 18th], and " send back immediately the American 2nd Division ".[2]

This counter-order General Fayolle reported personally to General Foch as the latter called at his headquarters at Noailles on his way to the conference with Sir Douglas Haig at Monchy le Châtel, already mentioned. " General " Foch did not view the situation in the same way as " General Pétain. He considered that nothing should be " changed in the arrangements made for the counter- " attack, and addressed to the French Commander-in-Chief

---

[1] On the right, next to the Reims sector, were the following divisions: Italian 3rd, Italian 8th, forming the Italian II. Corps, French 40th (which had been in the Chemin des Dames battle), 8th (which had been in the mid-June fighting east of Reims) of the V. Corps ; then along the Marne to Château Thierry, the 51st (which had been in the Chemin des Dames battle), 125th (which had been in the March offensive and the Matz) of the III. Corps, and the American 3rd Division, in the XXXVIII. Corps.

[2] F.O.A. vi. (ii.), p. 503. The American 2nd Division was on its way from the Sixth to the Tenth Army.

" the following message : ' Please understand that, until
" ' you inform me of some fresh crisis (événement) there
" ' can be no question of slowing down in any way, still less
" ' of stopping, Mangin's preparations. In case of urgent
" ' and absolute need, you may take from him the troops
" ' absolutely indispensable, letting me know at once.' "

General Pétain then decided to take the reserves (eventually only one division) intended for the counter-attack from the left of the Sixth Army; but so much progress had been made by the enemy in the centre of the Marne front, towards Epernay, that at 4.45 P.M. he asked General Foch for permission to employ the American 2nd Division, and suggested that the Mangin offensive might be postponed 24 hours. In an interview, however, that evening with the Generalissimo he agreed that, " according " to all probability, the 16th and 17th July would suffice " to break the enemy attack, and the counter-attack of " the G.A.C. could be launched on the 18th, as had been " decided ".

During the the 16th the Germans not only failed to make any progress against General Gouraud and to reach a good line which they could hold permanently (*Dauerstellung*), but the French, using the method of infiltration in many places, drove them back and re-established an outpost line.

On the Marne front heavy fighting continued, and the Germans " seized an important part of the 2nd Position " in the direction of Epernay, and made local attacks against Reims ; but on the west of the enemy bridgehead, three French divisions, with portions of the American 28th Division, counter-attacked at midday, and drove the Germans back over a mile and recovered the Intermediate Position ; whilst farther west the American 3rd Division cleared away all enemy troops which were across the Marne west of the Jaulgonne bend. The situation of the six German divisions in the bridgehead was meantime becoming precarious owing to gun and air attack on their bridges.[1] On the evening of the 16th the Crown Prince stopped further advance in that quarter and east of Reims, but ordered the two corps between the Marne and Reims

[1] The squadrons of the IX. Brigade R.A.F. co-operated with the French Air Division in this portion of the battlefield. They were mainly engaged in attacks on ground targets from low heights and, in particular, in attacks on the numerous foot-bridges thrown by the enemy on the Marne, some of which they destroyed in the face of strong opposition. During 15th-17th July fifteen planes were shot down or wrecked after damage in combat.

BRITISH REINFORCEMENTS

to continue the attack next day. No instructions came to him from O.H.L.

General Pétain, in looking round for reinforcements, again bethought himself of the British. On the 16th, whilst the 51st (Highland) Division (Major-General G. T. C. Carter-Campbell) and 62nd (West Riding) Division (Major-General W. P. Braithwaite), of the XXII. Corps (Lieut.-General Sir A. Godley)[1] were in process of concentration in the French Fourth Army area, some units having detrained near Revigny and being already in billets, whilst others were still on their journey, the corps was ordered back westwards by General Pétain to support the Fifth Army. Some confusion ensued, not only owing to the counter-order, but also because the assembly places of the two divisions were changed. It was not until the 18th that the 51st Division (less its artillery, which was marching from the original detraining station) and the 62nd Division were concentrated east and south-east of Epernay, the leading units marching from the detraining station and the later ones being brought up by lorry. They were then allotted to the reserve of the French Fifth Army.

General Pétain also asked that the British 15th Division (Major-General H. L. Reed) and the 34th Division (Major-General C. L. Nicholson),[2] the second pair of divisions of the XXII. Corps, which had entrained for Châlons during the night of the 15th/16th, might be handed over to him. General Foch, however, decided to keep them at his own disposal. The 15th Division, whilst en route on the 17th, was directed to detrain at Clermont (41 miles west of Soissons); it completed its concentration on the 18th in the French Third Army area, with headquarters at Liancourt (5 miles S.S.E. of Clermont). The 34th Division was similarly diverted to Chantilly, and, by the evening of the 18th, was concentrated around Senlis (10 miles S.S.E. of Liancourt). Thus the XXII. Corps had two divisions behind the eastern side and two behind the western side of the Château Thierry salient.

Sketch B.

On the 17th the British Chief of the General Staff, in view of the likelihood of a strong attack at an early date

---

[1] The 51st had been engaged in both the March and April battles in the Third and First Armies, respectively; the 62nd in the March battles in the Third Army.

[2] The 15th had been engaged in the March battle (Arras) in the Third Army; the 34th in the March battle in the Third Army, and in the April battle in the Second Army, and had been reconstituted, receiving 5 battalions from Palestine, which had arrived in France in June.

on the Second Army in Flanders, drafted a letter to General Foch, for Sir Douglas Haig's signature, pointing out that trench mortars and ammunition dumps were already installed on the whole front, and guns established well forward in close proximity to the British front line, and requesting that "the four divisions of the XXII. Corps may be "returned to me forthwith".

Before this letter was signed by the Commander-in-Chief, Lieut.-General Du Cane arrived with a letter from General Foch in which he wrote: " Independently of the " information regarding the situation and possible enemy " movements against the British front which you send me " daily, I have the honour to request that you will let me " know without delay, when you consider it would be " useful, which parts of this front seem threatened by early " attack, and also the steps which you have already taken " to meet the attack should it take place.

" Recent operations have shown that to nip an enemy " attack in the bud it is necessary to have brought up in " advance sufficiently large forces and placed them ready " in position. This deliberate and immediate call on the " reserves will save the far more considerable calls which " would be required to deal with a deep penetration into " our lines, should it have been effected.

" These forces can only be found by withdrawing them " from the fronts which are not threatened for the benefit " of that which is in danger. Such preventive movements " will naturally require the shifting of reserves and variation " in the strength of occupation of certain sectors inside " each of the Allied Armies, as well as the use in quiet " sectors of American troops and second-line divisions. It " is only when all formations, either those which exist or " which can be created, have been engaged that it is proper " to call on the Allied reserves, and the resistance organized " as suggested above will give them time to arrive.

" The information which I request from you is there-" fore indispensable to enable me to consider, prepare and " decide, should occasion arise, the despatch of any Allied " formations which may be required for the British zone."

Sir Douglas Haig entertained small expectation of the success of the French counter-attack, but felt certainty as to the enemy preparations on the Ypres front and was convinced that even should the Germans be hard pressed near Soissons, Crown Prince Rupprecht would at least try to take the Flanders hills (Mont des Cats, etc.) in order to

ATTACK STOPPED. 17TH JULY

improve his position for the winter. Since the General Staff letter already drafted very nearly appeared to meet the case, he decided to sign and send it. He told Lieut.-General Du Cane, however, to add verbally that if British troops were needed to exploit a success they should of course be used, but it must be borne in mind that after doing his utmost to collect troops to meet Crown Prince Rupprecht's attack against the Second Army, he could only muster nine divisions in front line and six in support, two of the latter being half-trained American and one a second-class division containing " C 3 " men. General Foch was delighted with the first part of the verbal message, and next day replied to the letter that: (1) the battle had been engaged under favourable conditions on an 80-mile front, and that its magnitude and place forbade the enemy to consider any large attack against the British front "*for the moment*"; (2) an attack on a reduced scale seemed to be in preparation on the Bailleul (10 miles south-west of Ypres)—Merckem (7 miles north of Ypres) front, and immediate measures to meet it should be taken; (3) since the rest of the British front was not threatened it could be "milked" without danger to provide troops to deal with the above attack; and (4) if the XXII. Corps were sent back it could not arrive for six or eight days; this would make it too late for the Flanders battle and also prevent it from continuing to play its part in the Marne battle.

On the 17th, east of Reims, General Gouraud gained a little more ground. Between Reims and the Marne the German attack made no progress, only one enemy regiment claiming to have made any advance. To the south of the Marne, although fighting continued in which both sides attacked and counter-attacked, no change took place in the situation; another division was sent to General Berthelot, and he was promised the British XXII. Corps. The destruction of the German bridges over the Marne continued, and the casualties among German engineers trying to repair them and among the troops and trains trying to cross the river "reached a terrifying height". At 5.30 P.M. (German time) the Chief of the Staff of the *Seventh Army* telephoned to the Crown Prince's headquarters that only one solution was possible: the speedy withdrawal of the three corps which were beyond the Marne. At 7.25 P.M. General von Boehn stopped further attacks by his Army. At midnight O.H.L. agreed to the gradual withdrawal of the troops in the bridgehead, " but withheld the final order "for the moment". Ludendorff still hoped at least to "pinch out" the Reims salient. General Mangin's counter-attack launched in the morning of the 18th was to render impossible the fulfilment of this last hope.

It was not finally settled until midday on the 17th, when it was evident that the German offensive was held up, that the French Tenth Army (General Mangin) and Sixth Army (General Degoutte) should attack early on the 18th, as originally arranged, and that the Ninth, Fifth and Fourth Armies (Generals de Mitry, Berthelot and Gouraud), farther east, should join in and that the Ninth should regain the ground near the Marne just lost to the Germans.[1] Agents' reports and prisoners' statements had led the Germans to expect a great attack on the 14th July, the French National Fête day, but, as nothing materialized either on that date or on the three following days, at *Seventh Army* headquarters "the situation was no longer "regarded as strained and an attack in grand style as no "longer probable". According to an entry in the war diary of the German Crown Prince's Group of Armies:[2] "The French attack against the west front of the *Ninth* "and *Seventh Armies* on a front of roughly thirty miles "was not expected either in such breadth or in such "weight. It was believed that the enemy would continue "his local attacks on the same scale as before our offensive "[of the 15th July], but it was not believed he had so far "recovered that he could so soon carry out an offensive "on so large a scale. The reports and prisoners' state- "ments of the assembly of tanks and troops in the woods "of Villers Cotterêts were thought to refer to movements "in connection with the continuation of local attacks, a "full-dress attack was not regarded as imminent."

General Pétain had on the 12th July laid down the outline of the attack as follows:[3]

"The operation has as its object the reduction of the "Château Thierry salient by means of the two lateral "thrusts towards the plateaux situated north of Fère en "Tardenois. It should, as a minimum, deprive the enemy "of the free use of the railway and road junctions in "Soissons and improve the trace of our front between "Reims and the Marne (freeing of Reims)." For this

---

[1] The Ninth Army was re-formed on the 17th of the XXXVIII. and III. Corps, the left wing of the Fifth Army, taken from General Berthelot, leaving him with the XIV., V., I. Colonial and Italian II. Corps.
[2] Monograph IV., p. 99.   [3] F.O.A. vi. (ii.), 438.

PREPARATIONS. 11TH–17TH JULY

purpose, the Tenth Army " is to break through the German " front south of the Aisne in the general direction [east- " ward] of Oulchy le Château ", whilst simultaneously the Sixth Army " is to attack [north-eastward] in the direction " of the plateau south of Brény—Armentières [2½ miles " east of Brény] ", and, on the other side of the salient, south of the Vesle, the Fifth Army " is to endeavour to " break the enemy's lines by pushing [north-westward] " towards Arcis le Ponsart [5 miles south of Fismes] ". The rupture of the enemy front was to be exploited with the maximum of speed, so that the inner flanks of the two attacking groups would meet in the neighbourhood of Fère en Tardenois ; the three Armies would then advance to the east-west line, Rosnay (7 miles west of Reims)— Arcis le Ponsart—plateaux north of Fère en Tardenois— Hartennes—Dommiers.

During the 11th-13th July, in a series of small attacks, the 128th and 48th Divisions, in the centre of the French Tenth Army, had again pushed forward, this time from the edge of the Forest of Villers Cotterêts to the eastern side of the Savières stream, a confluent of the Ourcq. General Mangin pressed for permission to attack at once. General Pétain fixed the 18th as the probable date for the attack of the Sixth and Tenth Armies ; but he sent no warning to the Sixth, in view of the expected German offensive.

The deployment of the Tenth Army was begun on the 14th ; it was interrupted for a few hours owing to General Pétain's counter-order, already mentioned, but was completed, as was that of the Sixth Army, with nearly five hundred tanks in all, during the 16th and 17th.[1] The great woods

---

[1] The Tenth Army (see Sketch 12), neglecting the XVIII. Corps, on its extreme left and not engaged in the attack, consisted of four corps with 16 divisions (including the American 1st and 2nd, Major-Generals C. P. Summerall and J. G. Harbord), one cavalry corps (3 divisions) and approximately 1,545 guns, 346 tanks and 581 aeroplanes.

The Sixth Army consisted of three corps (including the American I., Major-General Hunter Liggett), with 8 divisions (including the American 4th and 26th, Major-Generals H. Cameron and C. R. Edwards), and approximately 588 guns, 147 tanks and 562 aeroplanes.

In the Tenth Army the distribution of the tanks was : one groupement of medium tanks to each of the assaulting divisions, with 3 battalions of light tanks in reserve for exploitation. Of the total of 346 tanks, only 225 got into action. Of these 102 became casualties, 62 as a result of German artillery fire. On the second day, of the 195 tanks available, 50 were hit by shell-fire. On the third day, only small local attacks were carried out ; in these, 32 tanks took part, of which 17 were hit (" Tanks in the Great War ", pp. 192-3, by Brevet-Colonel J. F. C. Fuller).

Commandant Balland in the " Revue d'Infanterie " of October 1935 gives details of the employment of the tanks with the American 1st

around Villers Cotterêts, which have a frontage of 13 miles from La Ferté Milon to Dommiers, afforded excellent cover, but every measure of precaution was taken to hide the assembly of so many troops and so much apparatus. The superiority of the Allied air forces was invaluable in preventing the enemy from learning very much by air reconnaissance. Facing the 24 divisions of Generals Mangin and Degoutte, the four American divisions being double the strength of the others, were 19 German divisions, 11 in front line, 7 in second line, and 1 in Army reserve.

The night of the 17th/18th was sultry and dark after an evening of heavy rain, the roads through the forest were pitch-black tunnels, the trees dripping. The watercourses and ditches alongside the narrow tracks and roads were full, and the ground near them soft and wet. The final preparations were thus rendered difficult and much confusion ensued, so that the troops were in position only just in time.[1]

The Moroccan Division, with the American 1st and 2nd Divisions on either side of it, was the spearhead of the attack. Day dawned at 2.30 A.M., but until 9 A.M., when the morning mist dispersed, the light was poor.

The artillery of the French Armies opened first on the eastern wing, the Fourth Army at 4 A.M.; that of the Fifth and Ninth followed at 5 A.M., but only a certain number of local actions ensued; the Ninth Army was to make its effort next day. The artillery of the Sixth and Tenth Armies opened fire simultaneously at 4.35 A.M. In the case of the latter Army, where, owing to preliminary action no serious obstacle was to be expected, the barrage immediately crept forward, the infantry keeping close to it; the tanks followed and aided the infantry to encircle and then rapidly reduce the isolated resistance of the enemy outposts. In the Sixth Army the enemy's trenches were bombarded for three-quarters of an hour before the infantry advanced.

General Mangin had effected a complete surprise. The Germans did hear sounds as of motor vehicles from one

---

Division. They were deployed in three lines: one, a strong one, in advance of the infantry; one in the first line of infantry; and one with the infantry battalions in second line. No less than 80 per cent of the tanks engaged were knocked out on 18th July; " in one square of 1,500 metres side, there " were 23 tanks destroyed solely by artillery ".

[1] See a description (pp. 318 *et seq.*) in " The American Army in France ", by Major-General J. G. Harbord, commander of the American 2nd Division. He mentions that " the three regiments for the attacking line reached the " jump-off place designated for the assault at the double-time and ran " behind the barrage ".

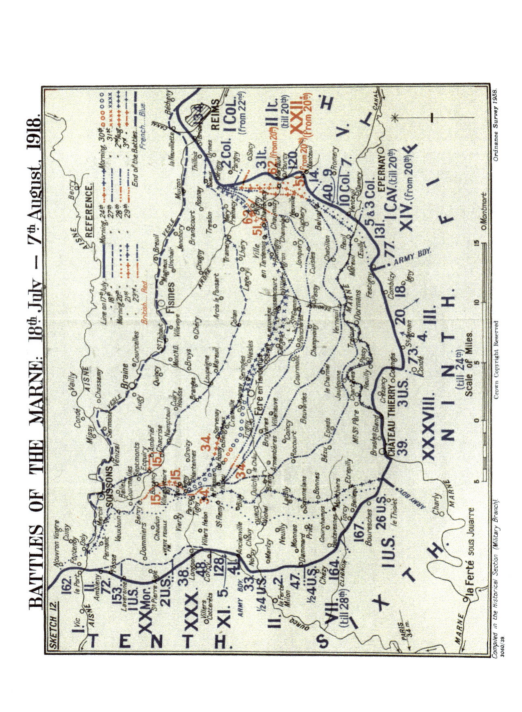

FRENCH SUCCESS. 18TH JULY

village near Dommiers on the extreme left of the attack, and had fired light balls and put down a barrage, but suspected nothing serious. After dawn the same sounds were reported by sentries farther to the north and to the south. Then at 3.15 A.M. two French deserters came over to the outposts of the *3rd Bavarian Regiment*,[1] and stated that there would be a general attack between 4 and 5 A.M. It was 3.30 A.M. before the company commander in Dommiers heard the news; 3.45 before it reached the battalion; 3.50, the regiment; 4.00, the brigade; and 4.10 before the division sent out the alarm, too late.

What happened is best and most easily grasped by a glance at the map. The French made steady progress. At 7.15 A.M. General Mangin ordered up the II. Cavalry Corps and directed General Robillot to make preparations to push through in advance of the infantry to Fère en Tardenois, in the rear of the Germans defending the Marne. "Before midday" it was evident at the German Crown Prince's headquarters that the divisions in the line on the west face of the salient had been driven in and even the supporting divisions heavily engaged. At 10.54 A.M. an order was sent to the *Seventh Army* to reorganize resistance "on the general line Soissons—Hartennes— "le Plessier Huleu—Latilly—heights north of Château "Thierry", actually occupied on the 21st. In giving this order, the Crown Prince pointed out that there was no question at present of the fighting divisions retiring to the line defined. If they did, they must hold it to the last. At the same time, he ordered a second back line to be prepared, about five miles in rear of the one above named; it started near Venizel, east of Soissons, and passed south by Droizy—Coincy—Epieds to Chartèves (5 miles E.N.E. of Château Thierry). Both back lines were to be strongly held with machine guns. At 11.45 A.M. he ordered the evacuation of the bridgehead south of the Marne, for which all preparations had been already ordered by General von Boehn at 9.40 A.M. A message was sent to General von Eben (*Ninth Army*) to make sure of the retention of Soissons and the heights to the south-east, as it was essential for the issue of the battle. They were held until the 3rd August.

By noon, the first Franco-American rush being over, there was a pause; the situation seemed to the Germans to be well in hand, and General von Eben began to make

Sketch 12.

---

[1] Of the *11th Bavarian Division*, which had the American 1st Division and Moroccan Division opposite to it.

R

arrangements for a counter-attack next day. But in the late afternoon the attack was resumed by General Mangin's right and centre, and the enemy reinforcements on the ground had to be used to form a south defensive flank.

The Fourth, Fifth and Ninth Armies were " not " altogether inactive " and made a little progress ; their turn was to come next day ; but when, towards 1 P.M., General Maistre [1] was informed by G.Q.G. that he must not count on the free disposal of the British XXII. Corps, he " telephoned and telegraphed [to G.Q.G.] that there was " a risk of a catastrophe, as the situation of the Italian " Corps rendered an immediate relief indispensable, and a " contrary decision might lead to the loss of Reims " ; he demanded that the British XXII. Corps should be placed at his free disposal.[2] Owing to General Pétain being away from his headquarters, there was some delay, but at 10 P.M. General Godley, who had been warned that he might have to relieve the Italian Corps, received orders from the French Fifth Army to concentrate the 51st and 62nd Divisions in rear of the Italians, who were reported to be " in an exhausted and shaken condition ", with a view to relieving them.[3] Accordingly, during the night of the 18th/19th and the early morning of the 19th, the two divisions, carrying two days' " debusing rations ", crossed the Marne at Epernay, and, after an arduous march, concentrated in the southern part of the Montagne de Reims forest, moving up in the evening to a preliminary position.

Sketch 13.

During the morning General Berthelot (Fifth Army) had met Lieut.-General Godley and his two divisional commanders at the headquarters of the Italian II. Corps, when arrangements for the impending relief were being discussed. He told them that, in view of the success of General Mangin's Army, all efforts must be made to prevent the Germans from withdrawing troops from the Fifth Army front to oppose the Tenth Army. He therefore called on the XXII. Corps, instead of carrying out a deliberate relief

---

[1] Commanding Fourth, Fifth, Ninth and Sixth Armies.

[2] The XXII. Corps in the following operations consisted of the 51st and 62nd Divisions, the 15th and 34th being diverted to the Soissons area, as will be seen.

[3] The Italian II. Corps had suffered very serious casualties. When relieved, out of a fighting strength of about 24,000, it had lost 9,334 (282 officers) ; of these, the share of the 8th Division was 6,792, and, by direct hits or by capture, it had lost all but 7 guns of its nine 4-gun batteries. Of the grand total, 3,936 men were prisoners and from 3,500 to 4,000 dead. Colonel M. Caracciolo's " Le truppe italiane in Francia ", pp. 102-3 and 132-3.

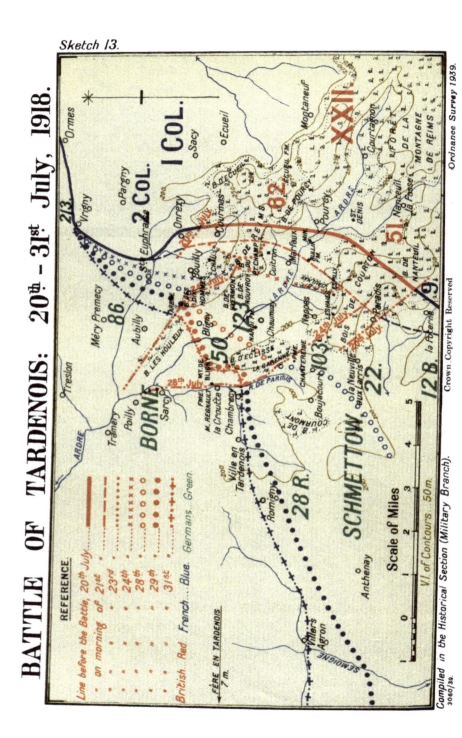

Sketch 13.

BATTLE OF TARDENOIS: 20th – 31st July, 1918.

XXII. CORPS ENTERS THE BATTLE. 20TH JULY

of the Italians, to attack through them on the following morning (20th). He produced a plan for an attack on a two-division front, based on the assumption that the German withdrawal was already in progress—but events showed that they intended to dispute every inch of ground. In spite of the short notice and obvious difficulties which this entailed, especially on account of the differences of language and staff methods, Lieut.-General Godley and his divisional commanders accepted the plan without demur and soon dispelled the prevalent French idea that the British could only act with great deliberation. Theoretically, the hinge of the German salient was the proper place to attack, but the originators of the scheme took no more account of the difficulties of the ground than had the drafters of Plan XVII., when they launched an offensive into the Ardennes in August 1914.

On the 19th there could be no surprise, and the French and Americans found themselves faced by rows of machine guns hidden in the high crops and bushes, with only field-gun barrages to aid in overcoming them. Notwithstanding, the French Tenth Army and left of the Sixth added another two or three miles' advance to the four-mile gain of the first day. In the Marne bridgehead the Germans during the night of the 18th/19th had got the greater part of their guns, transport and stores back across the river; the Ninth Army, however, did not attack on the 19th, as ordered, on account of " the non-arrival on the field of " two battalions of light tanks ",[1] so the German fighting troops south of the Marne maintained their position throughout the day, and all the wounded were removed and sent across the river. The Fifth Army on the 19th also made only slight progress, " always meeting with obstinate resist-" ance " and, similarly, the Fourth Army, east of Reims, gained but little ground, all interest being concentrated upon, and all reinforcements sent to, the Château Thierry salient.

On the 20th the Tenth and Sixth Armies continued their advance on the right and in the centre; but near Soissons, where the enemy put in two fresh divisions,[2] were unable,

[1] F.O.A. vii. (i.), p. 82; but F.O.A. vi. (ii.), p. 540 gives as reason: "the " hard fighting of the last three days had tried the troops and led to a " mix-up of units ".

[2] In order to strengthen the German western flank, at 11.15 A.M. on the 19th, General von Etzel (*XVII. Corps*) took over a front between Winckler and Watter (*XIII. Corps*), his troops consisting of the *40th Division* (Winckler's right) and the *51st Reserve* and *10th Divisions*, brought from the reserve of the southern front.

in spite of the use of tanks and attacks eight times renewed,[1] to break the German defence. General Mangin, however, had done more than the first task required of him : he had taken over 15,000 prisoners and 400 guns, and made it easy to prevent the Germans from using the junction of railways at Soissons, which was the principal cause of their evacuating the Château Thierry salient. On this day the Ninth and Fifth Armies were to join in, taking the offensive on the whole front from the Jaulgonne bend to five miles short of Reims. " In the Fifth Army the fighting was " extremely severe ; the Germans opposed an obstinate " resistance and at certain places counter-attacked." [2] The enemy having retired across the Marne in the course of the night, completing the evacuation by 4 A.M. on the 20th, "the Ninth Army found the ground in front of it empty" and " without difficulty, advanced to the banks of the " Marne ". Soon after 9 A.M. General Pétain directed that the maximum of troops should be withdrawn from the Ninth Army " to maintain with the utmost energy the " thrust of the Fifth Army on the one hand, and support the " right of the Sixth Army on the other ".

The British 62nd and 51st Divisions certainly found the fighting severe, and the conditions different from those to which they had been accustomed, owing to the woods and the almost total absence of trenches, and they did not enter the fray under favourable conditions. Owing to the delay of the French Fifth Army in issuing detailed orders, it was not until 4.45 P.M. on the 19th, when it was too late for much reconnaissance, that the corps orders for the attack at 8 A.M.[3] reached the divisions. They were to be supported on the right by the 2nd Colonial Division, and on the left by the French 9th Division. The ground ahead was that over which the British IX. Corps had operated seven weeks earlier, but it was unknown to the XXII. Corps and distinctly favourable to the defenders. The river Ardre was to be the directing line and the dividing line between the two divisions. Its valley, two to three thousand yards wide, was open, arable land, with standing

---

[1] According to Monograph IV., p. 157.

[2] Thus F.O.A. vi. (ii.), p. 542. F.O.A. vii. (i.), p. 88, also says little about the fighting on the 20th : all it states about the Fifth Army is, " the " divisions did not debouch until 9 A.M. [the British did so at 8 A.M.], and " encountered an obstinate resistance from the enemy in the Bois de " Courton and before Marfaux ". The former place was in the zone of the British 51st Division, and the latter of the British 62nd.

[3] The barrage map was not received until 3 A.M. on the 20th.

corn, two feet high, which concealed the German defences, but with soft marshy patches on both sides of the stream, here, in its upper course, only 6 to 8 feet wide and fordable. The valley was bounded on each side by ridges, the western buttresses of the Montagne de Reims, rising to a height of 200-300 feet, crowned with dense woods with very few rides in them, and with undergrowth so thick that the men had the greatest difficulty in forcing their way through it, whilst the bastion-like spurs on the edges of the woods afforded ideal positions for the German machine gunners to rake the valley. The main feature of the latter, indeed, as seen from the British lines, was that it seemed blocked by the spur, extending right down to the Ardre, on which stands the salient of the Bois de Reims projecting southwards towards Cuitron. Opposite, on the western side, the long hill on which is the Bois d'Eclisse flanked the valley. On the eastern side of the stream, the slopes of the ridge were steep and devoid of cover, but on the western they were more gradual and dotted with small copses. Sunken roads athwart the direction of attack offered ready-made facilities for defence. The villages of Marfaux and Chaumuzy in the valley, and the commanding bare summit of the Montagne de Bligny, an outlier of the Bois d'Eclisse ridge, lost since the IX. Corps had left the scene and now four miles from the front line, gave the enemy three strong centres of resistance; the smaller villages of Cuitron, Espilly, les Haies and Nappes, perched high on the spurs of the wooded ridges, also afforded useful assistance in this way. The houses in all of them were still standing and the cellars afforded good cover.

Owing to the amount of traffic on the roads, which were exceptionally dusty, the night approach march of over six miles was so slow and tiring that it was well after daylight before the troops reached the forming-up line. Intercommunication in the woods presented many difficulties, so the divisional engineers were directed to cut paths and lay tapes. The barrage provided by the French and Italian field and heavy artillery (39 batteries of 75-mm. and 14 of 155-mm.), already in action covering the Italian II. Corps, opened punctually at 8 A.M.; but, owing to uncertainty as to the exact jumping-off line, it fell too far ahead of the troops. In consequence, many enemy machine-gun posts were left untouched. Moreover, owing to the activity of these posts and the difficulties of the ground, the barrage, moving at a hundred metres in four minutes, was soon still farther ahead of the infantry.¹ It had been arranged that as soon as the barrage reached the "Green Line", about 1½ miles ahead, it should halt for twenty minutes, and the divisional artillery of the 62nd and 51st Divisions, acting on their own initiative, should then assume the main responsibility for covering the further advance, although the French and Italian guns would continue to fire up to their extreme range. Like the infantry, but without maps and without guides, consigned to destinations of whose names the inhabitants professed complete ignorance, so that many unnecessary miles were added to the march, the guns were hustled onto the field; but the opportunity for their independent action did not arise.²

The four French and British divisions of the Fifth Army went forward as in open warfare against a series of defended localities, just as the Germans in October 1914, during the Race to the Sea, had attempted to dislodge the French from the fortified villages of the Arras front, and similarly failed. The present difficulties were greater, for the enemy's front, a line of resistance covered by outposts which, where not overcome by the barrage, withdrew as the Allies approached, bristled with machine guns and presented a far greater volume of fire and fewer targets than in 1914. The barrage had gone on, there was no plan to deal with

---

[1] The infantry disliked a creeping barrage in densely wooded country: they could not keep close to it owing to the trees provoking premature bursts with the sensitive fuze used with the French H.E. shell, and the echoes were most disturbing.

[2] Of the two brigades of the 62nd Division (C.R.A. Br.-General A. T. Anderson), the 310th reached the position of assembly at Courtagnon, on the edge of the forest of the Montagne de Reims, 2 miles from the front line, at 6 A.M., and went into action on the edge of the woods to the north-westward about 10 A.M., in time to assist in the attacks against Marfaux, which was not captured. The 312th did not reach its position of readiness 2 miles east of Pourcy until 7.30 A.M., and there it remained with some Italian artillery until 5.30 P.M., when its batteries were pushed forward about a mile.

In the 51st Division (C.R.A. Br.-General L. C. L. Oldfield), after marching 80 miles in three days, the brigades did not reach Ay (on the northern bank of the Marne, a mile E.N.E. of Epernay) until about 2 A.M. on the 20th; but soon after they pushed on and reached their position of assembly, about half a mile south of Nanteuil la Fosse, by 6 A.M. Shortly after 10 A.M. the batteries of the 255th from in front of Nanteuil opened harassing fire on Chaumuzy, and by 11 A.M. the batteries of the 256th were in action five hundred yards south-west of Pourcy; but, as an enemy counter-attack was expected, the batteries of both brigades were withdrawn at dusk to the east of Nanteuil, leaving forward guns in close support of the infantry to carry on harassing fire during the night. No heavy artillery accompanied the XXII Corps.

THE 62ND DIVISION. 20TH JULY

each locality by concentrated artillery fire, no plan to gas the woods, and ten minutes after zero enemy artillery fire fell and continued to fall on all the avenues of approach.

The 62nd Division (Major-General W. P. Braithwaite)[1] had the 187th and 185th Brigades in front line, and the 186th in support, $2\frac{1}{2}$ miles in rear, ready to leap-frog the leading brigades when they had captured the first objective, five miles from the starting line.[2] The right of the 187th Brigade captured Courmas, which was almost in the front line, but no sooner did the troops emerge from the western edge than they came under devastating fire from Commetreuil Château beyond it,[3] as well as enfilade fire from the woods on the left. The 2/4th York and Lancaster actually captured the château, but was driven out again. This wing then attempted to work round by the right and reached Bouilly, but after arrival there was turned out by a counter-attack preceded by a severe artillery bombardment. Though supported by the greater part of the reserve brigade, no advantage could be gained. The left of the 187th Brigade could make little progress in the thick woods on the northern side of the Ardre valley, for although the enemy riflemen disappeared when the British came into view, the machine gunners remained. The 185th Brigade, too, was unable to overcome the defenders of the two villages of Cuitron and Marfaux, which formed a long, broadside-on continuous street, and to reach them meant crossing eight hundred yards of open ground under terrible machine-gun fire from the front and right. A few men are said to have pushed on to the latter village, but by 11 A.M. the brigade was brought to a standstill. A proposal was made in the afternoon to attack the Cuitron–Marfaux

---

[1] It had opposed to it the German *123rd Division*, part of which had been relieved during the night of the 19th/20th by the *50th Division*, of which two infantry regiments were in position. The *123rd* had taken part in no battle in 1918; the *50th* had been in the March and Chemin des Dames offensives.

[2] 185th Brigade (Br.-General Viscount Hampden): 8/West Yorkshire, 2/5th West Yorkshire, 5/Devonshire;
186th Brigade (Br.-General J. L. G. Burnett): 2/4th Hampshire, 2/4th and 5/Duke of Wellington's;
187th Brigade (Br.-General A. J. Reddie): 2/4th York & Lancaster, (Hallamshire), 5th and 2/4th K.O.Y.L.I., with the 9/Durham L.I. (Pioneers) attached.

[3] "From every bay window many rifle barrels faced the attacking "enemy. Below in the cellars our heavy machine guns were mounted. ". . . Every bullet found its mark. The attacking enemy fell in rows, "doubled up and collapsed silently in the high grass of the parkland." (From a letter in "Fus. Regt. No. 39" of the *50th Division*.)

line from the north, through the woods, with the remaining two fresh companies of the reserve brigade, after a howitzer bombardment; but reconnaissance showed that the attack would stand no possible chance of success. So, during the night, the 62nd Division was reorganized less than half a mile in front of its morning position. The French 2nd Colonial Division, on its right, had made no advance whatever.

The attack of the 51st Division [1] (Major-General G. T. C. Carter-Campbell) made better progress at first than that of the 62nd.[2] The early fighting had to be carried out entirely in the great Bois de Courton, which lies on a wide, flat ridge, with its northern slopes falling sharply down to the Ardre. About two thousand yards from the front line the Bois narrowed to the width of a mile; beyond lay open slopes dotted with villages, small collections of farm buildings and copses. The 154th Brigade and the 153rd Brigade, in the front line, with two miles of front to cover, each had its three battalions in column, the second having to pass through the first at an intermediate line and take the first objective, and, similarly, the third battalion to advance to the final objective. Progress at first was good; but direction was lost in the Bois—even beaters find it hard to keep line and direction in a wood which they know—and on reaching its northern edge Marfaux on the far side of the Ardre was mistaken for Chaumuzy, and some confusion arose. On the right, outside the Bois, Bullin Farm and Espilly, with the Bois d'Aulnay between them, prevented further headway being made, whilst enfilade fire from the uncaptured Marfaux swept the ground; so a defensive flank towards the river was formed. At one place only, in the zone of the 153rd Brigade, was the German line of resistance pierced, but there a counter-attack by two battalions restored the enemy situation. On the left, the French 9th Division (General Gamelin), one of the best French divisions, was unable, in spite of several attempts, to reach Paradis, a collection of

---

[1] It had opposed to it the *22nd* and *103rd Divisions*, the former from Russia; the latter had been in France since 1916 and had taken part in the March offensive.

[2] 152nd Brigade (Br.-General R. Laing): 1/5th and 1/6th Seaforth, 1/6th Gordon Highlanders;
153rd Brigade (Br.-General W. Green): 1/6th and 1/7th Black Watch, 1/7th Gordon Highlanders;
154th Brigade (Br.-General K. G. Buchanan): 1/4th Seaforth, 1/4th Gordon, 1/7th Argyll & Sutherland Highlanders.

FRENCH REINFORCEMENTS. 20TH JULY

buildings at the southern side of the Bois where it narrowed, and, falling back, exposed the flank of the 51st Division, which then had to give some ground. But counter-attacks were repulsed, and after a day of close fighting the 51st Division dug in a mile in front of its jumping-off line.

The attack of the two British divisions had done no more than drive in the enemy outposts and reach the line of resistance. Some five hundred prisoners and a large number of machine guns, fought to the very last, had been captured, but the casualties had been heavy.[1]

It was obviously the best policy to continue the pressure on the hinges of the German salient, particularly on the Soissons side, and during the 20th the French High Command was concerned in increasing the flow of reserves to the left of the Sixth Army, and even more to the Tenth Army. Permission was obtained from General Foch to employ the British 15th and 34th Divisions; the American 32nd Division (Major-General W. G. Haan) was ordered up from Alsace to move behind the Tenth Army; the American 42nd Division (Major-General C. T. Menoher), from Champagne, behind the Sixth; and the French 12th and 25th Divisions, which were en route from the eastern part of the front, were assigned to the Tenth Army.[2]

In a long telegram General Pétain directed the Fifth Army to march on Fismes by both banks of the Ardre; the Ninth Army, leaving only a minimum force south of the Marne, to endeavour on its two wings to push north of the river; the Sixth Army to take the direction first of Fère en Tardenois and then of Mareuil, farther to the northeast; and the Tenth Army, covering its left flank securely on the Soissons side, to make its principal effort towards the Vesle on either side of Braine. The telegram ended with the words, "Everyone will understand that no " respite must be allowed to the enemy until the objectives " have been attained ". Later, General Pétain transferred the XXXVIII. Corps from the Ninth to the Sixth Army, and left General de Mitry on the Marne with only the III. Corps in a " rôle d'expectative ". In communicating these instructions to the Sixth and Tenth Armies, General Fayolle added, " it is not merely a matter of driving the

Sketch 12.

---

[1] See p. 288.
[2] The 12th came from Lorraine, where it had been resting since early April, and the 25th from the Verdun area—it had not been in an important action since August 1917.

" enemy from the Château Thierry pocket, but also of
" cutting off his retreat to the north and capturing the
" bulk of his forces ".

During the day air reconnaissances reported important movement of enemy columns northwards and considerable traffic blocks at Fère en Tardenois and Oulchy.

The German commanders were quite aware of the dangers of the situation, and, as the Marne bridgehead had been evacuated, felt that " the time had come for the " reduction of the salient according to plan ". At 11.20 A.M. orders were issued to Winckler's, Schoeler's and Kathen's corps,[1] holding the line from near Chartèves on the Marne above Château Thierry to a few miles north of the Ourcq, to withdraw the front between these points some five miles during the night.[2] This new line was to be manned in the course of the afternoon by reserves ; the artillery was not to change position until after dark ; at 10 P.M. the line of resistance was to be abandoned, and an hour later the outpost position. How soon the next step of retirement would be initiated would depend, it was stated, on the state of evacuation of material, and the situation on the flanks. Directions were also given, in view of the later retirements, to prepare a number of back lines, to which code names were assigned.[3]

In view of the turn which the situation in the Château Thierry salient had taken, Ludendorff this day came to the conclusion that the " Hagen " attack, against the British, would not be possible within measurable time. Crown Prince Rupprecht had informed him by telegram that " the decision of the War could certainly not be " expected from a weakened, narrowed and considerably " less well mounted attack, particularly against a foe who " knew the German intentions, had made his preparations " accordingly near Ypres, and stood ready to counter- " attack near Arras ". Ludendorff, therefore, replied that

---

[1] See Sketch 16 which gives the position of the German corps and the names of their commanders.

[2] Roughly to the line reached by the Allies by the morning of the 23rd shown on Sketch 12.

[3] Monograph IV., p. 175, mentions that three divisions, the *115th*, *14th Reserve* and *47th Reserve*, withdrawn on account of their losses on General Mangin's front, were ordered northwards across the Aisne. The *47th Reserve Division* could assemble only 11 officers (excluding regimental staffs) and 220 men of its infantry ; the *115th Division* had an infantry total of 56 officers and 1,218 men (of these, 222 belonged to the machine-gun companies), and its artillery was reduced to two batteries of 5 guns each. The state of the *14th Reserve Division* is not given.

" in view of the situation of the German Crown Prince's
" Group of Armies, which, as far as can be foreseen, will
" absorb a still greater amount of troops, and in view of
" the possibility of a British offensive action, the Hagen
" operation will probably never come to execution ". He
reserved, however, the right to return to the plan and
carry it out " should the general situation permit; in the
" meanwhile Crown Prince Rupprecht's Group of Armies
" would remain on the defensive ".[1]

The success of the French counter-attack of the 18th
July was a severe blow to Ludendorff. As recently as
the 9th July, in reply to a question, he had assured Admiral
von Hintze, the Foreign Secretary, that his offensive of
the 15th would " finally and decisively conquer the enemy ",
and gave the reasons for his belief.[2] He admitted in his
memoirs [3] that " the attempt by means of German vic-
" tories to force the nations of the Entente to ask for
" peace had been shattered before the arrival of American
" reinforcements. . . ."

" The offensive powers of the Army had not been
" sufficient to beat the enemy decisively before the Ameri-
" cans were on the spot with large forces. I was clearly
" conscious that as a result our general situation had become
" very serious."

NOTE I

DATE OF GERMAN ATTACK AGAINST THE BRITISH IN FLANDERS

Ludendorff (ii., p. 667) defines this proposed attack against the British on the Lys front by Crown Prince Rupprecht's Group of Armies " as a continuation of that which had to be suspended at " the end of April ". It was to be made by the *Fourth* and *Sixth Armies*, north of the Lys, on a frontage of 27 miles, its objectives being the possession of the commanding heights between Poperinghe and Bailleul, as well as the high ground round Hazebrouck. It was estimated that 47 divisions and 1,100 to 1,200 batteries were required, and at the beginning of May 32 divisions were assembled for special training behind the front. Crown Prince Rupprecht gives the following particulars of the postponement of " Hagen ". On the 15th May he was informed that it would not take place " before " the end of June ". On the 3rd June, in consequence of the Chemin des Dames offensive of the 27th May having been carried too far, " by order of O.H.L., Hagen was put off for some weeks ". On

---

[1] For the various postponements of the date of the " Hagen " offensive see Note I.
[2] Schwertfeger, p. 85.   [3] Ludendorff, pp. 543 and 545.

the 19th June, O.H.L. stated that the attack on both sides of Reims could not take place before the 15th July, which entailed a corresponding postponement of " Hagen ". On the 3rd July, O.H.L. wrote that " Hagen offensive will be carried out, and that the " Kurfürst offensive [in the direction of Paris, proposed by the German " Crown Prince] would only be got ready ". On the 6th July, General von Kuhl, Rupprecht's Chief of the Staff, went to O.H.L. at Avesnes, where " Ludendorff said that he concurred in all our arrangements, " but wished, if possible, that there should be a diversion attack " before Hagen ". On the 11th July Rupprecht notes that " Hagen " might have to be put off on account of the influenza epidemic, " which would be unfortunate, as the quicker Hagen follows Reims " and Marneschutz [the attacks on either side of the Reims], the " better are the prospects of success ". On the 16th July, the " battering train ", having played its part in the opening of the German offensive on the previous day, " the railway transport of " artillery, trench mortars and planes from the Reims district [to " Flanders] had begun according to plan " (Ludendorff, p. 667). On the night of the 17th/18th, feeling that, although the Reims operations had failed, they might prove a very valuable assistance to the attack on the Flanders front by absorbing French reserves (Hindenburg, p. 378), Ludendorff left O.H.L. for Crown Prince Rupprecht's headquarters to make the final arrangements for " Hagen ". From the original reserve of 32 divisions in Crown Prince Rupprecht's Group, 14 had been employed in the Reims battle, leaving 18 ; O.H.L. could find 8 to replace them, and the rest of the 47 required would have to be made up from " position " divisions. On the 18th a conference was held at Mons, at which were present, besides Ludendorff and Crown Prince Rupprecht and his staff, General Sixt von Armin (commander of the *Fourth Army*) and the chief General Staff officers of the *Fourth* and *Sixth Armies*, and of the corps in those Armies. In spite of the fact that the " position " divisions were on the average 2,000 to 3,000 men below strength and had been overworked by having to hold long frontages,[1] " the discussion turned principally on the artillery preparation and " execution of Hagen ". Ludendorff had " the first days of August " in view for the Flanders offensive ". Whilst the conference was still sitting came news of the French counter-attack and Ludendorff at once ordered the *5th Division*, then in O.H.L. reserve, southwards to Laon, and the *76th Reserve Division* from the Verdun sector to Soissons. At 3.35 P.M., O.H.L., having received further news, ordered Crown Prince Rupprecht to send the *56th Reserve Division* at once, followed within 24 hours by the *24th Reserve*, to the Reims area. Later a telegram from O.H.L. was received at Mons, the contents of which were as follows : (1) All transfers from the *Seventh Army* [engaged at Reims] for " Hagen ", except super-heavy artillery and trench mortars, to be stopped and the material to be left at the free disposal of the *Seventh Army*. (2) The continuation of the attack against Reims to be stopped at once. On the 20th, as narrated in the text, Ludendorff stopped the execution of " Hagen ".

[1] Ludendorff was so hard pressed for men that he arranged for two Austrian divisions to be sent to the Western Front ; the *1st* and *35th* arrived early in July, but then had to be trained in the methods of the Western Front. Two others followed in September. An account of the German forces in the East is given in Note II.

NOTE II

German Troops left on the Eastern Front

According to Kuhl (p. 7) on the 22nd May 1918 there were in the East (including Rumania, but excluding Turkey and the Balkans) 38 divisions, 13 brigades and the " North Corps " (the garrison of the Oesel islands). One division was soon after sent to the Western Front where it was broken up to provide reinforcements. No others were transferred until September and October, when 9 divisions (including 3 Landwehr) were sent, one of them being diverted to the Balkans.

In March German forces had occupied the Ukraine, on the grounds of appeal for help against Bolshevism made by the pro-German local government of the moment. They had en route occupied Odessa. In the following months, leaving the Austrians in the South-western Ukraine and southward, they had worked their way forward to the Crimea, the Sea of Azov and the Donetz coal basin. They were opposed only by small local bands, except at Taganrog, on the Sea of Azov, where on the 14th June some 10,000 Russians in vain tried to check their progress. German and Turkish warships in the Black Sea followed up the advance, and on the 8th June landed troops at Poti, who on the 14th occupied Tiflis. The Caucasus and Western Russia from the mouth of the Don (Sea of Azov) to Riga were in German possession.

CHAPTER XIV

THE SECOND BATTLE OF THE MARNE (*continued*)

21ST–26TH JULY 1918

(Sketches 12, 13, 14, 15)

Sketch 12.
IN consequence of the German retirement from the Marne, in the centre of the front, during the night of the 20th/21st, the French Sixth Army (now including the XXXVIII. Corps of the Ninth Army) and the right of the Tenth Army, made good progress on the 21st.[1] Although the Ninth Army (now reduced to one corps, the III.) could not cross the Marne, part of the XXXVIII. Corps did so and re-occupied Château Thierry. General Fayolle, in great jubilation, sent forward the 6th Cavalry Division for the pursuit—it did not go farther than the front infantry line—and asked G.Q.G. for the I. Cavalry Corps for the same purpose. But on the flanks of the German salient, where a success on either might have brought about a decisive victory, no progress could be made. On the west, the Tenth Army attacked, but the Germans " had " brought up a number of new field and heavy batteries ",[2] which knocked out the tanks and inflicted heavy losses; whilst the *5th Division*, fresh from five weeks' rest after the Chemin des Dames battle, by a counter-attack completed the French discomfiture. General Mangin's first effort was obviously exhausted, and he decided to bring up the British 15th and 34th Divisions to relieve the American 1st and French 38th Divisions, which with a relief already in progress would give him four fresh divisions.[3]

---

[1] Almost to the line marked " morning 23rd " on Sketch 12.
[2] Monograph IV., p. 180. Details from the French side are lacking.
[3] The relief of the 153rd and Moroccan Divisions by the 69th and 87th Divisions was in progress and was completed during the night of the 21st/22nd. The 69th had been in the Matz battle, the 87th had had a long rest except for a skirmish on 12th and 13th June.

TACTICS OF XXII. CORPS. 21ST JULY

On the eastern shoulder of the salient General Berthelot had given orders at 8.20 P.M. on the 20th for the renewal of the attack. It was to be " poussée sans arrêt " by his troops, including the British 62nd and 51st Divisions, on the whole front between Vrigny and the Marne. " An " opportunity ", he said, " to obtain important results had " arisen ; it must not be allowed to escape. Let every " man put his heart into it. The general counts upon the " will and energy of all to give the enemy a blow which " may be decisive."

Sketch 13.

Lieut.-General Godley's orders, issued at 12.30 A.M. after a warning telegram had been sent, directed the continuation of the operation " by a process of successively " reducing the enemy's points of resistance until the " objectives are gained.

" The enemy should be engaged and worn down by a " continuous series of advances undertaken with sufficient " deliberation and artillery preparation to secure economy " of men, whilst giving him no rest.

" Successive objectives will be arranged by divisions " on the general principle that the enemy strongpoints and " machine-gun nests should be kept under fire whilst " progress is made in the direction of least resistance.

" The mopping up of strongpoints should not, as a rule, " be undertaken till the posts supporting them in rear can " be closely engaged.

" Divisions will be responsible for arranging their own " artillery support with all the artillery at their disposal, " both field and heavy (British and Allied)."

Soon after midnight a visit of Br.-General C. W. Gwynn, of the XXII. Corps General Staff, to St. Imoges,[1] where both the 51st and 62nd Divisions had their headquarters, made clear what was required : before attempting to advance down the Ardre valley it was necessary, as in mountain warfare, to crown, that is gain possession of, the wooded ridges on either side of it.

Major-General Braithwaite (62nd Division), in consequence, ordered the 187th Brigade—with the 1/9th Durham L.I. (Pioneers) attached since the brigade had lost so heavily on the preceding day—to push through the Bois de Reims as far as a track which passes through the hamlet of Bouilly. The wood, although it gradually narrowed, covered the entire top of the ridge. Half an

---

[1] Not on Sketch ; it is 3 miles E.S.E. of Nanteuil la Fosse.

hour's bombardment by all the available artillery was arranged, followed by a creeping barrage of field artillery, with suitable pauses, whilst the heavy artillery shelled the villages of Chaumuzy and Bligny, whose defenders flanked the projected advance. Zero hour was fixed for 10.30 A.M., which left none too much time, since the troops were not reported as being ready until 10.20 A.M. Even then it turned out that a mistake had been made in reporting the position of the front line, so that when the 9/Durham L.I., which was to lead, was brought up, it was halted by the guides six hundred yards in rear of the intended forming-up line for which the barrage had been planned. Nevertheless, some progress was made. The Durham L.I. came on at a steady double to catch up the barrage, until the machine guns in the woods, on the left flank, opened fire and held up the advance just as they had done on the previous day. Attempts made by the 2/4th York & Lancaster to approach Commetreuil Château, west of Courmas, and by patrols of the 186th Brigade to reach Cuitron and Marfaux, in the Ardre valley, failed, as these localities were found to be still strongly held. There was very little change during the day in the position of the 62nd Division front. The I. Colonial Corps, on its right, remained stationary.

Major-General Carter-Campbell (51st Division) similarly arranged to work along the ridge south of the Ardre, which is covered by the wide Bois de Courton and the narrower Bois d'Eclisse. He fixed three objectives: first, the west edge of the former wood; second, a line through the centre of the Bois d'Eclisse; and, third, the road beyond that wood. He detailed the 152nd Brigade for the operation, with the 153rd to protect its flanks as far as the first objective.

Zero hour was set at 8 A.M. in order to co-operate with the French 9th Division, on the left, which was starting at that hour; so there was no time to issue written orders to units.[1] Here, too, the advance was made on a frontage of one battalion, the 1/6th Gordon Highlanders, while a mistake was also made about the forming-up line. When the Highlanders moved forward at 6.45 A.M. they found that the line, chosen in haste and in ignorance of the true situation, lay about seven hundred yards beyond the front strongly held by the enemy. Thus when the barrage opened at 8 A.M. it was of little use. The Gordons managed

---

[1] Formal divisional orders were issued at 2.30. A.M.

to advance a little, but the right, owing to enemy infiltration and envelopment, had eventually to fall back to a line some two hundred yards in front of its position of deployment. The support and reserve battalions were put in and gaps filled, but it all ended in indeterminate wood fighting, with the French on the left faring no better.

The Germans, who expected from the Fifth Army an attack against the vital flank at least as heavy and on as wide a front as on the previous day, were agreeably disappointed on receiving only several strong partial attacks from the British.[1] During the day the enemy brought up to the battle front no less than six divisions, with four more to follow.[2]

Two short paragraphs in the French Official Account deal with the events of the following day. The first is :
" The fighting on the 22nd July, in the course of which " the Tenth and Fifth Armies obtained no marked success, " showed clearly that the enemy attached a very special " importance to the retention of the plateaux south-west " of Soissons and the heights of Vrigny, north-east of the " Ardre : these two positions were in fact the hinges on " which the Army of General von Boehn must be supported " if German O.H.L. was forced to draw it back."

The second paragraph states that the III. Corps (Ninth Army) forced passages of the Marne near Passy and Courcelles (both about 4 miles below Dormans).

The XXII. Corps was ordered to continue the attack, zero hour being fixed by the French at 12.15 P.M. Twenty-five French light tanks were placed at Lieut.-General Godley's disposal, but the soft ground was unsuitable for their use. Each division employed no more than one battalion, and that weak in numbers owing to previous losses. In the 62nd Division the 5/Duke of Wellington's (186th Brigade) was directed to capture a salient of the Bois de Reims which projects southwards between Marfaux and Chaumuzy, known as the Bois du Petit Champ, and believed to be full of machine guns commanding the valley of the Ardre. Owing to the density of the undergrowth and the weakness of the battalion, it was decided to proceed

---

[1] Monograph IV., p. 188.
[2] *50th Reserve, 222nd, 24th Reserve, Guard Ersatz, 1st* and *26th*, whilst the *4th Guard, 1st Bavarian, 18th*, and *Jäger Divisions* began detraining during the night of the 21st/22nd. Of these divisions, 4 came from the German Crown Prince's Group reserve and 6 from Crown Prince Rupprecht's Group. Monograph IV., p. 189.

in two columns, each of two companies on the front of a platoon, which were to work along the edges of the Bois de Reims, whilst a heavy artillery barrage combed through it. Each column was to drop posts about every three hundred yards, and from these posts patrols were to be sent into the wood to mop up enemy posts and gain touch with each other. Both attempts encountered severe opposition: the right column of the 5/Duke of Wellington's advanced nearly half a mile, captured two strongpoints one after the other and several isolated machine-gun posts, and reached the centre of the wood. It was then foiled by an unlocated strongpoint; so, withdrawing three hundred yards, it consolidated a line from the northern edge of the wood towards its centre.

The left column came against a strongpoint only fifty yards from the jumping-off line, but captured it and five others in succession on the southern edge of the wood. The leading company was then counter-attacked and retired to a line just outside the wood; but there it came under fire from Cuitron, until in the end only eight survivors managed to fight their way back to the support company. Two companies of the 5/Devonshire were sent up in reinforcement and with their help the line of the support company, about seven hundred yards in advance of the starting line, was consolidated and touch obtained with the right column. To this extent the day had been successful; in addition over two hundred prisoners had been brought in. The operations seemed to show that with larger forces and successive reinforcements the wood might have been cleared and the defenders of the villages cut off.

The 51st Division had only to provide one battalion to co-operate with the attack of the French 9th Division against Paradis, which it was not to make until 5 P.M.; it was later to advance on la Neuville. The 7/Black Watch (153rd Brigade) was detailed to move along the western edge of the Bois de Courton, to the north of Paradis; but, although it was supported by the 6/Black Watch, the volume of machine-gun fire was too great, as it also was opposite the French 9th Division; so that a gain of no more than one hundred yards could be made. During the night the French 14th and 120th Divisions, now on the right of the XXII. Corps, which had for a short time been under command of Italian II. Corps headquarters, were placed, for defensive purposes, under Lieut.-General Godley.

On the western flank of the salient the British 34th Division—the infantry had been moved up by lorry—

began the relief of the French 38th Division of the XXX. Corps, south-west of Hartennes, on the 22nd. Both infantry and artillery completed the relief by 3 A.M. on the 23rd, and at 7 A.M. Major-General Nicholson assumed command of the sector. The infantry of the British 15th Division similarly relieved that of the American 1st Division of the French XX. Corps, separated by a two-division front from the 34th Division. The change of artillery should have been carried out on the nights of the 22nd/23rd and 23rd/24th; so that at 10.35 P.M. on the 22nd, when Major-General Reed learnt that his division was to attack at 8 A.M. on the following morning, he found that at zero hour half of his divisional artillery would be in and half of it out of the line. Accordingly he arranged with Major-General C. P. Summerall that the artillery of the American 1st Division (Colonel L. R. Holbrook) should remain for 24 hours and cover the attack. Colonel Maybell, the A.D.M.S. of that division, also lent his motor ambulances and kept his hospitals open in rear of the 15th Division for four days after his own troops had gone out of the line. Without this help the British casualties could not have been evacuated, since the 15th Division had no casualty clearing station, nor motor ambulance convoy behind it.[1] On the other hand, the 15th Division artillery lent teams to the Americans to pull their guns out.

The infantry relief was no easy matter; for the maps provided were of the French small scale, 1 : 80,000 series, the line was not continuous, and extended along a front intersected by valleys and covered with woods. Here a sad sight lay ahead; for the American dead were lying in swathes in the cornfields, having obviously been cut down by machine-gun fire whilst in thick waves; the British divisions were yet to discover that in standing crops the use of scouts and the application of rifle and machine-gun covering fire may become a very difficult matter.

The enemy was found to have a most striking air superiority over the French in this quarter; German planes were over the French lines at all hours of the day, and at night they bombed the roads.[2] All movements had

---

[1] When the Americans left, many British "walking wounded" drifted into French ambulances, and some " lying down " cases were picked up by these and evacuated to the South of France, with the result that the men were reported missing.
[2] During this period of service with the French the divisional engineers were wholly employed on improving communications.

to be made after dark and the strictest orders enforced during the day as to concealment from air observation.

General Foch possibly heard of General Mangin's arrangements for the hurried engagement of the British divisions; for during the 22nd he sent him a note written by his own hand as follows:—"The attention of the "Tenth Army is called to the advantage which may " accrue if, without checking the offensive for long, it " prepares further operations with the new divisions which " are reaching the Army every day, so as to produce " strong combined action at the moment when the Army " wishes to inflict a serious reverse on the enemy."

During the course of the 22nd General Foch also addressed a letter to General Pershing confirming the decisions taken at an interview on the previous day, when it was agreed that an American First Army should be formed on the nucleus of the American I. Corps, then in the French Sixth Army west of Château Thierry.

Sketch 12.

The German reports of the 22nd speak of lively fighting and the repulse of attacks made by the French with the assistance of tanks near Oulchy. The diary of the *Seventh Army* puts on record that the crisis was considered to be over, the danger of complete envelopment and annihilation of the Army to be no longer imminent, and its strategic freedom regained. O.H.L. began to consider a counter-attack against Mangin's left flank from the north; but it was found that owing to the bad railway conditions it would require too much time to place the necessary troops in position, while it was impossible to foresee what counter-action Foch might not devise: if he considered that his Soissons offensive, begun on the 18th, had come to a standstill, he might, with the means at his command, launch a surprise offensive at some other place now shorn of good divisions and reserves: even a purely defensive attitude on the part of the Germans would require the provision of fresh and the removal of tired divisions: the transport difficulties, owing to Soissons railway junction being under heavy fire and no longer available, were becoming very great, indeed the diversion line via Missy was now exposed to long-range fire so that very soon its abandonment would have to be faced: the *Seventh Army* was already reduced to the supplies that road transport could carry, and petrol was running very short. On the 21st the German Crown Prince's Group of Armies had proposed to O.H.L. the withdrawal of the line between Reims and Soissons, so as to shorten the front, provide forces for attack and regain the initiative. Ludendorff was much disinclined to consider the proposal; but on the 22nd he verbally ordered the Chiefs of the Staff of the *Seventh* and *First Armies* to make all preparations for a retirement " behind the upper Ourcq with the left flank " in the direction of Marfaux [where the British 62nd " Division was fighting] " : that is for the abandonment of only the southern half of the great salient. Meantime, on the night of the 23rd/24th, the three centre corps (Wichura, Schoeler and Kathen) were to withdraw another stage to the line Verneuil (on the Marne)—Beauvardes—Bruyères. On the 22nd, however, the *Seventh Army* gave warning of a further retirement, probably on the night of the 24th/25th.

On the 23rd, as on the 22nd, some progress was made by the Sixth Army in the left sector, where the enemy had fallen back; but the German flanks held firm. Only the British 62nd and 51st Divisions on the east, and the 34th Division on the west, together with the French troops near them, gained ground. The French account of the day is : " In the Tenth Army the XX. Corps and left of the XXX. " in vain repeated their efforts, engaging the British 15th " and 34th Divisions, which were fresh, in relief of the " American 1st Division and the French 38th Division. " These attempts yielded little result, in spite of the " participation of about a hundred tanks—it is true before " their units had completed reorganization; the com- " mander of the Tenth Army therefore ordered the corps " to spend the next day in consolidating their positions, " except the XX. Corps [in which was the 15th Division], " which was to attack Villemontoire and Tigny. The " centre and right of the Fifth Army were in a similar " situation to that of the Tenth Army [the left was still " held up along the Marne]; the attacks made on the " 23rd did not result in the corps making any noticeable " progress towards their objectives." Sketch 12.

At 9.30 P.M. on the 22nd the French Fifth Army had issued operation orders reiterating that the mission of the Army remained offensive. After directing the XIV. Corps to continue passing " groupes de combat " over the Marne and the V. Corps to pursue its mission as before, the orders entered into details as regards the British XXII. Corps : " With its left division it will renew its effort between " Neuville aux Larris and Nappes with a view to securing Sketch 13.

" the whole of the Bois de Courton and pushing forward to
" the Bois d'Eclisse and Chaumuzy.

"With its right division it will pursue the success
" gained to-day and will keep in close liaison with General
" Mordrelle,[1] who will attack on its right.

" General Mordrelle, attacking between the Bois de
" Reims and Point 240 [2] in a north-easterly direction, will
" arrange for one regiment of the 168th Division to support
" and prolong the attack."[3]

Lieut.-General Godley, who earlier had been made aware of General Berthelot's intentions, in order to give plenty of time for preparation, had warned his divisions by telephone, so that, although his formal orders were timed 6.40 P.M., the divisional orders were out at 4.45 and 5 P.M., respectively. The 62nd and 51st Divisions were to co-operate in the capture of Marfaux and the Bois d'Aulnay, south of that village, when sufficient progress should have been made in the Bois de Reims on the northern flank. The advance was to follow the line of the valley of the Ardre. The 82nd Squadron R.A.F. was to provide contact and artillery planes. Zero hour was left to the divisional commanders to settle, and they fixed 6 A.M. The attack was completely successful except that Espilly, on the extreme left, where the French could not gain ground, remained in the enemy's hands. On the right, however, they made good progress and captured Commetreuil Château.

Major-General Braithwaite ordered the 186th Brigade (Br.-General J. L. G. Burnett) with the 9/Durham L.I. (Pioneers), the 8/West Yorkshire (185th Brigade) and two companies of the XXII. Corps cyclists attached, to carry out his part of the attack. The last-named battalion was detailed to clear the remainder of the machine-gun posts in the salient Bois du Petit Champ, on the capture of which the success of the attack depended. The first objective was the villages of Cuitron and Marfaux and the road between them; the second, a ridge five hundred yards beyond that road. Five French light tanks were to assist the advance. The divisional artillery (less two batteries) was used to support the attack in the Bois du Petit Champ,

---

[1] G.O.C. of the 2nd Colonial Division, commanding the left wing of the I. Colonial Corps.

[2] Half a mile south-west of Vrigny.

[3] The 168th Division had been in the reserve of the V. Corps, but passed this day to the I. Colonial Corps.

whilst French field artillery provided the creeping barrage for the main attack. There was no preliminary bombardment, but the heavy artillery swept the high ground and woods on either side of the Ardre valley.

All went according to plan in the 62nd Division, in spite of German artillery fire which caused seventy casualties, mostly in one company of the 9/Durham L.I., before zero hour. The barrage, being particularly accurate, intense and effective, allowed the first objective to be reached by 6.50 A.M., and the final one by 8 A.M., at the cost of a hundred casualties, and the loss of two tanks knocked out by gunfire.[1] But, although shortly after 11 A.M. the French 77th Division came up on the right and immediately went into action, it was evening before the Bois du Petit Champ was entirely cleared at the cost of 44 further casualties, including all the officers of one company of the 8/West Yorkshire. Nearly two hundred prisoners and 12 field guns (which turned out to be French 75's) were captured.

In the 51st Division (Major-General G. T. C. Carter-Campbell), the advance of the 152nd Brigade (Br.-General R. Laing), with parts of two battalions of the 154th on its left, was covered by a barrage fired by the divisional artillery and French field artillery. It was equally successful; so that the final objective, the Bois d'Aulnay. including the sunken road east of Espilly, was reached by 8.20 A.M. in the face of a heavy German barrage and of machine-gun fire, and in spite of much short shooting by the barrage guns.[2] The occupation of Espilly, although renewed efforts were made throughout the day, proved impossible to achieve, as the open slope down to the village was swept by fire from the northern edge of the Bois de Courton. German bombardments hampered all movement, but the 152nd Brigade maintained its position.[3]

Thus the result of the day's operations in the XXII.

---

[1] For the German account of the action of the tanks, see Note at end of Chapter.

[2] On the left the French barrage opened fire at the correct time, but fell on the forming-up line of the 8/Royal Scots; on the right, it was on the right line but 20 minutes late, so that it crept forward over the 6/Seaforth and 6/Gordons, which had captured the first objective. As a result, the French 75's were henceforth given a wider margin of safety 500 yards instead of 200.

[3] The brigade lost 9 officers killed and 16 wounded on this day; the other ranks casualties are not given for the 23rd separately, but for the period 21st-28th July; judging by the percentage of officer casualties, 25 out of 48 for the week, the loss must have been little under a thousand. About one hundred prisoners and 32 machine guns were taken.

Corps was an advance of about twelve hundred yards on a 2½-mile front. Some British soldiers wounded on the 20th were found in Marfaux; their wounds had been dressed and they had been given water, but no food, by the Germans.

On the Soissons side of the salient General Mangin had issued orders on the 22nd for the XXX. Corps (1st, 19th and British 34th Divisions) and XX. Corps (58th, 87th and British 15th Divisions) to make the principal attack at 5 A.M. and reach the line Orme du Grand Rozoy—Taux—Buzancy;[1] the XI. Corps (41st and 5th Divisions), on the right, was to render what assistance it could to the XXX., the Butte de Chalmont being assigned as its objective. As ulterior objective the line Saponay—Arcy—Maast was mentioned.[2]

For carrying these orders into effect the corps arranged that attacks, after a bombardment lasting ten minutes, should first be made against the flanks of the woods which lay on the front: the 19th Division, with the 1st covering its right, should first turn the Bois de St. Jean[3] from the south, whilst the 87th and British 15th Divisions, after a 40 minutes' bombardment, were to capture Villemontoire, Buzancy and Chivry Farm, so as to threaten the line of the woods from the north. This done, on signal from the Army, the centre, the British 34th and the 58th Divisions, the connecting link between the two attacks, was to join in and move forward.

It was not until 9.20 P.M. on the 22nd that General Berdoulat's orders (XX. Corps) reached Major-General Reed, who was to take over command of the former front of the American 1st Division at midnight. Consequently not until 11.55 P.M. could the 15th Division orders be issued. The infantry relief was completed by 3 A.M., as already mentioned, under the superintendence of French officers, but this was accomplished only after strenuous exertions, which left only two hours to zero, and had the result of attracting enemy artillery fire. Then a second difficulty arose: the line taken over, which was without trenches, did not coincide with that shown on the map, and when the bombardment fired by the artillery of the American 1st Division opened at 4.15 A.M. it was not only thin, but also several hundred yards ahead of the line from which the infantry was to start, so that the enemy's advanced machine

---

[1] The line shown on Sketch 14 as held on the morning of 2nd August.
[2] The whole order is translated in Appendix XI.
[3] The southern part is called Bois du Plessier.

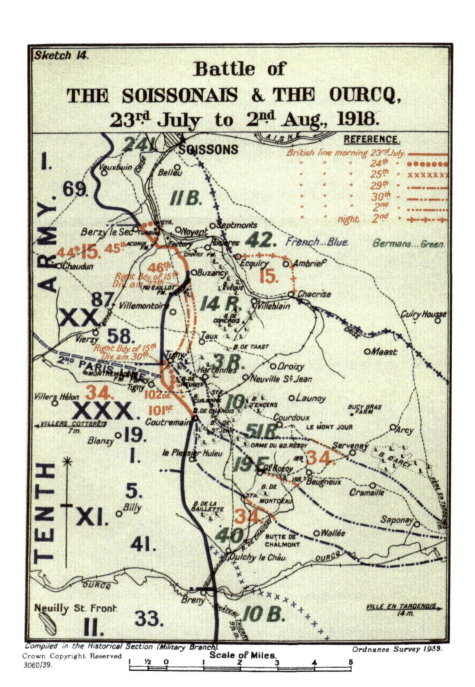

guns were untouched. At 4.55 A.M., when the barrage moved forward, after resting in front of the supposed jumping-off line during the last five minutes of the bombardment so as to enable the infantry waves to come close up to it, the 15th Division at once encountered fire.

The 46th and 45th Brigades (Br.-Generals V. M. Fortune and N. A. Orr-Ewing), whose front was facing ground cut into by the valleys of the Crise stream and its affluents, had, respectively, one and a half and two battalions in front line in waves; the 44th (Br.-General N. A. Thomson) was in reserve. Neither the 15th Division nor the French 87th Division could make any real progress, since they suffered not only from frontal fire at short range, but enfilade heavy-gun fire from the Soissons direction. The 7th/8th K.O.S.B., with two companies of the 10/Scottish Rifles, of the 46th Brigade, advanced about one hundred and fifty yards. The 6/Cameron Highlanders (right of the 45th Brigade), moving down the steep slope to the Crise, suffered heavily, but captured the sugar factory in the valley, and then extended to the left to cover the whole brigade front and form the defensive flank. The Highlanders beat off a counter-attack launched about 6 P.M.; but at night, the sugar factory being in advance of the general line, the men holding it were withdrawn. The French 87th Division, on the right of the 15th, had failed to capture either Villemontoire or Buzancy, and had come back on its original line.

On the right wing of the attack, the French 19th Division had likewise made no progress.

In the centre the attack was made by the British 34th and French 58th Divisions.[1] The former, as already mentioned, had just taken the place of the French 38th Division. The commander of that division, General Guyot d'Asnières de Salins, had made every possible preliminary arrangement and handed to Major-General Nicholson draft orders for the attack founded on his knowledge of the ground. He left in position the 32nd and 41st Field Artillery Regiments (each of three " groupes ") and a " groupe " of twelve 155-mm. howitzers, under Colonel Béranger, which were all placed by General Penet (XXX. Corps) under the command of Br.-General E. C. W. D. Walthall, C.R.A. of the 34th Division, when he found that the latter spoke French well. The 101st and 102nd

[1] Two of its three infantry regiments were composed of Africans, the 6th and 11th Tirailleurs.

Brigades (Br.-Generals W. J. Woodcock and E. Hilliam), with machine-gun companies, were each to attack on a one-battalion front, the former on a 500-yard and the latter on a 300-yard frontage, while a second battalion was to come up later on the right in order to encircle the Bois de Reugny. The rearward battalions were subsequently to pass through the front battalions. Two battalions of the 103rd Brigade (Br.-General J. G. Chaplin) and half a machine-gun company were in corps reserve, and the third, with half a machine-gun company and the 2/4th Somerset L.I. (Pioneers), in divisional reserve.

At 6.30 A.M., when reports tended to show that the attack on either wing was going well, a warning order was telephoned to the brigades to be ready to move at short notice. Three-quarters of an hour later the executive corps order was received. The divisional signal, timed 7.20 A.M., was at once transmitted by telephone, wireless and rocket; twenty minutes after that hour the infantry was to advance. But the rockets were not seen, the lines were down and the runners became casualties to a man, so that, although the artillery opened fire as arranged five minutes after the signal and the 102nd Brigade started at 7.40 A.M., the 101st did not get off until 8 A.M., and therefore lost the barrage.[1] When its leading battalion, the 2/L. North Lancashire, did move forward the Germans were ready, but owing to the many woods and copses and the standing corn little could be seen of them.[2] The leading wave of the right company, after advancing fifty yards, was almost annihilated by the fire of an advanced line of machine guns and by an artillery barrage; the remnants fell back. The left company, overcoming the advanced machine guns, went nearly a thousand yards, but the 2/4th Queen's, which attempted to come up on the left, was forced back; and about 9.30 A.M. a counter-attack compelled the advanced party of the 2/L. North Lancashire to return to the starting line.

In the 102nd Brigade both front line battalions, the

---

[1] The 18-pdrs. fired the creeping barrage with H.E. and 106 fuze, as the moves were at such short notice; the French 75's deepened it, whilst the 4·5-inch howitzers and French heavies were used to bombard localities and known strongpoints. Shrapnel was fired only to catch the retiring enemy in the open.

[2] This was the first general action in which the 2/L. North Lancashire had taken part since Tanga (East Africa) in 1914. The battalion remained in East Africa, suffering much from sickness until December 1916, when it was moved to Egypt. It left for France on 18th May 1918.

1/7th Cheshire and 1/1st Herefordshire, followed the barrage closely and reached a line twelve hundred yards from the starting point; they were then stopped by enfilade fire from right and left as well as by frontal fire from the Bois de Reugny.[1] But the position gained was consolidated and the flanks extended rearwards to connect with the 101st Brigade and the French 58th Division. Neither of the divisions on the flanks of the 34th had been able to make any progress, though they were seen to advance gallantly, only to be cut down by machine-gun fire. Corps orders for the preparation of an attack against the Bois de Reugny by the 34th Division, in conjunction with one directed against Tigny by the French 58th Division, were given in the afternoon, but subsequently cancelled owing to the losses of the latter division.

There was no result to show for the day except the advance made by the 102nd Brigade.

During the afternoon of the 23rd General Foch visited General Pétain at Provins and handed to him, and discussed, a long letter in which he laid down his conception of the situation. It may be summarized thus:[2] Owing to the tactics of the enemy the battle was slowing down: it must be set going again vigorously: the tactics employed by the enemy were to strengthen his flanks by means of fresh divisions supported by artillery, whilst attempting to delay progress against his front by the use of rear guards well provided with machine guns: to overcome this method of resistance one, at least, of the flanks must be broken, whilst everywhere else the troops were to push on as fast as they were able, in accordance with the Instruction of the 19th July[3]: the western flank near Soissons was that to be attacked: all available means (fresh divisions, artillery, tanks, etc.) should be allotted to the Tenth Army, and this Army, in conjunction with the left of the Sixth, must be ordered to prepare to execute the attack towards the region of Fère en Tardenois: the Fifth Army on the eastern flank, consequently reduced as to combatant resources, should act by successive concentrations "alternately "north and south of the Ardre", and, above all, avoid the dispersal of its forces evenly along its whole front.

[1] There was some short shooting on the part of the artillery, but it was impossible to signal the position of the infantry, as the French signal lights supplied could not be fired from the British rifle.
[2] A translation of the letter is given in Appendix XII.
[3] This directed General Pétain to exploit the success achieved.

The Generalissimo then informed Sir Douglas Haig that the two British divisions which he had requested on the 12th July might be sent south of the Somme were now free to go to any part of the British front.

As a fresh measure, General Pétain made arrangements to collect reserves, and he directed General Maistre (G.A.C. : Fourth, Fifth and Ninth Armies) to transfer to his general reserve two divisions from the right of the Fourth Army, to prepare three more to follow, and to send the Italian II. Corps to the Second Army (on the right of the Fourth) in order to relieve two more French divisions.

Sketch 12.

At 11.45 P.M. General Pétain addressed secret and personal instructions to General Maistre and General Fayolle (G.A.R. : Sixth, Tenth, Third and First Armies). In these he modified his orders given on the 20th July in accordance with the points raised by General Foch. Each group was to make one principal attack with the maximum of forces. The G.A.R. with the whole of the Tenth Army and the left of the Sixth was to carry out its effort south-eastwards instead of eastwards, towards the north of Fère en Tardenois instead of Braine, " between the upper Crise " [marked by Chacrise] and the Longpont [6 miles N.N.E. " of Villers Cotterêts]—Fère en Tardenois road, covering " the attack by action south of the Ourcq in the direction " of Fère en Tardenois via Villeneuve sur Fère [3 miles " south-west of Fère en Tardenois] ". The Fifth Army of the G.A.C. was to pursue its advance by successive attacks on both banks of the Ardre, so that it might finally reach a line through Tramery. Between the two attacks, and in conformity with them, the centre was to press on with tenacity, taking care to guard against enemy counter-attacks which might easily be attempted to throw parts of it back into the Marne. Finally both Groups of Armies were to maintain reserves on the flanks to guard against enemy local counter-strokes.

These orders were passed on by the G.A.C. and G.A.R. to the Armies, but did not cause any modification in the conduct of the operations in hand.

The Germans considered that the 23rd had been a satisfactory day which had " created favourable conditions " for a further retirement of the centre, and during the " night Schoeler's, Kathen's and Wichura's corps fell back " without any interference from the foe ".[1] The front

---

[1] See Sketch 15.

THE MARNE, 1918: The German Retirement.

being thereby reduced, General von Kathen handed over his sector to General Wichura as from 5 A.M. on the 24th. The eastern wing was strengthened by the *240th Division* relieving the *50th* during the night of the 23rd/24th.

The German retirement allowed the French left centre to make a small advance on the 24th between Dormans and Oulchy le Château, but elsewhere little happened, because, except for a single division sent to General Mangin, no reinforcements reached the fighting Armies. The Sixth Army, pressing on in the evening near Coincy (4 miles south-west of Fère en Tardenois), did force back the Germans, capturing ten field guns; but, as a battle, except for a few local affairs and a final " flare-up " on the 1st August, the Allied offensive was over, and it became no more than a " follow-up ", the Germans retiring in their own time " behind the Vesle and the Aisne below " Condé ",[1] covering their night marches by bombing of the Allied bivouacs, and leaving behind gas " booby traps " in the numerous large caves to be found in this part of the country.

On the 25th a little more ground was gained near Oulchy, Villemontoire was captured, and a German counter-attack from the eastern shoulder on a front from Vrigny down to Marfaux was repulsed after an initial success; but otherwise on that day and during the 26th there was a pause in the Allied offensive.[2]

NOTE

GERMAN ACCOUNTS OF FIGHTING ON THE EASTERN WING, 21ST–26TH JULY[3]

The *83rd Regiment* (*22nd Division*, Schmettow's corps), which was holding part of the line between Paradis and Espilly, speaks of repulsing attacks in the morning and afternoon of the 21st July, and another attack during the morning of the 23rd. At 7.30 P.M. on the 23rd the fighting strength of the three battalions of the regiment amounted to 27 officers and 735 other ranks, which was little more than a third of its establishment.[4] On the 24th warning was

Sketch 15.

---

[1] During the night of the 24th/25th Conta's and Schmettow's corps fell back from the Marne to the line Champlat—Chatillon—Verneuil.
[2] Lieut.-Colonel J. A. Turner, 13/Royal Scots, of the 15th Division, was, on the 26th, killed at his headquarters by a shell.
[3] A general account of the German retirement is given at the end of Chapter XVI.
[4] Before 21st March 1918 the total establishment of a German battalion

received that the right wing of the corps, of which the regiment formed part, would shortly be ordered to retire. It claims to have repulsed another attack about 10.30 A.M. on the 26th; during the afternoon orders came that the withdrawal would be begun at 1 A.M. on the 27th towards Lhery.

The *116th Reserve Regiment*, in the left sector of the *103rd Division* (*LXV. Corps*) just south-west of Espilly, claims, that on the 21st, although suffering from influenza, it repulsed an attack by Scottish, French and French Colonial troops. On the 23rd the *32nd Regiment* took over a sector of the divisional front extending from the northern edge of the Bois de Courton to just east of Espilly, with outposts pushed forward. It admits being heavily engaged on this day with the 51st Division. " At 6.20 A.M. the barrage moved westwards, " and infantry and machine-gun fire began. The enemy—Scottish " troops of the 51st Division—attacked. Tanks appearing through " the smoke advanced against the German line. Six of these tanks " [only 5 engaged] crawled towards the left sector and moved down " the main line of resistance which had to fall back westwards to " avoid destruction. Behind the tanks the hostile infantry advanced " in long waves, in places in bunches. Such losses were inflicted on " it that by the time the main line of resistance had been reached " the enemy's attacking power had vanished. . . . The men of " *I./32nd*,[1] on whose front the tanks first appeared, behaved " splendidly; they did not allow the monsters to intimidate them, " but opened machine-gun fire against them. . . . Three tanks were " disabled by artillery and machine-gun fire and the other three " turned and disappeared in the smoke. . . . By 8 A.M. the hostile " fire had decreased, and the infantry attack had come to a stand- " still. Touch on the left had been lost and was not regained until " evening. The Bois d'Aulnay and Marfaux had been lost. Scottish " troops from the Bois d'Aulnay had been able to get behind the " *I./32nd*, and the left flank had been thrown back."[2]

During the night of the 26th/27th the *103rd Division* fell back into reserve, near Savigny (7 miles south-east of Fismes), to the new position which ran north of Romigny, north of Ville en Tardenois, through Chambrecy and thence just north of Bligny.

The relief of the *123rd Division* by the *50th Division* began on the night of the 19th/20th and was completed during that of the 21st/22nd July. Between the 15th and 20th July the losses of the *106th Reserve Regiment*, which formed part of the division, were 6 officers and 101 other ranks killed; 11 officers and 435 other ranks wounded; 116 other ranks missing. On relief, the division left the *VI. Reserve* (Borne's) Corps.

The *39th Fusiliers* (*50th Division*) claims to have repulsed an attack on Commetreuil Château on the 21st, and gives an account of its capture on the 23rd by the French. In the evening two regi-

---

was fixed at 980 men (including the machine-gun company). From 1st July 1918, the establishment was 880 men (750 men for the 4 companies and 130 for the machine-gun company). In the autumn of 1918 the strength of an infantry battalion was estimated at 20 officers and 650 other ranks (excluding the machine-gun company).

[1] The *I./32nd* was holding the extreme left sector of the *103rd Division* front north-east of Espilly.

[2] In the sketch in the history of the *32nd Regiment*, the line is shown as running east and west through the wood just north of Espilly.

ments of the *240th Division*, which relieved the *50th Division*, counter-attacked and regained, so it is stated in the history of the *39th Fusiliers*, with the help of that regiment, all the ground that had been lost during the day except the château. During the night of the 24th/25th the *50th Division* withdrew to Chambrecy and Michel Renault Farm. Between the 14th June and 25th July the *53rd Regiment* (*50th Division*) lost 6 officers and 77 other ranks killed, 12 officers and 364 other ranks wounded. The fighting strength of the *39th Fusiliers* by the 25th was only 360 other ranks.

CHAPTER XV

THE SECOND BATTLE OF THE MARNE (*continued*)

27TH–28TH JULY 1918

BUZANCY

(Sketches 12, 13, 14)

Sketch 12.

THE 27th July witnessed a definite change for the better in the situation on the eastern and southern sides of the salient. An Allied attack planned for that day led to the discovery that the Germans had retired on the front from Vrigny right round to the Butte de Chalmont (exclusive), the latter place being a hill which overlooks Oulchy le Château on the east.

Conferences had taken place during the 25th and 26th in the Fifth Army (General Berthelot) in order to discuss General Pétain's instructions of the 23rd, and a general advance had been fixed for the 27th. As regards the British XXII. Corps (Lieut.-General Sir A. Godley), whose front had been diminished on the 24th to about three miles owing to the I. Colonial Corps taking over some twelve hundred yards on the right, and the V. Corps a similar length on the left, it was agreed that until the ridge south of the Ardre had been secured further advance north of the river was impossible. Accordingly, the 186th Brigade of the 62nd Division (Major-General W. P. Braithwaite), with the 185th in support, continued to hold the line from the Bois du Petit Champ, the southward projecting portion of the Bois de Reims, to the Ardre. The 187th Brigade and the 51st Division (Major-General G. T. C. Carter-Campbell), supported by the artillery of both divisions and the French guns which had been co-operating with them, as well as the French 14th Division, were all to advance south of the Ardre; they were to capture the Bois de Courton ridge as far as a line west of Nappes, about three-quarters of a mile ahead. The order of the troops from

Sketch 13.

right to left was, 152nd Brigade (Br.-General R. Laing), with the 5/Seaforth Highlanders in front line, on the low ground near the Ardre; 187th Brigade (Br.-General A. J. Reddie), with all three battalions, 5/K.O.Y.L.I., 2/4th York & Lancaster and 2/4th K.O.Y.L.I., in line; and the 153rd Brigade (Br.-General W. Green), with the 7/Gordon Highlanders and 6/Black Watch in the front line.

As the ground over which the 152nd and 187th Brigades were to move was commanded from the edge of the Bois de Courton on the south, and the progress of the 153rd Brigade through the wood must necessarily be slow, it was settled that the advance should be made in echelon from the left, the French 14th Division and the 153rd Brigade starting, after a 10 minutes' bombardment, at 6.10 A.M., the 187th Brigade at 6.56 A.M., and the 152nd about 7.30 A.M. (owing to delay in the barrage lifting it did not do so until 7.45 A.M.). The barrage, in view of the difficulties of ground, moved at a rate of only 100 metres in 8 minutes, with three 20-minute pauses, after the first pause quickening to 100 metres in 7 minutes. Twenty-four machine guns of the 51st Machine-Gun Battalion were to fire an intense barrage of 120,000 rounds against the edge of the Bois de Courton, west of Espilly. French tanks were to have taken part, but after the heavy rain of the previous night they were unable to move over the sodden ground.

No opposition worth mentioning was encountered, and the first objective was secured about 8.45 A.M. and the second about 10 A.M.; hostile guns maintained fire for an hour, but no contact was made with the German infantry, in fact the XXII. Corps saw little of it and made only one prisoner during the day. It was apparent that the enemy was in retreat—he had, in fact, withdrawn during the night to a new line—and, after consultation, Major-Generals Carter-Campbell and Braithwaite, with covering authority from Lieut.-General Godley, issued orders for an advance by the two divisions at 1 P.M. to a line which passed through Chaumuzy to the south-eastern corner of the Bois d'Eclisse, between a half and three-quarters of a mile ahead, whence patrols were to be sent out. The artillery and corps mounted troops [1] were moved forward, and the French on either flank were asked to conform, which they agreed to do.

North of the Ardre the new position was occupied by

---

[1] Composite Cavalry Regiment (2 squadrons of the 4th Australian Light Horse and 1 of the Otago Mounted Rifles) and 22nd Cyclist Battalion.

2.30 P.M. without opposition; south of the river, Chaumuzy was reached just before 3 P.M. and an hour and a half later the 152nd and 153rd Brigades were reported as consolidating. The 187th Brigade then reverted to the 62nd Division, and subsequently went into reserve near Chaumuzy.

There being fears of a trap, all too easy to lay in the wooded and broken country, a further general advance was not made immediately; when it did take place the brigades moved in depth, ready to meet any counter-attack. At 1.55 P.M. Major-General Braithwaite had directed the corps mounted troops, which had been placed at his disposal during the morning, to push forward rapidly and seize the line Bligny—Montagne de Bligny. As soon as the mounted troops should report this line to be in their possession the 186th and 185th Brigades were to advance and relieve them. The mounted troops left Nanteuil at 2.45 P.M. and passed through the line of the infantry; patrols of the 186th Brigade followed them. But both parties came under machine-gun fire from the woods on their right and their progress became very slow. At 7.40 P.M., the previous orders to send on only patrols having been modified, the 186th Brigade began to advance to the support of the mounted troops and found them heavily engaged, but still five hundred yards from their objective, so that their relief could scarcely be completed before midnight. The 185th Brigade also moved up, but remained around Chaumuzy.

It was not until 9.43 P.M. that a report of the situation near Bligny reached the 62nd Division, and until 10.30 P.M. that divisional orders were issued for a further advance at dawn in conjunction with the French 77th Division, on the right, which was to clear the woods on that flank.

South of the Ardre, there was little opposition to the second advance. At 4 P.M. Major-General Carter-Campbell ordered the 152nd and 153rd Brigades to send forward patrols to examine the Bois d'Eclisse, and as soon as it might be reported clear to push on and occupy an old French trench line west of the wood. It was after midnight before the patrols of the 153rd Brigade reported the wood to be free of the enemy. The brigade then moved forward until by 6.30 A.M. it occupied a north-south line through the centre of the wood, with outposts on the edge, in touch on the left with the French 14th Division, but not with the 152nd Brigade on the right, so a defensive flank was formed. The latter brigade received no reports from its patrols until early morning, except that the corps mounted troops were held up near Bligny. So, after a short advance in conjunction with the 186th on its right, it halted for the night. The men were so exhausted that although it became known that the 153rd Brigade was advancing to occupy the Bois d'Eclisse, no further move was made. But at 6.15 A.M. on the 28th patrols were sent out, and by 10.30 A.M. the 152nd Brigade had joined up with the 153rd, so that the latter's defensive flank could be withdrawn.

Thus during the 27th some ground had been gained on the eastern wing, whilst on the whole front as far as the neighbourhood of Oulchy le Château the French divisions had similarly gone forward.

The events of the 28th were somewhat similar to those of the 27th, and another general advance was made, with the addition that, on the western wing, the French XI. Corps captured the Butte de Chalmont, overlooking Oulchy le Château,[1] whilst the British 15th Division took Buzancy, but only to lose it again, as will be related. Sketch 14.

The 15th Division (Major-General H. L. Reed) had on the 26th/27th taken over half a mile more front from the French 87th Division on its right, so that its total frontage was over two miles, its right now facing Buzancy. Opposite were the German *50th Reserve* and *5th Divisions*. The 15th, with the 44th (vice 46th) and 45th Brigades in the line, had orders to attack Buzancy on the 28th. This village, covering, together with its château in the northwest, a quarter of a square mile, nestled in a slope of the western side of a large flat hill, yet it stood well above the Allied front line. The objective was the line Villemontoire (exclusive, now in French possession)—high ground east of Buzancy—point where the Allied front line cut the Château Thierry-Soissons road, that is, it had to make a bite about two thousand yards wide and twelve hundred deep into the German front. The 44th Brigade (Br.-General N. A. Thomson) was to make the attack, with the assistance of five companies of the French 91st Regiment (87th Division). Zero hour was fixed for 30 minutes after midday, when it was hoped that the Germans would be off their guard. Most careful preparations were made. Every company was given a special task by Br.-General Thomson, and the guns were massed under the commander of the artillery of the XX. Corps, who for the operation

[1] The Germans claim to have evacuated it during the preceding night, but British officers saw at least a rear guard driven off it.

added to the artillery of the 15th Division that of the French 87th Division, the 253rd Artillery Regiment (3 " groupes ") and 3 batteries of 155-mm. of the 69th Division; but here, as on other occasions, the infantry attack was handicapped by the allotment of the British 4·5-inch field howitzers for counter-battery work. To deceive the enemy bombardments of Buzancy and other villages near the front of attack and of various works were carried out during the afternoon of the 27th and morning of the 28th. The barrage, extending well beyond the flanks of the attack, fell two minutes before zero. Smoke was fired at the same time to screen Buzancy château, the south-western side of the village, three sides of the wood south-west of it and Noyant on the northern side of the Crise, so as to prevent observation from the neighbouring heights. Machine-gun barrages were also arranged and the French provided a section of flame-throwers. Fifteen minutes after zero a fighting aeroplane patrol flew over the objective to drive off hostile aircraft and engage ground targets.

Owing to the woods and the broken nature of the ground, the close support of the infantry was difficult, but was most satisfactory in the initial stages of the attack. The French companies advanced against the wood south-west of Buzancy, which had " Grenade Work ", a strong-point, in front of it, and the 8/Seaforth Highlanders and 1/5th Gordon Highlanders against Buzancy, with the 4th/5th Black Watch in reserve. Although the ground to be crossed was destitute of cover, the château was taken at once, but the village proved very troublesome, explosive charges carried by the engineers and flame-throwers having to be used, and the houses with their cellars cleared one by one; in a single cellar two officers and a hundred men were captured. The strongpoints north of Buzancy were also secured after a sharp bombing fight. By 1.30 P.M. the 44th Brigade had captured its objectives, but on its right there was no news or sign of the French, and the situation was obscure, so a second company of the reserve was sent to support the liaison company on that wing, and later a defensive flank was formed at Buzancy.

At 1.35 P.M. Major-General Reed received information from the French 69th Division, on the left, that a column of Germans could be seen moving north-eastward through Septmonts (1¾ miles N.N.E. of Buzancy), and it was at once engaged by the heavy artillery, with good results. At 2.10 P.M. he heard by wireless from the French artillery that German reinforcements (reserves of the *5th* and the *50th Reserve Divisions*) were advancing on Buzancy from the east. Forty minutes later he learnt by wireless that the progress of the French 91st Regiment was slow, and at 3.35 P.M. by message from his own troops that the French were back on their original starting line and could not renew their attack; lastly, came the news that the 44th Brigade was being subjected to heavy counter-attacks.

Major-General Reed made this known to General Berdoulat (XX. Corps), requesting him to find out the exact position as regards the French 91st Regiment; he instructed Br.-General Thomson to hold on to Buzancy and the château and strengthen his right. Before any action could be taken on this instruction, Br.-General Thomson heard direct from the 91st Regiment that it had not been able to advance at all from its original line; simultaneously at 4.35 P.M. the S.O.S. signal went up in the south-eastern corner of Buzancy. Outflanked and outnumbered, the Highlanders were driven first from the village, then from the château, but only got clear of artillery fire to find enemy machine gunners in rear of them. These they bombed with hand-grenades taken from a German dump in the château grounds, and, after having sent back as prisoners six officers and over two hundred other ranks, they regained their starting line soon after 6 P.M. The 15th Division, which had been in most of the heavy encounters of the War since Loos in September 1915, regarded the action on this day as the severest and " most gruelling " of them all.[1]

At 5.45 P.M. Major-General Reed had been informed by the XX. Corps that a new barrage would be fired, and that the 91st Regiment would launch a fresh attack at 6.45 P.M. This was of course all too late and the operation was cancelled. The attempt to extend the pressure upon the enemy to the northward which began so well had failed for want of co-operation.[2]

At 6 P.M. Major-General Reed was also warned by the liaison officer of the XX. Corps that his division was to change places with the 87th Division (which the British had known as a Territorial division at Ypres in October

---

[1] For the German account see Note at end of Chapter.
[2] On 27th August 1918 General Gassouin, commanding the French 17th Division, which on 2nd/3rd August finally relieved the 15th Division, wrote to General Reed to inform him that a monument to the division had been erected at Buzancy by his men as a mark of their admiration. See Appendix XVII.

1914), with a view to further operations. It was that night to take ground to the right as far as Tigny, relieving parts of the 12th and 87th Divisions, and then, during the following night, to hand over its left sector to the 87th Division; the artillery was to remain where it was. An immediate relief at such short notice was a formidable task, as many of the units were in confusion after the fight—and there was, as ever, the language difficulty—but the first relief was carried out.[1]

On the eastern wing the British were again the spearhead. The 62nd Division had issued orders at 10.30 P.M. on the previous evening for a further advance to take place at 4.30 A.M. by the 186th and 185th Brigades, the latter south of the Ardre, covered by the mounted troops, to the old trench line beyond Bligny and the Montagne de Bligny held by the 19th Division on the 4th June. Rain fell all night, making the fields and even the roads heavy going, while a cold mist formed in the morning; but when the 186th Brigade, with the 2/4th Duke of Wellington's and 2/4th Hampshire in front line, deployed on the starting line at 4 A.M. it was immediately struck by machine-gun fire, particularly from the Bois des Dix Hommes on the right, whilst the ground over which the advance was to be made was swept by an artillery barrage besides other fire. Touch could not be obtained with the French 77th Division on the right, for it started later; it did not inform the 62nd Division of the capture of the Bois des Dix Hommes until 4 P.M. Nevertheless, by persistent pushing forward of small parties under covering fire, ground was slowly gained. Bligny was entered during the morning but not entirely captured until 4 P.M., when the 77th Division came up and then the whole of the brigade objective was secured.

The 185th Brigade had better luck. The 5/Devonshire soon came under fire, but, advancing swiftly in the mist, by 7 A.M. had got to its objective between Bligny village and the Montagne. The 8/West Yorkshire, without a barrage, reached the slopes of the Montagne before it was quite light, surprised the Germans and drove them off the top of the hill by a charge, taking forty prisoners and three machine guns; but it could not complete the capture of the whole position.[2]

In the 51st Division a warning order was sent out at 8.35 A.M., that as soon as the 152nd Brigade came up in

Sketch 13.

---

[1] The 15th Division operation order is in Appendix XIII.
[2] The 8/West Yorkshire was awarded the "Croix de guerre".

line with the 153rd, although the German artillery was shelling the villages and had obviously registered the ground, the advance would probably be continued. At 11.5 A.M., in consequence of an erroneous report that the French 14th Division was in Chambrecy, the 153rd Brigade was ordered to advance in touch with it, and the divisional artillery, 255th and 256th Brigades R.F.A., moved forward through Chaumuzy under shell-fire.

An attack made on Chambrecy by the 14th Division at noon failed to capture it, and General Baston then sent information that it would attack Ville en Tardenois, farther to the west, at 3 P.M.; but this movement when initiated was soon checked by artillery and machine-gun fire. The 1/7th Gordon Highlanders and 1/6th Black Watch, of the 153rd Brigade, advanced about half a mile from their morning line—squeezing out the 152nd Brigade as the front was narrowed by the left boundary of the XXII. Corps, which turned northward; but the two battalions then ran into the German barrage and heavy machine-gun fire from the north-western slopes of the Montagne de Bligny. Though losing heavily, they continued to push on, and in the end the 6/Black Watch entered Chambrecy and took up position, entirely isolated on its northern side; but the 7/Gordon Highlanders came up on the right to the lower western slopes of the Montagne de Bligny, on top of which the 8/West Yorkshire was established. ,By now it was dark and the situation of the two battalions in contact with the enemy with the men dead tired was full of danger. Major-General Carter-Campbell dealt with it by sending up two battalions of the 154th Brigade to relieve both the 153rd and the 152nd Brigades. As the 7/Gordon Highlanders had not consolidated any line, the wing of the 1/4th Gordons which took its place decided to occupy the old trench west of the Bois d'Eclisse and fell back to it. All reliefs were completed by 3 A.M. (29th).

Thus a general advance of about a mile had been made by the XXII. Corps. The French 77th Division was up on the right and the 14th on the left, but the latter had not taken Ville en Tardenois, although farther west as far as Oulchy le Château the leading French units had closed up to the new German line. No change had taken place on the important western wing. Bad weather and continuous fighting had greatly fatigued the troops; notwithstanding, General Fayolle telegraphed to his Army commanders that the moment to stop had not yet come : that, whatever the state of fatigue of the troops, the Tardenois plateaux—the wide open stretches on the east and west of Fère en Tardenois—must be carried and the enemy prevented from effecting an undisturbed retirement: advanced guards of infantry and cavalry must follow him so as to keep close contact and secure all the ground which he abandoned.

NOTE

GERMAN ACCOUNTS OF BUZANCY

Sketch 14.

The following is the narrative of the fighting about Buzancy on the 28th July drawn from regimental histories.

The *52nd Regiment (5th Division)* held the eastern edge of the wood north-west of Buzancy, the western face of the village and the western edge of the wood south-west of it. On the right it was in touch with the *8th Leib Grenadiers (5th Division)* and on the left with *III./230th Reserve Regiment (50th Reserve Division)*. The history of the *8th Leib Grenadiers* states that after a violent barrage, beginning at 12.30 P.M., the British infantry attacked at one o'clock and succeeded in capturing Buzancy château and park and in advancing to the copse 800 yards east of the village (it lay on the eastern edge of the high ground). The *I. Battalion* counter-attacked and drove the attacking troops back to Buzancy château, and by 5 P.M. the original front line had been re-established. According to the history of the *52nd Regiment*, it was at 12.45 P.M. that the British attacked. The regiment and the *230th Reserve Regiment*, on the left, held firm, but farther north the enemy broke through and tried to encircle Buzancy from the north and east. Reserves were hurried up, but by 2 P.M. they had failed to restore the situation. Then a counter-attack by *I./52* and *II./230* drove the enemy from the village and the *8th Leib Grenadiers* also regained its original position.

The history of the *230th Reserve Regiment (50th Reserve Division)* is more detailed. Its *III. Battalion* was holding the front line with three companies. The right lay in the woods south-west of Buzancy and the left 200 metres south of them. A valley separated the Germans and the Allies. During the morning of the 28th July artillery fire increased considerably; about midday the barrage became very heavy. At 12.15 P.M. news reached battalion headquarters from the front line that the French were pushing forward small groups with the apparent intention of attacking. Just before 1 P.M. the *52nd Regiment* reported that the British had broken through, had captured Buzancy and were already gaining ground east of the German front line, and that only the southern part of the village was still held. By now the *III./230th Reserve* was also being attacked and the French reached the front line of the two right companies; but a counter-attack drove them back. At 2.45 P.M. battalion headquarters received a message from the front line that as far as the *230th Reserve* was concerned the attack might be considered as over; on the other hand, the company of the *52nd* on the right of the *230th Reserve* reported that the enemy had succeeded in breaking through that regiment, and was continuing his advance eastwards. About 3 P.M. machine-gun fire on the right of the *230th Reserve* indicated an attempt by Scottish troops coming from the direction of the *52nd Regiment* to turn the right flank of the *III./230th Reserve*. The last of the battalion reserves was put in, but the situation was critical. Great efforts were made to restore communications which had been destroyed, and by 3.25 P.M. touch had been regained by battalion headquarters with its companies and with regimental headquarters; the last-named informed the battalion that the *II./230th Reserve* would counter-attack in the sector of the *52nd*. This battalion was on the western edge of the Bois l'Evêque, and received orders to send an officer's patrol towards Buzancy to clear up the situation, whilst two companies were to be ready to counter-attack the village. Shortly afterwards the battalion received orders from regimental headquarters :—according to information received from the *5th Division*, on the right, the enemy had broken into Buzancy and through the line north of it, and was advancing towards the high ground east and north-east of the village : the *5th Division* was about to counter-attack Buzancy from the north-east : the *50th Reserve Division* had given orders that the *230th Reserve Regiment* was to support this counter-attack to the utmost : the *II./230th Reserve* was therefore to attack at once, two companies (*Nos. 5* and *8*), with their right flank working along the southern edge of Buzancy, the third company behind the right flank, was to occupy the high ground east of the village, and the fourth company was to remain in reserve on the western edge of the Bois l'Evêque.

In the face of the counter-attack the enemy fell back to Buzancy, and his resistance in the eastern outskirts was quickly overcome. The village was captured after house to house fighting, the Scottish troops defending the walls of the château to the last. " It was not " until *No. 5 Company* attacked the brave defenders in rear that " about fifty men surrendered ". *Nos. 5* and *8 Companies* then resumed their advance, and finally took up a defensive position 200 metres west of the park surrounding the château.

CHAPTER XVI

THE SECOND BATTLE OF THE MARNE (*continued*)

29TH–31ST JULY 1918

(Sketches 12, 13, 14, 15)

Sketch 12.

On the 29th activity was mainly confined to the right of the French Tenth Army. The Fifth Army, in which was included the British XXII. Corps, was to continue the pursuit : " if the enemy's halt is prolonged, the Fifth " Army will take all measures to attack him and throw " him on to the Ardre, making its principal effort in the " direction Lagery—Crugny "—that is northward. Little happened. The divisions of the XXII. Corps were worn out by previous fighting and made no advance except to improve the position of the 185th Brigade on the Montagne de Bligny, where another part of the objective was gained, at heavy loss, by the 2/5th West Yorkshire. The French 77th Division also made a small advance in the woods on the right of the XXII. Corps, but was driven back next morning. " The French High Command recognized the " impossibility, in the circumstances in which the Fifth " Army was situated, of mounting fresh attacks with the " insufficient means at its disposal." [1]

The French Sixth Army received " as minimum ob- " jective to be reached by the end of the day " a line 7 miles ahead and only $3\frac{1}{2}$ miles from the Vesle ; its advanced guards were to overlook the river. This Army made no progress whatever.

In the French Tenth Army the XXX. Corps, of which the British 34th Division formed part, was to make the principal attack and reach the high ground north of Grand Rozoy, between Servenay and the Bois de St. Jean, the XI. Corps coming up on its right, and the XX., in

[1] F.O.A. vii. (i.), p. 130.

which was the British 15th Division, and I. Corps, covering its left. General Mangin had received no reinforcements except the 128th Division from the Third Army in exchange for the tired 1st Division, but the 127th and 17th from the Second Army (Verdun) were expected to begin detraining on the 29th.

The operations of the XXX. Corps involved a left wheel, pivoting on Tigny, and the British 34th Division was now on the wheeling flank.

During the afternoon of the 26th Major-General Nicholson had been warned by General Penet (XXX. Corps) that the 34th Division would be shifted to the right to take part in the attack on the 30th. So during the night of the 27th/28th the infantry and the machine-gun battalion of the 34th Division had been relieved, after considerable difficulties, in the sector opposite Hartennes by the extension inwards of the flanks of the French 19th Division on the right, and the 12th (which had taken the place of the 58th) on the left.[1] With its artillery, withdrawn the same night, it was assembled by 2 A.M. among the woods south of Villers Helon. Verbal orders were received at 11 A.M. on the 28th from the XXX. Corps that the division was to concentrate some five miles to the south-east, about the Bois de la Baillette, during the ensuing night, with a view of attacking in the direction of Beugneux and Grand Rozoy on the morning of the 29th. The success of the French XI. Corps in capturing the Butte de Chalmont had caused the date of attack to be advanced by twenty-four hours. There was, however, time for reconnaissance.

Sketch 14.

The 34th Division, with the XI. Corps on the right and the 25th Division (XXX. Corps) on the left, was to capture the high ground mentioned in the Tenth Army instructions, Cramaille—Beugneux—Orme du Grand Rozoy—now held by German rear guards. The sector allotted to the 34th had its front line in the valley of a small stream, and the objective lay westwards of Servenay for a little over a mile. To reach it the division had to make an advance uphill and then cross the high ground marked by Point 189 and Orme du Grand Rozoy. The troops moved off at 9 P.M. and reached the position of assembly, west of a light railway, by 1 A.M. on the 29th without incident. Zero hour was 4.10 A.M.

The 103rd and 101st Brigades (Br.-Generals J. G.

[1] The 87th Division, previously mentioned, was on the left of the 12th.

Chaplin and W. J. Woodcock), each with a machine-gun company attached, were to lead the attack, supported by the divisional artillery and two French field artillery regiments, making a total of 108 field guns and 56 howitzers, under Br.-General E. C. W. D. Walthall, and three batteries of French heavy artillery. The barrage was to move forward, with pauses, at the rate of one hundred yards in 4 minutes. The 102nd Brigade (less one battalion in corps reserve) and the rest of the divisional troops were kept in reserve.

At 4.10 A.M. fog covered the ground, but the leading line, in which were the 1/8th Scottish Rifles and 1/5th K.O.S.B. of the 103rd Brigade, and the 4/R. Sussex and 2/4th Queen's of the 101st Brigade, each on a two-company front, pushed forward through a German barrage, which fell two hundred yards in front of the starting line and contained a belt of tear-gas. Good progress of over a mile was made; so towards 6 A.M. a short halt was ordered, during which two 18-pdr. batteries and two sections of howitzers were brought to advanced positions, amid cheers from the French gunners, whose front they had to cross. The French took Grand Rozoy on the left, but did not come up on the right : it subsequently transpired that the French XI. Corps did not start until 6 A.M. So the line ran from Grand Rozoy south-eastward. Difficulty in finding artillery support owing to failure of communication now occurred, and the German machine gunners stoutly opposed any further progress. The infantry considered that on this occasion an intermediate halt had been a mistake, as it gave the enemy time to bring up reinforcements. When further advances were made at a number of places, as far as the Bois de Beugneux (west of the village) and Point 189, north-west of the village, the Germans counter-attacked. After a long deadlock and a struggle against machine-gun fire, the troops fell back about 2 P.M. to the position gained at the first advance, although the 5/Argyll & Sutherland Highlanders, the reserve of the 103rd Brigade, had been engaged.

Before this hour, as the fog cleared, it had become evident that the attack had come to a standstill, and at 10.50 A.M. Major-General Nicholson had ordered the 102nd Brigade (two battalions) and the 2/4th Somerset L.I. (Pioneers) to move forward at 2.30 P.M. against the original objective and outflank Beugneux from the west, whilst the 103rd Brigade attacked the village from the south. This operation was anticipated by the Germans, who launched a heavy counter-attack at 2.10 P.M., driving the French 25th Division out of Grand Rozoy and uncovering the left of the 101st Brigade. A defensive flank was formed and the counter-attack driven off, but, as the right was also open, the 103rd and 101st Brigades fell back to the position of the Second Paris Line, half-way back to the jumping-off line. At nightfall the outposts were pushed up to the 6 A.M. line and the 2/L. North Lancashire (101st Brigade)—whose commander Lieut.-Colonel C. E. A. Jourdain was killed during the morning—was sent up to protect the left flank. But matters on that flank were put right at 6 A.M. next morning when the French recaptured Grand Rozoy.[1] As further sign of his retirement the enemy during the night shelled the 34th Division with mustard gas, and caused much inconvenience.

Disappointed with the progress made on the two wings, but encouraged by the relative success of the centre (Sixth Army), due to the retirement of the enemy, General Pétain on the 29th had issued a new Instruction to the Groups of Armies, of which the following is a summary.

Sketch 12.

" The enemy appears to be too strongly established on
" the plateaux south of Soissons and on the heights between
" the Vesle and the Ardre to admit of any hope that these
" two pillars of resistance can be broken and the German
" forces south of the Aisne destroyed. Henceforward our
" object must be to hustle their retreat so as to upset
" their plans of evacuation and devastation of the country,
" and to hasten the moment when the Marne railway can
" be made ready again for traffic.

" The Sixth Army, which now possesses the largest
" resources, is charged with the principal rôle : it will
" push forward vigorously without interruption on its
" whole front in the general direction of Fismes and
" Bazoches [3 miles west of Fismes], its left establishing
" itself in the Saponay area, so as to facilitate the advance

---

[1] The French Official Account of the 29th is slightly different : " The " XXX. and XI. Corps advanced to the attack at 4 and 6 A.M., respectively. " At the beginning of their engagement they obtained important successes : " at 8 A.M. the British 34th Division entered Grand Rozoy and the XI. " Corps, Wallée [on the east of the Butte de Chalmont]. But the enemy " did not delay to react vigorously against the right of the Tenth Army, " as well as against the fronts of the Sixth and Fifth Armies. Towards " the end of the day our tired troops were not able to develop their efforts " beyond the general line Grand Rozoy—southern outskirts of Saponay— " Seringes—Nesles—Cierges [the last three places had been reached on the " previous day]." F.O.A. vii. (i.), pp. 129-30.

" of the right wing of the Tenth Army towards Cramaille.
" From midnight of the 29th/30th the Sixth Army will
" take over the III. Corps, the left of the Fifth Army, so
" that the boundary between the Groups of Armies of the
" Centre and Reserve will be Verneuil—Ste. Gemme and
" thence northwards to the east of Fismes.

" The Tenth Army, which cannot count on any more
" reinforcements after receiving the 17th Division, will
" continue to act in the direction of Braine. It will make
" its principal effort with its right; but the centre will
" participate in the movement so as to occupy progressively
" the heights on the left bank of the Crise.

" The Fifth Army, which not only cannot count on
" any reinforcements but must also release the British
" XXII. Corps on the 31st, will act preferably south of
" the Ardre northwards on the axis Lagery—Crugny, so
" as to support the right of the Sixth Army.

" The commanders of Groups of Armies are requested
" to see that the forces are methodically employed, to
" insist that each Army engaged is echeloned in depth so
" as to facilitate the employment of reserves and to guard
" against enemy action, which might entirely compromise
" our advance by a counter-offensive suddenly launched
" either between Oise and Aisne, or against the Reims
" salient."

By a telegram timed 7.10 P.M., General Pétain withdrew the two cavalry corps into reserve pointing out that the form which the battle had assumed precluded any possibility of employing cavalry corps in the fighting. He was aware by now that General Foch had in his mind operations on another part of the front, as will be related later. Where this would be, even he, in the interest of secrecy, had not yet been informed; he had been personally and specially warned on the 25th by General Weygand, on behalf of the Generalissimo, not to come to a conference at Sarcus, Foch's headquarters. But in the afternoon of the 28th Colonel Desticker, Foch's Assistant Chief of the Staff, had brought to him a copy of a short Special Directive from which he learnt that the new offensive would be carried out by the French First Army and the British Fourth Army. The Generalissimo had come to the conclusion that the enemy in the Soissons salient " will without doubt occupy
" a defensive position behind a river, which we cannot
" attack immediately; this in all likelihood will permit
" him to reorganize his forces, so that in the course of time

PETAIN'S INSTRUCTION. 31st JULY

" he may make some of them available for use else-
" where ".

The only indications of future action so far visible were that General Foch, in spite of the battle, had accumulated two groups of reserves, one of 4 divisions behind the left of the G.A.R., around Conty (12 miles S.W. by S. of Amiens), and the other of 3 divisions behind the centre of the G.A.R., behind Compiègne; six tired divisions and the Italian Corps from the G.A.C. were in the course of transport to, or reorganizing behind, the G.A.E., where also the American 1st and 2nd Divisions were being sent to relieve French divisions and reorganize, after having been the spearhead of General Mangin's attack of the 18th July. Meanwhile the American Army of two corps (I. and III., the II. being with the British) was being constituted in the area of the French Sixth Army, where the American 3rd, 28th, 42nd, 32nd and 4th (portion) Divisions had taken part in the operations of the 28th and 29th July.[1]

What General Pétain had in his mind in issuing his Instruction of the 29th July is best explained by a telegram which he sent on the 31st to Generals Fayolle and Pershing:—

" The state of the forces at our disposal at the moment
" obliges us to give the battle a new turn (' allure ') which
" will economise infantry to the maximum. . . . In con-
" sequence regulate your efforts by your resources. The
" object to attain is to throw back the enemy on the Vesle
" gradually by successive efforts in accordance with my
" directive of the 29th July, giving the American forces of
" the Sixth Army more and more the principal rôle, so
" that towards the 15th August they will hold all the front
" of that Army."

There was no need, as it turned out, for any special effort to throw the Germans back on the Vesle, for in two great retirements on the nights of the 1st/2nd and 2nd/3rd August they withdrew behind it.

[1] The 42nd had relieved the 26th, which had taken part in the earlier fighting, on the 26th July, and the 77th arrived later : the I. Corps (Major-General Hunter Liggett) contained the 26th, 42nd and 77th Divisions; it had taken over the sector of the French III. Corps on 4th July : the III. Corps (Major-General R. L. Bullard) contained the 3rd, 28th and 32nd (earlier the 1st and 2nd) and took over from the French XXXVIII. Corps on 4th August. General Pershing assumed command of the American First Army relieving the French Sixth Army on 10th August.

The formation of a Second American Army (General R. L. Bullard) in the St. Mihiel area, headquarters Toul, was agreed to by General Foch on 28th July, and it took over a defensive sector in Lorraine on 12th October, Lieut.-General Hunter Liggett then replacing General Pershing in the First Army.

288 SECOND BATTLE OF THE MARNE

Sketch 13.

On the eastern wing, in the French Fifth Army little further happened on the 30th. In order to relieve the two divisions of the British XXII. Corps as quickly as possible General Berthelot arranged that the 77th and 14th Divisions should extend inwards, and on the night of the 30th/31st the former took over the front of the 62nd Division. But about 8 P.M. on the 30th, after heavy shelling lasting all day and culminating in fifteen minutes' intense bombardment, the Germans attacked the Montagne de Bligny held by the 154th Brigade, now the only infantry of the 51st Division in the front line. Thanks to a very good artillery barrage the attack was driven off by the 7/Argyll. After dusk on the 31st, the 51st Division was relieved by the French 14th. The divisional artillery began entraining for the British area on the 31st July, the remainder of the division on the 2nd August. In the 62nd Division, the artillery entrained on the 1st and 2nd August and the rest of the troops on the 3rd and 4th.

The net result of the operations of the XXII. Corps between 8 A.M. on the 20th July and 10 P.M. on the 31st had been an advance of about four miles commencing on a frontage of 7,000 yards which decreased to 4,000. The captures were 21 officers and 1,148 other ranks of seven different German divisions, with 135 machine guns and 32 recovered French and Italian guns.

The gross casualties were reported as 51st Division 115 officers and 2,950 other ranks; 62nd Division 118 officers and 3,865 other ranks.[1]

In an Order of the Day General Berthelot specially thanked the divisions of the XXII. Corps for their success; involved in heavy fighting in extremely difficult country, they had certainly done well.[2]

Sketch 12.

The French Sixth Army on the 30th, whilst preparing for future attack, made contact with the enemy on its whole front. But from the Bois Meunière, between Villers

---

[1] The strength (excluding artillery) at 6 P.M. on the 30th July was

	OFFICERS	OTHER RANKS
51st Division	220	5,598
62nd „	226	5,536

and the reinforcements received

51st Division	60	1,065
62nd „	69	1,712

The German losses are not yet available, but must have been very heavy: never had British divisions seen such a number of enemy dead as they found in the woods. French calculations place the total German casualties on the Marne battle front in July at 168,000 (Paquet, p. 132).

[2] For the Order of the Day see Appendix XV.

Agron and Ronchères, to the Ourcq it encountered lively resistance and made hardly noticeable progress. On the 31st this Army made an advance on the right averaging about a thousand yards on the front between Villers Agron and Seringes, occupying the greater part of Bois Meunière.[1] In the Tenth Army General Mangin decided not to renew the attack of the XI. and XXX. Corps (in the latter of which was the British 34th Division) supported on the left by the XX. Corps (in which was the 15th Division) until the 1st August, and this decision met with the approval of General Foch, who visited him during the day.[2]

NOTE

THE GERMAN RETIREMENT 25TH–31ST JULY

The German Crown Prince on the 24th July ordered prepara- **Sketch** tions to be made for a retirement on the night of the 25th/26th **15.** to what was called the "great bridgehead position", now defined as Ville en Tardenois—Romigny—Villers Agron—Bois Meunière —Cierges, and thence down the upper course of the Ourcq to Trigny and then to Grand Rozoy, roughly, on the east, the line occupied by the Allies on the 28th, and, on the west, that on the 30th. The Crown Prince on the 27th directed that the construction of a "Blücher Position", behind the Vesle to its confluence with the Aisne and thence behind that river, should be begun. Six "tired divisions", under a corps staff, were detailed by the *Seventh Army* for the work along the Vesle, leaving the Aisne portion to be dug by the *Ninth Army*. The "Blücher Position" was to be covered by an intermediate ("small bridgehead" or "Ziethen") position, running along the heights about four miles south of the Vesle from Jonchery to opposite Missy.

The date of the retirement to the "great bridgehead" was, however, postponed by order of Ludendorff. The Operations Staff of O.H.L. was not convinced of the necessity for withdrawal. It was obvious that the troops had recovered from "the nervous "breakdown" caused by General Mangin's attack on the 18th, and were now again resisting with all their old determination. The idea of restoring the situation by offensive action took form, and the

---

[1] The Germans claim to have withdrawn from the wood during the previous night. Officer prisoners declared that the German *Seventh Army* would soon retire on to a fortified position; one of the reasons for the retirement, they said, was the difficulty of railway communication, but the retirement would be of no great scope and only affect the plateaux running from Ville en Tardenois to Fère en Tardenois; others said that they had been ordered to hold the Grand Rozoy position to the last.

[2] Lieut.-Colonel J. G. Dooner, G.S.O.I. of the 34th Division, was killed on the 31st July whilst visiting the brigades to make arrangements for the attack.

Ninth Army was instructed by O.H.L. to prepare an attack on a 12-mile front, from Osly (5 miles west of Soissons) westwards, to be extended eastward later to include Soissons. An attack had been arranged by the *1st Division* on the 25th to recover the ground lost near Marfaux—and more if possible—in which other troops [1] were to join, so that the front of attack would extend from the Bois de Courton eight miles northward to Ormes, and Ludendorff was inclined to await the result of this effort. If it reached the edge of the heights overlooking the Reims basin the city might, after all, be captured.

The German Crown Prince took a different view of the situation. He was convinced of the necessity for retirement, and retirement right behind the Vesle and Aisne. He telegraphed to O.H.L. as follows :

" If the battle is to be fought out in the area south of the
" Aisne and Vesle, the despatch of fresh forces of all arms, including
" the general artillery reserve, is necessary. . . .

" It can be expected with all certainty that the enemy will
" continue the battle. He has sufficient forces at his disposal.

" In these circumstances the Group of Armies does not believe
" that it is expedient to fight the struggle out south of the Vesle.
" A large part of the Armies and of the transportation service would
" be destroyed and wasted.

" The Group of Armies therefore proposes to withdraw the
" *Ninth, Seventh* and *First Armies* gradually (*lit.* step by step) behind
" the Aisne and Vesle. . . .

" The Group of Armies will examine whether it would be advisable
" to retain an advanced position south of the Aisne and Vesle.

" The shoulders of the movement, the right wing of the *Ninth*
" *Army* [Soissons area] and the Reims area in particular, will have
" to be strengthened.

" The reconnaissances are in hand ; the material preparations
" can be begun without delay directly a decision has been made.

" As soon as the enemy recognizes our intentions he will no
" doubt proceed to further action. It is therefore of great importance
" to anticipate this by attacking on our own account."

The attack of Borne's (*VI Reserve*) corps on the 25th receives small mention in the French and British accounts.[2] According to the German, it " brought relatively slight success ; it only succeeded in regaining
" part of the ground lost on the 23rd [not the case] : to reach the
" line Marfaux—Ormes, or even the edge of the heights farther
" south, proved impossible ".

As for the suggested counter-offensive by the *Ninth Army*, its commander, General Fritz von Below, demanded five fresh attack divisions and ten fresh position divisions, and " of course, a con-
" siderable number of batteries, etc. " ; he also reported that if the construction of certain railway lines could be hastened the attack could begin in 14 days. Thus, on both sides, strategic theory had to give way to hard reality. On the 25th, therefore, O.H.L., after directing that preparations for the *Ninth Army* counter-attack

---

[1] *50th, 86th, 103rd* and *123rd Divisions.*

[2] The war diary of the 62nd Division speaks of a quiet day, only shelling of Marfaux, Cuitron and Pourcy ; that of the 51st describes continuous fighting in the Bois de Courton, by which the British line was advanced, and occasional heavy shelling, " otherwise quiet ".

should be begun on the understanding that only five fresh attack divisions in all could be allotted to it, ordered the arrangements for the retirement of the *Seventh Army* and the right wing of the *First* to the " great bridgehead " to be continued so that it could take place on the night of the 26th/27th ; the executive order was given at 11 A.M. on the 26th. General von Boehn directed four of his five centre corps (Schmettow, Conta, Wichura and Schoeler) to withdraw accordingly ; the left wing of Winckler's, the western one, was to conform, but its right wing was to hold on to the Butte de Chalmont (heights overlooking Oulchy le Château from the east) until further orders.

During the 26th Schmettow's, Conta's and Wichura's corps beat off strong attacks, and under cover of night the retirement, " favoured " by rainy weather ", was carried out, covered by machine-gun detachments, without interference and apparently unnoticed, for until late in the afternoon of the 27th the Allies continued to bombard the old positions, and only in the evening did French patrols follow up to the Ourcq.

During the 27th O.H.L. provisionally fixed the date of the next stage of the retirement to the final " Blücher Position "—but schemes for a withdrawal by sectors were to be prepared—for the night of the 1st/2nd August, the actual date being dependent on the progress of the evacuation of material, which presented great difficulties, as it had to be brought back over two rivers and two ridges, the Vesle ridge and the Chemin des Dames ridge. Later the *Ninth Army* was warned that its left wing would probably retire in one bound to the Aisne, but still retaining Soissons, whilst the *Seventh Army* and right of the *First* would occupy the " Ziethen " intermediate position for 24 hours, after which both this and Soissons would be abandoned. Parties to garrison the back lines were to be sent back a day ahead and weak mobile rear guards left to cover the retirements.

During the night of the 27th/28th the projecting Butte de Chalmont sector was evacuated and the line thereby shortened. General von Winckler's command was broken up, one tired division being withdrawn and the others taken over by the adjoining corps.

On the 28th there was heavy fighting on the southern front, and entry was made at several places into the position, but at night, after various counter-attacks, the Germans were in complete possession of their main line of resistance and most of the outpost zone ; Buzancy was lost to the British 15th Division, but recovered by the counter-attack of two divisions.

On the 29th there was again heavy fighting, the flattened centre position of the salient, not the flanks, being attacked frontally after a bombardment of several hours. The result was the same as on the previous day : parts of the outpost zone were lost, but the main position of the *Seventh Army* remained intact ; it was broken through near Grand Rozoy, but the situation had been restored by a counter-attack division which advanced exactly at the right moment. The right wing of the *First Army* is said to have " essentially " held its position, although the fighting lasted well into the night.

These successes in defence led Ludendorff to enquire whether, in view of the slow follow-up of the Allies, it would not be possible to hold the " Ziethen " or " small bridgehead position " for a considerable time. The German Crown Prince protested "energetically" against the idea, referring to the reasons which he had already given in his telegram of the 24th; he could not, he said, advise such a course unless O.H.L. desired, at high cost, to hold fast Allied reserves on this front whilst a blow was struck elsewhere. But to ensure success, as the French would certainly begin to withdraw divisions to deal with the blow, there must eventually be a sortie from the bridgehead, and, in view of the circumstances and of the difficulties of eventually converting a retirement into an advance, he was not in favour of the suggested halt.

On the 30th, therefore, O.H.L. definitely fixed the date for the beginning of the retreat as the night of the 1st/2nd August. In reply to Ludendorff's renewed question, whether the intermediate position could be held for more than twenty-four hours, both the *Ninth* and *Seventh Armies* and the Group of Armies replied in the negative. On this day there was lively fighting in the outpost zone of the southern front, especially near Fère en Tardenois and Grand Rozoy, and part of this zone was lost. At night, the front was straightened by a withdrawal from the wooded salient (Bois Meunière) north of Villers Agron and Ronchères and from Bois St. Jean north of Grand Rozoy.

On the 31st only attacks on the corps of Wichura and Schoeler on the southern front took place.

CHAPTER XVII

THE SECOND BATTLE OF THE MARNE (*concluded*)

1ST–6TH AUGUST 1918

(Sketches 12, 14, 15, 16)

THE Allied offensive of the 1st August, which caught the Germans making ready for a further retirement during the ensuing night, met with considerable success. Essentially a renewal of the attack of the 29th July with the same objectives, it extended a little farther to the left. The XXX. Corps of the Tenth Army, with the British 34th and the French 25th and 19th Divisions in line, and the 127th in support ready to pass through the 25th, was to secure, first, the high ground Servenay—Orme de Grand Rozoy, and later the next ridge, south of Droizy. These divisions were covered on the right by the XI. Corps of the same Army and by the II. Corps of the Sixth Army, which was to outflank Saponay from the east, whilst on the left the XX. Corps was to hold itself ready to press forward in the direction of Droizy as soon as the success of the main attack developed.

Sketch 14.

On the eve of the offensive General Pétain addressed a long letter to General Foch in which he reviewed the situation. He stated that the French Armies had 71 divisions in the line and 32 in reserve; of the former, 20 had been in the line for over a month and 13 more for over 2 months; of the 19 divisions in the Eastern group, 11 had been in action and suffered heavy losses; of the reserve, 27 divisions had been in the fighting since the 15th July. In the battle in progress 58 divisions had been engaged, " I have not a single fresh division in my pre- " cautionary reserve ". The quiet sectors, he continued, were very wide: a great deal of labour was needed to keep them in order, and effectives were very low: on the

30th July the total shortage of infantry was about 120,000, and only 19,000 mobilizable reinforcements were available, with the hope of 29,000 more in two or three months' time : the troops at the front or coming out of battle were in a state of excellent morale, but extremely tired. He concluded his letter with the words " we are at the limit " of our effort ".

Major-General Nicholson's orders to the 34th Division for the projected attack were issued at 5 P.M. on the 31st : the division would have the French 68th Division (XI. Corps) on its right and the 25th Division (XXX. Corps) on its left ; the objective was the same as on the 29th and the outpost line was to be the starting line ; the same artillery support and a forty-five-minute bombardment would be provided, followed by a four-minute barrage before the infantry advanced at 4.49 A.M. As in the previous attack the 103rd and 101st Brigades provided the leading battalions : 5/K.O.S.B., 5/Argyll & Sutherland Highlanders, 4/R. Sussex and 2/4th Queen's. They were weak in numbers owing to the previous fighting—the 5/Argyll had only 6 officers and 260 other ranks. Consequently in order to cover their frontages they each placed three companies in the front line instead of two. Beugneux and Hill 158 south of it were not to be attacked frontally but by encirclement, the 103rd Brigade being authorized to cross its right boundary line in order to make a sufficiently wide enveloping movement. Smoke from the barrage added to the morning mist made visibility very poor, so that platoon direction had to be kept by compass. Notwithstanding, the attack on Beugneux and Hill 158, carried out by the two right battalions, was entirely successful, 4 German officers and 60 other ranks being captured, but the Argyll lost all their officers. The K.O.S.B. with the remnants of the Argyll under two K.O.S.B. officers, then fought their way about seven hundred yards up the ridge beyond Beugneux, just short of the final objective, but were then brought to a halt by the severity of the fire from Servenay, on the right front, which the French had not yet reached. A company of the 8/Scottish Rifles (103rd Brigade) was therefore sent to protect the right flank, but soon after, about 9 A.M., the French 68th Division reached Servenay.

The 101st Brigade had advanced more rapidly, and before 6 A.M. reported that it was on the objective and in touch with the 103rd, although later reconnaissance showed its position to be about six hundred yards short of where it supposed that it was. The French 25th Division was not up, so a company of the 2/Loyal North Lancashire (101st Brigade) which had been following closely, was despatched to guard the left flank; it pushed on some fifteen hundred yards north-east of Grand Rozoy, handing over the captured ground to the French when they arrived soon after. Two field batteries had followed up the advance as soon as the barrage stopped, and the remainder of the divisional artillery came forward 3,000 to 4,000 yards.

To cover the advance of the French 127th Division through the line towards Launoy, the 34th Division had been instructed to occupy and hold in strength the high ground about the farms of le Mont Jour and Bucy le Bras, a thousand to fifteen hundred yards beyond the division's objective. The task was allotted to the 102nd Brigade, and it detached the 1/1st Herefordshire and 1/4th Cheshire, which followed the rear echelon of the attacking brigades and came up to pass through them when they halted. Owing to the severe machine-gun fire the Herefordshire were not able to go much beyond the line of the 103rd Brigade, but captured a detachment armed with a large-bore anti-tank rifle; the 1/4th Cheshire reported it had reached le Mont Jour, losing Lieut.-Colonel G. H. Swindells, killed; and it held this position, short of the farm, until relieved by the French 127th Division.

A long pause now ensued. Hostile artillery fire was never heavy and the work of consolidation proceeded without hindrance. About 11 A.M. the 2/L. North Lancashire was withdrawn into 101st Brigade reserve, and towards 2 P.M. the Herefordshire were also recalled, being relieved by a company of the 1/7th Cheshire, and the survivors of the 1/5th Argyll & Sutherland Highlanders were replaced by the 1/8th Scottish Rifles.

About 5 P.M. it became clear that the line was not sufficiently advanced to cover the valleys on either side of the hill on which stood Bucy le Bras Farm. In the easternmost of these valleys lay the village of Arcy, and here hostile action was causing considerable trouble to the troops of the 68th Division in Servenay, which stands at the head of the valley. Accordingly, at 5.50 P.M., after consultation with General Menvielle of that division, Major-General Nicholson issued verbal orders to his brigadiers (the written version was not ready until 7 P.M.) for an advance of from 300 to 400 yards to be made at 7 P.M. under a creeping barrage, as far as the le Mont Jour objective on the right, but somewhat short of it on the left. This movement, in which the left of the 68th Division co-operated, was successfully carried out against vigorous opposition by German rear-guards. By 10 P.M. the 2/L. North Lancashire and 4/R. Sussex had captured a hill which dominated the German line of retreat, and touch was obtained with the 127th Division, south-west of le Mont Jour.[1]

With this success the operations of the 34th Division in the Aisne area came to an end. At 10 A.M. on the 2nd Major-General Nicholson received orders from the XXX. Corps to remain in his position whilst the French 25th Division passed through to follow up the enemy, who was apparently retiring—the whole plain was, indeed, already blue with advancing French. At 7 P.M. he was ordered to concentrate his division, and during the 4th, 5th, 6th and 7th August it entrained for the British zone. It had lost since the 24th July 108 officers and 2,368 other ranks.

The 15th Division (Major-General H. L. Reed) also took part in the fighting on the 1st August. By the morning of the 30th July it had changed places with the French 87th Division, each leaving its artillery in position to cover the other. The new front of the 15th Division, from near Tigny (in enemy hands) to short of Buzancy (also in enemy hands), was overlooked. Opposite the right front lay a ridge a thousand yards long marked by three prominent hillocks—"Les Trois Mamelons"—which formed strong-points in the German front system. The left of the line was faced by the western side of the Buzancy plateau, the approach to which led up an open and regular slope without a scrap of cover.

Sketch 14.

During the morning of the 29th, Major-General Reed had received orders from the XX. Corps that his division would carry out an attack in conjunction with the French 12th Division on the right. The operation would begin by an encircling attack against the Bois d'Hartennes, between Hartennes and Taux, the 12th Division moving by the south and the 15th by the north; after joining hands beyond the wood the advance was to be continued eastward towards Droizy. The date, which depended on operations carried out farther south on the 30th, would

---

[1] A captured order showed that the rear-guards were not due to retire until midnight. See Appendix XIV.

probably be the 31st. It was later decided by General Mangin, as has been seen, to postpone the attack until the 1st August, when it could form part of the main operation.

During the 30th and 31st the 15th Division suffered heavy shelling, including much gas, both by day and night, but advanced headquarters being situated to a flank at Dommiers (6 miles west of Buzancy) escaped. At a conference in the afternoon of the 31st the details of the attack were arranged. The 46th Brigade on the right was to attack the two northern of Les Trois Mamelons,—the French 12th Division would deal with the third and mask the wood. After the capture of its first objective the brigade was to move straight on past the northern side of the Bois d'Hartennes but only as far as the Château Thierry—Soissons road, which traverses the wood from north to south about a third of its depth from the western edge. The 44th Brigade, in reserve, would then pass through the 46th to the eastern edge of the wood, where junction was to be made with the French 12th Division. The 45th Brigade, in front of Villemontoire, was to keep touch with the left of the attacking brigade and form a defensive flank. The troops were to be in position at 4.45 A.M., and as the enemy had observation over the area the 44th Brigade must be moved up by night and hide in the cornfields east of Vierzy. Zero hour depended on the progress of the attack of the XXX. Corps (in which the British 34th Division was engaged) on the right. The signal for the attack would be given by the XX. Corps, by rockets fired from aeroplanes and balloons, and salvoes of 155-cm. shells with black smoke from three places: at the first exact clock hour or half hour thirty minutes or more after the signal (*e.g.* 7 A.M. if the signal were given at 6.22 A.M.) the troops were to advance without any preliminary bombardment, under an artillery and machine-gun barrage, whilst the heavy artillery would bombard the enemy back areas.

As good reports of the initial progress of the XXX. Corps reached General Mangin, he ordered the XX. Corps to advance. The agreed signals were given at 8.25 A.M., which signified that 9 A.M. would be zero.

When the leading battalions of the 46th Brigade, the 9/Royal Scots and 7th/8th K.O.S.B. with the 10/Scottish Rifles behind them, began to advance they came under fire from heavy artillery and from machine guns hidden in derelict tanks in front of them and were checked, with severe casualties. On the left the 6/Cameron Highlanders and 13/Royal Scots of the 45th Brigade, forming the defensive flank, were able by 11 A.M. to reach the Château Thierry—Soissons road and dig in. The 12th Division on the right was at first reported to be making good progress, it had in fact captured the small Tigny salient, but otherwise the advance had been very slight. At 12.55 P.M. the commanding officers of the 9/Royal Scots and 10/Scottish Rifles informed Br.-General Fortune that unless the French could come up and engage the machine guns on the right flank, further attack held no prospect of success. In the meantime, however, Major-General Reed had arranged for another bombardment by artillery and trench mortars and an assault at 3.30 P.M. Help from the French was put out of the question by a German counter-attack against the left of the 12th Division; at 2.45 P.M. the S.O.S. was seen to go up from Tigny and French troops were seen leaving the village. Nevertheless the renewed bombardment was begun at 3 P.M. and at 3.27 P.M. the creeping barrage opened. The fire is said to have been more effective than in the morning, but when the 9/Royal Scots advanced towards the centre " mamelon " followed in echelon by the 10/Scottish Rifles which was to take the northernmost, fire from the right and right rear soon stopped all progress, and at 4.50 P.M. further attempts to push forward were abandoned; to use the words of the French Official Account : " the XX. Corps after some " progress towards Tigny and Taux was driven back " towards its starting position ".[1] Major-General Reed was then informed that his division would be relieved during the night of the 2nd/3rd August.

In the course of the morning, the French airmen, who throughout the day met with very active opposition, had noticed fires starting at Fismes, Soissons and other places in German possession. From mid-day onwards they reported that the enemy seemed to be evacuating material and supplies from the valley of the Vesle. General Fayolle (G.A.R.), in spite of the stout resistance of the enemy and the lack of fresh troops, at 5 P.M. ordered the operation to be continued on the 2nd with the same objectives as on the 1st, with the object of throwing the Germans back on to the Vesle, " but without playing their game, that is to say " without expending more men than they do ".

[1] F.O.A. vii (i), p. 141.

General Degoutte (Sixth Army) passed these orders on to his corps, but General Mangin (Tenth Army) after giving instructions for the relief of the British 34th and 15th Divisions, ordered that " for the continuation of the " operations, the right of the XXX. Corps and the XI. " Corps will dig themselves in solidly on the conquered " positions, the XI. Corps holding itself ready to support " the Sixth Army by taking Saponay ; the left of the " XXX. Corps will manœuvre with a view to the capture " of the Bois du Plessier ".[1] Active reconnaissances to watch the movements of the enemy and discover any symptom of retirement were recommended.

The Germans retired during the night to a position covering the Vesle, leaving weak rear-guards to delay pursuit, but still continued to hold Soissons. The first news of the retirement only reached General Mangin at 6 A.M. on the 2nd. Major-General Reed had received no orders, except as regards his relief; not until 8.30 A.M. did he hear from the artillery observers that on the right the French preceded by cavalry were pushing on eastwards following the retreating Germans. At 10 A.M. the French 12th Division reported to him that its right wing had advanced and that patrols were entering the Bois d'Hartennes without encountering opposition. Strong patrols were at once pushed out towards the " mamelons " and Taux. At 11.50 A.M. orders arrived from the XX. Corps for a general advance, and Major-General Reed then gave instructions for the 45th Brigade to swing forward its right, keeping contact with the 44th Brigade (now in the place of the 46th) which was to move due east through Taux and there get in touch with the French 12th Division. When this had been obtained, both brigades were to advance in a north-easterly direction, with the river Crise near Villeblain as the first objective.

Sketch 15.

At 3.30 P.M. a report came from the 45th Brigade that it had reached the edge of the Bois de Concrois, and soon after the 44th Brigade came up. Villeblain was entered at 6.45 P.M. The French 12th Division was next reported in Chacrise, to the right, and shortly after the 87th Division, to the left, on the Crise east of Buzancy ; farther north Rozières and Noyant were in French hands. The leading British troops then crossed the river and formed an outpost line.

[1] Bois de St. Jean on Sketch 14.

At 7.50 P.M. orders were issued for an advance to the next objective: the road from Soissons south-east to Cuiry Housse. It was then decided by General Mangin that the relief of the 15th Division which had been planned to take place on two successive nights, should be carried out forthwith. The two relieving infantry regiments of the 17th Division arrived at 1 A.M. on the 3rd and passed through the line of the 44th and 45th Brigades, which were then withdrawn. They left behind the two machine-gun companies attached to them: these were to remain until the afternoon. The 46th Brigade, which had moved up to the Bois de Concrois, was relieved at dawn by the third regiment of the 17th Division, and the artillery by batteries of the 87th Division.

It had been intended to transport the infantry by bus, but owing to the congestion on the roads the buses did not arrive and the men marched back 18 miles to the Vivières (3 miles north of Villers Cotterêts) area, whence they were sent in buses 35 miles westwards to the Liancourt area, where they entrained on the night of the 5th/6th and on the 6th.[1]

In appreciation of the services of the 15th and 34th Divisions General Fayolle, G.A.R., was moved to write a special letter to Sir Douglas Haig,[2] in which he said, "Both of them, by their dash, their courage, and their "devotion, have excited the admiration of the French "troops in whose midst they fought". They had indeed given of their best and worthily upheld the honour of the British Army in the ranks of our Ally, and in a country in which the defenders possessed all the advantages. Their share, as well as that of the 51st and 62nd Divisions, in the first victorious Allied offensive has been fully and gracefully acknowledged in France but almost entirely overlooked by their fellow-countrymen.

The placing of British corps and divisions under the orders of the higher French commanders revealed that

---

[1] The casualties of the 15th Scottish Division from noon 21st July to 3rd August had been:

	Officers	Other Ranks
killed,	34	441
wounded,	126	2,511
missing,	4	393
injured,	1	6
	165	3,351

[2] See Appendix XVI, where it is given in full.

although the Allied troops had been fighting alongside each other for four years they knew very little of each other's methods. The occasional mingling of troops which had taken place, notably at "First Ypres 1914", again during the attachment of the small French First Army to the British forces during the Passchendaele fighting in 1917, once more in the sector of General Gough's Army in March 1918, and lastly when the D.A.N. formed part of General Plumer's Army in April 1918, had brought to notice certain difficulties. Owing to some extent to the difference of language, co-operation at the junctions of the Allied contingents from August 1914 onwards had not as a rule been very satisfactory, except on the 1st July 1916, the first day of the Somme.[1] No general measures to obviate friction had been taken except by the formation of Missions at the respective G.Q.G. and G.H.Q., and the attachment of interpreters to units and of liaison officers to the corps and divisions near the " soudures ". No official attempts had been made to familiarize staff officers, still less the regimental officers, with the organization and methods of their Allies.

The French commanders and staffs were, with the one exception of the commander of the Sixth Army in May 1918, already referred to, consistently helpful and considerate. Representations were met in a sympathetic and practical manner. The relations of the French and British troops were at all times excellent, but the display of friendliness became more demonstrative after operations actually carried out in common, as they had been at " First " Ypres " and were now again in the Château Thierry salient. Heavy demands were made on the four divisions of the XXII. Corps, but they responded to them all, and thus completely effaced the bad impression of British fighting powers which they found prevalent among the French owing to the unfortunate events of March 1918.

It may be as well to summarize some " lessons learnt " by the staff of the XXII. Corps and others. Very few British and French officers understood each other over the telephone, so liaison officers were called upon to speak— this also enabled national abbreviations, code words and slang to be used. It was almost impossible, except with long delays, to get English telegraphic messages through

[1] By July 1918 most of the English-speaking French officers had been attached to the American Army, which certainly increased the difficulties of the IX. and XXII. Corps.

on French lines. French despatch riders seemed casual as to whom they delivered messages and their system of obtaining receipts was not as strict as with the British Signal Service. It was even more necessary than between entirely British staffs to enquire frequently by telephone if orders were on the way. Liaison officers found it advantageous to keep themselves informed as to when orders would be going out, so as to notify, if possible, British addressees by telephone. Practice was required in reading the unfamiliar, black and white hachured French maps.

The very elaborate French operation orders were frequently not received until very late. The French General Staff seemed averse to issuing warning orders—for reasons of secrecy—but the intention was usually discussed some time before orders were drafted. It was therefore most necessary that good and intelligent liaison officers should be selected for the headquarters of the higher French formations, who would gain the confidence of the French staffs, learn their intentions early and possess sufficient knowledge and experience of military operations to enable them, with due permission, to send warning of what was coming. The French liaison officer was the actual representative of his commander, gave his orders and was empowered to vary them to meet local conditions and circumstances; sometimes, in anticipation of the arrival of the written orders, he gave verbal orders which were acted on, and on every occasion they were found to conform to the formal orders. Mere facility in the foreign language was not sufficient qualification for a liaison officer. It was discovered that far fewer French officers possessed a working knowledge of English than British officers a similar acquaintance with French, so that the French language was generally used.[1]

[1] General Blin, head of the Service Historique, made the following remark on this chapter :—
"Je partage tout à fait votre manière de voir quant aux difficultés "qui se produisent lorsque des unités de pays différents sont appelées à "travailler ensemble. Vos observations, notamment en ce qui concerne "les liaisons à réaliser, sont tout à fait judicieuses. Il est certain qu'il "y a trop peu d'officiers français à parler anglais et vice versa. Quant à "ceux qui possèdent bien la langue du pays allié parce qu'ils sont dans "les affaires, ce sont en général des officiers de réserve trop souvent in- "capables de bien remplir leur rôle si important de liaison parce que, ne "connaissant rien de la tactique, ils ne peuvent pas interpréter les ordres "qu'ils transmettent. Il y a là une question très délicate. On peut s'en "tirer avec de la bonne volonté, mais il est certain que cette situation "n'est pas pour activer les choses."

It may be noted that French divisions were better provided with motor cars than the British; in view of the French methods of inter-communication, at least two extra cars should have been allotted to any division serving with our Ally.

The French as a rule did not put a distribution list on their orders, so it was not always certain, unless enquiry were made, whether flank divisions or divisions temporarily under the command of British formations had received orders.

Co-operation when French artillery covered British infantry and vice versa was good, but naturally took longer to arrange than in normal circumstances. It was learnt that a French barrage might have its corners turned back, so that the infantry were boxed in and the flank troops could not edge round any obstacle, whether human or topographical.

The French system of movement by train and bus differed from our own, and required study. The loading ramps were often of insufficient width for British methods. As men had sometimes to be put into railway vehicles previously occupied by horses, cleaning apparatus was required. Information as to " halte repas " and use of latrines was vague and untrustworthy. Buses were smaller than the British; debusing frequently took place at a considerable distance from the concentration area, and the marches proved a hardship to men of " B " class detailed for baths, salvage, and similar duties; yet unless the British officers held written authority from the French staff concerned, they could not alter route or destination. The French could not supply transport for laundry stores and the usual surplus baggage, so clean clothing was brought up as opportunity offered. Billets were often allotted by villages in which it was difficult to discover what the accommodation might be, unless it had been ascertained earlier from some local town-major. Previous personal reconnaissance by an officer was found desirable.

On occasions when coal supplies did not arrive the French were always ready to assist and hand over in bulk —on payment—and they cashed officers' cheques. What the troops missed most were the ordinary Expeditionary Force Canteen supplies, particularly cigarettes and tobacco. It should be added that the local estaminets on the line of march of the XXII. Corps on the 17th July dispensed a clear brown liquid which looked like beer and was treated as such by a whole brigade that had never heard of still champagne, with disastrous results.

The concluding operations on the Aisne after the British divisions had left the line do not call for lengthy description. During the night of the 2nd/3rd August the German *Seventh Army* and the flanks of the *First* and *Ninth* on either side of it, retired behind the line of the Vesle and the Aisne, abandoning Soissons, but leaving the usual machine-gun rear parties. The commanders of the three French Armies, the Fifth, Sixth, and Tenth, had in the afternoon and evening of the 2nd independently ordered a general pursuit and the pushing forward of the divisional cavalries, followed by advanced guards or " groupes de combat " of all arms, " the main bodies " proceeding by successive bounds from position to position " in accordance with the progress of the advanced guards ".

_{Sketch 15.}

To these orders General Fayolle (G.A.R.) added that to prevent surprise reserves should be collected as the front was narrowing and the reduction of the numbers engaged thus became practicable : the pursuit should be continued " by advanced guards supported by the mass of the " batteries, but the main bodies held ready to constitute a " battle-front quickly ".

_{Sketch 12.}

Towards midday on the 3rd the French centre and left nearly reached the line of the Vesle and Aisne between Fismes and Soissons ; but the right, that is the greater part of the Fifth Army and the right of the Sixth, could not push their main bodies as far as the Vesle, because the enemy artillery, after being silent, woke up about the middle of the afternoon and severely shelled the plateaux south of Muizon, Jonchery and Fismes. Neither General Maistre (G.A.C.) nor General Fayolle (G.A.R.) was prepared to risk an immediate assault of a position which might be strongly occupied and defended. Nothing could be done but reconnoitre, reorganize the divisions, reconstitute reserves, bring up the mass of the field artillery to cover the passage of the rivers, and then, if possible, form small bridgeheads.

The 3rd August was therefore passed in closing up, so that on the 4th, in spite of gun and machine-gun fire, a few patrols managed to cross the Vesle to the east and west of Fismes and to the east and west of Braine. On the 4th General Pétain issued a General Instruction to the effect that the mission of the three Armies remained as before to throw

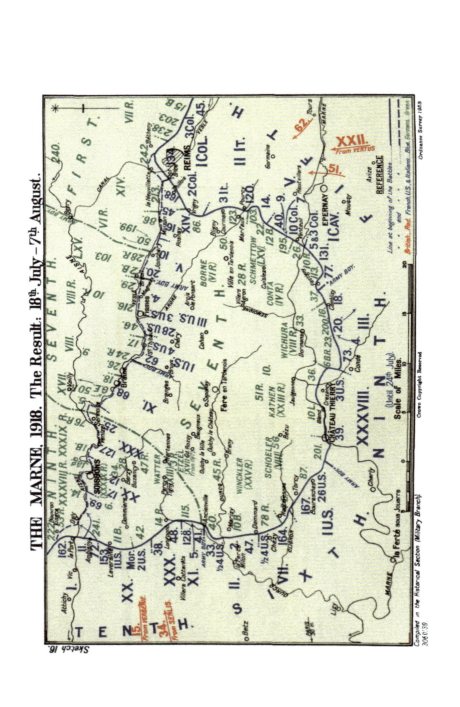

the enemy north of the Vesle and the Aisne, " but without " exposing themselves to useless losses or to failure with a " river behind them " : that endeavour should be made to discover the intentions of the enemy so as not to allow him—without, however, attacking prematurely—to continue the retirement of his main bodies under cover of a weak screen left on the Vesle and the Aisne: that if only rear-guards were found to have been left on these rivers, they were to be hustled back and an advance made to the Aisne and later the Ailette, always in considerable depth; but that if the enemy was found to be established in force, the Armies were to dig in thoroughly in front of him, and postpone all general action until a decision had been reached by the High Command.

Both air and ground reconnaissances on the 4th and 5th gave the impression that the enemy was well entrenched behind the Vesle and Aisne. On the evening of the 6th, therefore, General Pétain came to the decision that the Fifth, Sixth and Tenth Armies should establish themselves south of the rivers, but must continue offensive preparations, so as to give the enemy the impression that a serious attack was about to take place, particularly on the 8th August, the date fixed by General Foch for the Franco-British offensive elsewhere. General Pétain telegraphed at 10.10 P.M.: " Until further orders, no attempt will be " made north of the Vesle to carry the enemy positions ".

The Second Battle of the Marne was over. Between the 15th July and 5th August, the French Armies and the Allied divisions engaged with them had taken prisoner 659 officers and 28,708 other ranks, had captured 793 guns and 3,723 machine guns. The French casualties in the battle had been 2,539 officers and 92,626 other ranks. The enemy losses are not yet known.[1] The Germans attribute their defeat to the surprise by General Mangin's Army on the 18th July, and to the numerical and physical weakness of their infantry. Battalion trench strength (excluding machine gunners) had, it is stated, fallen to 200-240 rifles, with 15-20 light machine guns, with a fatal lack of regimental officers and N.C.O.'s: one regiment, reduced to two battalions, had only four of its companies led by officers, and both battalion commanders were second lieutenants.

Sketch 16.

---

[1] Monograph IV. gives neither the losses nor the prisoners and booty captured. French Intelligence calculations put the German losses on the fighting front in July as 168,000, and elsewhere at 50,000 to 55,000. (Paquet, pp. 132-3.)

Physical fitness had been reduced by poor rations and influenza.[1]

The state of the German *Second Army* at the beginning of August has been revealed, and the others were hardly in better condition: on the 3rd August, of its 13 divisions, only 2 were "fully fit for battle"; 5 only fit for position warfare; 3 only fit for defence on a quiet front; and 3 required relief, having a trench strength of about one-quarter of their establishments.[2] French and British Intelligence calculations agreed that the Germans had lost almost exactly a million men in battle on the Western Front since the 21st March (450,000 in March and April, and 550,000 in their subsequent diversion offensives), plus 350,000 on other fronts; the depôts were nearly empty and men with two months' training, drawn in anticipation from the 1920 class, were being sent to the front.[3]

On the 7th the French Commander-in-Chief in a congratulatory order to his Armies, summed up the result as:

" Four years of effort aided by our faithful Allies, four
" years of trial stoically accepted, commence to bear their
" fruit.

" Broken in the fifth of his attempts in 1918, the
" invader has recoiled. His effectives are falling, his
" morale is weakening, whilst on our side, our American
" comrades, just disembarked, have already made our
" disconcerted enemy feel the vigour of their blows.

" Yesterday I said to you: Obstinacy, Patience, your
" American comrades are coming. To-day I say to you:
" Tenacity, Boldness, and Victory must be yours."

The Allies had been very slow in adopting suitable methods to meet the great German offensives, only learning by experience that neither the first position nor the intermediate line could as a whole be maintained. Even to

---

[1] Monographs III., p. 23 (f.n.), and IV., pp. 222-3.

[2] The official monograph, "Die Katastrophe des 8. August 1918 ", pp. 26-7.

[3] The statistics of the *Reichsarchiv* (quoted by Mr. Winston S. Churchill in "The World Crisis", p. 823, abridged edition) give the German losses on the Western Front for March-June as 688,341. This figure, it is assumed, does not include the wounded "likely to recover within a reason-" able time." The enemy losses in July, in the unsuccessful offensive of the 15th and the French counter-offensive which began on the 18th, were certainly greater than in the successful Chemin des Dames offensive, which are admitted to have been 130,370 (Monograph II., p. 192); they were probably greater than the French estimate of 168,000. This figure added to 688,341 makes 856,341, not much short of a million if the lightly wounded are added.

TACTICS OF DEFENCE

the last the French relied on stopping the enemy on the second position, on which the forward troops retired whilst a counter-attack from a flank was prepared—whereas, after adopting " elastic yielding " the Germans depended upon a proportion at least of the troops in the forward zone sticking to their posts to embarrass the attackers and an immediate counter-stroke by divisions kept near at hand for the purpose of recovering the lost ground. The system adopted by some old Regular divisions in early 1915 of sign-boarding their support trenches as " counter-attack " trenches " had in the course of time been forgotten. The selection of a single good line, covered by outposts, any part of which if lost was to be recovered by local counter-stroke, as exhibited by Major-General H. S. Jeudwine in the defence of Béthune in April 1918, proved remarkably effective. No system, of course, should be made of universal application, for, next to surprise, variety of tactics is of supreme importance. Further, the system selected must be the best suited to ground, not a rigid system applied to all types of country. It is unnecessary to emphasize the advantages of a reverse slope position, on which the enemy has no ground observation, whilst its foreground can be covered by our own field-gun fire. Few counter-attack troops are required in such a case. But on a long front many varieties of contour will be encountered and a continuous reverse slope out of the question.

It may be suggested that in the end all was for the best. Had not the great and carefully prepared offensive of the 21st March met with a considerable measure of success, Ludendorff might earlier have realized the immense difficulties of a strategic break-through, and instead of dashing the German Armies to ruin, with loss of numbers, morale and prestige, as he did, he might by a series of retirements have lured the Allies on to one position after another, have inflicted on them losses of trained men, for which even the American contingents would scarcely have been adequate compensation; or if the Allies refused to attack, have established a stalemate in which time was not altogether in the Allies' favour, for the French and British civil populations were suffering considerable hardships.

No one knew better than the Germans that victory can be obtained only by attack. In theory Ludendorff's plan for drawing the Allied reserves away from Flanders by a series of offensives elsewhere before delivering the final blow was perfect; but misled by his experience of offensive warfare on the Eastern Front—though his strategic adviser, Lieut.-Colonel Wetzell, had warned him against the danger of such miscalculation [1]—he failed to reckon the cost of offensives against French, American and British troops in 1918. And it is the best and bravest who fall in attack. With more pertinacity, such as Sir Douglas Haig showed in 1917, Ludendorff might perhaps have hammered through to Amiens or Hazebrouck in March or April; for he had driven the British from their fortified zones, and they were fighting on unprepared ground; but having in mind his own methods, he conjured up a vision of impending counter-attacks; and ordered a halt. In order to draw away from Flanders the dreaded Allied reserves, he attacked elsewhere against fully prepared positions and with many weeks' fatal interval between the different operations, each of the new offensives being a separate major operation which required as an indispensable preliminary the presence of the "battering train" of heavy guns, trench mortars and aeroplanes: hence unavoidable delay. It has several times been pointed out in these volumes that in the old days of the assault of fortresses reliance was not entirely placed on an attack on the main breach, but that simultaneous subsidiary and feint attacks were carried out, and that as often as not the main attack failed, for the besieged were ready for it, and one of the minor assaults effected an entry. For even one such subsidiary attack Ludendorff said in March 1918 that he had not the men and material; he could stage only one attack at a time. Foch was to show him that in modern times the old theory of the attack of fortified lines can be modified by executing a series of attacks following each other closely at different places instead of several simultaneous assaults.

General Foch was not slow to take advantage of the situation which the German failure at the Second Battle of the Marne had gradually created, and for which the Allies had so long waited. The prospect of success had dawned. Enemy morale was at last beginning to break, and all who knew the Germans expected that once it did show signs of "cracking" it would collapse rapidly. In the later part of July, Intelligence reports had shown the radical difference between the state of mind of the prisoners captured in the recent operations and that of

[1] See "1918", Vol. I., p. 141.

those taken in the earlier offensives of the year. Time after time from the 21st March onwards the prisoners stated they had been told that this particular offensive would be the last, and after it a victorious peace would be concluded. The majority of those taken after the 15th July, however, retained only a much shaken confidence in these promises of success. They showed signs of war-weariness and often of complete indifference; only a few exhibited the old arrogant attitude and spoke of having been " betrayed " by deserters revealing the secret of the operations, in itself an indication of falling morale. On seeing American troops, of whose presence they had been kept in ignorance, some admitted that victory was no longer possible.

The grave crisis through which the German Homeland was passing could be detected even in the closely controlled German Press. In July the newspapers contained such phrases as " the hour has come when the faith of the nation " in the future and in victory requires to be sustained with " a strong heart "; " it is the resistance of the nerves " which will win the War ". Some spoke of "a serious " moral depression "; although the heavy cost of the unsuccessful offensives in France, the gravity of the defeat of the Austrians in Italy, the failure of submarine warfare, and the arrival of the Army of the United States were all either concealed or minimized. Even without great Allied victories, when the peace promised before autumn did not come, a final collapse might well be expected. Obviously the time had come to accelerate the process of disintegration by the counter-offensives of which Maréchal Foch [1] had spoken earlier in the year.

NOTE

The German Retirement 1st–2nd August

On the 1st August the intensity of the fighting again rose to that of a great battle on the southern front between Bois Meunière and the Oulchy le Château—Hartennes road. In the fog, tanks, followed by infantry, broke through the position on the extreme west, north of Grand Rozoy, and captured a number of field batteries. But again the situation was restored and the guns recaptured by the counter-attack of the last reserves of two divisions. Elsewhere the

Sketch 15.

---

[1] He had received the baton of Maréchal de France on 6th August. Henceforward he will be given this style.

main position was not reached, and, in spite of the heavy fighting, troops were sent back during the afternoon and evening to man the " small bridgehead position " as previously arranged. At 11 P.M. the infantry began its retirement to the " Blücher Position " behind the Aisne and Vesle. The *First* and *Seventh Armies* left 13 divisions in the " small bridgehead " covered by " pursuit commandoes " *(Jagdkommandos)* ", with single guns pushed well out in front of the outposts. At 2 P.M. on the 2nd August Soissons was evacuated, and at 2.30 P.M. its bridges blown up. On the " small bridge-" head " position no contact with the Allies took place, and when darkness fell on the 2nd August the troops left it and completed the retirement to the " Blücher Position " undisturbed. The casualties of the campaign are not stated, but it is mentioned that, owing to lack of reinforcements, ten divisions had to be broken up ; but " much worse was the loss of confidence in final victory ". The effects of the great victory of the Chemin des Dames operation had not only been wiped out, but the Germans had lost the initiative, had suffered heavy casualties which they could not replace, and were thrown on the defensive.

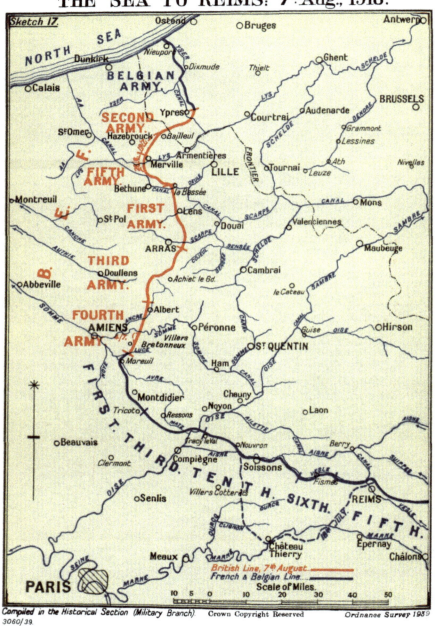

CHAPTER XVIII

PLANS FOR AN ALLIED OFFENSIVE

(Sketch 17)[1]

IT remains to explain the plans which were in Maréchal Foch's mind when he not only refused to accede to General Pétain's requests for further reinforcements in order to achieve a striking success against the Germans in the Château Thierry salient, but also withdrew from him the British XXII. Corps (15th, 34th, 51st and 62nd Divisions) for return to Sir Douglas Haig's command.

It will be recalled that on the 12th July [2] Maréchal Foch, by letter, after a personal interview with Lieut.-General Sir H. Lawrence, the Chief of the General Staff, had suggested that the British Armies, besides recovering Kemmel (between Bailleul and Ypres) as planned on the 20th May as a task for the D.A.N., should be prepared to launch an offensive from the Festubert—Robecq (La Bassée—Merville) front.

The Commander-in-Chief was not due to return from England until the 14th; so, on the 13th, Lieut.-General Lawrence on his way back to G.H.Q. from the Generalissimo's conference, knowing his Chief's objections to the Robecq scheme and his ideas for the future, had called at Fourth Army headquarters at Flixecourt (13 miles north-west of Amiens). As early as the 17th May, Sir Douglas Haig had directed General Rawlinson to begin studying, in conjunction with General Debeney, the preparation of an attack from the French front south of Roye. Lieut.-General Lawrence now instructed him that he should draft plans at once for an attack east of Amiens on the lines of

---

[1] To save overcrowding, some of the smaller places mentioned in documents quoted in this chapter have not been shown on Sketch 17; in such cases the nearest towns which are marked are given in brackets, or the distance from a marked place is added.

[2] See p. 223.

the operations for an advance south of the Somme, which the Fourth Army commander had suggested after the success at Hamel (12 miles east of Amiens) on the 4th July. He added that the Fourth Army would be reinforced for this purpose and that fuller details and orders would be sent after the return of Sir Douglas Haig.

During the 15th the Commander-in-Chief was busy dealing with the question of the transfer of British reserves to the French zone; but on the 16th he visited the Third Army headquarters at Hesdin (13 miles south-east of Montreuil), where he met both General Byng and General Horne (First Army) and after his return to G.H.Q. summoned General Rawlinson (Fourth Army) there in order to discuss the situation and future plans.

According to the Intelligence Branch the distribution of the 204 German divisions on the Western Front (it was assumed that the balance had been broken up) was:—
(1) Crown Prince Rupprecht's Group of Armies, 81 divisions (of which 23 were in reserve and available for immediate operations), with the greater part of the front, particularly the Lys—Ypres sector, prepared for the launching of an attack, all information pointing to the 20th July as the date of its commencement; (2) German Crown Prince's Group of Armies, engaged on the Reims—Soissons front, 92 divisions (of which 21, in reserve, were fit); (3) the smaller eastern Groups, 31 divisions (with 1 in reserve available for immediate operations).

Both Generals Horne and Byng were opposed to making an attack to retake Orange Hill and Monchy le Preux ($5\frac{1}{2}$ miles east of Arras), because, unless Henin Hill, to the south, were also captured, the new position would be very costly to hold: to attack the two hills involved a large operation, for which troops were not available. So the idea of an immediate attack was abandoned, but Sir Douglas Haig instructed General Horne to arrange for the Canadian Corps to reconnoitre and work out a scheme; in the meantime it should advance its line, step by step, as opportunity occurred. General Byng was to prepare a scheme for retaking the ridge between Ablainzevelle and Moyenneville (11 and 7 miles south of Arras respectively), with $2\frac{1}{2}$ divisions; if all went well he was to make dispositions to seize Serre ridge (5 miles south of the Ablainzevelle ridge and 7 miles north of Albert). To the Second Army he sent the Chief of the General Staff to inform General Plumer of his belief that the enemy would attack the Hazebrouck—Ypres front at an early date, and to ask him to consider the possibility, if a check were inflicted on the enemy, of counter-attacking with the object of regaining Kemmel. In view of Crown Prince Rupprecht's large reserves, an attempt on the hill, he believed, could not be made until the enemy had first attacked and been repulsed.

To General Rawlinson, the Commander-in-Chief confided that the orders for attack which he had given to the commanders of the First and Third Armies were for the purpose of distracting the enemy's attention from the preparations for the main operation. This, he told him, would be the task of the right of the Fourth Army in front of Amiens, and he proposed to ask Maréchal Foch to order the French First Army, which was on the Fourth Army's right, to co-operate: as soon as Maréchal Foch sent back the XXII. Corps of four divisions, and as soon as Crown Prince Rupprecht's reserve of 23 divisions had been engaged, he intended to move the Canadian Corps from the First to the Fourth Army to assist the Australian Corps to carry out the Fourth Army's operation, which, if successful, would cut the enemy communications and force him to fall back in front of the French.

The formal reply to the Generalissimo's proposals of the 12th was not sent from G.H.Q. until the 17th July. In his letter Sir Douglas Haig said that he could " see no " object in pushing forward over the flat and wet country " between Robecq and Festubert [La Bassée and Merville]. " . . . The operation which to my mind is of the greatest " importance, and which I suggest to you should be carried " out as early as possible, is to advance the Allied front " east and south-east of Amiens so as to disengage that " town and the railway line.[1] This can best be carried " out by a combined French and British operation, the " French attacking south of Moreuil and the British north " of the river Luce." He asked for the return of the XXII. Corps to take over the front as far south as the river Luce.[2]

To this letter of the 17th Maréchal Foch replied on the 20th after the successful commencement of General Mangin's counter-offensive at Soissons. He expressed himself as particularly pleased to hear of the different British offensive schemes in contemplation; he gave precedence to the Kemmel operation by the Second Army, since the

[1] This had been included in Directive No. 3 of 20th May. See p. 23.
[2] The whole of this important letter is given in Appendix XVIII.

concentration of forces in the north to meet the threat of a great attack by Crown Prince Rupprecht would permit of an offensive in that area without any loss of time should the threat not materialize. An enemy attack in the north was now, he considered, unlikely, as the enemy had already engaged 32 divisions [1] from his reserve in the Aisne battle and was pinned down there. He begged, however, that the preparation of the Festubert—Robecq (La Bassée—Merville) operation might be continued by the First Army, as it would free a particularly valuable area. This, however, was the last heard of the proposal for the British to advance into " the water-logged basin of the Upper " Schelde ". The letter continued : " the combined opera- " tion of the British Fourth Army and the French First " Army intended to free Amiens and the railway seems to " me also one of the most profitable to execute at the " moment by reason of the prospects which it offers. . . . " General Debeney, on his part, has been studying an " offensive with the same objectives, but his proposals " differ a little from yours "—they were, in fact, only for a small operation south of the Luce. Maréchal Foch concluded by pointing out the weakness of certain parts of the enemy front and the seriousness of the check to the recent enemy offensive, which presented an opportunity which must not be missed.[2]

On the 17th General Rawlinson had, in the form of a memorandum, submitted to G.H.Q. his proposals for an attack east and south-east of Amiens to free the railway. They were for an advance in three stages, with due care for the flanks, by the Canadian, Australian and III. Corps, to a line about 3 miles east of the front at Villers Bretonneux (11 miles east by south of Amiens), thence north across the Somme to the Ancre near Morlancourt (4 miles south of Albert), and south-westwards to Moreuil. The conditions, he considered, were extremely favourable : the enemy's defences were poor, he having no well organized system, as was shown by the trenches captured on the 4th July which had been protected by very little wire : not many reserves were stationed behind this sector of the German front : the spirit of the German divisions, which were known to be weak in numbers, had sunk low, and in the past three months the Australian troops had gained a

---

[1] Crown Prince Rupprecht's reserves had since 24th May actually fallen from 56 to 29 divisions (23 opposite the Hazebrouck area).
[2] The whole letter is given in Appendix XIX.

distinct moral ascendancy over them : the country, open in character, free from shell craters, and with its surface rendered hard by the spell of fine weather, was particularly favourable to the movements of cavalry and tanks : excellent observation could be obtained from the present front line and good artillery positions behind it : finally, facilities for covered approach existed which would render a surprise attack comparatively easy.

General Rawlinson went on to express a wish to take over an additional 4 miles of front as far south as Moreuil, so as to make the attack with the Fourth Army alone and thus keep the conduct of the operations entirely in the hands of one nationality. Experience in previous combined attacks by the French and British had certainly shown that difficulties as regards zero hour and general co-ordination were bound to arise. He suggested that if the French wished to take part they might launch an attack northwards from the Montdidier area, where success might lead to great strategic results, if the attack were delivered when the advance of the Fourth Army should have thrown the enemy into confusion.

On the 23rd Sir Douglas Haig gave general approval to General Rawlinson's plan, except as regards taking over the front down to Moreuil; but he told him not to communicate with General Debeney until the general lines of co-operation with the French had been agreed upon with Maréchal Foch. The Commander-in-Chief was now more easy in his mind with regard to the Hazebrouck—Ypres front; for he felt certain, in view of the German Crown Prince being in command on the Marne front, that O.H.L., in order to prevent any failure on his part, would send him reserves from the north. Actually on the 23rd a prisoner revealed that he had been told by a high medical officer that the Hazebrouck—Ypres attack had been ordered for the 18th, then postponed to the 25th and finally indefinitely postponed.[1]

An important Commander-in-Chiefs' conference took place on the 24th at Bombon Château (30 miles south-east of Paris), Maréchal Foch's new headquarters, at which, besides Maréchal Foch and General Weygand, were present General Pétain and General Buat,[2] Field-Marshal Sir Douglas

---

[1] Ludendorff made this decision on the afternoon of the 20th. See Chapter XIII., Note I.
[2] General Buat had on 5th July succeeded General Anthoine as Major-General (Chief of the Staff) of the French Armies.

Haig and Lieut.-General Lawrence, and General Pershing and Colonel Boyd. In a preliminary talk held before the meeting, between Maréchal Foch and Sir Douglas Haig, at which their Chiefs of Staff were present, it was agreed that, as the expulsion of the Germans from the Château Thierry salient was making good progress, the operations east of Amiens should be proceeded with as soon as possible. Maréchal Foch accepted the scheme suggested by the Fourth Army commander on the 17th, with the modification that the French First Army (as proposed in G.H.Q. letter of the 17th) should co-operate in conjunction with the Fourth Army and be responsible for the right attack; it was settled that Generals Rawlinson and Debeney should be directed to meet to co-ordinate their plans. Furthermore, it was suggested by Maréchal Foch—but not decided until two days later—that if affairs continued to go well on the Marne, the objective of the right of the attack from Amiens might be put forward so that the right wing, instead of forming a defensive flank facing south-east from Moreuil to a point in front of Villers Bretonneux, should conform to the north-south line of the left wing, and its objective become Hangest (6 miles east by south of Moreuil) —Villers Bretonneux.

At the formal conference after this conversation the proceedings were opened by General Weygand reading a memorandum prepared under Maréchal Foch's direction,[1] which, though only tentative, formed the basis of future Allied action. A turning-point, it was stated, had arrived. Taking advantage of the situation in which the enemy had been placed by the ill-success of his defence on the Marne, of the rising superiority of the Allied Armies in men and material as well as in morale, and of their recovery of the initiative, Maréchal Foch intended to pass from the general defensive attitude lately adopted to the offensive. Without promising an immediate decisive result he proposed a series of operations which would facilitate later action and benefit the economic life of the country. These operations were, first, the freeing of three railways: of the Paris—Avricourt line in the Marne area, as a result of the battle then in progress; of the Paris—Amiens line, by means of the British-French offensive proposed by Sir Douglas Haig; and of the Paris—Avricourt line near Verdun, by a reduction of the St. Mihiel salient, to be undertaken by the American Army, proposed by General Pershing.

[1] See Appendix XX. for the translation.

Secondly, he proposed the driving of the enemy from the northern coal mining area and the neighbourhood of Calais and Dunkirk. These operations were to be carried out at short intervals so as to prevent the enemy from having time to shift his reserves and reorganize. After their conclusion the Maréchal looked forward to a further offensive which should be launched at the end of the summer or during the autumn.

Sir Douglas Haig entirely agreed with the general outline suggested, as did General Pétain, who asked for time to consider the possibilities ; while General Pershing stated that the details of organization and supply in regard to the American operation were already receiving every preparatory consideration, since what was now proposed was merely a restatement of the plans to which he had been leading up ever since the entry of the United States into the War.

The conference, as General Pershing subsequently wrote,[1] " decidedly confirmed the principle of co-operation " and emphasised the wisdom of having a co-ordinating " head for the Allied forces ".

After an interchange of views, Maréchal Foch requested the three Commanders-in-Chief to send him the statistics of the forces which each of the Allied Armies would be able to put into the field on the 1st January and the 1st April 1919—they were to include the number of divisions present and the prospect of reinforcements ; the amount of artillery of the three main categories and rate of flow of ammunition supply ; the number of aeroplanes (pursuit, observation and bombing) ; tanks of three categories ; and motor transport.

On the 26th, after a discussion with General Rawlinson on the previous day, Sir Douglas Haig with Lieut.-General Lawrence attended another conference held by Maréchal Foch, at which also General Debeney and General Rawlinson, with his chief General Staff officer, Major-General A. A. Montgomery, were present. General Debeney proposed to execute a small operation south of the river Luce ; but the Generalissimo gave his decision that the larger operation suggested by the British should be carried out.[2] General

---

[1] Pershing Experiences, p. 506.
[2] On 23rd July the IX. Corps (General Garnier-Duplessix) of General Debeney's Army had carried out a very successful minor operation two miles south of Moreuil on a front of 3,000 yards, and to the same depth in the centre, in order to secure a spur which gave observation over the Avre valley. Three divisions attacked side by side with a fourth in

Rawlinson was still anxious to make the attack without French co-operation; but, in view of the limited number of divisions available, Sir Douglas Haig agreed to the French First Army taking part. This he regarded as the more desirable in view of the French reserves (4 divisions) which Maréchal Foch was moving to the Beauvais area behind the French First Army and which therefore would be available to exploit a success. It was settled that Generals Debeney and Rawlinson should meet next day and settle details of co-operation, and the 10th August was fixed as the date of the offensive.

No reports had come to hand of any further diminution—indeed there seemed to have been a slight increase—of Crown Prince Rupprecht's reserves; but prisoners confirmed the statement that his Hazebrouck—Ypres offensive had been definitely abandoned, because, as they said, the British had received warning of it. It was calculated that the total German reserves were now down to 34 divisions. Train movements from Lille to Douai were observed by fliers, which seemed to indicate that the enemy was strengthening his front near Arras, as G.H.Q. hoped that he might be persuaded to do. Prisoners also said that the Germans expected to be attacked south of the La Bassée canal.

In bringing the contents of Maréchal Foch's memorandum of the 24th to the notice of the five Army commanders, personally, not even any of their staff officers being present, Sir Douglas Haig handed them a G.H.Q. Note drawing special attention to one paragraph in it, in which it was said that the Germans, in order to evade battle and shorten their front when the numerical and moral superiority of the Allies became sufficiently marked, might make successive withdrawals to previously prepared positions. The Note enumerated the communications and positions which O.H.L. might not willingly evacuate

reserve. The area contained a number of small woods, but otherwise the ground was suitable for tanks, and Sir Douglas Haig gave assistance by lending the 9th Tank Battalion, with 42 Mark V. Tanks and 4 supply tanks, as well as the 12th Division artillery. The attack was carried out in three stages, with zero at 5.30 A.M., after an hour's bombardment; visibility was poor. The French infantry followed the tanks in small fighting groups, but the bombardment had given the Germans warning, the pace of the barrage was too slow for tanks, the liaison, particularly between the infantry fighting in the woods and the tanks outside, was not good, and there was 1½ hour's wait on the second objective. The general result was that the objective was gained but 14 of the 35 tanks which started, although none was ditched, were knocked out by artillery fire, and the tank personnel suffered 78 casualties (22 killed).

owing to their vital importance. From north to south these were :—

(a) The Flanders coast, their base for submarines and bombing aircraft.
(b) The defended area of Lille, essential for the security of the Flanders coast and a most important railway centre.
(c) The Lille—Valenciennes—Hirson—Mezières—Metz railway, which was the only effective means of communication across the front of the Ardennes.
(d) The defended area Metz—Thionville, of great railway importance and forming a bastion which protected the German frontier.
(e) The front line from Metz to Switzerland, which almost coincided with the German frontier.

To protect these important places, frontiers, and communications, so that they should not be disturbed by accurate gun-fire, the enemy would try to keep the Allies at a distance, say, of 12 miles. The Note suggested that the enemy could without disadvantage withdraw as far back as the line Metz—Lille, but that south of Metz and north of Lille he would have to accept battle, and he seemed to have prepared rear lines in the winter of 1916–17 with this strategic idea in view. The result would be that the British Armies would have either to follow up the enemy across a devastated area, as in 1917, or to attack on certain limited fronts well prepared for defence. In the first case, the Note continued, early information of the enemy's intentions was most essential; but if he were to retire in the late autumn or winter he should be followed up only by strong advanced guards, whilst immediate preparations should be made to repair roads and railways. In the second case, there would, in the British area, be little hope of capturing the positions by surprise attack and the matter was left for later decision.

On Sunday, the 28th, came an agreeable invitation for the British Commander-in-Chief. General Weygand arrived with a letter from the Generalissimo asking him to take command of the French First Army and combine its action with the Fourth Army in the forthcoming operations. At the same time General Weygand handed him another letter and a " Directive particulière ". In the former, in view of the rapid accentuation of the Allied progress towards the Ardre and the Aisne and the probability that the enemy would take up a position behind the rivers which could not be immediately attacked, Maréchal Foch asked that the preparation for the offensive of the British Fourth and French First Armies might be expedited, and offered to send back the XXII. Corps earlier in accordance with the new date. Sir Douglas accepted the invitation to assume command, and in his reply said that he would try and gain two days if the XXII. Corps with all its four divisions could be sent back two days earlier than requested. This was at once arranged.

Maréchal Foch's " Directive particulière " ran :

" 1. The object of the operation is to disengage Amiens and the Paris—Amiens railway, also to defeat and drive back the enemy established between the Somme and the Avre.
" 2. To do so, the offensive, covered on the north by the Somme, will push as far as possible in the direction of Roye.
" 3. It will be executed by :
(i) the British Fourth Army, composed at the start of 12 divisions and 3 cavalry divisions, supported by
(ii) the French First Army, reinforced by 4 divisions.
" They will act the one north, the other south of the Roye road, once debouchment south of the Luce and east of the Avre is assured."

Thus it was that the 8th August 1918 became the date of the great turning-point in the War.

NOTE

German Plans after the Retirement behind the Vesle

The following is an extract from an appreciation of the situation drawn up by General Ludendorff on the 2nd August and sent to the Commanders of the four Groups of Armies on the Western Front [1] :—

" The situation requires, first, that we stand on the defensive and, secondly, resume the offensive as soon as possible.
" Since the Entente has engaged large forces between the Vesle and the Marne, full-dress attacks by the enemy within a short time at another place are as little to be expected as is a counter-attack by us to be taken into account by him. The continuation at an early date of the attack near the Vesle is not improbable. Later on enemy full-dress attacks may naturally be expected against many parts of our front. In all probability they will be directed against :—

I. Kemmel and the salient of the Sixth Army ;
II. our positions between the Somme and the Oise, as far east as Soissons ;
III. the Moronvillers position [12 miles east of Reims] ;

[1] The extract is in Monograph IV.

GERMAN PLANS

  IV. the south front of Army Detachment " C " [that is the southern front of the St. Mihiel Salient] ; and
  V. finally against the Lorraine front and in the Sundgau [the district west of Mulhausen].[1]

" Whilst the defence is being organized at these places, we must simultaneously prepare to attack. The following will be considered :—

  I. The Hagen [Hazebrouck—Ypres] attack in a small form ;
  II. the Kurfürst attack on both sides of the Oise, say between Montdidier and Soissons ;
  III. perhaps smaller attacks eastwards of Reims against Fort Pompelle and near Vauquois [12 miles north-west of Verdun] as well as on the front of Army Detachment " C " ; and
  IV. attacks from the sector of Duke Albrecht of Württemberg [Alsace], on wide or small frontages.

" In these attacks, especially west of the Moselle, it is of less importance to conquer much ground than to inflict loss on the enemy and gain better positions. East of the Moselle the gain of more ground would certainly be advantageous ; but even there we shall have to be content with something less.

" We must adhere to surprise attacks, others cost us too many men. Too much importance cannot be laid on the rapid assembly of troops and attack material, and on the simplification of the preparations ; by these means it will be possible to obtain important partial successes, particularly on narrow fronts and at selected places where the enemy is weak. All attacks are to be prepared as measures of defence only. Nothing is to be said about attacks."

[1] It will be noted that the Amiens front, except south of the Somme, is not included.

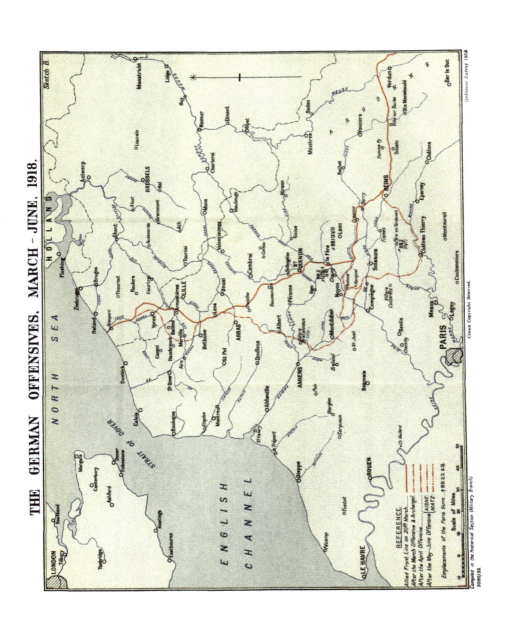

THE GERMAN OFFENSIVES, MARCH – JUNE, 1918.

APPENDICES

APPENDIX A

ORDER OF BATTLE

BRITISH FORCES

BATTLE OF THE AISNE, 27TH MAY–6TH JUNE 1918

IX. CORPS

Commander	Lieut.-General Sir A. H. Gordon.
Br.-General, General Staff .	Br.-General W. J. Maxwell-Scott.
Br.-General, Royal Artillery	Br.-General G. Humphreys.
Br.-General, Heavy Artillery	Br.-General G. B. Mackenzie.
Chief Engineer . . .	Br.-General G. S. Cartwright.

8TH DIVISION : Major-Gen. W. C. G. Heneker.

G.S.O. 1	Lieut.-Col. C. C. Armitage to 5th June; then Lieut.-Col. A. G. B. Bourne.
C.R.A.	Br.-General J. W. F. Lamont.
C.R.E.	Lieut.-Col. C. M. Browne.
23rd Brigade . . .	Br.-General G. W. St. G. Grogan, V.C.
2/Devonshire	2/West Yorkshire 2/Middlesex
24th Brigade . . .	Br.-General R. Haig to 4th June; then Br.-General L. M. Stevens.
1/Worcs.	1/Sherwood For. 2/Northampton
25th Brigade . . .	Br.-General R. H. Husey, wounded and captured on 27th May; died wounds 30th May; 29th May-3rd June, Major H. P. Allaway, acting; then Br.-General J. B. Pollok-McCall.
2/East Lancashire	2/R. Berkshire 2/Rifle Brigade
R.F.A. Bdes. . . .	XXXIII., XLV.
Field Coys. R.E. . .	2, 15, 490.
Pioneers	22/Durham L.I.

19TH DIVISION : Major-Gen. G. D. Jeffreys.

G.S.O. 1	Lieut.-Col. H. F. Montgomery.
C.R.A.	Br.-General W. P. Monkhouse.
C.R.E.	Lieut.-Col. P. E. Hodgson.

APPENDIX A

56th Brigade	. Br.-General R. M. Heath.	
9/Cheshire	1/4th K.S.L.I.	8/N. Staffordshire
57th Brigade	. Br.-General A. J. F. Eden, who had assumed command on the 24th May from Br.-General T. A. Cubitt.	
10/R. Warwick	8/Glo'ster	10/Worcs.
58th Brigade	. Br.-General A. E. Glasgow.	
9/R. Welch Fusiliers	9/Welch	2/Wiltshire
R.F.A. Bdes.	. LXXXVII., LXXXVIII.	
Field Coys. R.E. . . .	. 81, 82, 94.	
Pioneers	. 5/S. Wales Borderers.	

21st Division : Major-Gen. D. G. M. Campbell.

G.S.O. 1	. Lieut.-Col. H. E. Franklyn.	
C.R.A.	. Br.-General H. W. Newcome.	
C.R.E.	. Lieut.-Col. G. H. Addison.	
62nd Brigade . . .	. Br.-General G. H. Gater.	
12th/13th North'd Fus.	1/Lincoln	2/Lincoln
64th Brigade . . .	. Br.-General H. R. Headlam.	
1/East Yorkshire	9/K.O.Y.L.I.	15/Durham L.I.
110th Brigade . . .	. Br.-General H. R. Cumming.	
6/Leicestershire	7/Leicestershire	8/Leicestershire
R.F.A. Bdes.	. XCIV., XCV.	
Field Coys. R.E. . . .	. 97, 98, 126.	
Pioneers	. 14/Northumberland Fus.	

25th Division (*From VIII. Corps*) : Major-General Sir E. G. T. Bainbridge.

G.S.O. 1	. Lieut-Col. R. T. Lee.	
C.R.A.	. Br.-General K. J. Kincaid-Smith.	
C.R.E.	. Lieut.-Col. R. J. Done.	
7th Brigade	. Br.-General C. J. Griffin.	
10/Cheshire	4/S. Staffordshire	1/Wiltshire
74th Brigade . . .	. Br.-General H. M. Craigie Halkett.	
11/Lancs. Fus.	3/Worcestershire	9/L.N. Lancs.
75th Brigade . . .	. Br.-General A. A. Kennedy, assumed command on 27th May vice Lieut.-Col. A. M. Tringham, acting since 22nd May.	
11/Cheshire	8/Border Regt.	2/S. Lancs.
R.F.A. Bdes.	. 110, 112.	
Field Coys. R.E. . . .	. 105, 106, 130.	
Pioneers	. 6/S. Wales Borderers.	

APPENDIX A

50TH (NORTHUMBRIAN) DIVISION : Major-Gen. H. C. Jackson.

G.S.O. 1	Lieut.-Col. E. C. Anstey.
C.R.A.	Br.-General W. Stirling.
C.R.E.	Lieut.-Col. J. A. McQueen.
149th Brigade	Br.-General E. P. A. Riddell, wounded 27th May; Major I. M. Tweedy acting till 3rd June; then Lieut.-Col. L. D. Scott, acting till 7th June; then Br.-General P. M. Robinson.

4/North'd Fus.	5/North'd Fus.	6/North'd Fus.

150th Brigade	Br.-General H. C. Rees, captured 27th May; Brigade H.Q. ceased to exist; re-formed 31st May. Br.-General F. J. Marshall assumed command 1st June.

4/East Yorkshire	4/Green Howards	5/Green Howards

151st Brigade	Br.-General C. T. Martin, killed 27th May; Lieut.-Col. F. Walton acting till 7th June; then Br.-General R. E. Sugden.

5/Durham L.I.	6/Durham L.I.	8/Durham L.I.

R.F.A. Bdes.	250, 251.
Field Coys. R.E.	7, 446, 447.
Pioneers	7/Durham L.I.

BATTLES OF THE MARNE 1918, 20TH JULY–2ND AUGUST

XXII. CORPS

Commander	Lieut.-General Sir A. J. Godley.
Br.-General, General Staff	Br.-General C. W. Gwynn.
Br.-General, Royal Artillery	Br.-General E. W. M. Powell.
Br.-General, Heavy Artillery	Br.-General A. S. Jenour.
Chief Engineer	Br.-General A. E. Panet.

BATTLE OF THE SOISSONNAIS AND OF THE OURCQ, 23RD JULY–2ND AUGUST

15TH (SCOTTISH) DIVISION : Major-Gen. H. L. Reed, V.C.

G.S.O. 1	Lieut-Col. W. H. Diggle.
C.R.A.	Br.-General E. B. Macnaghten.
C.R.E.	Lieut-Col. J. M. Arthur.
44th Brigade	Br.-General N. A. Thomson.

4th/5th Black Watch	8/Seaforth	5/Gordons

APPENDIX A

| 45th Brigade | . | . | . | Br.-General N. A. Orr-Ewing. |
| 13/R. Scots | | 6/Camerons | | 8/A.&S.H. |

| 46th Brigade | . | . | . | Br.-General V. M. Fortune. |
| 9/Royal Scots | | 7th/8th K.O.S.B. | | 10/Scottish Rifles |

R.F.A. Bdes. . . . . LXX., LXXI.
Field Coys. R.E. . . . 73, 74, 91.
Pioneers . . . . . 9/Gordon Highlanders.

34TH DIVISION: Major-Gen. C. L. Nicholson.

G.S.O. 1 . . . . . Lieut.-Col. J. G. Dooner.
C.R.A. . . . . . . Br.-General E. C. W. D. Walthall
C.R.E. . . . . . . Lieut.-Col. A. C. Dobson.

| 101st Brigade | . | . | . | Br.-General W. J. Woodcock. |
| 2/4th Queen's | | 4/R. Sussex | | 2/L.N. Lancs. |

| 102nd Brigade | . | . | . | Br.-General E. Hilliam. |
| 4/Cheshire | | 7/Cheshire | | 1/Herefordshire |

| 103rd Brigade | . | . | . | Br.-General J. G. Chaplin. |
| 5/K.O.S.B. | | 8/Scottish Rifles | | 5/A.&S.H. |

R.F.A. Bdes. . . . . 252, 260.
Field Coys. R.E. . . . 207, 208, 209.
Pioneers . . . . . 2/4th Somerset L.I.

BATTLE OF TARDENOIS, 20TH–31ST JULY

51ST (HIGHLAND) DIVISION: Major-Gen. G. T. C. Carter-Campbell.

G.S.O. 1 . . . . . Lieut.-Col. R. S. McClintock.
C.R.A. . . . . . . Br.-General L. C. L. Oldfield.
C.R.E. . . . . . . Lieut.-Col. N. W. Napier-Clavering.

| 152nd Brigade | . | . | . | Br.-General R. Laing. |
| 5/Seaforth | | 6/Seaforth | | 6/Gordons |

| 153rd Brigade | . | . | . | Br.-General W. Green. |
| 6/Black Watch | | 7/Black Watch | | 7/Gordons |

| 154th Brigade | . | . | . | Br.-General K. G. Buchanan. |
| 4/Seaforth | | 4/Gordons | | 7/A.&S.H. |

R.F.A. Bdes. . . . . 255, 256.
Field Coys. R.E. . . . 400, 401, 404.
Pioneers . . . . . 8/Royal Scots.

62ND (2/WEST RIDING) DIVISION: Major-Gen. W. P. Braithwaite.

G.S.O. 1 . . . . . Lieut.-Col. C. R. Newman.
C.R.A. . . . . . . Br.-General A. T. Anderson.
C.R.E. . . . . . . Lieut.-Col. L. Chenevix-Trench.

APPENDICES A AND B 329

185th Brigade	Br.-General Viscount Hampden.	
1/5th Devon	2/5th W. Yorks	8/W. Yorks
186th Brigade	Br. General J. L. G. Burnett.	
2/4th D.W.R.	5/D.W.R.	2/4th Hampshire
187th Brigade	Br.-General A. J. Reddie.	
2/4th K.O.Y.L.I.	5/K.O.Y.L.I.	2/4th York & Lanc.
R.F.A. Bdes.	310, 312.	
Field Coys. R.E. . . .	457, 460, 461.	
Pioneers	1/9th Durham L.I.	

APPENDIX B

ORDER OF BATTLE [1]

FRENCH FORCES

MAY–JULY 1918

GROUP OF ARMIES OF RESERVE. (G.A.R.)
(General Fayolle.)

Third Army. (General Humbert.)
First Army. (General Debeney.) Until 27th July, transferred to Sir Douglas Haig's command.

Tenth Army. (General Maistre, from 10th June General Mangin.) From 1st June, previously in General Reserve.
Sixth Army. (General Duchêne, from 10th June General Degoutte). From 21st July, transferred from G.A.C.

GROUP OF ARMIES OF THE NORTH. (G.A.N.)
(General Franchet d'Espérey, until 9th June, then General Maistre.)

(On 6th July became Group of Armies of the Centre.)

Sixth Army. (see G.A.R.)
Fourth Army. (General Gouraud.)
Fifth Army. (General Micheler, from 10th June General Buat, from 5th July General Berthelot.) From 29th May, previously in General Reserve.

[1] From F.O.A. Order of Battle volumes. Divisions occasionally attached to Corps are omitted.

APPENDIX B

GROUP OF ARMIES OF THE CENTRE. (G.A.C.)
(General Maistre.)

(Dissolved 1st December 1917, reconstituted 6th July by change of name of G.A.N.)

Sixth Army. (See G.A.R.) — Until 20th July, then to G.A.R.
Fourth Army. (See G.A.N.)
Fifth Army. (See G.A.N.)
Ninth Army. (General de Mitry.) — From 17th July to 24th July then dissolved.

THIRD ARMY

Corps

27th May. II (General de Cadoudal, from 11th June General Philipot.)
XVIII (General de Pouydraguin.)
XXXIV (General Nudant.)
XXXV (General Jacquot.)

5th June. — plus XV (General de Fonclare) from Eighth Army.
11th „ — less XVIII to Tenth Army.
19th „ — less II to Sixth Army.

FOURTH ARMY

27th May. III (General Lebrun.)
IV (General Pont.)
V (General Pellé.)
VIII (General Hély d'Oissel.)
I Colonial (General Mazillier.)

28th „ — less I Colonial to Fifth Army.
30th „ — less V to Fifth Army.
21st June. — less III to Sixth Army.
21st „ — plus XXI (General Naulin) from Sixth Army.
14th July. — plus XVI (General Corvisart) from Second Army.
24th „ — less XVI to Eighth Army.

FIFTH ARMY

27th May. I (General Lacapelle.)
28th „ — plus I Colonial from Fourth Army.
30th „ — plus V from Fourth Army.
17th July. — plus XIV from Ninth Army.
25th „ — plus III from Ninth Army.
30th „ — less III to Sixth Army.

APPENDIX B

SIXTH ARMY

27th May.	XI (General de Maud'huy, from 3rd June General Niessel, from 19th July General Prax.)	
	XXI (General Degoutte, from 10th June General Naulin.)	
	XXX (General Chrétien, from 10th June General Penet.)	
29th ,,		plus I from Fifth Army.
30th ,,		plus VII (General de Bazelaire, from 4th June General Massenet.) from First Army.
30th ,,		plus XXXVIII from Tenth Army.
2nd June.		less I to Tenth Army.
2nd ,,		less XI to ,,
2nd ,,		less XXX to ,,
19th ,,		plus II from Third Army.
21st ,,		plus III from Fourth Army.
21st ,,		less XXI to Fourth Army.
17th July.		less III to Ninth Army.
17th ,,		less XXXVIII to Ninth Army.
20th ,,		plus XXXVIII from Ninth Army.
30th ,,		plus III from Fifth Army.
31st ,,		less VII to Tenth Army.

NINTH ARMY

6th July.	XIV (General Marjoulet.)	
17th ,,		plus III and XXXVIII from Sixth Army; less XIV to Fifth Army.
20th ,,		less XXXVIII to Sixth Army.
25th ,,		less III to Fifth Army.

TENTH ARMY

27th May.	XX (General Berdoulat.)	
	XXXVIII (General Piarron de Mondésir.)	
30th ,,		less XXXVIII to Sixth Army.
2nd June.		plus I, XI, and XXX, all from Sixth Army.
11th ,,		plus XVIII from Third Army.
31st July.		plus III from Sixth Army.

Appendix C

BATTLE OF THE AISNE

FRENCH FORCES ENGAGED

compiled from the text of F.O.A. vi. (ii.) and F.O.A. x. (i.)

Originally in the line
  Fourth Army
    I. Colonial Corps . 45th Division.
  Sixth Army
    XI. Corps . . . 22nd Division.
                  21st Division.
                  61st Division.
    XXX. Corps . . 151st Division.
Original reserves of the Sixth Army :
                  157th Division.
                  39th Division.
                  74th Division.

Arrived on 27th May . . 13th Division from Fourth Army.

Arrived on 28th May . . 154th Division from Fourth Army.
                  1st Division from Fifth Army.
                  43rd Division from Fifth Army.

Arrived on 29th May . . Moroccan from Fifth Army.
                  131st Division from First Army.
                  170th Division from Fifth Army.
                  20th Division from Second Army.
                  4th Division from Third Army.

Arrived on 30th May . . 164th Division from Fifth Army.
                  10th Colonial from Fourth Army.
                  162nd Division from Third Army.
                  120th Division from Fourth Army.
                  40th Division from Fourth Army.
                  28th Division from Fifth Army.
                  167th Division from Fifth Army.
                  3rd American.

Arrived on 31st May . . 35th Division from Third Army.
                  51st Division from Fifth Army.
                  73rd Division from Tenth Army.
                  26th Division from Tenth Army (from Fifth).

Arrived on 1st June . . 128th Division from Third Army.
                  15th Division from Third Army.
                  2nd American.
                  133rd Division from D.A.N. (through Seventh).
                  47th Division from Tenth Army.

APPENDICES C AND I

Arrived on 2nd June . 87th Division from Fourth Army (through Third).
Arrived on 3rd June . . 153rd Division from Tenth Army.

Summary

From D.A.N. (with British)	1
From First Army (on right of British)	2
From Second Army (Verdun)	1
From Third (on left of Sixth)	5
From Fourth (on right of Sixth)	5
From Fifth (general Reserve)	8
From Tenth (general Reserve)	4
From American	2
	28

APPENDIX I

WAR COMMISSIONS AND COMMITTEES

By the end of March 1918 no less than 165 Commissions, Committees and other bodies had been appointed to consider questions arising from the War. The list given below does not include Committees appointed to consider questions of post-War problems formed under the Ministry of Reconstruction. There were in addition 118 sub-committees and sub sub-committees formed from the main Committees.

A.—FINANCE AND INSURANCE—
    I.—Committee to Consider and Advise upon Applications received by the Treasury for Approval of Fresh Issues of Capital.
    II.—American Dollar Securities Committee.
    III.—Foreign Trade Debts Committee.
    IV.—Enemy Debts Committee.
    V.—Excess Profits Duty (Board of Referees).
    VI.—Munitions Exchequer Payments (Board of Referees).
    VII.—National War Savings Committee.
    VIII.—Scottish War Savings Committee.
    IX.—Irish War Savings Committee.
    X.—War Office, Soldiers' Dependants. Appeals Assessment Committee.
    XI.—Board of Trade Advisory Committee on the National Insurance of British Ships' Cargoes.
    XII.—Board of Trade Committee for Carrying into Operation the Government Scheme of Insurance against Bombardment and Aircraft Risks.

XIII.—War Office Contracts Advisory Committee.
XIV.—Inter-Ally Council on War Purchases and Finance.
XV.—Departmental Committee on Contracts.
XVI.—Committee on Contracts.
XVII.—Committee on Staffs of Public Departments.
XVIII.—New Issues of Capital Committee.
XIX.—Soldiers' and Sailors' Pay Committee.
XX.—Insurance Intelligence Department.
XXI.—Air Raid Compensation Committee.

B.—TRADE—
XXII.—Ministry of Blockade:
    (i.) The War Trade Department.
    (ii.) The War Trade Intelligence Department.
    (iii.) The War Trade Statistical Department.
XXIII.—Ministry of Blockade Committee.
XXIV.—War Trade Advisory Committee.
XXV.—Department of Import Restrictions.
XXVI.—Restriction of Enemy Supplies Department.
XXVII.—Fish Purchase Advisory Committee.
XXVIII.—Prohibition of Industrial Diamonds Committee.
XXIX.—Foreign Office Committee on Contraband Trade.
XXX.—Cornhill Committee on German Trade and other Financial Questions.
XXXI.—Trading with the Enemy Committee.
XXXII.—Prize Claims Committee.
XXXIII.—Oversea Prize Disposal Committee.
XXXIV.—Foreign Office Committee on Enemy Exports.
XXV.—Board of Trade Executive Committee for Dealing with Cargo which, though possibly liable in law to Condemnation as Prize, might with Advantage be Released.
XXXVI.—Foreign Trade Department.

C.—SHIPPING AND TRANSPORT—
XXXVII.—Tonnage Priority Committee.
XXXVIII.—Shipping Control Committee.
XXXIX.—Shipbuilding Advisory Committee.
XL.—Port and Transit Executive Committee.
XLI.—Inter-Ally Chartering Committee.
XLII.—National Maritime Board.
XLIII.—Mercantile Marine Conciliation Committee.
XLIV.—Neutral Tonnage Conference.
XLV.—Inter-Ally Ship Purchasing Committee.
XLVI.—Shipping and Coal Co-ordinating Committee.
XLVII.—Greek Ships Committee.
XLVIII.—Merchant Ships Gratuities Committee.
XLIX.—Hire Claims Committee.
L.—Railway Executive Committee.
LI.—Railway Executive Committee (Ireland).
LII.—Departmental Committee on Road Locomotives and Heavy Motor-Cars.

APPENDIX I

    LIII.—Horse Transport Department.
    LIV.—Horse Transport Advisory Committee.
    LV.—Canal Control Committee.
    LVI.—Road Transport Board.
    LVII.—Shipbuilding Council.
    LVIII.—Diversion of Traffic (East to West Coast Ports) Committee.
    LIX.—Tramways (Board of Trade) Committee.

D.—SUPPLIES—
    LX.—Commission Internationale de Ravitaillement.
    LXI.—Joint Propaganda Committee of the Board of Agriculture and Fisheries and the Ministry of Food.
    LXII.—(A.) Board of Agriculture and Fisheries Committees:
        (1.) Flax Production Committee.
        (2.) Fish, Food, and Motor Loan Committee.
        (3.) Freshwater Fish Committee.
        (4.) Advisory Committee on Poultry.
        (5.) Live Stock Committee.
    (B.) Food Production Department:
        (1.) Advisory Committee on Food Production.
        (2.) Technical Committee.
        (3.) Seeds Advisory Committee.
        (4.) Cereal Seeds Advisory Committee.
        (5.) Potato Advisory Committee.
        (6.) Phosphates and Potash Distribution Committee.
        (7.) Sulphate of Ammonia Distribution Committee.
    LXIII.—Ministry of Food Committees:
        (1.) Flour Mills Control Committee.
        (2.) Food Control Committee for Ireland.
        (3.) Central Feeding Stuffs Advisory Committee.
        (4.) Rabbits and Game Advisory Committee.
        (5.) Jam Advisory Committee.
        (6.) Advisory Committee on Live Stock and Meat Supplies.
        (7.) Advisory Committee for the Control of Butter and Cheese Supplies.
        (8.) Bacon Advisory Committee.
        (9.) Tea Advisory Committee.
        (10.) Dried Fruits Advisory Committee.
        (11.) Coffee Advisory Committee.
        (12.) Cocoa Advisory Committee.
        (13.) Consumers' Council.
    LXIV.—Army Cattle Committee.
    LXV.—Royal Commission on Wheat Supplies.
    LXVI.—Wheat Executive.
    LXVII.—Royal Commission on the Sugar Supplies.
    LXVIII.—Forage Committee.
    LXIX.—Central Wool Advisory Committee.
    LXX.—Raw Wool Advisory Committee.
    LXXI.—Board of Control of Wool Textile Production.
    LXXII.—Road Stone Control Committee.
    LXXIII.—Leather Supplies Central Advisory Committee.

LXXIV.—The American Board.
LXXV.—His Majesty's Petroleum Executive.
LXXVI.—Petrol Control Department.
LXXVII.—Irish Petrol Committee.
LXXVIII.—Pool Board (Petroleum Supplies).
LXXIX.—Coal Mines Department.
LXXX.—Coal Mines (Controller of) Advisory Board.
LXXXI.—Timber Supplies Department.
LXXXII.—Tobacco and Match Control Board.
LXXXIII.—Paper Control Department.
LXXXIV.—Department of Surveyor-General of Supply:
    (i.) National Salvage Council.
    (ii.) Executive Board.

E.—MUNITIONS AND ARMAMENTS, INCLUDING INVENTION AND RESEARCH—

Ministry of Munitions Committees:
LXXXV.—The Ordnance Committee.
LXXXVI.—Munitions Inventions Panel.
    Sub-Committees of Munitions Inventions Panel:
        (1.) Ordnance and Ammunition.
        (2.) Gunsights, Rangefinders, &c.
        (3.) Instruments.
        (4.) Fortifications.
        (5.) Field Service.
        (6.) Transport.
        (7.) Chemical Inventions.
        (8.) Machinery and Metals.
        (9.) Nitrogen Products.
LXXXVII.—(A.) War Priorities Committee of the War Cabinet.
    (B.) Permanent Sub-Committee of the War Priorities Committee.
    (C.) Allocation Sub-Committees of the War Priorities Committee:
        (i.) Steel Allocation Sub-Committee.
        (ii.) Oxy-Acetylene and Hydrogen Sub-Committee.
        (iii.) Timber Allocation Sub-Committee.
        (iv.) Non-Ferrous Materials Allocation Sub-Committee.
        (v.) Machine Tools and Ball Bearing Allocation Sub-Committee.
        (vi.) Explosives and Chemicals Allocation Sub-Committee.
        (vii.) Linen and Fabric Allocation Sub-Committee—Flax Control Board.
    (D.) Other Sub-Committees operating under War Priorities Committee:
        (i.) Information Sub-Committee.
        (ii.) Works Construction Sub-Committee.
        (iii.) General Services Sub-Committee.
            (*a*.) Industries Committee (Sub-Committee of General Services Sub-Committee).

APPENDIX I

LXXXVIII.—Anti-Aircraft Equipment Committee.
LXXXIX.—Chemical Warfare Committee.
    XC.—Sulphuric Acid Advisory Committee.
   XCI.—Board of Management Executive Committee.
  XCII.—Munitions Financial Advisory Committee.
 XCIII.—Trade Union Advisory Committee.
 XCIV.—Ministry of Munitions Hours of Labour Committee.
  XCV.—Committee on Building Labour.
 XCVI.—Mineral Resources Advisory Committee.
XCVII.—Lubricating Oil Advisory Committee.
XCVIII.—Committee on Scottish Shale Industries.
 XCIX.—Advisory Committee on Alcohol Supplies for War Purposes.
    C.—Munitions Works Board.
   CI.—Causes of Explosions at Government and Controlled Factories Standing Committee.
  CII.—Employers' Advisory Committee.
 CIII.—Chemical Employers' Advisory Committee.
 CIV.—Special Arbitration Tribunal on Women's Wages.
  CV.—Women's Trade Union Advisory Committee.
 CVI.—Central Billeting Board.
CVII.—Admiralty Board of Invention and Research.
CVIII.—Air Ministry Committees:
    (A.) Advisory Committee for Aeronautics.
        (1.) Internal Combustion Engine Sub-Committee.
        (2.) Light Alloys Sub-Committee.
        (3.) Aerodynamics Sub-Committee.
        (4.) Special Committee on the Electrification of Balloons.
    (B.) Air Inventions Committee.
        (1.) Engine Sub-Committee.
        (2.) Aeronautics Sub-Committee.
        (3.) Armament Bombs Sub-Committee.
        (4.) Instruments Sub-Committee.
        (5.) Procedure Sub-Committee.
 CIX.—Tank Design Committee.
  CX.—Nitrate of Soda Executive.

F.—COMMITTEES DEALING WITH QUESTIONS ARISING OUT OF RECRUITING AND THE MILITARY SERVICE ACTS:—

 CXI.—Ministry of National Service Committees:
    (1.) Reserved Occupations Committee.
    (2.) Recruiting Advisory Board.
    (3.) Medical Advisory Board.
    (4.) Registration Advisory Board.
    (5.) Labour Advisory Board.
    (6.) National Labour Priority Committee.
    (7.) Aliens Advisory Committee.
    (8.) Labour Advisory Committee.
    (9.) Advisory Committee on Part-Time Labour &c.

CXII.—Ministry of Labour Committees :
    (1.) Labour Resettlement Committee.
    (2.) Demobilization Priority Committee.
CXIII.—Central Colliery Recruiting Court (Home Office).
CXIV.—Railwaymen and Enlistment Committee.
CXV.—The Military Service (Civil Liabilities) Department.
CXVI.—Committee on Work of National Importance.
CXVII.—Committee on Employment of Conscientious Objectors.

G.—COMMITTEES DEALING WITH QUESTIONS ARISING OUT OF THE DEFENCE OF THE REALM REGULATIONS—

CXVIII.—Committee to consider Proposed Amendments of the Defence of the Realm Regulations.
CXIX.—Central Control Board (Liquor Traffic).
CXX.—Defence of the Realm (Licensed Trade Claims) Commission.
CXXI.—Defence of the Realm Losses Commission.
CXXII.—Cocaine Committee.
CXXIII.—Committee on Destruction of Material seized under No. 51 of the Defence of the Realm Regulations.

H.—ALIENS—

CXXIV.—Home Office Committee on Alien Restrictions.
CXXV.—Home Office Aliens Advisory Committee.
CXXVI.—Civilian Internment Camps Committee.
CXXVII.—Inter-Departmental Advisory Committee on the Administration of Article 22 (*b*) of the Aliens' Restriction Regulations.
CXXVIII.—Scottish Advisory Committee on Aliens.
CXXIX.—Committee on Claims of Neutral Subjects to Compensation on Account of Illegal Detention.

I.—PRISONERS—

CXXX.—Central Prisoners of War Committee.
CXXXI.—Government Committee on the Treatment by the Enemy of British Prisoners of War.
CXXXII.—Prisoners of War Inter-Departmental Committee.
CXXXIII.—Committee on Proposals for Employment of Prisoners of War.

J.—RELIEF OF DISTRESS—

CXXXIV.—Co-ordinating Committee appointed by the Cabinet.
CXXXV.—Local Government Board Committee on the Prevention and Relief of Distress for London.
CXXXVI.—Professional Classes Committee.
CXXXVII.—Central Committee on Women's Employment.

APPENDICES I AND II

CXXXVIII.—Committee on Cases of Hardship (Seamen's Effects).
CXXXIX.—Belgian Refugees Committee (Ireland).
CXL.—Committee on Repatriation of Belgian Refugees.
CXLI.—War Refugees Committee.
CXLII.—Advisory Committee on the Welfare of the Blind.
CXLIII.—Institutional Survey Committee.
CXLIV.—Committee on Housing (Building Construction).
CXLV.—Conference on Housing.

K.—MISCELLANEOUS—

CXLVI.—Home Office Advisory Committee on Passenger Traffic between United Kingdom and Certain Foreign Countries.
CXLVII.—Colonial Office Committee in connection with the War Contingents of the Dominions.
CXLVIII.—Committee on Production.
CXLIX.—Conciliation and Arbitration Board for Government Employés.
CL.—Committee on Revision of Treaties with Enemy Countries.
CLI.—Committee on National Registration.
CLII.—Vulnerable Points Committee.
CLIII.—Civil Aerial Transport Committee.
CLIV.—The Committee of the Imperial War Museum.
CLV.—War Cabinet Committee on Accommodation.
CLVI.—Official History of the War Committee.
CLVII.—Departmental Committee on Building Bye-Laws.
CLVIII.—Graves Commission.
CLIX.—Artificial Limbs Committee.
CLX.—Recognition for Next-of-Kin Committee.
CLXI.—War Trophies Committee.
CLXII.—Committee on the Interpretation of the Term " Period of the War ".
CLXIII.—Foreign Office Committee on the League of Nations.
CLXIV.—International Law Committee.
CLXV.—National War Aims Committee.

APPENDIX II

GENERAL FOCH'S GENERAL DIRECTIVE NO. 3

G.Q.G.A. 20TH MAY 1918

(Translation)

I.

After an effort without precedent against the whole of the battle-front the enemy has halted ; for three weeks he has not attacked anywhere in force.

It is probable that he cannot remain inactive except under pain of admitting that he has been checked, and that his effort will be continued. But whatever attitude he may take up in the future, whether he resumes the attack or not, the Allied Armies must be ready to pass to the offensive.

The offensive alone, in fact, will permit the Allies to end the battle victoriously, and then to recover, by the initiative in operations, moral ascendancy.

This offensive can be undertaken now under conditions particularly effective, due to our superiority in aircraft, tanks and artillery.

This superiority may only be temporary; we must profit from it without delay.

II.

In order that this offensive may attain the objects proposed it must—particularly in the actual circumstances which compel strict economy of our forces—obtain results commensurate with the sacrifices we are prepared to make.

Between the Oise and the North Sea, important results can be sought, so important that they of themselves alone impose the offensive. These are:

(i) Between the Oise and the Somme, the freeing of the railway Paris—Amiens and the Amiens area, and the restoration to the Nord Railway of facilities over its line which carries most traffic; this will improve both the supply of the country at large and the liaison between the French and British armies, and thus will have profitable results both economic and strategic.

(ii) In the Lys region, the freeing of the mines which will enable the intensive exploitation to be resumed which was carried out in the months which preceded the German attack, and [sic] will place Flanders definitely beyond the reach of enemy enterprises.

On the other hand in the actual state of affairs there is every reason to discard the idea of any offensive enterprise upon our part between the Oise and Switzerland, even in the sectors already prepared for attack; for in order to be always ready to parry an enemy offensive we are under the obligation of maintaining our reserves near enough to intervene on the battle-front, that is north of the Oise.

III.

Each of the objects indicated above, in each of the areas under consideration, can be pursued by making use of envelopment, which the form of front admits, so as to combine attacks capable of producing, even with forces relatively small, very important results.

Thus, for instance, in the area between Oise and Somme, the French attack launched northward from the front Montdidier—Lassigny combined with an Allied attack launched from the front between Somme and Luce, but later directed southwards, may be expected to produce a sufficiently deep disorganization of the enemy system between Montdidier and the Somme to free at the same time both Amiens and the railway Paris—Amiens.

Thus also, in the Lys area, a British attack launched from the front Festubert—Robecq, in the direction of Estaires, combined with a French attack having Mount Kemmel as its first objective, will drive the enemy out of his Hazebrouck salient, and consequently free at the same time both our mining region and the line of hills which are the bastion of Flanders.

Nevertheless, although in the area between Oise and Somme, the two combined actions cannot be dissociated one from the other because they are seeking results which complete each other—freeing Amiens and the railway Paris—Amiens—on the other hand the attack in the direction of Estaires, which is intended to push the enemy away farther from Béthune, is for itself susceptible of furnishing a result of importance : the freeing of the mines, and may for that reason be undertaken separately. The same may be said of the Kemmel operation.

IV.

In the situation in which we find ourselves facing an enemy on guard and in force, surprise is a factor of capital importance. Everything must therefore be used to obtain the advantage of it : tanks, the employment of the new gas, Yperite (lethal) on a large scale will add to all the usual elements of surprise : secrecy, rapid placing in position of the attacking divisions, concealed movements, false news, . . . not one of these must be neglected.

It is equally important that by rapid exploitation every possible advantage should be drawn from the temporary disorganization in the enemy's ranks thus obtained.

V.

It remains to consider what moment should be chosen to launch the offensive. If the enemy does not attack, he must be surprised by a powerful attack : the operation proposed between Somme and Oise provides us with the means : it demands fairly considerable forces (about 20 divisions not counting those already in the line)—the inaction of the enemy will permit us to find them.

If the enemy attacks, our own offensive will be a " riposte " returning blow for blow to the " parade "—but the forces required for the " parade " may leave us without any for the " riposte ". We shall be obliged to do something on a smaller scale. The Lys operation, less costly, part of which only, if necessary, can be carried out, will be ready for the purpose.

Both of these two operations must therefore be prepared without delay, so that the High Command will have at its disposal a series of offensive combinations, of which it can make use according to circumstances, always bearing in mind that it is the effort between Oise and Somme which must be got ready as soon as possible.

The two attached Notes[1] give general directives referring to each of these operations.

F. FOCH.

[1] Not reproduced.

Appendix III

MESSAGES SENT BY GENERAL DUCHENE, COMMANDING THE FRENCH SIXTH ARMY, 8.45 A.M., 27TH MAY 1918, AT THE BEGINNING OF THE BATTLE OF THE AISNE.

(Translation from F.O.A. VI (ii.) Annexe 385)

To G.O.C.'s 61st Division and XI. Corps:

The artillery should remain as long as there is any infantry in front of it. In the present case, it should fight by echelons to defend the Intermediate Position.

Hold on for the moment like scabs (teignes), but with prudence as the necessities of the battle demand. Echelon the artillery.

To G.O.C. 22nd Division:

Try and keep touch, using your divisional squadron, the only means which you still have; make the artillery retirement by echelons. Hold the Intermediate Position to give time for divisions to arrive.

Command by the use of officers and men on foot and on horse.

To the G.O.C. XI. Corps:

Organize the battle, if the infantry has to retire, by withdrawing the artillery by echelons.

To the G.O.C. 21st Division:

Order the colonel of the 146th to cross the water with his three battalions, and occupy the Intermediate Position.

To the G.O.C. XI. Corps:

To sum up: Hold all you can, if possible the Intermediate Position. Echelon the artillery.

APPENDIX IV

OPERATION ORDER OF THE FRENCH XI. CORPS [1]

(Translation)

XI. Corps
3rd Bureau
No. 1244/3

H.Qrs. 27th May 1918.
Handed to despatch rider
12 noon.

GENERAL ORDER No. 105

First Part

I. The corps has received orders to transfer the defence to Map 2. to the 2nd Position.

II. For this purpose, the 157th, 39th and 74th Divisions come under my orders to defend the 2nd Position; supported by the 22nd, 21st and 61st Divisions they will counter-attack any enemy body which may cross the Aisne or penetrate into the 2nd Position.

III. The 157th and 22nd Divisions will defend the 2nd Position between the eastern boundary of the corps (1 km. west of Maizy) and the bridge of Cys la Commune—Chavonne (exclusive).

The sector will be divided into two half-sectors; the 22nd Division taking the right as far as Villers en Prayères inclusive.

Command Post : 157th Division, Courcelles
,,   ,,   22nd   ,,   Paars.

IV. The 39th Division with the 21st Division will hold the sector included between the bridge of Cys la Commune (inclusive) and Condé (inclusive) where it will make liaison with the left sector.

The 21st Division will occupy the left half-sector separated from the right half-sector (39th Division) by the line : Vailly—Chassemy—Ciry Salsogne road, allotted to the 21st Division, which should keep a strong detachment in Condé in order to ensure liaison with the 74th Division.

Command Post : 21st Division, Sermoise.
,,   ,,   39th   ,,   Couvrelles.

V. The left sector will be held by the 74th and 61st Divisions from Condé (liaison will be 21st Division) to the western boundary of the sector, that is to say : Neuville sur Margival (inclusive)—Clamency (exclusive), where liaison with the 151st Division will be made.

The 61st Division will occupy the left half-sector separated from the right half-sector of the 74th Division by the line :

---

[1] Sent to British IX. Corps " for information ".

Maubeuge—Pont Rouge—Nanteuil La Fosse road, and will make liaison with the 151st Division.

The 2nd Field Artillery Brigade, whose arrival has been notified, will be put at the orders of the 61st Division as soon as it appears.

VI. The troops of the fresh divisions (157th, 39th, 74th) will hand over the responsibility for guarding the half-sectors to the tired divisions as the latter are gradually reconstituted, in order to ensure their defence. The generals commanding the divisions concerned will arrange the matter between themselves. In the meantime until this is carried out, the responsibility for the command of each sector will rest with the G.O.C. of the fresh division.

The G.O.C. XI. Corps
DE MAUD'HUY.

APPENDIX V

OPERATION ORDER OF THE FRENCH SIXTH ARMY FOR THE 28TH MAY 1918

(Translation)

GENERAL OPERATION ORDER No. 3101

H.Qrs. 27th May 1918.

No. 887/3

Map 2. The mission for all remains unchanged : hold on and as soon as possible attack any troops which have crossed the 2nd Position.

XXX. Corps : no change of orders already given.

XI. Corps : no change of orders given, will cover Soissons at all costs on the 2nd Position.

XXI. Corps : will bar the Vesle where the Germans are along it, and defend it to the last man, whilst keeping all the portions held beyond it.

Will continue to hold all the ground possible in front, maintaining liaison with the XI. Corps on the left and the British IX. Corps on the right.

As soon as the corps has collected its resources, it will attack and throw the enemy who is threatening the Vesle back on the Aisne.

The 43rd Division is arriving at Ste. Restitue [4 miles N.N.W. of Fère en Tardenois] by bus by the route Compiègne —Vic sur Aisne during the course of the night ; the G.O.C. XXI. Corps will send orders for it to Ste. Restitue.

British IX. Corps : will continue to defend its position maintaining close liaison on the left with the XI. Corps and on the right with the 45th Division, and covering all approaches to and passages of the Vesle.

45th Division : keeping in liaison with the left of the [French] Fourth Army, will defend its position connecting its left to the right of the British IX. Corps.

GENERAL DUCHÊNE.

[no time.]

APPENDIX VI

OPERATION ORDER OF THE FRENCH SIXTH ARMY

(Translation)

GENERAL OPERATION ORDER 3115.

H.Q. 28th May 1918.

I.   The enemy has continued his pressure to-day along our whole front ; detachments entered Soissons this evening ; the Mont de Soissons has been occupied and Arcis le Ponsart has been entered. It is more than ever necessary to stop all movements to the rear ; the imperative watchword for all, already given, remains good : hold on " coûte que coûte ".

Map 2. Sketch 14.

II. The XXX. Corps will maintain its actual front, will form a right defensive flank for protection between the Ailette and the Aisne, and on the other flank will keep very close liaison with the left of the XI. Corps towards Pommiers. It will direct all its available reserves to its right and prevent, at all costs, any infiltration of the enemy on the right bank of the Aisne which would threaten its rear.

III. The XI. Corps, having at its disposal the troops actually under its orders : 170th, 61st, 74th, 39th and 1st [headquarters and two regiments] Divisions, and in addition the Moroccan Division (N.Q. Pommiers), will hold the front from the Aisne (near Pommiers ; liaison with the XXX. Corps) to Cuiry Housse (exclusive).

Its first business is to try and defend Soissons, and, at a minimum, its imperative task, to prevent the enemy from debouching from the town and from creeping forward either by the southern valley of the Aisne or by the valley of the Crise. For this purpose it will occupy strongly the Montagne de Paris, facing North and East.

IV. The XXI. Corps will hold the front from Cuiry Housse (inclusive ; liaison with XI. Corps) to Arcis en Ponsart (inclusive), having at its disposal all the troops already in line on this front : 1 regiment of the 1st Division, 43rd Division, portions of the I. Cavalry Corps and of the 1st Division already in line on this front, and in addition the 4th Division (Headquarters Grand Rozoy).

V. General Féraud, whose headquarters will be in Villers Agron, will hold the front from Arcis en Ponsart (exclusive) to the western boundary of Branscourt (boundary to be settled with the British IX. Corps), having at his disposal his own [I. Cavalry] corps staff, 13th Division (less portions in the line of the XXI. Corps), 154th Division and 20th Division.

VI. The British IX. Corps and the 45th Division will keep the fronts and tasks already allotted to them.

VII. An annexe attached to this order [1] fixes the lateral boundaries of the corps zones and their rear limits, as well as the areas allotted to the units which are to be relieved (21st, 22nd and 157th Divisions) for reconstitution and are to be reconstituted with utmost urgency in order to permit of their return to the line as soon as possible.

VIII. The instructions in this order will enter into force at midday 29th May as far as modifications of sector commands are concerned, it being understood that the Moroccan Division and the 4th Division are at the disposal of XI. and XXI. Corps as soon as the present order is received.

GENERAL DUCHÊNE.

[no time]

APPENDIX VII

OPERATION ORDER NO. 111 OF THE IX. CORPS

Headquarters IX. Corps,
28th May 1918.

Sketch 15.

1. G.O.C. 50th Division will hand over to G.O.C. 8th Division responsibility for his front and for all fighting troops in action which are under his command. On handing over, 50th Divisional Headquarters will move to Jonquery to-night.

2. The 50th Division, less fighting troops handed over to 8th

[1] Not reproduced.

APPENDICES VII AND VIII 347

Division, will collect to-night in the Area Jonquery—Cuisles—Baslieux sous Chatillon where they will re-organize.

3. All troops of 25th Division, less fighting troops, attached to 8th and 21st Divisions will be collected in the area Villers Argon—Ste. Gemme-Goussancourt. Divisional Headquarters Goussancourt.

4. (*a*). 8th Division Report Centre opens to-night at Romigny.
   (*b*). 21st Division Report Centre is at Sarcy.
   (*c*). 52nd Sqdn. R.A.F. is at Athenay.

5. 19th Division is being placed under orders of IX. Corps and will be concentrated to-night and to-morrow in IX. Corps Reserve in the area Chaumuzy—Bligny—Chambrecy. H.Q. 19th Division Chaumuzy.

6. D.A. & Q.M.G. IX. Corps is arranging for stragglers' posts on the line Courmais—Chaumuzy—La Neuville aux Larris—Cuchery—Baslieux sous Chatillon—Ste. Gemme.
All stragglers will be collected by 50th and 25th Divisions.

7. IX. Corps School and Reinforcement Camp will be at Ste. Gemme.

8. Acknowledge.

W. J. MAXWELL-SCOTT,
Br.-General,
General Staff, IX. Corps.

[no time

APPENDIX VIII

GENERAL FOCH'S MEMORANDUM OF THE 1st JUNE 1918

(Translation)

I.

The Allied Armies are engaged in a defensive battle with forces inferior to those of the enemy.

They can only obtain a successful issue by the intervention of their reserves which must therefore be kept as large as possible.

On March 21st the situation of both armies was the following :

APPENDIX VIII

ALLIES.		ENEMY.
American	4 [1]	
Belgian	12	
British	57	
French	99	
Portuguese	2	
	174	195

that is an inferiority of 21 Divisions on the side of the Allies. On May 30th, the situation was modified as follows :—

ALLIES.		ENEMY.
American	4 [2]	
Belgian	12	
British	53 [3]	
French	103 [4]	
Italian	2	
	174	207

That is an inferiority of 33 Divisions on the Allied side.

This inferiority is made worse by the fact that the 12 Belgian Divisions, whose action is limited to their own front, and in spite of the extension of this front as far as YPRES, are only opposed by 7 German Divisions — which fact amounts to this : viz. 162 Allied Divisions are opposed to 200 German Divisions, thus giving the enemy the advantage, to the extent of 38 Divisions.

On the other hand, the increasing development of the battle, the extension of the fronts of attack, compel the Allies to engage on these fronts and therefore to keep there an ever increasing number of units, with the result that there is a corresponding decrease of units in reserve.

The grave danger which threatens the Allies to-day is to see this number of units being reduced to such an extent that it may be impossible to keep sufficient reserves to meet fresh attacks which are sure to take place.

Also to maintain the necessary strength to feed the battle and insure the relief of tired units.

It is therefore of vital importance, that at all costs, the total number of French and British Divisions should be maintained and that the whole of the Allied forces should be progressively and rapidly increased by the entry into the line of American forces.

II.

The measures taken or to be taken in order to achieve these results are considered below :—

[1] Divisions with full strength.
[2] Divisions up to strength, to which the infantry of 3 Divisions should be added.
[3] +4 (2 from Italy ; 2 from the East) −8 broken up.
[4] +4 from Italy.

APPENDIX VIII

1st   As regards the FRENCH ARMY.

France, in spite of her shortage in man power has done everything in her power to avoid any reduction in the number of her Divisions. The measures taken are summed up :—

(*a*) Breaking up of battalions or regiments in excess of the normal number of battalions or regiments which standard units consist of, whether this number is attained by means of French units or Allied ones (Black, American, Polish or the Tczech-Slav regiments).

(*b*) Delay in making up to strength units which have been engaged so as to keep a sufficient margin, in order that the return to their units of the slightly wounded, evacuated in the Army zone, shall not create any surplus of strength in some formations.

(*c*) Utilization of creole and colonial natives to replace French effectives of the same importance, not as drafts.

The measures in (*a*), (*b*), and (*c*) are taken not successively but simultaneously, so as not to be reduced at a given moment to break up units, in order to make others up to strength, or to stop the creation of new artillery formations with a view of keeping up the effectives of artillery units in existence.

(*d*) Increasing man power by :
  The intensive training of class 1919.
  Combing out of men employed in factories on national work.

These measures, of which some may be called expedients, will enable France to keep all her Divisions, provided that the total casualties of the French Army from May 1st to October 1st do not amount to more than 500,000.

But one realizes what the cost is !

2nd   As regards the BRITISH ARMY.

As early as the end of January, 1918, the attention of the SUPREME WAR COUNCIL was drawn, in a pressing manner, to the insufficiency of the man power obtained by British recruiting in order to keep up the British Armies in France.

At the same Session of the Supreme War Council, the Field-Marshal, Commander-in-Chief of the British Armies, stated that if he had to meet an important offensive, he would have to consider the breaking up of 30 of his Divisions, owing to shortage in effectives.

In fact, before March 21st, no measures had been taken to increase these effectives, with the result that in the month of April, Marshal Haig had to break up successively 9 Divisions.

On May 14th, the attention of the Marshal was called by General FOCH on the necessity of reconstituting these units. The Field-Marshal agreed and applied to the War Office for drafts to be sent especially for the purpose.

The Chief of the Imperial Staff gave hopes for the sending of the following drafts :—4 to 5,000 men belonging to class A., 15,000 men belonging to class B., and 50,000 men of classes not stated.

In fact, from May 1st to 31st, there only arrived in France 28,000 [1] men of class A., and 7,000 of class B.

Only one of the 9 Divisions which were to be broken up was kept up. None of the other 8 were reconstituted. What is more, owing

---

[1] That is, the number provided normally.

APPENDIX VIII

to heavy losses sustained by units of the 9th British Corps on the AISNE, the British General Staff contemplates breaking up 2 other Divisions, which would mean the suppression of 10 Divisions.

So that, at the moment of a decisive effort, on the part of the enemy, the strength of the British Army is decreasing day by day. It even decreases more rapidly than that of the American Army increases. (The entry of the American Army into the line can only be made progressively.) The result is a decrease in the total strength of the Allies.

This consequence is exceptionally grave; it may mean the loss of the war. The most drastic and quickest measures must be taken in order to avert this danger which has been pointed out for some considerable time. That is to say : British effectives must be supplied without delay, either by the home country or by Armies operating in distant countries, in order to make up the total number of British Divisions.

3rd As regards the AMERICAN ARMY.

The programme of American arrivals in France for the month of June was decided at ABBEVILLE on May 2nd.

It includes, as that of May, the transportation by priority of 120,000 men (infantry strength of 6 divisions).

When this programme is carried out, there will be 24 Divisions landed in France (totally, or infantry only).

The programme of transportation for July is not yet decided on.

Circumstances which demanded for May and June the arrival of infantry before anything else, still demand to-day and more imperiously than ever, that during the month of July, infantry would be sent first and that the strength of this infantry should be increased from 120 to 200,000 men; that is, the infantry of 10 new Divisions.

A similar programme is contemplated for the month of August.

But, after having fulfilled the immediate requirements of the Coalition, one must consider further.

As soon as the Programme for July is realised, 34 Divisions will be in France, that is to say almost the total number of Divisions for the formation of which provision has been made by the American Government (42 ?).

The United States, who, when they joined the war, expressed their will to obtain the victory and who have already shown, by the results obtained in May (184,000 men transported or on the way) their energy in the realisation of this main idea, the United States cannot limit their efforts to this programme.

They must now consider a greater effort in order to pursue a war, which will last a long time. For this object, they must contemplate a progressive increase of their army, up to 100 Divisions, and achieve this result by using their available shipping.

If they do so, then we can expect to turn the scales in our favour as regards the strength of the opposing Armies and thus insure victory for the Allies.

Under these circumstances, the Supreme War Council is asked to decide:

1st. The total number of French Divisions will be maintained in accordance with means provided for.

2nd. The total number of British Divisions will be made up

again without any delay, by means of resources drawn from the Home Country and from Armies fighting on fronts out of France : these Divisions will be kept up to strength, by means of resources obtained through the carrying into effect of the new laws.

3rd. To ask the UNITED STATES

(a) For the transportation over to France, during July with priority of transport of the infantry of 10 more Divisions (200,000 infantrymen or machine gunners). A similar programme must be considered for August.
(b) To undertake, at once, the increasing of their Army up to 100 Divisions, the transportation of which will be carried on without a stop so as to utilize all available tonnage : the training of these troops will be intensified in France as well as in United States.

The General Commander-in-Chief,
The Allied Armies.
F. FOCH.

APPENDIX IX

INSTRUCTIONS OF THE SECRETARY OF STATE FOR WAR TO THE FIELD-MARSHAL COMMANDING-IN-CHIEF, BRITISH ARMIES IN FRANCE

(WAR OFFICE, 21st JUNE 1918.)

In consequence of the concurrence of His Majesty's Government in the appointment of General Foch as Commander-in-Chief of the Allied Forces on the Western Front, it has become necessary to modify in some respects the instructions given to you in War Office letter No. 121/7711 dated 28th December, 1915.[1]

(1) The general objects to be pursued by the British Armies in France remain the same as those set forth in the first and second paragraphs of that letter.

(2) In pursuit of those objects you will carry out loyally any instructions issued to you by the Commander-in-Chief of the Allied Forces. At the same time, if any order given by him appears to you to imperil the British Army, it is agreed between the Allied Governments that you should be at liberty to appeal to the British Government before executing such order. While it is hoped that the necessity for such an appeal may seldom, if ever, arise, you will not hesitate in cases of grave emergency to avail yourself of your right to make it.

---

[1] See "1916" Vol. I., Appendix 5.

(3) It is the desire of His Majesty's Government to keep the British forces under your command as far as possible together. If at any time the Allied Commander-in-Chief finds it necessary to transfer any portion of the British troops to the French area in order to release French troops for purposes of roulement, it should be distinctly understood that this is only a temporary arrangement, and that as soon as practicable the troops thus detached should be re-united to the main body of the British forces.

(4) You will afford to the American troops forming part of the Allied Armies in France such assistance in training, equipment, or administrative matters as may from time to time be required of you by the Commander-in-Chief of the Allied Forces.

(5) Subject to any special directions you may receive from the Commander-in-Chief of the Allied Forces, the principles laid down in the fourth paragraph of War Office letter No. 121/7711 of the 28th December 1915, are to be regarded as still holding good.

(6) The fifth, sixth and seventh paragraphs of that letter are maintained in their entirety.

MILNER.

APPENDIX X

GENERAL FOCH'S NOTE OF THE 16TH JUNE 1918

(Translation)

The results obtained by the Germans in their " attaques brusquées " executed since the 21st March show the necessity to adapt our methods of defence to this kind of attack.

In order to determine these methods, it is necessary first to recall the German procedure, which was practically uniform in all these attacks.

1—Attack.

The German method of attack is characterized by:
- surprise;
- violence;
- rapidity of execution;
- manœuvre;
- depth of penetration sought.

I. Surprise is obtained by the shortness of the artillery preparation (3 to 4 hours); and by the deployment of the attacking divisions at the very last moment, the approach marches of these divisions being effected by night and across country.

Until the night preceding the attack, nothing is therefore

changed in the habitual appearance of the front ; calm reigns there ; the divisions in line remain the same.

The attack always takes place at dawn, the infantry being preceded by a barrage which includes a strong proportion of smoke shell ; as a result of the cloud thus produced, our infantry and even our artillery do not perceive the enemy until he is within a few yards of them.

II. Violence is obtained by the intensity of the bombardment, all calibres and all kinds of shell being employed simultaneously, to a depth of 4,000 to 5,000 yards ; and by the attack in mass of the infantry, which during the artillery preparation is assembled 200 or 300 yards from the first line to be stormed.

III. The rapidity of execution is due to the speed of the infantry.

As soon as it has stormed the first position, it echelons itself in depth and shakes out—the units in front move as fast as possible against the successive objectives which have been assigned to them, troubling neither about the protection of their flanks nor mopping up behind them, these matters being attended to by other units.

The allotment of successive objectives does not mean any halt at these objectives, which simply mark the direction to be followed.

During its advance, the infantry is first protected by the artillery rolling barrage, after that by the artillery and trench mortars which accompany it. The infantry also makes large use of its own fire, particularly of light machine guns.

If an infantry unit strikes against resistance which it cannot overcome by its own means, it halts and is immediately passed by the units on either side of it, these having the duty of capturing by envelopment the strong point that resists.

IV. The Germans usually detail their best divisions for the centre of the attack, so as to have all the chances of producing a rapid and deep advance in the central sector.

The manœuvre consists of rapidly enlarging the breach thus made by attacks on the sides of the breach.

The frontal attack is nevertheless continued whilst these flank attacks are being developed.

V. The depth of the penetration is obtained by the rapid and resolute march of the troops on the objectives fixed beforehand and a long way ahead.

This has the effect of promptly disorganizing a defence which is not entirely complete, by capturing, in these objectives, the essential points of its organization.

Such a method of attack has succeeded when it has only encountered feeble resistance on account of the occupying troops being insufficient in number. It has then obtained important results both tactical and material.

It has failed, with heavy losses, when it encountered energetic troops, sufficiently numerous and suitably disposed in depth.

In any case, it is indispensable to arrange our forces so that they will be in a position to stop an enemy attack, and

2—Defence.

I. Surprise can only be avoided by having information about the enemy.

It is this information therefore that must be sought by every possible means and on every part of the front.

In spite of the precautions taken by the enemy, certain indications may always reveal the preparation of an attack: increase in the number of hospitals, dumps of ammunition, development of the communications of all kinds etc.

The Air Force operating day and night should discover these indications.

In addition, prisoners and deserters always give important information.

The Command, if it exercises vigilance and insists upon the activity of the troops in the line, ought not to be taken unawares.

But, whatever knowledge there may be of the projects of the enemy, the shortness of the preparation and the suddenness of the attack make it certain that troops which are not close up cannot be utilized at the beginning of the battle. The first position, badly damaged by fire, cannot probably hold for its whole length, and the second position will be easily carried by the enemy, in his rapid advance, if it is not at the moment sufficiently strongly held by the troops charged with its defence.

This means that the assault should be met by the troops already in place, echeloned in the first and second positions, and by their immediate reserves.

How much resistance will be offered by the troops actually occupying the position at the moment of the assault, depends on the course of the battle, that is to say whether it comes to an end immediately or develops further.

It should be noted, that the violence of the bombardment is such that from its very commencement all communication between the Command and the troops becomes impossible; and that any decision taken at this moment for the direction of the troops in occupation cannot be possibly carried out.

From the above it results that the Commander must:

(a) As soon as an attack is foreseen, allot to the threatened sector and send up such forces that the first and second positions can be occupied simultaneously by sufficient effectives before the attack.

Better send effectives in good time, that is to say before the attack, than send a greater number at a later period.

(b) Assign to the troops in occupation the sole duty of resisting where they stand, no unit having the right to retire, even if it is outflanked by the enemy. These troops are the garrison with the duty of defending the positions which they hold to the last man.

It is only after having made sure that the enemy has been

stopped in front of our positions that general counter-attacks can be executed, and by troops reserved for that purpose.[1]

(c) But whatever foresight has been exercised and however appropriate are the measures laid down in the Defence Scheme, they do not form more than preparatory measures, are, as it were, merely taking guard.

As soon as the attack has begun it is the duty of the Commander to take charge of the battle, rapidly obtaining information as to its development and moving the troops at his disposal in good time.

Position warfare comes to an end when a position has been taken; the war of movement then resumes all its rights and all its exigencies; in particular it demands rapid decision as well as rapid execution.

It is then the business of the Commander to make his plans for the employment of the troops which will be sent up to him as reinforcements, in such a manner that his decision of the subject of this employment may be taken as soon as the first results of the attack become known to him.

The first object to be sought is to hold up the enemy on the flanks of his initial progress; it will thus at the same time be possible to limit the depth of his advance, because an advance cannot be deep if it is kept narrow.

The greater part of the forces should therefore be assigned to supporting the flanks of the breach, the rest serving to contain the enemy in front and to stop him. (Second object.)

By making his decision on this subject at the beginning of the attack and in accordance with a preconceived idea, by communicating his decision without delay to his subordinates by a precise order, by sticking to his decision in spite of the fluctuations of the combat, and by avoiding the dispersal of his forces in every direction, the Commander will be certain to check the progress of the enemy before it has had serious consequences.

He can then, in the minimum of time, proceed to execute counter-attacks, notably on the flanks, which will re-establish the situation, by using all the troops which remain at his disposal to block one part or other of the breach.

In a word, our Commanders should prepare a defensive battle which corresponds to the practice of the enemy.

This method aims before all at disorganizing us and not leaving us time to make judicious dispositions; it will not be effective if our Commanders have made up their minds beforehand on an appropriate line of conduct, if they have drawn up a programme which can be executed as rapidly and surely as possible, and if then they have the firmness to stick to it and never lose control of the battle for an instant.

This firmness in the Command will be instantly communicated to the troops; it is the security that the most difficult tasks will be carried out.

FOCH.

---

[1] It is of course understood that besides these general counter-attacks, partial counter-attacks still remain indicated for driving out an enemy who has succeeded in penetrating into the position of resistance.

APPENDIX XI

OPERATION ORDER OF FRENCH TENTH ARMY
22ND JULY 1918
(Translation)

I.

Sketches 14, 15.
During the 21st July the Tenth Army attacked on its whole front with great vigour. In spite of strong enemy counter-attacks carried out by fresh divisions, we maintained our line in the western outskirts of Buzancy and Contremain and at le Plessier Huleu; we are in front of Oulchy la Ville.

II.

After having reorganized its divisions during this day, 22nd July, and advanced its artillery, the Tenth Army will attack tomorrow the 23rd.
Principal objective : Orme du Grand Rozoy.

III. Mission of the Corps.

XX. Corps . Capture of the plateau Buzancy, Taux. Investment of the Bois d'Hartennes. Further objective of the attack : Maast et Violaine.

XXX. Corps . Will make its principal effort by le Plessier Huleu against Orme du Grand Rozoy.
Principal objective : Bois d'Arcy.

XI. Corps . Will join its action to that of the XXX. Corps by seizing la Butte Chalmont. It will further if possible seek to manoeuvre by the flank with the help of the artillery of the Sixth Army.
Further objective : Saponay.

IV.

Corps Commanders will make their own arrangements for artillery preparation. Attack at 5 A.M.

V.

The action of the I. Corps against the plateau Vauxbuin will be carried out when in the opinion of the Corps Commander all is ready, after artillery preparation.

VI. Tanks.

XX. Corps . The reconstituted groupements Chanoine and Herlaut. (about 37 tanks.)

XXX. Corps	The reconstituted units of groupement X. and of the 1st, 2nd, and 3rd battalions of light tanks. (about 62 tanks.) Commandant Velpry, commander of 20th Tank Wing, will co-ordinate the action of the tanks of the two Corps. Make large use of smoke shell.

MANGIN.
General Commanding Tenth Army.

[No time.]
HERGAULT.
Chief of the Staff.

APPENDIX XII

LETTER FROM GENERAL FOCH COMMANDER-IN-CHIEF OF THE ALLIED ARMIES TO THE GENERAL COMMANDING-IN-CHIEF THE ARMIES OF THE NORTH AND NORTH-EAST

(Translation)

G.Q.G.A.
23rd July 1918.

Today 23rd July, the battle has slowed down as a result of the tactics employed by the enemy.

Sketch 15.

It is now important to recover by vigorous action and without delay the control of the operations, in order to derive from the battle now in progress all the results which it may still produce.

The tactics employed by the Germans consist:
  (a) of making their flanks very strong, using fresh divisions supported by artillery for this purpose.
  (b) of slowing down our frontal advance, by the help of rear guards provided with numerous machine guns.

The action which we must take must therefore aim at:
  (a) driving in the enemy flanks, or at least one of his flanks;
  (b) pushing ahead elsewhere, as quickly as possible.

The means to be employed in order to realise these objects are:
  (i) mounting a powerful attack against one of the flanks: in conformity with the directive No. 2206 of 19th July, this flank is still the one being attacked by the Tenth Army.

All available means should therefore be allotted to this Army; but these means may be too limited to be effective if they are applied on the whole front of this Army. The consequent result is therefore that this Army should concentrate them on a part of its front, in order to execute a powerful attack in a particularly important direction, the region North of Fère en Tardenois.

Supported on the right by the Sixth Army, having concentrated on its left wing all forces available, this attack may result in the enemy being obliged to evacuate, under difficult conditions, all the region south of Fère en Tardenois. Thus it is necessary:

(a) to allot to the Tenth Army all the means still available (fresh divisions, artillery, tanks);

(b) to instruct this Army to prepare and execute as soon as possible an attack combined with the left of the Sixth Army and directed against the region of Fère en Tardenois, under the conditions of concentration laid down above.

(ii) As a result of the allotment of all available means to the Tenth Army, the Fifth Army will have only limited means at its disposal. To disperse these means along the whole front of this Army would only result in wearing out its forces, without appreciable result.

It is therefore necessary, for the Fifth Army, to execute successive operations, concentrating the means available for the benefit for each of them in turn and determining the order of succession in such a way that each of them places the following one in a favourable situation. Thus an advance on the heights north of the Ardre will facilitate a later attack south of that river, and this latter in its turn will oblige the enemy to evacuate the region north of the Marne.

This succession in the operations is all the more necessary for the Fifth Army, as the nature of the ground over which it has to operate renders difficult an advance against an enemy provided with very numerous machine guns. On such ground, our infantry cannot attack with success unless it is supported by a sufficient number of tanks, and these, being limited in number, will not be effective unless they are concentrated.

(iii) It is of course understood that these conditions of action of the Tenth and Fifth Armies must not reduce the activity of the divisions which are not dealt with above, whether they belong to the Tenth, to the Fifth or any other Army.

FOCH.

Appendix XIII

OPERATION ORDER No. 8 OF THE 15TH DIVISION

28th July, 1918.

1. The 15th Division (less Artillery) will take over the front held by the 87th Division and a portion of the front held by the 12th Division. **Sketch 14.**

   The 87th Division (less Artillery) will take over the front now held by the 15th Division.

   New boundaries are shown on the attached map.[1]

2. Tonight, 28th/29th July—
   1 Battalion 46th Inf. Bde. will relieve 1 battalion 67th Regiment, and 1 Company, 54th Regiment, 12th Division.
   1 Battalion 46th Inf. Bde., will relieve 1 battalion 72nd Regiment, 87th Division.
   1 Section " C " Company 15th Battn. M.G.C. will move with each of the above battalions, 46th Inf. Bde. and will be under the orders of O's C. those battalions.
   Battalions 46th Inf. Bde. will come under the orders of Regimental Commander on arrival in the respective regimental areas.

3. 2 Battalions, 72nd Regiment will move tonight to the areas vacated by the two battalions 46th Inf. Bde. and come under the orders of G.O.C. 46th Inf. Bde.

4. The following is a forecast of moves and reliefs which are to take place on the 29th/30th July :—
   - (a) 1 battalion 46th Inf. Bde. will relieve 1 battalion 72nd Regiment. Command of the front held by troops 46th Infantry Brigade will pass to G.O.C. 46th Inf. Bde. from O's.C. 72nd and 67th Regiments at an hour to be notified later.
   - (b) 45th Inf. Bde. will be relieved by troops of the 87th Division and will take over that portion of the front held by 156th and 91st Regiments, 87th Division.
   - (c) 44th Inf. Bde. will be relieved by troops of the 87th Division and will be in Divisional Reserve in the new area.

5. 15th Battalion M.G.C. (less 2 sections) will be withdrawn from the line on the night 29th/30th July and will be allotted tasks in the new sector under arrangements to be made by O.C. 15th Battalion M.G.C.

6. (a) R.E. will move under orders of C.R.E.
   (b) 9th Gordons (Pioneers) will be allotted an area in the new sector which will be notified later.
   (c) A.D.M.S. will arrange to relieve medical units in the 87th Divisional area.

7. All moves and reliefs are to be completed by 3 A.M. 30th July,

[1] Not reproduced.

at which hour the command of new Divisional Sector will pass to G.O's.C. concerned.

8. Divisional H.Q. will remain at the Caves 400. N.W. of COEUVRES. G.S. and R.A. report centre will be established in the trench system near LA GLAUX FME, 400 yards N. of DOMMIERS at an hour to be notified later.

9. G.O.C. will hold a conference of B.G's.C. Infantry Brigades, at a time and place to be notified later.

10. Acknowledge.

W. H. DIGGLE.
Lieut.-Colonel,
General Staff, 15th Division.

Issued at 11.0 P.M.

APPENDIX XIV

TRANSLATION OF A CAPTURED GERMAN OPERATION ORDER

Guard Ersatz Div. I.a.1515 Op.   31-7-18   11 A.M.

SECRET
DIVISIONAL ORDER

Sketch 15.

1. The Division will evacuate its sector keeping in touch with its flank divisions at midnight X/Y day. At this time the front line will be abandoned and the movement to the rear will commence.

2. The O.C. Artillery will give detailed orders so that the first batteries can begin to move at night fall. The time table must be arranged in precise detail so that the batteries can follow one another at very short intervals. Experienced and energetic officers must be detailed to superintend the movement of the columns.

In order to veil the departure the artillery will fire until the last moment. Several batteries must be left in position after midnight.

The batteries detailed for accompanying Infantry Regiments will remain with those Regiments.

3. The Guard Ersatz Infantry Brigade will organize the retreat of the Infantry Regiments, including the 29th Machine Gun Marksmen Detachment which is attached to it, and also the 7th Trench Mortar Company. It will also arrange for the movement of the forward detachment of the 18th Infantry Division.

APPENDIX XIV

The 7th Trench Mortar Company will, as far as possible, be withdrawn during the night 31st July-1st August (it will be warned by telephone). March route will be via BRAINE to the Forest to the West of ST. AUDEBERT Farm [*i.e.* N. of the Vesle]. The Brigade can, if circumstances permit, withdraw the Machine Gun Marksmen Detachment before the date fixed.

4. The Infantry will hold itself in readiness at midnight to move on the road LAUNOY–LES CROUTTES, and to the South of LAUNOY WOOD. [Area S.E. and E. of Droizy].

    The forward detachment of the 18th Infantry Division will be ready to move at 10.45 P.M., the head of the column near BOVETTES. As the Heavy Artillery passes through LES CROUTTES it will follow very closely behind.

    The departure of the Artillery must be arranged so that the Infantry can follow the road leading from LAUNOY at midnight. If there is any delay, which must be expected, the Infantry must continue its march alongside the roads.

    The Infantry must allow batteries which have been firing up to the last moment to come into the column if they should not arrive until late.

    I would again remind Commanders that in order to obviate the crowding of roads, all vehicles which are not indispensable should be immediately sent back, and that the strictest march discipline must be observed.

5. The Infantry retreat from the battle position will be made under the protection of small rear-guards, who will follow immediately the retreat has commenced.

    Small garrisons are to be left in the line N.E. of LAUNOY, western edge of the Wood east of LAUNOY, the road from LAUNOY to BUSSY LEBRAS Farm; these detachments must stop the enemy after our retirement and must not withdraw until hard pressed. They will keep touch with the detachments of flank divisions who will operate on the same heights.

6. The Artillery will move without stopping to North of the VESLE and the Infantry at least to the area CERCEUIL [1 mile S. of Augy] and AUGY; no halt will be made before reaching these points. Precautions must be taken against enemy aircraft.

7. The pass-word of the 10th Infantry Division when crossing the " ZIETHEN " position is " HOCHAUFEN ".

8. The removal of the most recently wounded will be made by red cross vehicles, which must be held in readiness beforehand according to a separate order issued.

9. In the new sector north of the VESLE, the 6th Guard Infantry Regiment will be on the right, the 399th Infantry Regiment in the centre, and 7th Guard Infantry Regiment on the left. Maps (1/25,000) will be distributed showing the exact boundaries after a reconnaissance of the area. The O.C. Artillery will send in his plans for the distribution of his guns.

10. The General Staff of the Guard Ersatz Infantry Brigade will first of all on " Y " day have their headquarters near St. AUDEBERT Farm, which will be in telephonic communication with Divisional Headquarters at MONT-DE-GONFREMONT, via the telephone exchange of the Corps at CHAVONNE.

11. The G.O.C. of the Division and the O.C. Artillery will be kept continually informed by telephone of the progress of the retreat.

12. O.C. Signals will despatch all available signal detachments to the new divisional area. The details of the telephonic organization will be prepared.

13. A separate order will be issued in regard to the move of the 5th Squadron of the 2nd Guard Uhlan Regiment; also for the Pioneer Battalion and the Sanitary Section. On the evening of " X " day the General Staff of the Division will move to Hauptstrasse 40, Braine, where the signal detachment will report on " Y " day at 11 a.m. During the afternoon of " Y " day the General Staff will move to its new headquarters at Mont-de-Gonfremont.

Issued to all units, including those attached, down to regiments.

Appendix XV

ORDER OF THE DAY BY GENERAL BERTHELOT

Q.G., le 30 juillet 1918

Ve Armée
État-Major
3e Bureau
No. 1863/3

Ordre Général No. 63

Au moment que le XXII. C.A. britannique est appelé à quitter la Ve Armée, le Général Commandant l'Armée lui exprime toute la reconnaissance et toute l'admiration qu'ont mérité les hauts faits qu'il vient d'accomplir.

A peine débarqué, tenant à honneur de participer à la contre-offensive victorieuse qui venait d'arrêter la furieuse ruée de l'ennemi sur la Marne et commençait à le rejeter en désordre vers le Nord, précipitant ses mouvements, réduisant a l'extrême la durée de ses reconnaissances, le XXII. C.A. s'est jeté avec ardeur dans la mêlée.

Poussant sans répit ses efforts, harcelant, talonnant l'ennemi, il a, pendant 10 jours successifs d'après combats, fait sienne cette vallée de l'Ardre largement arrosée de son sang.

Grâce au courage héroïque et à la ténacité proverbiale des fils de la Grande Bretagne, les efforts continus et répétés de ce brave Corps d'Armée n'ont pas été vains.

21 officiers, plus de 1,300 soldats prisonniers, 140 mitrailleuses, 40 canons enlevés à l'ennemi, dont 4 divisions ont été successivement malmenées et refoulées, la haute vallée de l'Ardre reconquise avec les

hauteurs qui la dominent au Nord et au Sud, tel est le bilan de la participation britannique à l'effort de la Ve Armée.

Écossais de la Montagne, sous le commandement du Général Carter-Campbell, Commandant la 51e Division.

Enfants du Yorkshire, sous le commandement du Général Braithwaite, Commandant la 62e Division.

Cavaliers Néo-Zélandais et Australiens.

Vous tous, officiers et soldats du 22e C.A., si brillamment commandés par le Général Sir A. Godley, vous venez d'ajouter une page glorieuse à votre histoire.

Marfaux, Chaumuzy, Montagne de Bligny, ces noms prestigieux pourront être écrits en lettres d'or dans les annales de vos régiments.

Vos amis Français se souviendront avec émotion de votre brillante bravoure et de parfaite camaraderie de combat.

Le Général Commandant la Ve Armée
BERTHELOT.

APPENDIX XVI

LETTER FROM GENERAL FAYOLLE, COMMANDING G.A.R., TO FIELD-MARSHAL SIR DOUGLAS HAIG

GROUPE D'ARMÉES DE RÉSERVE.

Le 2 août 1918.

État-Major

4077.   Le Général Fayolle
Commandant la Groupe d'Armées de Réserve
à Monsieur le Maréchal Sir Douglas Haig.
Commandant en Chef les Armées Britanniques.

Monsieur le Maréchal,

Au moment où les 15° et 34° Divisions britanniques vont quitter le Groupe d'Armées de Réserve, je tiens à vous exprimer toute la satisfaction et la fierté que j'ai éprouvée à avoir ces deux belles divisions sous mes ordres.

Elles ont pris une part brillante aux opérations victorieuses de l'Armée du Général Mangin qui ont abouti à la retraite des Allemandes et reconquis une partie du territoire français.

La 15° Division écossaise a mené l'attaque très dure de BUZANCY et participé, en liaison avec les troupes françaises, à l'enlèvement du village de TAUX.

La 34° Division a attaqué, avec beaucoup de vaillance, les formidables positions allemandes au Nord de GRAND-ROZOY.

Toutes deux, par leur allant, leur courage et leur abnégation, ont excité l'admiration des troupes françaises au milieu desquelles elles combattaient. Je suis heureux de vous le dire au nom de ces dernières en vous exprimant notre reconnaissance pour la part qui leur revient dans la victoire remportée en commun par les troupes alliées.

Veuillez agréer, Monsieur le Maréchal, l'assurance de mes sentiments personnels de respectueuse considération.

E. M. FAYOLLE.

APPENDIX XVII

LETTER FROM G.O.C. FRENCH 17th DIVISION TO G.O.C. 15th (SCOTTISH) DIVISION

(Translation)

17th Infantry Division. S.P. 66.
27th August 1918.

Dear General,

After relieving your division in the pursuit on the Vesle, I established my Headquarters at Buzancy. I found there the traces still fresh of the exploits of your Scottish soldiers, and the officers of my staff were able to see clearly what hard fighting you had had to gain possession of the village, and above all, of the park.

Wishing to leave on the spot some lasting tribute to the bravery of your soldiers, I entrusted to one of my officers, Lieutenant Réné Puaux, the task of erecting there, with the material at hand, a small monument emblematic of the homage and admiration of my division for yours.

This monument has on it "a medallion" on which are inscribed thistles and roses, and beneath, the words:—

"Here the noble thistle of Scotland will flourish for ever among the roses of France."

and beneath

"17th French Division"

to

"15th (Scottish) Division".

This monument was erected on the highest point of the plateau where we found the body of the Scottish soldier who had advanced the farthest (on 28th July, 1918 — BUZANCY).

The photograph of this monument has appeared in the last number of the journal "L'Illustration". I thought you would be glad to have a few copies of the photograph which I send you herewith. They convey to you, together with the memories which I have kept of our short meeting at Vierzy, the expression of my esteem and my admiration for your valiant division.

Will you please accept, dear General, the expression of my sincere regards.

C. GASSOUIN,
Commanding French 17th Division.

APPENDIX XVIII

LETTER FROM FIELD-MARSHAL SIR DOUGLAS HAIG TO GENERAL FOCH

17th July 1918.

O.A.D. 895

My dear General,

With reference to paragraph 3 of your letter No. 2021, of the 12th July, on the subject of offensive operations on the British front,[1] I beg to inform you that, owing to the despatch of so many reserves from the British to the French front, I am not in a position to carry out an attack on the Festubert—Robecq front as suggested by you, combined with an attack on Kemmel. Such an operation would absorb more troops than I have or am likely to have at my disposal. Moreover, I see no object in pushing forward over the flat and wet country between Robecq and Festubert, when the capture of the high ground about Kemmel alone would render the German positions in the low ground most difficult in winter. I have therefore issued instructions to my Second Army to study and prepare for an operation for the capture of Kemmel. I will carry this out when I can furnish the troops and the opportunity is suitable.

2. The operation which to my mind is of the greatest importance, and which I suggest to you should be carried out as early as possible, is to advance the Allied front east and south-east of Amiens so as to disengage that town and the railway line. This can best be carried out by a combined French and British operation, the French attacking south of Moreuil and the British north of the river Luce.

In order to give effect to this I am secretly preparing plans to push forward north of the Luce river in an easterly direction. For this purpose I should have to take over the front temporarily as far south as the Luce river. To enable me to do this it will be necessary that the XXII. Corps at present with the French should be returned as early as possible. The French troops thus set free would be available to take part in the operation, further south, as indicated below.

Combined with this operation north of the river Luce the French

Sketch 17.

[1] See p. 223.

forces should, I consider, carry out an operation between Moreuil and Montdidier in the direction of Hangest. In this way the high ground immediately east of Moreuil would be cut off and the Allied line could be advanced to approximately the front Chipilly—Caix—Hangest, thus freeing the St. Just—Breteuil—Amiens railway. Secrecy and surprise in this operation will be of the greatest importance.

3. In order that both the enemy and our own troops may be misled as to the real intentions described above, I have instructed my First and Third Armies to prepare offensive operations with a view to advancing their line to a more satisfactory position south of the Scarpe towards Monchy le Preux and between Ablainzeville and Moyenneville, and possibly later with a view to cutting off the German salient at Serre and Puisieux. This would involve operations on a front of ten to fifteen miles. The Army commanders concerned are now formulating the plans and making all necessary arrangements, but it is not the intention that these operations should actually be carried out, unless circumstances render them possible and advisable at a later date.

4. I should be glad to know whether the French Army on my right is prepared to co-operate generally on the lines I suggest.

Yours very truly,
D. HAIG
Field-Marshal.

APPENDIX XIX

LETTER FROM GENERAL FOCH TO FIELD-MARSHAL SIR DOUGLAS HAIG, 20TH JULY 1918

(Translation)

Sketch 17.

At the point at which we now are, it is indispensable to go for the enemy and to attack him everywhere we can do so with advantage. I was therefore particularly pleased to receive your letter of the 17th informing me of the different offensive schemes, which you contemplate on your front.

As regards the operations to be undertaken in the North, that against Kemmel should be prepared with greater speed than the others. If the threats of attack in this area do not materialize, the concentration of force which you are making there at this moment in reply to these threats should permit you without loss of time to take the initiative in the attack. It is most important to do so whilst the enemy—who since the 15th July up to last evening had already engaged 32 fresh divisions in the battle of the Aisne—the Argonne—is strongly pinned down and likely to be forced to modify the movement of reserves on your front, which he had prepared, in order to meet our counter-offensive. Although I am absolutely of your manner of thinking as regards the capture of Kemmel I request that you will with the greatest speed also continue the preparation of the attack starting from the front Robecq—Festubert in the direction Estaires, so that your First Army will be ready to execute it on the first order. This attack of itself has the indisputable advantage of freeing a particularly valuable area. It gives hope besides of more important results should the enemy anticipate you by an offensive towards the Flanders hills.

The combined operation of the British Fourth Army and the French First Army intended to free Amiens and the railway seems to me equally one of the most profitable to execute at this moment by reason of the results it offers. The advance recently made by your Australian troops north-east and east of Villers Bretonneux and the gain of ground made by the French First Army west of the Avre are of the nature to facilitate this operation.

You indicate in your letter to me how you consider this operation should be mounted : General Debeney on his part has been studying an offensive with the same objective, but his proposals differ a little from yours. I therefore suggest that the Generals Commanding the British Fourth Army and the French First Army should be invited to meet and come to an understanding without delay on a scheme of attack on which we can then definitely agree. The studies will naturally be carried out with the greatest secrecy.

The enemy seems now to be reduced to two Armies. One to garrison positions and to be sacrificed, and therefore without great value, as is proved by the complete success of the numerous small operations recently undertaken and the large total of prisoners captured in these operations ; the other Army of shock troops, specially trained, but already seriously knocked about.

There is in this situation a source of weakness to be exploited, and several offensives to be undertaken without delay against the parts of the front held only by garrison troops.

In the check of the recent enemy offensive, the seriousness of which becomes daily more apparent, there is an opportunity to be seized. We must not miss it.

APPENDIX XX

MEMORANDUM BY GENERAL FOCH READ AT THE CONFERENCE HELD BY THE COMMANDERS-IN-CHIEF OF THE ALLIED ARMIES, 24TH JULY 1918

(Translation)

I.

The fifth German offensive, checked at the outset, has been a failure from the very start. The offensive taken by the French

Tenth and Sixth Armies has turned that failure into defeat. This defeat must be exploited to the full, in the first place on the actual battlefield, and this is the object we have in view in attacking there without cease and with the greatest energy.

The consequences of the defeat, however, will extend beyond the battle itself.

II.

The enemy's defeat also determines the general attitude which the Allied Armies must take up.

The position to-day is as follows :—Although we are not yet superior as regards the number of divisions, we have at least reached an equal number of battalions, and more generally speaking number of combatants.

For the first time, owing to the number of divisions which the Germans have been forced to engage, we are superior in the number of reserves ; and, moreover, since the enemy will have to relieve a large number of tired divisions on the battle front, we shall shortly have superiority in the number of fresh reserves also.

On the other hand, all our information agrees in showing that the enemy has been reduced to having two armies ; an army sacrificed to trench holding, below strength and kept at the front for long periods ; and manœuvring behind this poor screen, an army of shock troops on which Supreme Headquarters lavishes all its care, but already seriously depleted.

Further, in material the Allies have an undoubted superiority, for instance in aeroplanes and tanks. In artillery the superiority is still very small but destined to increase in proportion as the American artillery arrives.

Finally, in rear of the Armies, on the Allied side, is the tremendous reserve of power which America is pouring, each month 250,000 men, on the soil of France ; on the enemy's side we know to what exceptional measures he was driven to deal with the crisis of effectives in May, and it is evident from the difficulty that he is experiencing in keeping up the strength of his formations that a new crisis is impending.

To all the manifestations of the swing of the pendulum to our side as regards " material strength " must be added the moral ascendancy maintained on our side ever since the opening of the battle, as is shown by the fact that the enemy despite unprecedented exertions has not been able to attain the decisive result which was so necessary to him : a moral ascendancy enhanced by the victory gained by the Allied Armies.

The Allied Armies have therefore reached a turning point ; by sheer fighting they have just regained the initiative ; their strength will allow them to keep it ; the principles of war command them to do so. <u>The moment has arrived to abandon the generally defensive attitude forced on us hitherto by numerical inferiority, and to pass to the offensive.</u>

III.

This offensive without seeking a decision will, by a series of actions to be undertaken from now onwards, aim at useful results :—

(1) for the development of later operations.

APPENDIX XX

(2) for the economic life of the country; and will keep the initiative of the operations in the hands of the Allies.

It should be possible to carry out these operations under conditions which will permit of rapidly striking the enemy repeated blows. This condition will, of course, limit their scope.

This scope will also be limited by the smaller number of formations which the Allied Armies will have at their disposal after four months of battle.

Taking these facts into consideration the programme of forthcoming offensive operations will take the following form :—

(1) Operations intended to free railways of vital importance to the future manœuvres of the Allied Armies, *i.e.* :—

    (*a*) The freeing of the Avricourt—Paris railway in the R. Marne area. That is the minimum result to be obtained from the fighting now in progress.

    (*b*) The freeing of the Paris—Amiens railway by means of a combined British and French operation.

    (*c*) The freeing of the Avricourt—Paris line in the Commercy area by the reduction of the St. Mihiel salient.[1] The Americans should make preparations for this operation at once and carry it out directly they have the necessary means to do so.

(2) Operations intended to free the coal mining area in the north and to drive the enemy finally from the neighbourhood of Calais and Dunkirk.

These operations will involve two attacks which may be delivered separately or in conjunction.

As mentioned above these operations should be carried out with only a short interval between them, so as to upset the enemy arrangements for the use of reserves and give him no time for reorganization of his formations.

They must be amply provided with the necessary means so as to avoid any risk of failure.

Finally, at all costs they must achieve surprises. Recent fighting has shown this to be an indispensable condition of success.

IV.

How long these different operations will take and how far they will carry us cannot be determined now. Nevertheless, if the results at which they aim are attained before too late in the year, we can from now onwards look forward to an offensive to be launched at the end of the summer or during the autumn of such importance as will increase our advantages and leave no respite to the enemy.

It is as yet too early to be more definite.

V.

Finally we must take into account that during these operations the enemy, in order to avoid our clutch, or to economize his effectives.

---

[1] This operation, apart from the advantage to be gained by shortening the front which, however, would benefit both sides, would bring us within range of the Briey area and put us into the position of having room to manœuvre on a large scale between the Meuse and Moselle, which we might find it necessary to do later.

may be led to make successive retirements to shorten lines prepared in advance.

Such manœuvres should not take the Allied Armies by surprise. Each Army therefore must :—

- (*a*) Study the trace of the rearward organizations of the enemy so as to determine what withdrawals he can make.
- (*b*) Watch the enemy closely for signs of retirement.
- (*c*) Have all the necessary measures prepared to prevent the enemy from executing such manœuvres at his leisure.

GENERAL INDEX

Abbeville, 217
Addison, Lieut.-Col. G. H. (C.R.E., 8th Div.), 326
Ailette, river, 33
Air Bombing, 3, 11, 162, 163, 202, 230
Air, Independent Force, 12 ; assistance, 35, 43, 44, 64, 66, 74, 104, 136, 150, 155, 156 ; Independent Force, 163 ; 174, 189, 196, 199, 200, 202, 208, 212, 221 ; assistance requested by French, 222 ; 15th July, 229, 232, 234, 240 ; German superiority over French, 259 ; 262, 276, 298, 318
Aisne, Battle of the. *See* Chemin des Dames
Aisne, river, 33 ; crossed, 88, 90, 92, 95, 97
Albert, King of the Belgians, 132, 220
Allaway, Major H. P. (25th Bde.), 325
American Army, distribution, 2 ; training, 5 ; numbers in May, 7 ; Milner-Pershing agreement, 8 ; sea-transport, 8-9 ; under one flag, 9 ; purchase of supplies, 14; expects attack against Chemin des Dames, 17-18 ; Cantigny fight, 115 ; 3rd Division, 131 ; 5th Division, 141 ; 2nd Division, 148 ; 3rd enters line, 147 ; 2nd brought up, 151 ; discussion at Supreme War Council, 152 ; programme of arrival, 154 ; divisions withdrawn from British, 160 ; replaced, 168 ; distribution in July, 188 ; II Corps goes to Plumer's Army, 190 ; divisions with British, 197, 202; Belleau Wood and Vaux, 213 ; speeding up, 214 ; transport of, 220 ; lack of horses, 220 ; 15th July, 233, 234 ; 18th July, 240 ; reinforce French, 249 ; 1st Division relieved by British, 259 ; First Army to be formed, 260 ; First and Second Armies formed, 287
Amiens offensive first proposed, 23, 313 ; Rawlinson's memo., 314 ; Foch's memo., 316 ; date, 320
Ammunition, dumps bombed, 3-4 ; situation, 6 ; expenditure, 82 ; plenty but uncertain, 195
Anderson, Br.-Gen. A. T. (C.R.A., 62nd Div.), 246, 328
Anderson-Morshead, Lieut.-Col. R. H., 56, 57
Anthoine, Gen. (French Chief of Staff), 39, 187
Ardre river, 34, 108, 131 ; nature of valley, 244
Armin, Gen. Sixt von (*First Army*), 252
Armitage, Lieut.-Col. C. C. (G.S.O.1., 8th Div.), 325
Arthur, Lieut.-Col. J. M. (C.R.E., 15th Div.), 327
Artillery, at Battle of the Aisne, distribution, 38, 42 ; lost, 55, 59, 60, 63, 81, 82, 97, 98, 99. *See also* Ammunition, Barrages *and* Bombardments
Austrian divisions, 252
Axford, Lce.-Corpl. T. L., V.C., 206

Bainbridge, Major-Gen. Sir Guy (25th Div.), 31, 46, 68, 69, 326
Barescut, Gen. (French G.Q.G.), 31
Barrages, 167, 194, 197, 202, 204, 206, 210, 211, 240, 245, 263, 266, 273, 276, 284
Baston, Gen. (French 14th Div.), 279
Beadon, Col. R. H., 15
Belgian Army, distribution, 1 ; 132 ; relations with Foch, 220
Bell, Major-Gen. G., junior (American 33rd Div.), 198
Belleau Wood, 213
Below, Gen. Fritz. v. (*Ninth Army*), 115, 290

371   2 B 2

GENERAL INDEX

Bennett, Br.-Gen. H. G. (3rd Aus. Bde.), 210
Berdoulat, Gen. (French XX. Corps), 264, 277
Berry au Bac, 99
Berthelot, Gen. (French Fifth Army), 231, 237, 238, 242, 255, 262, 264, 272, 277, 288
Bingham, Lieut.-Col. Hon. D., 201
Birdwood, Gen. Sir William (Fifth Army), 194
Blamey, Br.-Gen. T. A. (B.G.G.S. Aus. Corps), 198
Bligny, 146, 274, 275, 278
Bligny, Montagne de, 158, 275, 278, 279, 282, 288
Blin, Gen. (Head of French Historical Section), 302
Bliss, Gen. T. H. (American Military Representative at Supreme War Council), 220
" Blücher " position, 289, 291, 310
Boehn, Gen. v. (*Seventh Army*), 115, 157, 229, 237, 241, 257, 291
Bois des Buttes, 56, 96
Bombardments, German, 48, 177 ; British, 196, 202 ; German, 232 ; British, 263, 264
Booby traps, 269
Borne, General von (*VI. Reserve Corps*), 270, 290
Bouleuse ridge, 129, 139
Bourne, Lieut. - Col. A. G. B. (G.S.O.1., 8th Div.), 325
Braithwaite, Major-Gen. W. P. (62nd Div.), 235, 247, 255, 262, 272, 274, 328
Brand, Br.-Gen. C. H. (4th Aus. Bde.), 202
Branscourt, 121, 124, 125, 126
Breton, Gen. (French 154th Div.), 75, 121, 127, 129
Bridge demolition, 38, 51, 58, 60, 61, 68, 76, 85, 88, 89, 90, 91, 92, 94, 95, 97, 98, 104, 117, 118, 119, 121, 136, 149 ; German bridges bombed, 237
British Army, reduction of divisions, 5 ; distribution 1st May, 25 ; reserves shifted, 161, 163, 165 ; strength 5th June, 165 ; reinforcements, 166 ; use of reserve, 167 ; man-power, 168 ; reconstitution of divisions, 168 ; strength 11th June, 187 ; order of battle 2nd June, 193 ; position of reserves, 219, 224 ; use of reserves, 224-6 ; four divisions sent to French, 235 ; reserves on 15th July, 237 ; relations with French, 301
Browne, Lieut.-Col. C. M. (C.R.E., 8th Div.), 325
Bruchmüller, Col. (German artillery expert), 48, 232
Buat, Gen. (French Chief of Staff), 187, 231, 315
Buchanan, Br.-Gen. K. G. (154th Bde.), 248, 328
Buckle, Lieut.-Col. C. G., 57
Budworth, Major-Gen. C. E. D. (M.G.R.A., Fourth Army), 201
Bullard, Major-Gen. R. L. (American III. Corps and Second Army), 287
Bundy, Major-Gen. O. (American 2nd Div.), 148, 151, 213
Burnett, Br.-Gen. J. L. G. (186th Bde.), 247, 262, 329
Butler, Lieut.-Gen. Sir Richard (III. Corps), 200
Butte de Chalmont, 264, 272, 275, 283, 291
Buzancy, French fail to capture, 265 ; British attack, 272-7 ; German account, 280, 291
Byng, Gen. Hon. Sir Julian (Third Army), 208, 312

Cadre, reduction to, 5, 6
Californie plateau, 33, 36, 52, 93
Cameron, Major-Gen. H. (American 4th Div.), 239
Camouflage, 211
Campbell, Major-Gen. D. G. M. (21st Div.), 31, 35, 62, 120, 126, 326
Campbell, Major-Gen. J. (31st Div.), 195
Cannan, Br.-Gen. J. H. (11th Aus. Bde.), 202
Carter-Campbell, Major-Gen. G. T. C. (51st Div.), 235, 248, 256, 263, 272, 274, 279, 328
Cartland, Major J. B. F., 57
Cartwright, Br.-Gen. G. S. (C.E., IX. Corps), 59, 325
Casualties—
  British. March and April, 4, 31 ; 27th May-19th June, 159 ; La Becque, 197 ; Vaire and Hamel, 208 ; Meteren, 212 ; 152nd Brigade, 263 ; 51st and 62nd Divisions, 288 ; 34th Division, 296 ; 15th Division, 300
  French. Aisne and Matz, 160 ; Second Battle of the Marne, 305
  German. 27th May-13th June, 160 ; Second Battle of the Marne, 288 ; 305, 306

GENERAL INDEX

Casualties—*continued*
  Italian. II. Corps, in France, 242
Cavalry, for pursuit, 241, 254, 286, 299, 304
Cavan, Gen. Lord (Commander British Forces in Italy), 189
Champagne, Fourth Battle of, 228
Chance, Lieut.-Col. E. S., 129
Channel Ports, 167, 177
Chaplin, Br.-Gen. J. G. (103rd Bde.), 266, 328
Château Thierry, 149, 215, 238; reoccupied, 254
Chemin des Dames, Battle of, 17, 21, 24; German plans, 27; situation before battle, 30; description of ground, 32; British dispositions, 36; defences, 37; distribution of artillery, 42; indications of attack, 43; bombardment, 47; assault, 50; situation 9 A.M., 67; Allied reinforcements, 83; summary of 27th May, 84; German account, 86; 28th May, 102; 29th May, 120; 30th May, 135; 31st May, 143; comes to end, 155, 157; casualties, 159
Chenevix - Trench, Lieut.-Col. L. (C.R.E., 62nd Div.), 328
Chrétien, Gen. (French XXX. Corps), 32, 104, 133, 135; superseded, 171
Clemenceau, M. (French Prime Minister and Minister of War), 6, 8, 15, 24, 113, 133, 141, 144, 147, 153, 166, 170, 190, 220
Clive, Br.-Gen. G. S. (British Mission at G.Q.G.), 115
Collingwood, Br.-Gen. C. W. (H.A., XV. Corps), 196, 210
Commetreuil Château, 247, 256, 262, 270
Composite Battalions formed, 128, 158
Concealment, German orders for, 69
Condé, Fort, 104
Conferences. Army commanders, 5th July, 208, 221; Commanders-in-Chief, 315; inter-Allied, 153, 226
Connaught, Field-Marshal H.R.H., Duke of, 190
Conta, Gen. v. (*IV. Reserve Corps*), 92, 118, 122, 124, 136, 149, 156, 291
Cope, Major A. H., 109
Courage, Br.-Gen. A. (5th Tank Bde.), 199

Courmas, 247
Cowans, Gen. Sir John (Q.M.G. to Forces), 14
Cox, Br.-Gen. E. W., 20
Coxen, Br.-Gen. W. A. (M.G.R.A., Aus. Corps), 201
Craigie Halkett, Br.-Gen. H. M. (74th Bde.), 68, 75, 326
" Croix de guerre " awarded to British units, 57, 159, 278
Crookshank, Major-Gen. S. D'A. (D.G.T.), 16
Cubitt, Br.-Gen. T. A. (57th Bde.), 326
Cumming, Br.-Gen. H. R. (110th Bde.), 45, 62, 326
Cuninghame, Lieut.-Col. W. W. S., 145
Currie, Lieut.-Gen. Sir Arthur (Canadian Corps), 165

Dalziel, Driver H., V.C., 206
D.A.N. (Détachement d'Armée du Nord), 2, 12, 113, 132, 133, 163, 168, 170, 188; dissolved, 190
Davidson, Major-Gen. J. H., 30
Dawes (Br.-Gen., U.S.A.), 14
Deane, Lieut.-Col. L. C. W., 126
de Bazelaire, Gen. (French VII. Corps), 145
Debeney, Gen. (French First Army), 19, 23, 186, 311, 314, 315, 316, 317
de Cadoudal, Gen. (French II. Corps), 178
Defensive systems, April, 38, 39; June, 175, 177, 186; 15th July, 230-1; general, 306
Degoutte, Gen. (French XXI. Corps), 83, 122, 133, 141, 171, 215, 238, 299
de Lasbourde, Commandant (French 22nd Regiment), 150
de La Tour, Gen. (French 5th Cav. Div.), 122, 123, 136, 137, 145
de Lisle, Lieut.-Gen. Sir Beauvoir (XV. Corps), 209
de Maud'huy, Gen. (French XI. Corps), 32, 67, 74, 133; superseded, 171
de Mitry, Gen. (French D.A.N., later Ninth Army), 113, 163, 187, 190, 222, 228, 238, 249
Depôts bombed, 162
Deserters, 172, 232, 241
d'Espérey, Gen. Franchet (G.A.N.), 35, 40, 43, 46, 67, 84, 111, 112, 130, 140, 146, 148, 152; sent to Salonika, 170; objection to, 220

GENERAL INDEX

Desticker, Gen. (Foch's Assistant Chief of Staff), 286
des Vallières, Gen. (French 151st Div.), 104
Deverell, Major-Gen. C. J. (3rd Div.), 194
Diaz, Gen. (Italian C.G.S.), 189, 214
Dickman, Gen. J. T. (American 3rd Div.), 131, 147
Diggle, Lieut.-Col. W. H. (G.S.O.1., 15th Div.), 327
Dobbie, Col. W. G. S. (G.H.Q.), 43
Done, Lieut.-Col. R. J. (C.R.E. 25th Div.), 326
Dooner, Lieut.-Col. J. G. (G.S.O.1., 34th Div.), 289
Du Cane, Lieut.-Gen. Sir John (at Foch's Headquarters), 152, 161, 167, 185, 236
Duchêne, Gen. (French Sixth Army), 30; disregards General Pétain's orders, 39; snubs Lieut.-General Gordon, 44; forbids counter-measures, 46; forbids withdrawal, 61; sends up reserves, 66; demands reinforcements, 67; orders withdrawal, 67; 102, 103, 105, 111, 112, 115, 116, 121, 124, 129, 130, 131, 133, 141, 144, 147, 151, 152; superseded, 171
Dunkirk, proposed demolitions, 17; proposed evacuation, 147; value, 164

Eben, Gen. v. (*Ninth Army*), 229, 241
Eden, Br.-Gen. A. J. F. (57th Bde.), 127, 326
Edwards, Gen. C. R. (American 26th Div.), 239
Engineer-in-Chief, civilian proposed, 17
Etaples bombed, 162
Etaples bridge, 3
Etzel, Gen. v. (*XVII. Corps*), 243
Evacuation, of northern area, 16-17
Executive War Board dissolved, 8

Fayolle, Gen. (French G.A.R.), 157, 173, 174, 176, 179, 186, 188, 233, 249, 254, 268, 279, 298, 300, 304
Féraud, Gen. (French I. Cavalry Corps), 123, 125, 130, 133, 137, 150
Festubert-Robecq offensive proposed, 18, 23, 223, 311, 313, 314
Fismes, 92, 105, 118
Flame thrower, 276

Foch, Maréchal, 8, 24, 28; refuses help to Gen. Duchêne, 113, 132; puts his General Reserve at Pétain's disposal, 141, 143; 146, 147, 153, 154; asks for reciprocal air assistance, 155, 222, 224; withdraws troops from British area, 163, 165, 167, 169, 171, 179, 191, 223, 226, 235; 174, 175; pleads for an Italian offensive, 189; 195, 213, 215, 220; orders French counter-attack, 233; 237, 249, 268, 289, 293; Amiens Battle, 305, 309, 311, 313-20; created Maréchal de France, 309. *See also* Foch's Directives, Foch's Notes, *and* Reserve, General
Foch's Directives, No. 3, 23; No. 4, 217; particulière, 320
Foch's Notes, 18, 23, 38, 114, 149, 161, 166, 177, 182, 183, 185, 236, 260, 267, 286; memorandum of 24th July, 316
Ford, Major-Gen. R., 15
Fortune, Br.-Gen. V. M. (46th Bde.), 265, 298, 328
Fowke, Lieut.-Gen. Sir George (Adjutant-General), 4, 5
François, Gen. v. (*VII Corps*), 86, 136, 149, 173
Franklyn, Lieut.-Col. H. E. (G.S.O.1., 21st Div.), 326
Fraser, Br.-Gen. L. D. (H.A., Aus. Corps), 201
Frazier, Mr. A. H. (U.S.A.), 8
French Army, distribution in May, 2, 3; reinforcements, 3; casualties, 3; strength 15th June, 182; Pétain's complaints, 187; position of reserves, 219; distribution 15th July, 228; reserve groups 1st August, 287; forces 1st August, 293; shortage of men, 294; relations with British, 301; casualties in Second Marne, 305
" Friedensturm " offensive, 232

Gamelin, Gen. (French 9th Div.), 248
Garnier-Duplessix, Gen. (French IX. Corps), 317
Gas, 11, 19, 20, 48, 49, 50, 195, 196, 208, 284 (tear), 285 (mustard), 297
Gassouin, Gen. (French 17th Div.), 277
Gater, Br.-Gen. G. H. (62nd Bde.), 45, 61, 130, 158, 326
Geddes, Rt. Hon. Sir Eric, 147
Gellibrand, Major-Gen. J. (3rd Aus. Div.), 199

GENERAL INDEX

G.H.Q. bombed, 162
" George " offensive, New, 27
German Army, distribution in May, 26 ; casualties to May, 10 ; plans, 19, 27 ; preparation for attack of Chemin des Dames, 69 ; 27th May, 86 ; orders for 28th May, 101 ; result of 27th-28th May, 115 ; 28th May, 117 ; excesses, 118, 119 ; 29th May, 133 ; extension of attack, 140 ; 30 May, 142 ; plan, 143 ; situation 3rd June, 156 ; 4th June, 157 ; casualties, 159 ; deserters, 172 ; Battle of the Matz, 172 ; "Hammerschlag" offensive, 181 ; distribution 12th July, 192 ; morale, 215 ; evacuates Marne salient, casualties, 250 ; forces on Eastern Front, 253 ; plans, 22nd July, 260 ; retirement, 23rd/24th, 269 ; account of 21st-26th, 269 ; battalion establishment, 269 ; casualties 270-1 ; Buzancy, 280 ; retires behind Vesle, 287 ; account of 25th-31st, 289 ; probable casualties in Second Marne, 305, 306 ; battalion strength, 305 ; state of *Second Army*, 306 ; morale, 308 ; retirement to the Vesle, 309 ; ten divisions broken up, 310 ; distribution 15th July, 312 ; morale, 314 ; possible lines of defence, 318 ; future plans, 320
Gernicourt, 38, 41, 45, 59, 60, 99
Gibson, Lieut.-Col. B. D., 54
Gibson, Lieut. J. L., 55
Gillain, Lieut.-Gen. (Belgian C.G.S.), 220
Glasgow, Br.-Gen. A. E. (58th Bde.), 127, 139, 326
Glasgow, Major-Gen. T. W. (1st Aus. Div.), 209
" Gneisenau " offensive, 29, 155, 156, 172, 173, 182
Godley, Lieut.-Gen. Sir Alexander (XXII. Corps), 163, 225, 235, 242, 243, 255, 257, 258, 262, 272, 273, 327
" Goertz " offensive, 29
Gordon, Lieut.-Gen. Sir Alexander H. (IX. Corps), 12, 30, 35, 37, 43, 44, 46, 51, 58, 61, 62, 66, 68, 69, 75, 79, 81, 84, 106, 108, 112, 120, 127, 130, 160, 163, 171, 325
Gough, Gen. Sir Hubert, 31
Gouraud, Gen. (French Fourth Army), 30, 229, 230, 232, 234, 237, 238
Green, Br.-Gen. W. (153rd Bde.), 248, 273, 328

Green Line, 37, 38, 66, 67 ; defence of, 68, 73, 74, 75, 83, 88, 89, 92, 97, 98
Griffin, Br.-Gen. C. J. (7th Bde.), 68, 126, 326
Grogan, Br.-Gen. G. W. St. G., V.C. (23rd Bde.), 45, 55, 107, 108, 109, 125, 129, 325
Guillaumat, Gen., recalled from Salonika to succeed Pétain, 170 ; Military Governor of Paris, 190
Guyot d'Asnières de Salins, Gen. (French 38th Division), 265
Gwynn, Br.-Gen. C. W. (B.G.G.S., XXII. Corps), 255, 327

Haan, Major-Gen. W. G. (American 32nd Div.), 249
" Hagen " offensive, 27, 156 ; expected, 187, 222 ; preparations, 189 ; postponed, 250-1 ; stopped, 252
Haig, Field-Marshal Sir Douglas, 6, 7, 12, 17, 18 ; warns French of probability of Chemin des Dames offensive, 21 ; 23, 30 ; views on 28th May, 115 ; 133, 141 ; on impending German offensive in Flanders, 143, 146, 167, 187, 221, 222, 236, 312 ; 147, 152, 153, 160 ; sends divisions to help French, 161, 163, 185, 186 ; appeals to Cabinet on question of moving troops to French area, 166, 167 ; asks for modification of instructions, 169 ; 184 ; movement of reserves, 188, 191, 219, 225, 268 ; Amiens offensive, 190, 195, 208, 311-18 ; 220, 223, 226, 300
Haig, Br.-Gen. R. (24th Bde.), 45, 57, 325
Haking, Lieut.-Gen. Sir Richard (XI. Corps), 195
Hamel, action of, 197
" Hammerschlag " offensive, 181
Hampden, Br.-Gen. Viscount (185th Bde.), 247, 329
Hankey, Col. Sir Maurice, 8, 153
Harbord, Major-Gen. J. C. (American 2nd Div.), 213, 239
Harding-Newman, Br.-Gen. J. C. (D.A.Q.M.G., IX. Corps), 82
Harington, Major - Gen. C. H. (Deputy C.I.G.S.), 188
Headlam, Br.-Gen. H. R. (64th Bde.), 45, 107, 110, 126, 326
Heath, Major-Gen. G. M. (Engineer-in-Chief), 17
Heath, Br.-Gen. R. M. (56th Bde.), 129, 139, 158, 326

Heneker, Major-Gen. W. C. G. (8th Div.), 31, 55, 76, 107, 120, 121, 129, 130, 325
Hennocque, Gen. (French 2nd Dismounted Cav. Div.), 104, 121, 135
Hickie, Br.-Gen. C. J. (7th Bde.), 126
Hilliam, Br.-Gen. E. (102nd Bde.), 266, 328
Hindenberg, Field-Marshal v., 132
Hintze, Admiral v. (German Foreign Minister), 251
Hobbs, Major-Gen. Sir Talbot (5th Aus. Div.), 200
Hodgson, Lieut.-Col. P. E. (C.R.E., 19th Div.), 325
Holbrook, Col. L. R. (American 1st Div. Artillery), 259
Horne, Gen. Sir Henry (First Army), 208, 312
" Hubertus " offensive, 27
Humbert, Gen. (French Third Army), 172, 174, 175, 176, 177, 180, 181
Humphreys, Br.-Gen. G. (B.G.R.A., IX. Corps), 325
Hunter-Weston, Lieut.-Gen. Sir Aylmer (VIII. Corps), 30, 171
Husey, Br.-Gen. R. H. (25th Bde.), 45, 58, 325
Hussey, Br.-Gen. A. H. (C.R.A., 5th Div.), 196
Hutier, Gen. v. (*Eighteenth Army*), 172, 173

Infiltration, 85, 103, 104, 105, 179, 234, 257
Influenza, 189, 215, 252, 270, 306
Intelligence, forecasts ; American re Chemin des Dames, 17 ; 20, 22, 146, 172, 189, 190, 221, 225, 230, 308, 312
Italian Corps, 2, 31 ; 8th Division, 159 ; 231, 233 ; casualties, 242 ; 245, 246, 287
Italian Fleet, inaction of, 154

Jackson, Major-Gen. H. C. (50th Div.), 31, 51, 75, 327
Jacquot, Gen. (French XXXV. Corps), 178
James, Lieut.-Col. B. C., 59
Jaulgonne, 137, 149, 156
Jeffreys, Major-Gen. G. D. (19th Div.), 31, 126, 127, 129, 145, 151, 325
Jenour, Br.-Gen. A. S. (B.G.H.A., XXII. Corps), 327
Jeudwine, Major-Gen. H. S. (55th Div.), 307

Jonchery, 108
Jones, Br.-Gen. L. O. W. (13th Bde.), 196
Jourdain, Lieut.-Col. C. E. A., 285

Kathen, Gen. v. (*XXIII. Reserve Corps*), 250, 261, 268
Kemmel, 313
Kennedy, Br.-Gen. A. A. (75th Bde.), 68, 78, 326
Kennedy, Br.-Gen. J. (26th Bde.), 210
Kent, Lieut.-Col. R. E. D., 53
Kincaid-Smith, Br.-Gen. K. J. (C.R.A., 25th Div.), 326
Kirwan, Br.-Gen. B. R. (B.G.R.A., XV. Corps), 196
Kuhl, Gen. v. (Crown Prince Rupprecht's Chief of Staff), 27, 216, 252
Kühlmann, Herr v. (German Foreign Minister), 190
" Kurfürst " offensive, 252

La Becque, action of, 196
Lacapelle, Gen. (French I. Corps), 136
Laing, Br.-Gen. R. (152nd Bde.), 248, 263, 273, 328
Lambert, Br.-Gen. E. P. (C.R.A., 31st Div.), 196
Lamont, Br.-Gen. J. (C.R.A., 8th Div.), 59, 325
Language difficulties, 301, 302
Larisch, Gen. v. (*LIV. Corps*), 86, 100, 149, 155, 156, 157, 173 ; superseded, 181
Lawrence, Lieut.-Gen. Hon. Sir Herbert (C.G.S.), 153, 167, 223, 224, 235, 311, 316, 317
Lee, Lieut.-Col. R. T. (G.S.O.1., 25th Div.), 326
Lhéry, 127, 128
Liaison officers, 302
Liggett, Gen. Hunter (American I. Corps and First Army), 239, 287
Lloyd George, Rt. Hon. D., 5, 6, 147, 152, 153, 166, 220, 223, 225
Ludendorff, Gen., 1 ; orders Chemin des Dames offensive, 27 ; 28, 30 ; on German morale, 215 ; 238 ; cancels Flanders offensive, 250, 251, 315 ; his views on retirement behind Ourcq, 261, 289, 291 ; his strategy, 307 ; his appreciation of situation, 2nd Aug., 320
Luthernay farm, 80, 108

McClintock, Lieut.-Col. R. S. (G.S.O.1., 51st Div.), 328

GENERAL INDEX

McCulloch, Br.-Gen. R. H. F. (H.A., XI. Corps), 195
Machine Guns at Battle of the Aisne, number of, 42
Mackenzie, Br.-Gen. G. B. (H.A., IX. Corps), 325
Macnaghten, Br.-Gen. E. B. (C.R.A., 15th Div.), 327
McQueen, Lieut.-Col. J. A. (C.R.E., 50th Div.), 327
Madelin, Gen. (French 28th Div.), 139
Maistre, Gen. (French Tenth Army, later G.A.N.), 114, 152, 157, 180, 181, 242, 268, 304
Maizy, 94, 95
Malmaison Fort, 88
Mangin, Gen. (French Tenth Army), 180, 181, 214, 215, 233, 238, 239, 240, 241, 242, 244, 254, 260, 269, 283, 289, 296, 297, 299, 300, 305
Maps, 259. 301
Marfaux, 247, 248, 262, 264
Marne, river, 123 ; defences, 131 ; Germans reach, 135, 136, 137, 140 ; 145, 149
Marne, Second Battle of the, 238
Marshall, Br.-Gen. F. J. (150th Bde.), 158, 327
Martin, Br.-Gen. C. T. (151st Bde.), 45, 53, 327
Martin de Bouillon, Gen. (French 13th Div.), 75
Massenet, Gen. (French 39th Div.), 105
Matz, Battle of the, 172
Matz, river, 173
Maxwell-Scott, Br.-Gen. W. J. (B.G.G.S., IX. Corps), 325
Maybell, Col. (A.D.M.S., American 1st Div.), 259
Mazillier, Gen. (French I. Colonial Corps), 110
Medical, 82 ; hospitals bombed, 162 ; influenza and malaria, 189 ; American help, 259
Menoher, Major-Gen. C. T. (American 42nd Div.), 249
Menvielle, Gen. (French 68th Div.), 295
Merris, 194, 213
Metcalfe, Br.-Gen. S. F. (B.G.R.A., XI. Corps), 195
Meteren, action of, 209
" Michael " offensive, New, 27
Michel, Gen. (French 43rd Div.), 122
Micheler, Gen. (French Fifth Army), 130, 131, 140, 144, 146

Milner, Rt. Hon. Viscount, 8, 152, 154, 167, 168, 169
Missy, railway diversion, 260
Monash, Lieut.-Gen. Sir John (Aus. Corps), 194, 198
Monkhouse, Br.-Gen. W. P. (C.R.A., 19th Div.), 137, 325
Montagne de Reims, groupement, 113, 116, 131, 132, 245
Montazin farm, 108, 109, 119, 124, 125
Montgomery, Major-Gen. A. A. (M.G.G.S., Fourth Army), 317
Montgomery, Lieut.-Col. H. F. (G.S.O.1., 19th Div.), 325
Montigny ridge, 78, 79, 81, 100
Mordacq, Gen. (Chief of M. Clemenceau's Military Cabinet), 24, 113, 114, 144, 153
Mordrelle, Gen. (French 2nd Colonial Div.), 262
Morlancourt, 194
Mountain batteries, 88, 89

Napier-Clavering, Lieut.-Col. N. W. (C.R.E., 51st Div.), 328
Naulin, Gen. (French 45th Div.), 32
Newcome, Br.-Gen. H. W. (C.R.A., 21st Div.), 63, 326
Newman, Lieut. Col. C. R. (G.S.O.1., 62nd Div.), 328
Nicholson, Major-Gen. C. L. (34th Div.), 235, 259, 265, 283, 284, 294, 295, 296, 328
Nieppe Forest, operations at, 195
Norton, Br.-Gen. C. B. (95th Bde.), 196
Nudant, Gen. (French XXXIV. Corps), 178

Oil drums fired, 211
Oldfield, Br.-Gen. L. C. L. (C.R.A., 51st Div.), 246, 328
Orr-Ewing, Br.-Gen. N.A. (45th Bde.), 265, 328

Page, Lieut.-Col. C. A. S., 55, 56
Palestine, reinforcements from, 169, 235
Panet, Br.-Gen. A. E. (C.E., XXII. Corps), 327
Paris, Line, 103, 117, 122, 174 ; Fortress as objective, 186, 190, 217 ; 285
Paton, Br.-Gen. J. (6th Aus. Bde.), 204
Payot, M. (Head of French Services of Supply and Transport), 14
Pear Trench, 206, 207
Pellé, Gen. (French V. Corps), 140

GENERAL INDEX

Penet, Gen. (French XXX. Corps), 265, 283
Percy, Major-Gen. J. (M.G.G.S., Second Army), 188
Pershing, Major-Gen. J. J., 7, 8, 9, 13, 15, 131, 141, 154, 155, 160, 182, 190, 214, 220, 260, 287, 316, 317. *See also* American Army
Pétain, Gen., asks for drafts to replace wastage, 3 ; 18, 22 ; general instructions for defensive action, 39, 66, 102, 175, 176 ; action in Chemin des Dames battle, 66, 83, 102, 110, 112, 120, 130, 132, 135, 136, 141, 144, 147, 151, 152, 157, 164, 174 ; Directives of 28th May, 111, 116, 130 ; attacked in French Parliament, 170 ; presses Foch for British troops, 179 ; action in Battle of the Matz, 179, 180 ; 186 ; urges British should do more, 187, 223 ; 188, 190, 214, 219, 222, 224 ; action in Second Battle of the Marne, 231, 233, 234 ; asks for help of British XXII. Corps, 235 ; orders for counter-offensive, 238, 242, 244, 249, 268, 285, 287 ; appreciation of 1st August, 293 ; General Instruction of 3rd August, 304 ; instructions on 5th August, 305 ; order of 7th August, 306 ; 315, 317
Pévy, 80, 81, 107, 118
Piarron de Mondésir, Gen. (French XXXVIII. Corps), 32, 145
Piave operations, 214
Pinon, Forêt de, 65
Plumer, Gen. Sir Herbert (Second Army), 17, 23, 163, 188, 312
Polish contingent, 3
Pollitt, Lieut.-Col. G. P., 106
Pollok-McCall, Br.-Gen. J. B. (25th Bde.), 325
Pompelle, Fort de la, 150
Pope, Captain E. B., 150
Portuguese Corps, 5, 169, 194, 224
Powell, Br.-Gen. E. W. M. (B.G.R.A., XXII. Corps), 327
Prichard, Lieut.-Col. W. C. H., 4

Rawlinson, Gen. Sir Henry, Bt. (Fourth Army), 23, 197, 198, 208 ; his plan for Amiens offensive, 311
Read, Major-Gen. G. W. (American II. Corps), 161, 188, 190
Reddie, Br.-Gen. A. J. (187th Bde.), 247, 273, 329
Reed, Major-Gen. H. L. (15th Div.), 235, 259, 264, 275, 276, 277, 296, 298, 299, 327
Rees, Br.-Gen. H. C. (150th Bde.), 45, 52, 53, 327
Reims, proposal to evacuate, 146 ; 150, 226, 231, 233, 234, 238, 242, 290
Reinforcements, 4, 6, 7, 13 ; Foch's discontent, 153 ; 166, 168, 195
Reserve, General, 2, 6, 12, 114, 132, 133, 141, 142, 152, 157, 179, 186, 188
Riddell, Br.-Gen. E. P. A. (149th Bde.), 45, 53, 54, 55, 327
Ridge Wood, actions at, 194
Robillot, Gen. (French II. Cav. Corps), 145, 151, 241
Robinson, Br.-Gen. P. M. (149th Bde.), 327
Roques, Gen., 40
Rosenthal, Major-Gen. C. (2nd Aus. Div.), 194, 199
" Roulement ", 5, 12, 30
Rouvroy, Bois de, 77, 78
Rozoy, Grand, 285
Rupprecht, Crown Prince of Bavaria, 27, 132, 143, 163, 166, 183, 215, 225, 226, 236, 237, 251, 252, 314

St. Auboeuf ridge, 79, 80
Salonika, reinforcements from, 169 ; General Guillaumat recalled from, 170
Schmettow, Gen. v. (*LXV. Corps*), 96, 100, 118, 122, 123, 137, 150, 151, 291
Schoeler, Gen. v. (*VIII. Corps*), 250, 261, 268, 291
Scott, Lieut.-Col. L. D. (149th Bde.), 327
Searchlights, 4
Short shooting, 204, 206, 263, 267
Signal communication, 66
Signal for attack, 266, 297
Sinclair-MacLagan, Major-Gen. E. G. (4th Aus. Div.), 199
Smoke, 196, 200, 210, 211, 212, 233, 276, 294
Smuts, Gen. Rt. Hon. J. C., 226, 227
Soissons, 105, 117, 118, 121, 213, 214, 241, 243, 244, 291, 299 ; abandoned by Germans, 304, . 310
Staabs, Gen. v. (*LIV. Corps*), 181
Stephens, Major-Gen. R. B. (5th Div.), 195
Stevens, Br.-Gen. L. M. (24th Bde.), 325
Stirling, Br.-Gen. W. (C.R.A., 50th Div.), 55, 327

GENERAL INDEX

Strength, of battalions, 5
Sugden, Br.-Gen. R. E. (151st Bde.), 327
Summerall, Major-Gen. C. P. (American 1st Div.), 239, 259
Supply, 13 ; pooling, 14-15 ; evacuation, 16-17 ; during Battle of the Aisne, 36, 82 ; evacuation, 170 ; of British troops with French, 227
Supreme War Council, meeting 1st May, 8 ; pooling of supplies, 13 ; meeting 1st June, 152 ; meeting 2nd-4th July, 219
Surprise, 199, 201, 210, 212, 240, 315
Swindells, Lieut.-Col. G. H., 295

Tanks, number of, 7 ; German, 42, 54, 58, 96, 129, 144, 150, 174, 180 (tactics), 181, 198, 199, 200-7 ; casualties, 208 ; German, 229, 233 ; French 18th July, 239 ; 243, 244, 254, 260, 261, 262, 263, 270, 273, 297, 309, 318
Tanner, Br.-Gen. W. E. C. (South African Bde.), 210
Tardieu, M. (French Commissaire Général), 220
Taylor, Br.-Gen. S. C. (93rd Bde.), 196
Thomson, Lieut.-Col. J. A. R., 52
Thomson, Br.-Gen. N. A. (44th Bde.), 265, 275, 277, 327
Transportation, civil control abandoned, 15
Trenchard, Major-Gen. Sir Hugh, 12, 163
Treslon, 125, 126
Tringham, Lieut.-Col. (75th Bde.), 326
Tudor, Major-Gen. H. H. (9th Div.), 209
Turner, Lieut.-Col. J. A., 269
Tweedy, Major I. M., 55

Ukraine occupied, 253
United Kingdom, troops in, 6

Vailly, 88
Vaire wood, action of, 198

Vesle ridge, 34, 83, 84, 89, 90, 91, 98, 106, 107
Vesle, river, 34, 84, 91, 92, 95, 96, 102, 105, 107, 108, 110, 119
Villers Bretonneux, 198
Vindictive, H.M.S., 11

Wainewright, Br.-Gen. A. R. (C.R.A., 9th Div.), 210
Walthall, Br.-Gen. E. C. W. D. (C.R.A., 34th Div.), 265, 284
Walton, Lieut.-Col. F. (151st Bde.), 327
War Cabinet, message, 225
Wastage. *See* Reinforcements
Watter, Gen. v. (*XIII. Corps*), 243
Watts, Lieut.-Gen. Sir Herbert (XIX. Corps), 165
Wemyss, Admiral Sir Rosslyn, 147, 167
Weygand, Gen. (Foch's Chief of Staff), 31, 152, 153, 167, 286, 316, 319
Wichura, Gen. (*VIII. Reserve Corps*), 87, 117, 122, 136, 149, 156, 157, 181, 261, 268, 291
Wilhelm, Crown Prince of Germany, 28, 215, 225, 234, 241, 289, 290, 292
" Wilhelm " offensive, 27
Williams, Br.-Gen. O. de L. (92nd Bde.), 196
Wilson, Gen. Sir Henry (C.I.G.S.), 6, 14, 17, 152, 167, 168, 225
Winckler, Gen. v. (*XXV. Reserve Corps*), 89, 117, 122, 136, 149, 156, 250, 291
Winterberg. *See* Californie plateau
Wire cutting, omitted, 201
Wireless, 44
Woodcock, Br.-Gen. W. J. (101st Bde.), 266, 328
Wood fighting, 246, 257
Wounded, treatment by Germans, 264

" Yorck " offensive, 29, 134, 142

" Ziethen " position, 289, 291

INDEX TO ARMS, FORMATIONS AND UNITS

Armies—
  First—10, 11, 25, 193, 224, 312, 313
  Second—2, 11, 25, 27, 28, 193, 224, 312, 313
  Third—10, 11, 18, 19, 20, 25, 193, 224, 312, 313
  Fourth—10, 25, 193; action of Hamel, 197; 224; preparations for Amiens offensive, 312
  Fifth—31; re-formed, 194; 224
Artillery—
  Batteries, Field—
    1st—59; 3rd—59; 5th—59; 32nd—59; 33rd—59; 36th—59; 55th—59; 57th—59; B/XCV.—63; D/XCV.—63; A/110th—60; B/110th—60; C/110th—60; D/110th—60; C/112th—81
  Brigades, Field—
    XXXIII.—59, 196, 210, 325; XLV.—59, 325; LXX.—328; LXXI.—328; LXXXVII.—326; LXXXVIII.—326; XCIV.—63, 81, 326; XCV.—63, 81, 326; 110th—60, 68, 73, 81, 98, 326; 112th—63, 81, 326; 250th—55, 327; 251st—55, 327; 252nd—328; 255th—246, 279, 328; 256th—246, 279, 328; 310th—246, 329; 312th—246, 329
  Brigades, Heavy—
    XXVIII.—196; XXXVI. (Australian), 196, 210; XLI.—35, 42, 64, 81, 137, 150; XLIX.—196; LXXVII.—35, 42, 63, 124; LXXIX.—196
Cavalry—
  Corps, 25, 219

Divisions—
  1st—25; 2nd—25; 3rd—25
Regiments—
  XXII. Corps Cavalry Regiment, 273
Squadrons—
  4th Australian Light Horse, 273
  Otago Mounted Rifles, 273
Corps—
  I.—11, 25, 193
  II.—25, 193
  III.—25, 193, 200
  IV.—25, 193
  V.—11, 25, 193
  VI.—25, 193
  VIII.—25, 30, 31, 170
  IX.—move to French area, 12, 21, 30, 31; at Chemin des Dames, 36, 42, 44, 47, 63, 68, 73, 86, 102, 106, 120, 123, 137, 145, 150; casualties, 27th May-19th June, 159; return to British area, 163, 165, 188; 175, 325
  XI.—25, 193, 194, 195
  XIII.—25, 193, 194
  XV.—25, 193, 195, 209
  XVII.—25, 193
  XVIII.—25, 193
  XIX.—165, 166, 191, 219
  XXII.—11, 12, 25; move to French area, 163, 165, 174, 179, 186, 188, 191, 224, 227; at Second Battle of the Marne, 229, 235, 236, 237, 242, 244, 255, 257, 261, 264, 272, 278, 282, 288, 293; casualties, 288, 300; 301, 303; return to British area, 311, 320; 327
  Australian—25, 193; in action of Hamel, 197; casualties, 4th July, 208; 313

382 INDEX TO ARMS, FORMATIONS AND UNITS

Corps—*continued*
  Canadian—18, 25, 165, 219, 312, 313
Cyclist Corps, Army—
  9th Bn.—75, 84, 127 ; 22nd Bn.—262, 273
Divisions—
  Guards—25, 193
  1st—25, 193
  2nd—25, 193
  3rd—11, 25, 193, 194
  4th—25, 193
  5th—11, 25, 193, 195 ; in action of La Becque, 195 ; casualties, 27th/28th June, 197
  6th—25, 193, 194
  7th—189
  8th—5 ; move to French area, 12, 31, 35, 41, 45 ; 25 ; 27th May, 47, 50, 52, 55-61, 63, 66, 68, 76, 78, 79, 81, 82, 97, 98 ; 28th May, 102, 106 ; 29th May, 120, 121, 124, 127 ; 145 ; casualties, 27th May-19th June, 159 ; withdrawn and reconstituted, 168, 169, 188, 224 ; 325
  —— Composite Battalion, 139, 158, 159
  9th (Scottish)—25, 193 ; in action of Meteren, 209-12 ; casualties, 19th July, 212
  11th (Northern)—25, 166, 193
  12th (Eastern)—25, 163, 193, 223, 224, 318
  14th (Light)—5, 6, 25, 169, 188, 194
  15th (Scottish)—25, 193 ; move to French area, 227, 235, 242 ; in Second Battle of the Marne (Soissonnais), 249, 254, 259, 261, 264, 265, 275 (Buzancy), 283, 289, 296 ; casualties 21st July-3rd Aug., 300 ; return to British area, 311 ; 327
  16th (Irish)—5, 6, 25, 169, 188, 194
  17th (Northern)—25, 193
  18th (Eastern)—25, 193, 223, 224
  19th (Western)—5, 25 ; move to French area, 31 ; 27th May, 81 ; 28th May, 102, 113 ; 29th May, 120, 126, 131 ; 30th May, 137 ; 31st May, 145 ; 1st June, 150, 151 ; 2nd-5th June, 157 ; casualties, 27th May-19th June, 159 ; withdrawn and reconstituted, 163, 169, 188 ; 325
  20th (Light)—25
  21st—5, 25 ; move to French area, 31, 35, 38, 41 ; 25 ; 27th May, 47, 50, 61, 67, 73, 77, 78, 79, 84, 99, 100 ; 28th May, 106, 107, 109, 119 ; 29th May, 120, 121, 123, 126, 129 ; casualties, 27th-29th May, 130 ; casualties, 27th May - 19th June, 159 ; withdrawn and reconstituted, 168, 169, 188 ; 326
  —— Composite Brigade, 130, 158
  23rd—189
  24th—25
  25th—5 ; move to French area, 12, 31, 35, 42, 46 ; 25 ; 27th May, 63, 66, 68, 73, 81, 82 ; 28th May, 102 ; 29th May, 120, 127, 129 ; 145 ; casualties, 27th May-19th June, 159 ; withdrawn and sent to United Kingdom, 169, 188 ; 326
  —— Composite Battalion, 151, 158, 159
  29th—25, 193, 194
  30th—5, 6, 9, 25, 169, 188, 194
  31st—5, 25, 193 ; at action of La Becque, 195-7 ; casualties, 27th/28th June, 197
  32nd—25, 193
  33rd—25, 193, 194
  34th—5, 6, 9, 25, 169, 188, 194 ; move to French area, 227, 235, 242 ; in Second Battle of the Marne (Soissonnais), 249, 254, 258, 261, 264, 265, 282, 289, 293, 294 ; casualties, 24th July-2nd August, 296 ; 299, 300 ; return to British area, 311 ; 328
  35th—25, 193
  36th (Ulster)—25, 193
  37th—11, 163, 179, 193
  38th—25, 165, 193
  39th—5, 6, 9, 25, 169, 194
  40th—5, 6, 25, 169, 188, 194
  41st—25, 165, 193
  42nd (1st East Lancashire)—25, 193
  46th (1st North Midland)—25, 193
  47th (2nd London)—25, 193
  48th—189
  49th (1st West Riding)—25, 193
  50th (Northumbrian)—2, 5, 25 ; move to French area, 35, 41, 45 ; 27th May, 47, 48, 50, 51, 63, 66, 68, 73, 75, 77, 78, 79, 81, 82, 92, 93 ; 28th May, 102, 106, 107 ; 29th May, 120, 121, 127 ; 145 ; casualties, 27th

INDEX TO ARMS, FORMATIONS AND UNITS 383

May-19th June, 159; withdrawn and reconstituted, 169, 188; 325
50th (Northumbrian) Composite Brigade, 158, 159
—— Lewis Gun School, 76, 94
51st (Highland)—25, 193; move to French area, 224, 225; in Second Battle of the Marne (Tardenois), 235, 242, 244, 246, 248, 255, 261, 263, 270, 272, 278, 290; casualties, 20th-31st July, 288; 300; return to British area, 311; 328
52nd (Lowland)—5, 25, 166, 193
55th (1st West Lancashire)—25, 193
56th (1st London)—25, 193
57th (2nd West Lancashire)—25, 166, 193
58th (2/1st London)—25, 163, 193
59th (2nd North Midland)—5, 6, 25, 169, 188, 193
61st (2nd South Midland)—25, 193
62nd (2nd West Riding)—25, 193; move to French area, 224, 225; in Second Battle of the Marne (Tardenois), 235, 242, 244, 246, 247, 255, 257, 261, 262, 272, 274, 278, 290; casualties, 20th-31st July, 288; 300; return to British area, 311; 328
63rd (Royal Naval)—11, 25, 193
66th (2nd East Lancashire)—5, 6, 9, 25, 169, 194
74th (Yeomanry)—5, 165, 166, 193
1st Australian—25, 193, 194, 196, 209, 211
2nd Australian—11, 25, 194; in action of Hamel, 199
3rd Australian—11, 25; in action of Hamel, 199
4th Australian—10, 25; in action of Hamel, 199
5th Australian—25, 200
1st Canadian—25, 165, 193
2nd Canadian—25, 193
3rd Canadian—25, 165, 193
4th Canadian—25, 165, 193
New Zealand—25, 193
Engineers (R.E.)—
Field Companies—
2nd—45, 59, 325; 7th—45, 327; 15th—45, 58, 59, 325; 73rd—328; 74th—328; 81st—326; 82nd—326; 91st—328; 94th—326; 97th—45, 80, 107, 326; 98th—45, 80, 107, 326; 105th—68, 76, 326; 106th—68, 128, 326; 126th—45, 80, 107, 326; 130th—68, 78, 79, 326; 207th — 328; 208th — 328; 209th — 328; 400th — 328; 401st — 328; 404th — 328; 446th—45, 58, 327; 447th—45, 324; 457th—329; 460th—329; 461st—329
Special Brigade (Gas)—
No. 1 Company—200
Flying Corps, Royal (R.A.F.)—
Brigades—
IX., 174, 224, 229, 234
Squadrons—
No. 3—202; No. 8—199, 202; No. 9—199, 202; No. 52—35, 64; No. 82—262; No. 101—202; No. 205—202
Flying Corps, Australian—
Squadron No. 3, 199
Infantry Brigades—
4th Guards—193
7th—46, 68, 69, 73, 77, 78, 79, 107, 120, 326
9th—194
13th—196
15th—196
18th—194
23rd—45, 55, 96, 97, 107, 325
24th—45, 57, 96, 97, 325
25th—45, 58, 96, 325
26th—210
44th—275, 276, 277, 297, 299, 300, 327
45th—275, 297, 298, 299, 300, 328
46th—265, 297, 298, 299, 300, 328
56th—129, 137, 139, 145, 146, 150, 151, 326
57th—127, 128, 137, 138, 139, 145, 150, 151, 326
58th—127, 128, 137, 138, 139, 145, 326
62nd—45, 61, 77, 79, 99, 107, 126, 326
64th—45, 61, 62, 77, 79, 80, 107, 108, 326
74th—46, 68, 69, 75, 76, 77, 78, 79, 97, 106, 118, 121, 128, 137, 138, 145, 146, 326
75th—46, 68, 69, 76, 77, 78, 79, 98, 106, 109, 118, 121, 326
76th—194
86th—194
92nd—196, 197

384 INDEX TO ARMS, FORMATIONS AND UNITS

Infantry Brigades—*continued*
  93rd—196
  95th—196
  98th—194
  101st—265, 267, 283, 284, 285, 294, 295, 328
  102nd—265, 266, 267, 284, 328
  103rd—266, 283, 284, 285, 294, 295, 328
  110th—45, 61, 62, 77, 79, 80, 107, 126, 326
  149th—45, 54, 57, 96, 327
  150th—45, 52, 75, 92, 95, 327
  151st—45, 53, 92, 94, 327
  152nd—248, 256, 263, 273, 274, 275, 278, 279, 328
  153rd—248, 256, 258, 273, 274, 275, 279, 328
  154th—248, 263, 279, 288, 328
  185th—247, 262, 272, 274, 278, 282, 329
  186th—247, 256, 263, 272, 274, 278, 329
  187th—247, 255, 272, 273, 274, 329
  3rd Australian—194, 209, 210, 212, 213
  4th Australian—202, 203, 204
  6th Australian—199, 203, 204
  7th Australian—194
  12th Australian—202
  11th Australian—202, 203, 207
  13th Australian—202
  South African—210
Infantry Regiments—
  Argyll & Sutherland Highlanders, 1/5th Bn., 284, 294, 295, 328
  —— 1/7th Bn., 248, 288, 328
  —— 1/8th Bn., 328
  Berkshire, Royal, 2nd Bn., 45, 58, 325
  Black Watch (Royal Highlanders), 4th/5th Bn., 276, 327
  —— 1/6th Bn., 248, 258, 273, 279, 328
  —— 1/7th Bn., 248, 258, 328
  —— 8th Bn., 211, 212
  Border Regt., 8th Bn., 77, 78, 121, 128, 326
  Cameron Highlanders, 5th Bn., 211, 212
  —— 6th Bn., 265, 298, 328
  Cheshire, 1/4th Bn., 295, 328
  —— 1/6th Bn., 128, 158
  —— 1/7th Bn., 267, 295, 328
  —— 9th Bn., 139, 145, 146, 158, 159, 326
  —— 10th Bn., 77, 78, 79, 326
  —— 11th Bn., 76, 77, 97, 326

Devonshire, 2nd Bn., 45, 55, 56, 57, 96, 109, 325
—— 1/5th Bn., 247, 258, 278, 329
Duke of Wellington's (West Riding), 2/4th Bn., 247, 278, 329
—— 1/5th Bn., 247, 257, 258, 329
Durham L.I., 1/5th Bn., 45, 53, 54, 55, 97, 327
—— 1/6th Bn., 45, 53, 327
—— 1/7th Bn. (Pioneers), 45, 53, 327
—— 1/8th Bn., 45, 53, 327
—— 1/9th Bn. (Pioneers), 247, 255, 262, 263, 329
—— 15th Bn., 45, 62, 80, 108, 329
—— 22nd Bn. (Pioneers), 45, 59, 121, 128, 325
East Lancashire, 2nd Bn., 45, 58, 59, 325
—— 11th Bn., 197
East Yorkshire, 1st Bn., 45, 61, 62, 80, 107, 329
—— 1/4th Bn., 45, 52, 327
Gloucestershire, 8th Bn., 138, 150, 151, 158, 326
Gordon Highlanders, 1/4th Bn., 248, 279, 328
—— 1/5th Bn., 276, 327
—— 1/6th Bn., 248, 256, 263, 328
—— 1/7th Bn., 248, 273, 279, 328
—— 9th Bn. (Pioneers), 328
Green Howards, 1/4th Bn., 45, 52, 53, 327
—— 1/5th Bn., 45, 52, 327
Hampshire, 2/4th Bn., 247, 278, 329
Herefordshire, 1/1st Bn., 267, 295, 328
King's Own Scottish Borderers, 2nd Bn., 197
—— 1/5th Bn., 284, 294, 328
—— 7th/8th Bn., 265, 297, 328
King's Own Yorkshire L.I., 2/4th Bn., 247, 273, 329
—— 1/5th Bn., 247, 273, 329
—— 9th Bn., 45, 61, 62, 80, 81, 107, 329
Lancashire Fusiliers, 11th Bn., 76, 105, 106; casualties, 107; 326
Leicestershire, 6th Bn., 45, 62, 108, 129, 326
—— 7th Bn., 45, 61, 62, 326
—— 8th Bn., 45, 61, 62, 326
Lincolnshire, 1st Bn., 45, 61, 62, 126, 326

INDEX TO ARMS, FORMATIONS AND UNITS 385

Lincolnshire, 2nd Bn., 45, 61, 326
Loyal North Lancashire, 2nd Bn., 266, 285, 295, 296
—— 9th Bn., 75, 76, 95, 121, 326
Middlesex, 2nd Bn., 45, 55, 56, 57, 325
Northamptonshire, 2nd Bn., 45, 57, 325
North Staffordshire, 8th Bn., 129, 139, 158, 159, 326
Northumberland Fusiliers, 1/4th Bn., 45, 54, 327
—— 1/5th Bn., 45, 54, 55, 97, 327
—— 1/6th Bn., 45, 54, 327
—— 12th/13th Bn., 45, 61, 326
—— 14th Bn. (Pioneers), 45, 62, 80, 107, 326
Queen's (R. West Surrey), 2/4th Bn., 266, 284, 294, 328
Rifle Brigade, 2nd Bn., 45, 58, 325
Royal Scots, 1/8th Bn. (Pioneers), 263, 328
—— 1/9th Bn., 297, 298, 328
—— 13th Bn., 298, 328
Scots Fusiliers, Royal, 2nd Bn., 210, 211, 212
Scottish Rifles, 1/8th Bn., 294, 295, 328
—— 9th Bn., 210
—— 10th Bn., 265, 297, 298, 328
Seaforth Highlanders, 1/4th Bn., 248, 328
—— 1/5th Bn., 248, 273, 328
—— 1/6th Bn., 248, 263, 328
—— 7th Bn., 212
—— 8th Bn., 276, 327
Sherwood Foresters, 1st Bn., 45, 57, 60, 325
Shropshire L.I., King's, 1/4th Bn., 129, 139, 146, 158, 159, 326
Somerset L.I., 2/4th Bn. (Pioneers), 266, 284, 328
South Lancashire, 2nd Bn., 77, 78, 326
South Staffordshire, 4th Bn., 77, 78, 326
South Wales Borderers, 5th Bn. (Pioneers), 138, 326
—— 6th Bn. (Pioneers), 68, 77, 80, 81, 107, 126, 158, 326

Sussex, Royal, 1/4th Bn., 284, 294, 296, 328
Warwickshire, Royal, 10th Bn., 138, 150, 158, 326
Welch, 9th Bn., 138, 326
Welch Fusiliers, Royal, 9th Bn., 138, 326
West Yorkshire, 2nd Bn., 45, 55, 57, 325
—— 2/5th Bn., 247, 282, 329
—— 1/8th Bn., 247, 262, 263, 278, 279, 329
Wiltshire, 1st Bn., 77, 78, 79, 125, 326
—— 2nd Bn., 139, 146, 151, 326
Worcestershire, 1st Bn., 45, 57, 325
—— 3rd Bn., 76, 97, 138, 326
—— 10th Bn., 137, 138, 158, 326
York & Lancaster, 2/4th (Hallamshire), Bn., 247, 256, 273, 329
—— 13th Bn., 196
Australian, 9th Bn., 212
—— 13th Bn., 202, 204, 205, 206
—— 14th Bn., 205
—— 15th Bn., 202, 204, 206
—— 16th Bn., 204, 205, 206
—— 21st Bn., 204
—— 23rd Bn., 204
—— 42nd Bn., 207
—— 43rd Bn., 207
—— 44th Bn., 207
South African Composite Bn., 210, 211, 212
Machine Gun Corps—
  Battalions—
    9th—211 ; 34th—283 ; 51st—273 ; 2nd Australian—201 ; 3rd Australian—201 ; 4th Australian—201 ; 5th Australian—201
Tank Corps—
  Brigade—
    5th—199, 202
  Battalions—
    9th—318 ; 17th (Armoured Car)—163
Trench Mortar Batteries—
  74th—76, 121

Lightning Source UK Ltd.
Milton Keynes UK
UKHW02f0346270218
318537UK00007B/53/P